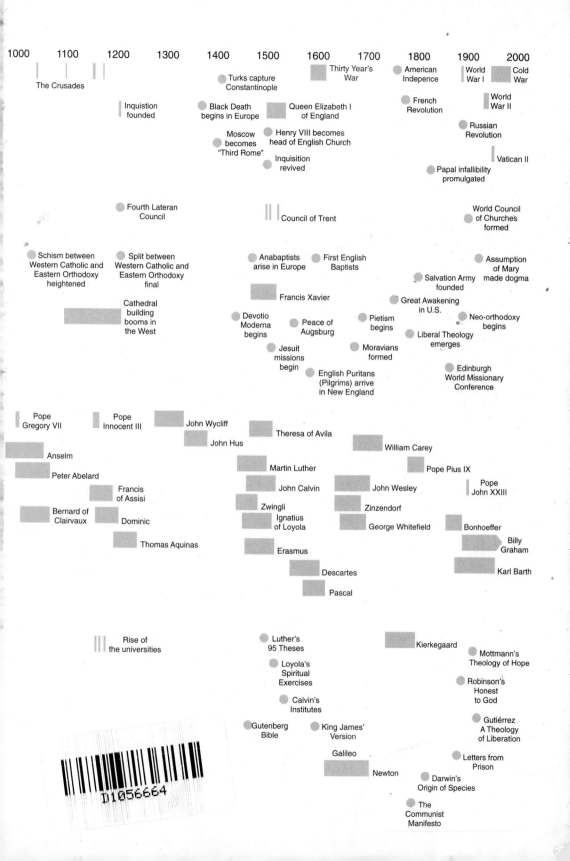

| 1000 | 1100 | 1200 | 1300 | 1400 | 1500 | 1600 | 1700 | 1800 | 1900 | 2000 |

The Crusades

Turks capture Constantinople

Thirty Year's War

American Indepence

World War I

Cold War

Inquistion founded

Black Death begins in Europe

Queen Elizabeth I of England

French Revolution

World War II

Moscow becomes "Third Rome"

Henry VIII becomes head of English Church

Russian Revolution

Inquisition revived

Vatican II

Papal infallibility promulgated

Fourth Lateran Council

Council of Trent

World Council of Churches formed

Schism between Western Catholic and Eastern Orthodoxy heightened

Split between Western Catholic and Eastern Orthodoxy final

Anabaptists arise in Europe

First English Baptists

Assumption of Mary made dogma

Salvation Army founded

Cathedral building booms in the West

Francis Xavier

Great Awakening in U.S.

Neo-orthodoxy begins

Devotio Moderna begins

Peace of Augsburg

Pietism begins

Liberal Theology emerges

Jesuit missions begin

Moravians formed

English Puritans (Pilgrims) arrive in New England

Edinburgh World Missionary Conference

Pope Gregory VII

Pope Innocent III

John Wycliff

Theresa of Avila

William Carey

John Hus

Anselm

Martin Luther

Pope Pius IX

Peter Abelard

John Calvin

John Wesley

Pope John XXIII

Francis of Assisi

Zwingli

Zinzendorf

Bernard of Clairvaux

Ignatius of Loyola

George Whitefield

Bonhoeffer

Dominic

Billy Graham

Thomas Aquinas

Erasmus

Karl Barth

Descartes

Pascal

Rise of the universities

Luther's 95 Theses

Kierkegaard

Mottmann's Theology of Hope

Loyola's Spiritual Exercises

Robinson's Honest to God

Calvin's Institutes

Gutenberg Bible

King James' Version

Gutiérrez A Theology of Liberation

Galileo

Letters from Prison

Newton

Darwin's Origin of Species

The Communist Manifesto

A Concise History of Christianity

THIRD EDITION

R. Dean Peterson

College of DuPage

Australia • Brazil • Japan • Korea • Mexico • Singapore • Spain • United Kingdom • United States

WADSWORTH
CENGAGE Learning™

A Concise History of Christianity, Third Edition
R. Dean Peterson

Publisher/Executive Editor: Holly J. Allen

Acquisitions Editor: Steve Wainwright

Assistant Editor: Lee McCracken

Editorial Assistant: Gina Kessler

Technology Project Manager: Julie Aguilar

Marketing Manager: Worth Hawes

Marketing Assistant: Alexandra Tran

Marketing Communications Manager: Stacey Purviance

Project Manager, Editorial Production: Megan E. Hansen

Creative Director: Rob Hugel

Executive Art Director: Maria Epes

Print Buyer: Linda Hsu

Permissions Editor: Bob Kauser

Production Service: Mona Tiwary, International Typesetting and Composition

Photo Researcher: Terri Wright

Copy Editor: Christine Andreasen

Cover Designer: Yvo Riezebos

Cover Image: Andre Gallant/ Image Bank/Getty Images

Compositor: International Typesetting and Composition

For product information and technology assistance, contact us at
Cengage Learning Customer & Sales Support, 1-800-354-9706

For permission to use material from this text or product, submit all requests online at **www.cengage.com/permissions**
Further permissions questions can be e-mailed to **permissionrequest@cengage.com**

Library of Congress Control Number: 2006922146

ISBN-13: 978-0-495-13030-7

ISBN-10: 0-495-13030-3

Wadsworth
10 Davis Drive
Belmont, CA 94002-3098
USA

Cengage Learning is a leading provider of customized learning solutions with office locations around the globe, including Singapore, the United Kingdom, Australia, Mexico, Brazil, and Japan. Locate your local office at:
www.cengage.com/global

Cengage Learning products are represented in Canada by Nelson Education, Ltd.

To learn more about Wadsworth, visit
www.cengage.com/wadsworth

Purchase any of our products at your local college store or at our preferred online store **www.ichapters.com**

Printed in the United States of America
2 3 4 5 6 7 8 11 10 09 08

Contents

Early Christianity

Christianity in the Middle Ages

Chapter 7   The Church in the High Middle Ages: Reform and Decline (1000–1500 C.E.)   166

The Reformation

Chapter 10   The Aftermath of the Reformation: War, Piety, and Reason (1600–1800 C.E.)   247

Christianity in the Modern and Global Eras

Tables, Boxes, and Maps

Preface to the Third Edition

It is always with a deep sense of gratitude that I work on a new edition of my *Concise History of Christianity.* I am always pleased that my teaching colleagues continue to find it useful for expanding the understanding of their students.

I have reviewed contemporary research and made changes in various chapters of the current edition as were necessary. I have paid special attention to the helpful reviews of the second edition conducted at Wadsworth's request. I am very grateful for the reviewers' insight, probing questions, and astute suggestions. I have incorporated most of their assessments into the new edition.

To me, the biggest change since the publication of the second edition involves the emergence of a body of literature that elaborates on the dynamics of globalization as well as its impact on all religions, including Christianity. Various developments in the Catholic Church in the last few decades are momentous as well and deserve special attention. Specifically, the continuing effort to interpret the Second Vatican Council as a key to responding to modernism and globalization merits further expansion. This development would not be complete without a discussion of the truly remarkable papacy of John Paul II. Finally, the increasing importance of the Latin American, African, and Asian branches of Christianity in determining the future direction of Christianity needed to be discussed. It is these "churches of the dispossessed" that are providing the hope for a revitalized global Christianity. As a result, the bulk of the revisions of the second edition are in Part IV, which focuses on the modern period along with emerging global society.

I trust that this new edition will improve *A Concise History of Christianity* and make it an even more useful instrument for enhancing the classroom experience.

R. Dean Peterson
College of DuPage
Glen Ellyn, Illinois

Introduction

Jesus teaching in a synagogue

This book examines a religion that is both old and new. Christianity is old because it has a history of almost 2000 years. Millions of men and women have lived and died according to its principles through the ages. At the same time, it is relatively young when compared to other great religions of the world. Christianity is a living religion that is continually being reformed.

This book explores the history of the Christian church.[1] It examines dates, places, people, and ideas that have played roles in the development of Christianity. More important, the book tries to provide a "feel" for history and the historical process. **History** is what has happened to people, institutions, or countries in the past. The **historical process** refers to the interactions among people, places, and events throughout history. This book focuses on the development of the church as an institution and on the development of Christian thought. A basic understanding of these developments is necessary before we can grapple with the complex issues of church history. This understanding also is necessary before we can properly assess contemporary conflicts in the Christian community.

This chapter introduces the study of history and the historical setting of early Christianity. To clarify the relation of the church to the historical process, this chapter discusses a Christian view of history, examines how historians may help in the discovery of the Christian past, and offers some thoughts on the study of church history. We then turn to a brief outline of Jewish history and to a short description of the Roman and Jewish worlds in which Jesus lived.

CHRISTIANITY AND HISTORY

Modern historical writing attempts to present history as "objective facts." It tries to describe actual events and persons. This "scientific" approach is less than 200 years old. Most introductory students believe all history, including religious history, is written from an objective viewpoint. In fact, until recent times, most histories were written with little regard for factual history. Many were written to prove specific points. The accuracy of material was secondary to what writers were trying to prove. If we are to recover the "facts," we must take care to sort out fact from interpretation. To begin this process, it is important to understand the assumptions of writers who present historical materials.

Christianity has operated on some basic religious assumptions about history. These assumptions underlie the Bible and many other Christian writings. Christianity, like Judaism, presents a **linear view of history,** which means that history has a definite beginning and will reach a definite end. For Christians, history originates with God and moves toward the goal that he has established. Beyond this, history is the stage on which God reveals himself. The Christian faith teaches that sin so affects humans that they cannot come to understand the full truth about God no matter how hard they try. In love, God chose to correct this situation by revealing his ways to humans.

This **revelation,** or self-showing, occurred through God's involvement with individuals and nations in the real world of historical events. God uses both the faithful and his enemies to reveal his truth to humans. God comes to be known against the historical backdrop of the rise and fall of actual empires, battles, and the struggles of ordinary people. The exact meaning of God's activity in history seldom is clear. For centuries men and women have struggled to interpret and reinterpret what God was up to in specific situations. However, there is general agreement that God's self-showing is closely related to the history of the Israelites. This history progresses through Abraham, Moses and the Exodus, David and Solomon, the prophets, the Babylonian Captivity and return to Jerusalem of a faithful remnant, the founding of Judaism, the Maccabean Rebellion, and Jesus of Nazareth.

Many Christians believe that God was fully revealed in Jesus, who is the central point in history. All earlier historical events led up to Jesus' coming; all events since must be interpreted in light of his earthly appearance. God's revelation did not stop with Jesus' death on the cross or even his rebirth in the Resurrection. It has continued in the world outside the church as well as in the life of the Christian community.

Christianity teaches that history is building to God's appointed end. The end for the Christian faith is the creation of a new heaven and new earth where there will be peace, harmony, and plenty. Above all, every creature will exist in proper relationship with God the Creator and Heavenly Father. The earth and its history will not be abandoned by God, but will be re-created and perfected.

HISTORIANS AND HISTORY

The above section gives a religious interpretation of history. Historians cannot say whether this interpretation is correct or whether an event shows the truth about God. However, historians can attempt to separate the "beliefs" of faith from the "objective facts" of history. They may help clarify the difference between what is believed to be true and what can be proved to be true.

History and the Problem of Interpretation

Discovering objectively what is true is very difficult, if not impossible. Modern historians often argue that the "facts" of history do not exist apart from the various interpretations placed on occurrences. For instance, many historians mark the beginning of the Protestant Reformation from the posting by Martin

Luther of his *Ninety-five Theses* on the Wittenberg church door in 1517. Other historians say this posting is a nice legend, but it never really happened. Therefore, it is not a historical fact.

If we establish that Luther did nail his *Ninety-five Theses* to the Wittenberg church door, we are still left with a number of different interpretations of why this happened and what it means. Although modern Protestant Christians may see the posting as a heroic act by a man of God challenging a corrupt pope, this does not seem to be what Luther intended. Instead, Luther and his early supporters saw this as the act of a faithful Catholic asking for reasonable discussion on issues of concern to all true believers.

To the contrary, the pope and his supporters took the public position that Luther's action was an act of subversion attempting to undermine the authority of Christ's representative on the earth (the pope). Even if this represents the public position of the pope and his supporters, was this religious concern a reflection of their true motivation? Or was the religious defense of papal authority a mask to cover their real motivation—protection of the financially rewarding trade in indulgences and relics?

And what of Luther himself? Could he have presented different understandings of the posting as he aged and saw how subsequent events unfolded? Would Luther's writings about the posting present the same sequence of events, explanations of his motivation, and interpretation of the importance of what happened throughout his life? Finally, how have "layers" of interpretation by Lutherans and other Protestants, Roman Catholics, Orthodox Christians, Marxists, economists, and "scientific" historians added to or completely changed the understanding of Luther's posting? In short, when historians look at documents or other materials, can the "facts" of history ever be recovered?

The Historian's Toolbox

Fortunately, historians have developed a number of tools to assist them in approximating the "facts" of history when sifting through interpretations. It is beyond the scope of this book to extensively review how historians "do history." Instead, a few key tools are outlined below. When a historian is attempting to understand a document or other piece on historical material, he or she:

1. **Places the document or other evidence within its context.** One of the most powerful tools historians have is an awareness of the context in which events occur. This context includes the historical developments leading up to a particular period; an awareness of the ideas, questions, and problem that have been inherited from previous ages as well as those that have recently emerged; and an awareness of existing social structures and changes in those structures that are taking place. For example, a change

may be occurring in the economy which is significantly impacting religion, politics, or family life. Historians may also be aware of the religious, philosophical, political, and social movements that are impacting the era in question. Finally, a historian may know about existing technology and changes in technology which in turn may influence the evidence being studied.

2. *Has knowledge of the existing literature and range of interpretations which may impact the understanding of the evidence being studied.* This knowledgeable approach to the literature helps the historian understand how people in the past have viewed the piece of evidence being investigated or, at least, how they have viewed similar data. Not only does this assist the historian by making him or her aware of options for understanding of the evidence, but it also helps the historian to be aware of questions and problems that may lead to misunderstanding the material being investigated. Armed with this background, the historian can make knowledgeable decisions about the evidence.

3. *Searches for the earliest available sources.* Ideally, the material can be investigated by employing original sources, meaning sources that are unpolished, uncopied, or untranslated. These sources are less likely to be contaminated by subsequent layers of interpretations. For example, when translating sources the translator often has to make decisions about "rough equivalents" of words, phrases, or concepts. They also have to make decisions about how to "translate" complex cultural ideas into the "closest cultural fit" in the new language. All of this means that translators must in some way or another redefine what they are translating. The translated document may lose or change the meaning of the original document. As a result, the earliest available version of the document and the document in the original language likely has the least possibility of change from the original author's ideas.

4. *Is aware of her or his own biases and predispositions, which may influence understanding the evidence.* While complete objectivity is not possible, some approximation of objectivity is possible if the historian is able to hold these biases in check and conduct detached and impartial investigation of the evidence. To the greatest degree possible the historian attempts to let the evidence "speak for itself."

5. *Questions and requestions conclusions.* The historians question their conclusions about the evidence as well as the conclusions of others. As new information comes to light, historians are willing to reassess earlier conclusions about existing materials. This leads to a continual growth in historical knowledge along with a sharpening of our understanding of the era being studied.

Understanding the Historical Process

Using such tools, historians can help us learn about the development of the Christian church by tracing the historical process to show how certain events or ideas happened and, in turn, how they contributed to later events. The historical process helps us see that the events of history do not occur in isolation. Neither did the Christian faith develop in isolation. Instead, history occurs within the context of culture. Sociologists say a culture is the way of life characteristic of a group. A culture includes the physical creations of a people and their learned and shared behaviors and beliefs.

As cultures become complex, numerous norms, values, beliefs, and symbols gather around major human activities, forming very complicated and interrelated patterns. These patterns are called institutions. The basic institutions of complex cultures and societies are family, politics, education, economics, and religion, and they touch almost every human activity. These institutions are also interrelated, which means what happens in one institution affects the others. For example, a change in politics may well change families, the economy, education, and religion. Or changes in a religious institution may produce changes in the political, familial, educational, and economic institutions.

In addition, changes in a culture's physical creations and technology may radically alter the less concrete elements of the culture. For example, the introduction of the computer over the last three decades has changed the way Americans do business, produce literature, diagnose illnesses, educate children, and conduct religion. Finally, cultures seldom exist in isolation from one another. Inventions, political upheavals, new ideas, economic shifts, and religious developments in one culture often affect others.

Historians know that this web of complex, changing patterns extends beyond the present moment. Something that happens now may be related to events and changes in the distant past. Certain links between these present and past events can be established. It might even be said that the present "grew out of" the past. Thus, historians see the historical process as an interrelated web of people, ideas, and institutions in which exist both change and continuity. It is in this dynamic web that the events of history occur.

THE HISTORICAL PROCESS AND CHURCH HISTORY

It is in this web of history that the Christian church developed. Changes in church structure or beliefs were as often influenced by political or economic concerns as by spiritual motives. Technological changes, a new discovery, or an emerging philosophy might call for a revamping of an important Christian practice or teaching.

When Christianity moved into a new culture, it often adopted the beliefs and symbols of that culture, at least in modified forms. These encounters with different cultures produced widespread changes in Christianity and brought about great diversity within the church. So it is that the Roman Catholic church in America is similar to the Roman Catholic church in Latin America, Africa, France, and Italy. But the Catholic church in each of these countries is still somewhat unique in its beliefs, customs, and philosophy. The same thing is true with any other denomination. The culture within which any church group operates may have more influence on the practices, beliefs, and morals of followers than do denominational ties.

On the other hand, the church has strongly influenced the cultures where it has been present. The teachings of Jesus of Nazareth have set the tone for day-to-day life in numerous societies. Additionally, the church frequently has "Christianized" the other institutions of society. This process has had its greatest impact in the Western world. It has been said that Western civilization was built upon Christianity.

Change and adjustment generally do not proceed smoothly. Jesus frequently found himself in conflict with the religious leaders of his day. Christianity itself was born through the great conflict of the cross. Every major teaching of the church was hammered out on the anvil of conflict. The many conflicts involving the church today indicate that Christianity is alive. People are struggling to live out their faith in the modern setting, and religion is being reformed.

THE JEWISH BACKGROUND OF CHRISTIANITY

Christianity developed from Judaism and shares much with it. Their histories are intertwined, and their faiths have similar views of God, revelation, creation, human duty to God and other humans, sin, salvation, and final judgment. In fact, they are so closely related that scholars sometimes refer to the Judeo-Christian tradition. Like Christianity, Judaism has had a long and constantly changing past—a history that is found in the Jewish, or Hebrew, Scriptures. These Scriptures are called the Old Testament by many Christians. Many of the books that make up the Scriptures are collections of spoken traditions handed down over many generations. As a result, it is often difficult to separate historical facts from legends. This book does not explore the many controversies created by efforts to uncover the details of Hebrew history.[2] Instead, a summary of key figures and periods in Jewish history is presented based on biblical material.

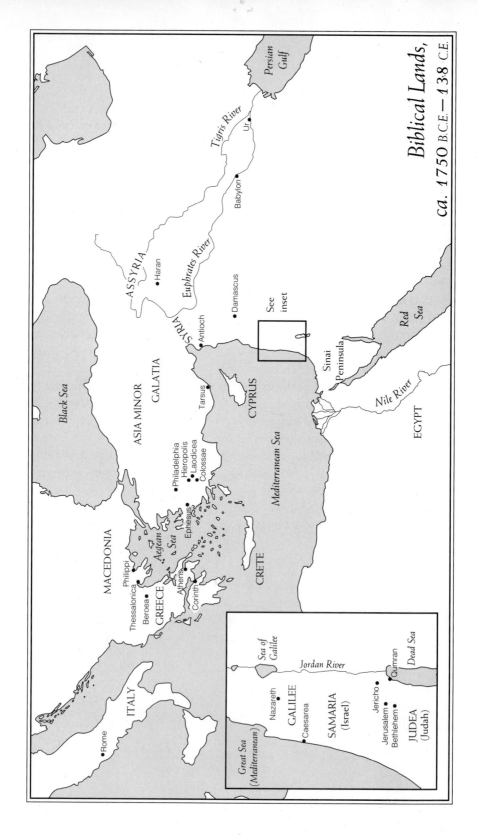

Biblical Lands,
ca. 1750 B.C.E. — 138 C.E.

Persian Gulf

Tigris River

Ur

Babylon

ASSYRIA

Haran

Euphrates River

Damascus

See inset

SYRIA

Antioch

Red Sea

Sinai Peninsula

GALATIA

CYPRUS

Tarsus

Nile River

ASIA MINOR

Black Sea

EGYPT

Mediterranean Sea

Philadelphia
Hieropolis
Laodicea
Colossae

Ephesus

Aegean Sea

MACEDONIA

Philippi

Thessalonica

Beroea

GREECE

Athens

Corinth

CRETE

ITALY

Rome

Inset:

Great Sea (Mediterranean)

Sea of Galilee

Jordan River

Qumran

Dead Sea

Nazareth

GALILEE

Caesarea

SAMARIA (Israel)

Jericho

Jerusalem
Bethlehem

JUDEA (Judah)

The Founding Fathers and the Exodus

The first era in Jewish history is called the period of the **Patriarchs** (founding fathers). According to the Hebrew tradition found in the Book of Genesis, the founder of the faith that became Judaism was Abraham, who may have lived about 1750 B.C.E. (**B.C.E.** means before the common era, or before the beginning of the time that Jews and Christians share, that is, before Jesus' birth.) The Jews believe God established a **covenant,** or **testament,** with Abraham (Gen. 12:1–3). This contract became the basis of the Jewish religion. It promised that, in return for faithfulness, Abraham's descendants would become a great nation, would enjoy God's special favor, and would be the means by which all the families of the earth would be blessed. The covenant was renewed several times in different periods and with different leaders, and the events of Jewish history were measured against it by their holy men. The keeping of their covenant with God was seen as the reason for prosperous times, and the tragedies that befell the Jews often were seen as the result of violations of their agreement.

Abraham and his people were originally called **Hebrews.** This name changed as God's special relationship with Abraham was passed on to his son Isaac and then to Isaac's son, Jacob. The Bible tells of Jacob's wrestling with a divine stranger (an "angel") at Peniel (Gen. 32:22–32), when he received the name *Israel,* which means "he who strives with God." Eventually, Jacob's descendants were called **Israelites** and their nation was called Israel. Jacob had twelve sons who were the fathers of the twelve tribes of Israel.

The Israelites eventually migrated to Egypt, where they became slaves. This slavery resulted in the **Exodus,** a formative event in Jewish history. The Exodus (ca. thirteenth century B.C.E.) refers to the Israelites' departure from Egypt under the leadership of Moses and the group's subsequent wandering in the wilderness and arrival at the "Promised Land." This area, roughly encompassing the modern nation of Israel, was promised to the Jews as a reward for their faithfulness to God.

During the Exodus a renewed covenant was established with God, whose Law was "received" on Mount Sinai. As the Jews later came to understand it, the **Law** consists of those commandments God told them to keep. Although it is popular to associate the Law received at Mount Sinai with the Ten Commandments (Exod. 20:3–17), or the various regulations appearing throughout the Book of Exodus, it is probably impossible to recover its exact content. Of equal importance, it was during the Exodus that the several isolated tribes wandering in the wilderness came to see themselves as an identifiable people.

Important Events in Jewish History

APPROXIMATE DATE	EVENT	BIBLICAL REFERENCE
1750 B.C.E.	Abraham called to his role	Gen. 12
1250	Exodus led by Moses	Exod. 13–15
1210	Invasion of Canaan led by Joshua	Josh. 1–24
1210–1020	Period of tribal confederacy (Judges)	Judg. 1–21
1020–922	Period of United Kingdom	
1020	Saul becomes first king of Israel	1 Sam. 10
1000	David becomes king	2 Sam. 2–21; 1 Kings 2
961	Solomon becomes king	1 Kings 3–11
922	Israel and Judah divide	1 Kings 12
850	Elijah prophesies	1 Kings 17 through 2 Kings 2
825	Elisha prophesies	1 Kings 19; 2 Kings 2–13
742	First Isaiah prophesies	Isa. 1–39
722	Israel falls to Assyria	2 Kings 17

Source: Adapted with modifications from J. Benton White, *From Adam to Armageddon: A Survey of the Bible,* 2d ed. (Belmont, CA: Wadsworth, 1991), 37. © by Wadsworth, Inc. Reprinted by permission of the publisher.

The Judges and the United Kingdom

Upon Moses' death, Joshua became leader of the Hebrews, and he began to wrest the land from the native Canaanites. The Promised Land was not completely secured for the Israelites for some time. The conquest probably involved initial military victories and a gradual expansion of the area controlled by the Jews. During this expansion, Israel was a loose confederation of tribes presided over by a judge. A judge was a part-time leader who periodically would leave his regular work to raise an army to deal with outside threats or sit in judgment on disputes between Israelites. The period of Judges lasted from ca. 1210 to 1020 B.C.E.

Important Events in Jewish History

APPROXIMATE DATE	EVENT	BIBLICAL REFERENCE
627	Jeremiah prophesies	Jer.
593	Ezekiel prophesies	Ezek.
586	Judah falls to Babylon	2 Kings 24
540	Second Isaiah prophesies	Isa. 40–55
538	Jewish exiles return to Jerusalem	Ezra 1
520–515	Temple rebuilt	Ezra 3–6
515	Third Isaiah prophesies	Isa. 56–66
458 or after	Period of Ezra and Nehemiah	Ezra 7–10; Neh. 1–13
332	Alexander the Great conquers Palestine	1 Macc.
167	Maccabean War	1 Macc.
63	Palestine becomes a Roman protectorate (Pompey)	
6(?)–4(?)	Birth of Jesus	
70 C.E.	Temple destroyed (after rebellion against Rome)	
90	Canon of Jewish Scripture established	
135	Jews expelled from Palestine (after second rebellion)	

Toward the end of this period, a new threat arose that could not be managed by judges and citizen-soldiers. The Philistines emerged from the northeastern Mediterranean to occupy large sections of the plains around the eastern end of the sea. They became a powerful military force because their iron-forging abilities allowed them to produce superior weapons and armor.

Israel had to unite under a single leader to counter this threat. The period of the United Kingdom ran from ca. 1020 to 922 B.C.E. The first king of Israel was Saul (ca. 1021–1000 B.C.E.), who met with limited success in subduing the Philistines. David (ca. 1000–961 B.C.E.) followed Saul. Through military power and treaty, David countered the Philistines and other groups and established a fairly extensive empire. His son Solomon (ca. 961–922 B.C.E.) was even more

Who Were the Hebrews?

Genesis states that Abraham was from the city "Ur of the Chaldeans" (Gen. 11:31) near the northwest corner of what is now the Persian Gulf. The home of his ancestors is said to be Haran in northwest Mesopotamia at the headwaters of a branch of the Euphrates River. Yet Abraham and his descendants are sometimes called Hebrews. Historians and biblical scholars have tried to understand why Abraham and his people came to be called Hebrews and how Hebrews related to other groups in the area.

These issues are still hotly debated. However, one explanation is that the biblical word for Hebrew ('ibri) is closely related to the terms Apiru or Habiru, which are found in other languages of the region. Apiru/Habiru are mentioned in several ancient texts from different groups living in the eastern Mediterranean area. The Apiru/Habiru do not seem to be particular peoples or tribes but a "class" of people. They were landless clans who lived on the edges of society, wandering from place to place and feeding their flocks of sheep on uninhabited lands. They may have occasionally hired themselves out as soldiers to powerful warlords or raided caravans and border villages. During famines, some may have migrated to Egypt, which served as the "breadbasket" of the region. This description conforms to the biblical portrait of the patriarchs.

Not all Apiru/Habiru were associated with Abraham and the group that came to be called the Hebrews. It seems that the Hebrews were a group of Apiru/Habiru who traced their beginnings back to Abraham. The Hebrews were likely a part of a larger migration of Apiru/Habiru who came from Egypt and conquered the Promised Land.[3]

successful at expanding boundaries, establishing peace with surrounding tribes, and bringing prosperity to Israel. Solomon also helped centralize worship in Jerusalem by constructing a temple in the city.

The Prophets

After Solomon's death, the nation separated into two kingdoms. The ten tribes to the north were called Israel. The two southern tribes banded together under the name Judah. This period of the Divided Kingdom ran from ca. 922 to 722 B.C.E., when Assyria conquered the north and destroyed Israel.

During this time there arose many prophets who brought new develop-ments to the religion of the Israelites. The most important prophets were Elijah (ca. 850 B.C.E.), Elisha (ca. 825 B.C.E.), first Isaiah (ca. 742–695 B.C.E.), Jeremiah (ca. 627–580 B.C.E.), Ezekiel (ca. 593–570 B.C.E.), second Isaiah (ca. 540 B.C.E.), and third Isaiah (ca. 515 B.C.E.).

The word **prophet** roughly means "speak for." Prophets assumed a special authority because they claimed to speak for God. They criticized both the reli-gion and culture of their day, usually by claiming they were recalling a straying people to keeping the covenant of Moses. In reality, they introduced several new concepts to the Jewish faith. They made it a faith rooted in history and introduced the idea that history is the stage of God's activity. They grounded true religion in ethics, meaning that religion would always have an effect on how a believer treats other people. Believers could not mistreat others and be a follower of God. True religion also involved having a pure heart, not just fol-lowing set rituals. The prophets held that Israel was not special to God because God loved her above others, but because she was chosen to be a witness about God to all nations.[4]

When Israel ceased to exist in 722 B.C.E., Judah survived as the "bearer of the covenant." This southern kingdom gave its name (Judaism) to the religion traced to Abraham. The people who practice this faith were eventually called Jews because at one time most of them were citizens of Judah.

The Babylonian Captivity

Another major point in Jewish history came in 586 B.C.E. when Judah was con-quered by Babylon, a city in modern Iraq near the Euphrates River. The leading citizens of the country were taken into captivity. The temple and the walls of Jerusalem were destroyed, and the country was left destitute. The Babylonian Captivity lasted until 538 B.C.E. when Cyrus, a Persian who had recently defeated the Babylonians, permitted Jewish captives to return to their homeland. The people who returned became the faithful "remnant," who carried the future of Judaism.

Many scholars claim that during the Babylonian Captivity the practices and beliefs associated with Judaism actually emerged. Certainly it was during this time that the forms of the Jewish religion of Jesus' day appeared. Judaism became radically monotheistic, which means the Jews developed a strong belief that there was only one God. Their rallying cry became "Hear, O Israel: The Lord our God is One Lord" (Deut. 6:4). Although there had been earlier advo-cates of monotheism, from this point on faith in one God became the identifying mark of Jews. To be a Jew was to be a monotheist.

The Torah was written in its present form during the captivity.[5] The Torah is the first five books of the Hebrew Bible: Genesis, Exodus, Leviticus, Numbers,

King David

David is of great importance in the Hebrew Scriptures. In fact, with the possible exception of Moses, no biblical character is held in such high regard. Although he had many faults, he was an accomplished musician, a great warrior, a shrewd politician, and a man of deep religious feeling. He could inspire people and hold their devotion. He is painted as a "man after God's own heart." Many Jews at the time of Jesus were expecting God to establish a kingdom "like David's," with Israel at its center.

David's story is found in 1 Samuel 16 through 2 Samuel 24, 1 Kings 1:1 to 2:10, and 1 Chronicles 11:1 to 29:30. He was from the family of Jesse, which lived in Bethlehem. The Scriptures say that after God rejected Saul as king because of his disobedience, the prophet Samuel was told by God to anoint (pour oil on to set aside for a high office) David as the next king. David was eventually noticed by Saul and taken into his court where he became an "armor bearer" to the king. Because of his victories over Israel's enemies and his winsome personality, he became a great favorite of the people. This attention made Saul very jealous. He attempted to kill David, forcing him to flee.

David and a band of followers found refuge among the Philistines, who were powerful enough to protect him. For several years, he worked in the service of the Philistine king and controlled much of the southern kingdom of Judah. After the death of Saul and his son Jonathan, leadership of Israel fell to Saul's son Ish-bosheth, who proved to be inept. When Ish-bosheth died, David asserted his kingship over the northern kingdom of Israel. One of his first acts was to move the capital to Jerusalem, a town on the border between Israel and Judah and not associated with either kingdom. In addition to making Jerusalem the political capital, he had the Ark of the Covenant (the symbol of God's presence) moved to Jerusalem, making the city the center of worship for the Israelites. Thus, Jerusalem was both "the city of David" and "the city of the God."

The later part of David's life was characterized by much conflict and sorrow, including the rebellion and the death of one of his sons at the hands of his army. Yet through conquest and treaty, David controlled the Philistines and other groups in the area. His kingdom stretched from Lebanon in the north, to Egypt in the south, and to the east past the Jordan River toward the Euphrates. Because of the weakness of surrounding "nation" and because major trade routes passed through the United Kingdom, David was one of the most powerful rulers of his day.

and Deuteronomy. Because these books contain the "Law of Moses," they also were called simply the Law. The Torah became the guide to Jewish faith, practice, and life. Obedience to the Law and the resulting legalism became central features of Judaism. Legalism is the tendency to make religion a matter of following certain rules.

One of the most important rules that developed during the Babylonian Captivity was observing the Sabbath. The Sabbath was the last day of the week (Saturday) and was a time of rest and worship. No work or business could be conducted. An elaborate set of laws eventually emerged that carefully defined what was work and what was not. Following the many rules of the Jewish faith came to be a fulfilling passion for some and a heavy burden for others.

The synagogue, a local congregation where believers gathered for worship and study, also appeared during this time. Rabbis emerged along with the development of synagogues. The word rabbi means "my master." They were teachers of the Jewish Law who settled disputes regarding the Law or rituals and performed other duties such as weddings. Often the rabbis were the heads of local synagogues. Later the term was applied by disciples to their teachers, although the teachers might not have been ordained. It was in this sense that the word rabbi was applied to Jesus.

An important new religious understanding also arose from the captivity and is found in the thought of the second (or Deutero) Isaiah. Second Isaiah is an unknown figure whose writings (Isa. 40–55) were added to those produced by the first Isaiah, the great eighth-century B.C.E. prophet. Second Isaiah was a radical monotheist with a strong sense of God's activity in history. He believed that Jews and Gentiles (all people who were not Jews) alike were the instruments of God. Yet he was troubled with a difficult question: If the Jews were God's chosen people, why did they suffer at the hands of Gentiles?

The answer to this question is presented in four poems about the "suffering servant" or "servant of the Lord" found in Isaiah 42:1–4, 49:1–6, 50:4–5, and 52:12 to 53:12. Isaiah holds that the Jews were to endure suffering because that was how the knowledge of the true God was taken to all the world. The servant's mission also was the method by which God's "healing" entered the world.[6] Isaiah says of the servant,

> **Who has believed what we have heard?**
> **And to whom has the arm of the Lord**
> **been revealed?**
> **For he grew up before him like a**
> **young plant,**
> **and like a root out of dry ground;**
> **he had no form or comeliness that**
> **we should look at him,**

> and no beauty that we should
>> desire him.
> He was despised and rejected by men;
>> a man of sorrows, and acquainted
>> with grief;
> and as one from whom men hide their faces
> he was despised, and we esteemed him not.
> Surely he has borne our griefs
>> and carried our sorrows;
> yet we esteemed him stricken,
>> smitten by God, and afflicted.
> But he was wounded for our transgressions,
>> he was bruised for our iniquities;
> upon him was the chastisement that made
>> us whole,
>> and with his stripes we are healed.
> All we like sheep have gone astray;
>> we have turned every one to his own way;
> and the Lord has laid on him the iniquity
>> of us all. (Isa. 53:1–6)

The servant was initially identified with Israel, later with a minority of faithful people in Israel, and then with a "remnant"—those who returned after the edict of Cyrus to rebuild Jerusalem. Finally, the suffering servant was an idea that Christians came to associate with the mission of Jesus.

The Greek Period

After the faithful remnant returned to Judah, the walls of Jerusalem and the temple were rebuilt. However, the Jews were not the masters of their own homeland but were dominated by the Persians. After Alexander the Great, a Greek, conquered the Middle East, Judah was captured from the Persians and placed under the control of a series of Greek rulers. The Hellenistic (Greek) era ran from 332 to 167 B.C.E. One of the more important occurrences of this era was the introduction of Greek culture and thought into the region. This process is called **hellenization.** Greek gymnasiums and statues to Greek gods appeared in many towns. Greek language, law, and philosophy became well known in the region. This hellenization left Jews bitterly divided between those who supported it and those who opposed it. This feud continued until the time of Christ.

After Alexander's death in 323 B.C.E, his empire was divided among his generals. Seleucia and Egypt are the two most important divisions of the empire for Jewish history. Seleucia contained Syria, Phoenicia, and areas north of Judea. Because the region was called Seleucia, rulers from that area are sometimes called Seleucids, but because the "capital" of the region was in Antioch, they also were referred to as Antiochus. Egypt was ruled by the Ptolemies. Both the Seleucids and the Ptolemies strongly favored Greek culture and sought to impose it in Judea (the name now applied to Judah).

For much of the time from 323 to 198 B.C.E., the Ptolemies and the Seleucids were at war with each other and fought each other for control of Judea. Domination of Judea passed to the Seleucids in 198 B.C.E. when Antiochus III took over the region. Trouble erupted in Judea when Antiochus IV sold the office of high priest of the Jews. This sparked near-warfare between hellenistic Jews and those Jews who sought to maintain the integrity of their faith by opposing selling the office. Antiochus IV saw the Jewish religion as the source of opposition to his policies and sought to eradicate it. Many Jews submitted to Antiochus' demands, but others did not.

Jewish Independence and Roman Domination

A rebellion was touched off in the small village of Modein when an old priest, Mattathias, killed a Jew and a Syrian officer who were about to perform a sacrifice to Zeus. One of Mattathias' sons, Judas Maccabees, led a successful war that wrestled control from the Syrians. Judas and his followers cleansed the Jewish Temple in 165 B.C.E. and rededicated it to God. The Jewish festival of Hanukkah celebrates this event.

The Maccabee family founded the Hasmonaean dynasty and controlled Judea for many decades. Eventually, internal political struggles and competition between the Sadducees and Pharisees (discussed below) resulted in civil war with neither side winning a clear advantage. Both sides then appealed to the greatest power in the area, Rome, to settle their differences. In 63 B.C.E., the Roman general Pompey took control of Jerusalem, thus ending the period of Jewish independence. The taking of Jerusalem established Roman domination of the Jews. It also corresponded to a rapid expansion of the Roman Empire. This empire played a decisive role in Christian history.

THE ROMAN WORLD OF JESUS OF NAZARETH

Jesus was born into a Judea controlled by Rome. The Roman Empire stretched north to south from England to North Africa and east to west from Syria to Spain. In this widespread region, the *pax Romana* ("peace of Rome") was enforced by tough legions. Highways constructed for the army linked the empire. Greek was the language of commerce and was spoken throughout the empire. These matters were all important for the spread of Christianity.

They allowed Christian missionaries to travel safely throughout the empire with relative speed and permitted believers to communicate the **gospel** (good news) of Jesus wherever they went.

The cultural and political situation was favorable to the development of many new religions. The official Roman religion was borrowed from Greek mythology. Although average citizens might have performed established rituals, they probably got little personal satisfaction from the state religion. Traditional cults dedicated to local gods also failed to satisfy the religious needs of many people.[8] As a result, new philosophies and religions had emerged around the time of Jesus and were spreading throughout the empire.

An important new religion was the cult of the emperor. A **cult** is a system of religious worship. The Emperor Augustus had been pivotal in bringing peace to the Roman Empire. He came to be viewed as a god incarnate (made flesh). An official state cult developed that required citizens to make offerings to a statue of the emperor. Romans saw this cult as necessary to establish order, law, and prosperity. In many ways religion and politics were intertwined. Making an offering to the emperor was more of a matter of showing loyalty to the state than it was a religious duty. If citizens refused to follow this practice, they were seen as traitors.

Another development was the spread of **mystery religions,** which were a group of faiths that originated in Greece and the eastern areas of the empire. These religions included the cults of Dionysus, Isis, *Magna Mater* (the Great Mother), and Mithra, as well as the Eleusinian mysteries. They promised salvation through the participation of believers in secret ceremonies and rites. Little is known of their specific beliefs and practices because they were kept secret by followers. We do know that stories of the virgin birth of a god, death and resurrection, and being born again appeared in several mystery religions. The rituals of some included a sacramental meal and baptism (at times, in the blood of a freshly slain bull).

Some early Christian teachers may well have borrowed from these cults in their attempts to explain the work and person of Christ. The growth of the mystery religions indicates a spiritual hunger in the first century. It also indicates that Christianity had competition in filling religious needs within the empire. In fact, for the first hundred or so years of Christianity, most average citizens probably could not distinguish between it and mystery religions.

Stoicism and Gnosticism were popular philosophies in Jesus' world and played important roles in the emergence of Christianity. The **Stoics** believed that God was a powerful energy that created and sustained the world. God also was the world reason, or **Logos,** that was seen in the order and beauty of the world. Human duty was to live "naturally" or according to the law of the universe, which was the embodiment of Divine Reason.

Another great competitor of to the Christian worldview was **Gnosticism,** which is a term used to describe several tendencies found in the Greco-Roman world that shared common ideas.[9] Gnosticism comes from the Greek word *gnosis,* which means knowledge. Secret knowledge revealed to a few was a key to Gnosticism. Those people who received this secret knowledge were freed from bondage to the physical and made spiritually alive. The Gnostics sharply separated the material world from the spiritual world. Matter was evil; spirit was good. Being trapped in the physical world caused humans to lose their ability to live forever. Because the material world was evil, it could not have been created by a good God. The world was created by the **Demiurge**, a lesser god who came out of the supreme, unknowable, and good God. Because the Demiurge was a flawed lesser god, the world he created was imperfect and at odds with the truly spiritual.

These concepts had dramatic effects when applied to understanding the mission of Jesus. It became popular to say Jesus was the Logos. Yet many Christians influenced by Gnosticism felt that because the world was evil, the Logos could not have become flesh. The incarnation and death of Christ was only apparent. It was not real. Other Christians believed strongly that if God had not become flesh in Jesus and if there had not been an actual death on the cross, the world could not have been saved. Gnosticism was eventually rejected. Still, Gnostic ideas were struggled with for many centuries before orthodox (officially accepted) understandings of God, creation, the material world, the Logos, and salvation were established.

THE JEWISH WORLD OF JESUS OF NAZARETH

Years of domination by Babylonian, Persian, Greek, and Roman masters had left God's "chosen people" extremely frustrated. Many expected to be delivered by God and to be restored to their proper place as a political power.

The Messiah and the Kingdom

During the time between the Babylonian Captivity and the birth of Jesus, Jewish hopes were linked strongly with two symbols: the Messiah and the kingdom of God. The Hebrew word *Messiah* is *Christ* in Greek. The **Messiah,** or **Christ,** was a figure in the Scriptures and other writings who was linked to the **Day of the Lord.** The Day of the Lord was that period at the end of time when God would judge the just and unjust from all nations and would create a new age in which God's rule would be eternal and supreme. This age was referred to as the **kingdom of God.**

The coming of the Messiah was closely related to the establishment of the kingdom. Some believed the Messiah would be an earthly king from the family of David who would make Israel the ruler of the world. Others thought that his coming could be hastened by strict observance of the Law. Others were determined to fight Rome as a means of bringing in the kingdom. Some believed the kingdom was spiritual and the Messiah was strictly a religious figure.

Even though views about the Messiah and the kingdom differed, the Jewish world of Jesus' time was filled with overwhelming excitement about the nearness of God's intervention for them and the approaching kingdom. Countless parents named their sons Joshua (*Jesus* in Greek) in the hope their child would be the chosen one from God who would deliver his people. The atmosphere was charged with expectation of the Messiah's coming.

Jewish Groups

Judaism was far from unified at the time of Jesus. In fact, some scholars have used the term "Judaisms" to stress this diversity, just as others speak of "Christianities" to emphasize Christian differences. Four main groups are important for our studies: Sadducees, Pharisees, Essenes, and Zealots.

The **Sadducees** were a small but wealthy ruling party closely associated with the temple and Jerusalem. They controlled the important office of the high priest and had great political influence in the **Sanhedrin** (the Jewish ruling body).[10] They taught a strict observance of the Torah as "it was given to Moses" and would permit no new doctrines apart from those found in the original Torah. As a result, they rejected oral interpretations of the Torah along with new ideas about life after death, the resurrection of the body, and angels and spirits. They tended to accept older interpretations of the afterlife found in the Torah. To them, life after death consisted of semi-lifeless ghosts confined to the gray underworld known as **sheol.** The Sadducees cooperated closely with the Romans. They were very active in having Jesus crucified, possibly because they saw him as a threat to Roman rule and their high position.

The **Pharisees** were the chief competitors of the Sadducees and were largely artisans and merchants. They were the descendants of the group that had opposed the hellenization of Jewish culture after Alexander the Great's conquest. They sought to protect Jewish purity by strictly following the Law in every area of life. The Pharisees used a large body of oral interpretation of the Law to apply it to day-to-day situations. They also accepted such new ideas as life after death and resurrection.

The Pharisees rejected foreign rulers but did not seem to be leaders in various rebellions against Rome. Their understanding of the Messiah was probably more religious than political. They had influence among common people who admired their disciplined lives and their rejection of foreign control of Judea. Their approach to religion involved living the Law, worshiping in synagogues, and being instructed by rabbis. This made Judaism more available and relevant to ordinary people than did the Temple-centered approach to Judaism favored by the Sadducees.

In the New Testament, Jesus is shown as having frequent conflicts with the Pharisees. He believed that their following of the Law was too external and felt that many of them missed the real spirit of the Law. Recently, scholars have questioned the New Testament picture of the relation of Jesus to the Pharisees. They point out that many of the teachings of Jesus about the spiritual nature of the Law are also found in Pharisaic writings. It may be that Jesus did not conflict with all Pharisees, but only with those who misapplied the Law.

The **Essenes** were another group that arose from the rejection of hellenization. They retreated to the desert where they lived in communes. There they practiced strict observance of the Law and waited for the overthrow of Rome by the coming Messiah. They believed that when the kingdom arrived God would establish a new covenant with them because they were the true Israel. There may have been only about 4000 Essenes at the time of Christ.[11]

The **Zealots** were more involved in Jewish society. They were an underground political party that actively sought to overthrow Rome by force, and they expected the Messiah to be a warrior-king who would lead the rebellion against the Romans. It is possible that one or more of Jesus' twelve original disciples were Zealots. Certainly the Zealots were disappointed by Jesus' understanding of messiahship.

CONCLUSIONS

This book tells about Christianity, a religion that is rooted in the past but that is alive and constantly changing today. It gives us insight into the history of this religion as well as into the forces that are now active in it. An appreciation of the historical process assists us in keeping the past and present in proper perspective. The church, along with its beliefs and practices, has emerged over a long time within the web of history. The same types of forces that were active in bygone ages are shaping the future of the Christian community now.

Christianity grew out of Judaism and owes many of its most important ideas to that faith. Jesus was a Jew and drew heavily upon his Jewish history in his teachings. Ideas about the Law, the kingdom of God, the suffering servant, and the Messiah all played a part in his thought. At the same time, the new religion that formed after his death developed in a world dominated by Roman political strength and Greek culture. The new church had to turn to both the

Jewish and the Roman worlds to understand itself and explain its faith to outsiders. This same process operates today as each new generation of Christians tries to apply the traditional faith to the world in which it lives.

Notes

1. In this book the terms *Christianity, the Christian church,* and *the church* are used interchangeably. Technically, there are differences among them. The Christian church is an institution. Christianity is the religion the church practices. Also, there has been debate on how "Christian" the church really is. Some have argued that the institutional church is a perversion of the true Christian faith.

2. For a discussion of biblical literature and studying the Bible, see Christian E. Hauer and William A. Young, *An Introduction to the Bible: A Journey into Three Worlds.* Englewood Cliffs, NJ: Prentice-Hall, 1986, 1–45. For a discussion of oral traditions, their formation into Scripture, and some problems with these, see Bernhard W. Anderson, *Understanding the Old Testament,* 4th ed. Englewood Cliffs, NJ: Prentice-Hall, 1986, 18–27, 151–156.

3. A classic on this problem is Moshe Greenberg, *The Hab/piru.* New Haven, CT: American Oriental Society, 1955.

4. For a good discussion of the prophets and the religious development of Israel, see John Carmody, Denise Lardner Carmody, and Robert Cohn, *Exploring the Hebrew Bible.* Englewood Cliffs, NJ: Prentice-Hall, 1988, 176–262.

5. For a discussion of the Babylonian Captivity, see Anderson, *Understanding,* 425–465.

6. For a discussion of the servant of God, see Anderson, *Understanding,* 488–506.

7. For a discussion of the time from the Exile to Jesus, see Edwin D. Freed, *The New Testament: A Critical Introduction.* Belmont, CA: Wadsworth, 1986. 1–36, and Hauer and Young, *Journey,* 189–209.

8. For a discussion of the moral and religious hunger of the age, see Kenneth Scott Latourette, *A History of Christianity,* vol. 1, *Beginnings to 1500,* rev. ed. New York: Harper & Row, 1975, 22–23.

9. Scholars used to believe that Gnosticism was a philosophical movement the among Christians and non-Christians alike. Many are now beginning to believe that tendencies like the belief in special knowledge or the Demiurge were found among non-Christians, but there was no organized Gnosticism outside of the Christian church. Gnosticism as such seems to have developed within Christianity.

10. For a discussion of early Jewish groups, see Mary Jo Weaver, *Introduction to Christianity.* Belmont, CA: Wadsworth, 1984, 22–24.

11. For a discussion of the Essenes, see "Essenes," in *Oxford Dictionary of the Christian Church,* 3d ed., ed. F. L. Cross (Oxford: Oxford University Press, 1997), 562. There is a great deal of debate about the number of Essenes. However, many agree that this was a fairly small party.

Additional Readings

Barnett, Paul. *Jesus and the Logic of History.* Grand Rapids, MI: Eerdmans, 1998.

Baston, John. *Reading the Old Testament: Method in Biblical Study.* Philadelphia: Westminster, 1984.

Bickerman, Elias. *From Ezra to the Last of the Maccabees: Foundations of Post-Biblical Judaism.* New York: Schocken Books, 1962.

Bright, John. *History of Israel*. 3d ed. Philadelphia: Westminster, 1981.

Bultman, Rudolf. *Primitive Christianity in Its Contemporary Setting*. New York: Meridian, 1956.

Ceresko, Anthony. *Introduction to the Old Testament: A Liberation Perspective*. Maryknoll, NY: Orbis. 1992.

Danielou, Jean. *The Dead Sea Scrolls and Primitive Christianity*. Translated by Salvator Attanasio. Baltimore: Helicon, 1958.

Eichrodt, Walter. *Theology of the Old Testament*. Vol. 1. Translated by J. A. Baker from the 6th German ed. Philadelphia: Westminster, 1961.

Feldman, Louis H. *Jew and Gentile in the Ancient World: Attitudes and Interactions from Alexander to Justinian*. Ewing, NJ: Princeton University Press, 1997.

Fisher, James A. *Interpreting the Bible: A Simple Introduction*. Mahwah, NJ: Paulist. 1996.

Friedman, Richard E. *Who Wrote the Bible?* New York: Harper & Row, 1989.

Grant, F. C. *Roman Hellenism and the New Testament*. New York: Scribner's, 1962.

Harding, Mark. *Early Christian Life and Thought in Social Context: A Reader*. T. and T. Clark, 2003.

Harvey, Van A. *The Historian and the Believer*. New York: Macmillan, 1966.

Horsley, Richard A. *Galilee: History, Politics, People. Place*. Harrisburg, PA: Trinity International. 1995.

Kee, Howard C. *Christian Origins in Sociological Perspective: Methods and Resources*. Philadelphia: Westminster, 1980.

Liberman, Saul. *Greek in Jewish Palestine/Hellenism in Jewish Palestine*. New York: Jewish Theological Seminary. 1994.

Nardo, Don. *The Rise of Christianity*. Turning Points in World History series. San Diego: Greenhaven, 1999.

Rad, Gerhard von. *Old Testament Theology*. Vol. 1, *The Theology of Israel's Historical Traditions*. Vol. 2, *The Theology of Israel's Prophetic Traditions*. Translated by D. M. G. Stalker. New York: Harper & Row, 1962, 1965.

Russell, D. S. *Method and Message of Jewish Apocalyptic*. Philadelphia: Westminster, 1964.

Wilson, Robert R. *Sociological Approaches to the Old Testament*. Philadelphia: Fortress, 1984.

Williams, Robert C. *The Historians Toolbox: A Student's Guide to the Theory and Craft of History*. Armonk, NY: Sharpe, 2003.

Websites

www.bible-history.com [Site provides access to a wide range of materials on ancient cultures, the Bible, and Church history.]

www.oldtestamentstudies.net [Site provides access to sites with materials on Old Testament topics.]

www.questia.com/library/religion/christianity/the bible/ [Site provides a host of articles and books, and links a gold mine of relevant topics.]

EARLY CHRISTIANITY

INTRODUCTION: THE GROWTH AND DECLINE OF THE ROMAN EMPIRE

The fate of the church throughout its first 500 years is linked with changes in the status of the Roman Empire. This section briefly traces the history of Rome from its creation as a republic, to its appearance as a world power, and then to its decline as a stable empire in Western Europe. The chapters that follow in this section show how these changes impacted the Christian community.

Republic to Empire

During most of the thousand years before the birth of Jesus, the lands around the eastern end of the Mediterranean Sea were dominated by Greek culture and military might. This influence spread west in part through the establishment of Greek city-states in southern Italy around 800 B.C.E. Around this time, the Etruscans, a group of people from Asia Minor, moved into what is now northern Italy and created a powerful civilization on the northwest coast. Shortly after 600 B.C.E., several villages near the mouth of the Tiber River united politically under a single Etruscan king who was advised by a council of 300 men called the *senate*. Other free citizens also participated in the government.

Rome was the center of this cluster of villages, and it soon became a powerful political force. When the Etruscans' power weakened around 500 B.C.E., high-ranking Romans succeeded in overthrowing the Etruscan king. This rebellion marked the beginning of the Roman Republic.

During its early centuries, the Roman Republic struggled for survival against foes within its borders and invaders from the outside. By 265 B.C.E., however, Rome became the master of all of Italy from the Po Valley to the south. The success of Rome soon resulted in conflicts with other powers in the area. Rome was victorious in several large land and sea wars. By 44 B.C.E., it controlled Spain, Gaul (France), northern Italy, Sicily, Greece, Crete, Cyprus, and parts of Asia Minor, eastern Mediterranean territories, and northern Africa.

World power brought wealth to Rome, but it also put the republic under terrible strain. The traditional citizens' army had to defend long frontiers and deal with hostile people within Roman borders. There were drastic changes in the economy and the social structure. To make matters worse, Hellenistic ideas and mystery cults from the East that stressed individual salvation tended to undermine traditional Roman values of commitment to work and citizenship.

This strain led to a period of struggle within the republic among a number of men vying for control. In 31 B.C.E., Octavian (or Augustus as he came to be known) won this struggle. He was able to claim autocratic powers unknown by any previous Roman ruler. His rule marked the beginning of the imperial period, and from this time on, Rome in effect was ruled by an emperor. Augustus took steps to end the civil warfare and chaos that tended to occur after the death of a leader by establishing a system in which able men from his family would continue to rule.

The first four emperors of the first century were from Augustus' family: Tiberius (ruled 14–37 C.E.),[1] Caligula (37–41), Claudius (41–54), and Nero (54–68). However, all were less-able rulers than Augustus, and Caligula and Nero were cruel, vain, wasteful, and, quite possibly, insane. For a brief period after Nero's death, the army tried to control the imperial office. But when Vespasian (69–79) took control, he reestablished the practice of passing the throne to his sons Titus (79–81) and Domitian (81–96). Despite their weaknesses, several of the rulers—especially Tiberius, Claudius, and Vespasian—were capable and extended the boundaries of the empire, increased the power of the emperor, administered the provinces effectively, and undertook large public works in Rome.

The High Point of the Empire

By the time of Domitian's death, imperial rule was firmly established. The empire reached its peak under rulers that following generations would call the "good emperors": Nerva (96–98), Trajan (98–117), Hadrian (117–138), Antoninus (138–161), and Marcus Aurelius (161–180). All named their successors early and worked closely with the senate. They encouraged an imperial **bureaucracy** (a hierarchy of professional government officials) to administer the empire, created a single body of law for the whole realm, met the monetary needs of the empire, gave local regions considerable freedom, and undertook projects to help the needy throughout the empire.

Because the number of slaves decreased, large estates began to rely more heavily on **tenants** (people who worked the land and paid rent). Small-scale industry flourished and trade was vigorous. Numerous public buildings, public baths, roads, aqueducts, and private homes were constructed. Through taxes on the provinces, the government maintained the bureaucracy, paid the army, and assisted the large numbers of poor in Rome. There were many holidays, religious festivals, games, and cultural events. Architecture, art, philosophy, science, and literature flourished under the *pax Romana* (Roman peace).

Yet the empire had problems that would soon cause difficulties. The boundaries of the empire were too extensive to be defended adequately by the army, and their defense strained public funds. The empire still had much poverty, injustice, and oppression.

A Declining Empire

After the death of Marcus Aurelius, the peace that had been common in the empire for almost 100 years was destroyed. From 193 to 284 there were continual wars as the army tried to control the state. Strife and rebellion were common as units of the army fought the ruling emperor and tried to place their general on the throne. Successful rebellions would result in great benefits to the army units in the form of money, government positions, land grants, and pensions. The rulers during this period are often called "barrack emperors" because their main concern was the well-being of the military.

The traditional role of Roman citizens in the government diminished. The emperor was in the process of becoming the absolute lord over the realm and the people were regarded as nothing but mere subjects. Agricultural output declined and trade was disrupted. To make matters worse, Persia to the southeast and German tribes to the northeast were increasing their pressure on the frontiers. The only Romans who benefited from this situation were the great landlords and the army. The values that had made Rome great were severely questioned and the whole society was troubled. People increasingly sought escape from this turmoil through nontraditional religions. Among these religions was Christianity.

Reforms of Diocletian and Constantine

The period from 284 to 500 saw the continued decline and eventual destruction of the Roman Empire. In 284, the general Diocletian (284–305) was placed in power by the army. He and his successor, Constantine (306–337), undertook reforms to try to stop the empire's decline. Diocletian ignored the senate and divided the empire into four areas ruled over by an *augustus*. He also reformed the tax system to obtain new revenues and undertook a fateful attack on Christians as a threat to the Roman way of life.

When Constantine assumed the throne he made a number of moves that would have important consequences for the history of the church. In 313 he issued the **Edict of Milan,** which gave religious toleration to all groups, including Christians, throughout the realm. This edict resulted in part from Constantine's conversion to Christianity before a battle in 311. Although he was not baptized until he was on his deathbed in 337, he used Christian teachings as the basis of many of his policies. He promoted Christian causes and saw Christianity as a force that could unite the empire.

For some time the city of Rome had been losing political importance and it was poorly positioned to defend itself against threats from the German tribes to the north. These reasons, together with other factors, led Constantine to establish a new capital at Byzantium, an ancient Greek city on the straits at the entrance of the Black Sea. The new capital, which Constantine named Constantinople (and is now called Istanbul), was dedicated in 330. The empire thus had two competing political centers, which aggravated an existing conflict between Western (Latin) and Eastern (Greek) Christianity. From this point on, the Christian world would have two centers.

The period from Constantine's death until the end of the rule of Theodosius I (379–395) was one of relative peace, although the western realm still had problems. The financial requirements of the government and the military placed an increasingly heavy burden on the people. The economy remained depressed. Large self-sufficient estates became more and more important. The army became more inefficient, especially those units on the frontiers. Many people remained loyal to the older pagan religions, and they resented the advantages given to Christians. This resentment led to a brief time of persecution of Christians under Julian the Apostate (361–363), who tried to reestablish the older pagan faith.

These internal tensions and weaknesses were made even more threatening by the rising power of the "barbarian" German tribes. Although the tribes were referred to as *barbarians,* they actually possessed a developed culture that depended on agriculture and that gave men and women considerable rights. Through the generations, they had become efficient in war. They lacked the "high" culture of the Romans, however, with its emphasis on art, literature, law, and architecture.

From the time of Augustus, small groups of Germans had been allowed to settle in the empire. Some of their members had risen to high positions in Roman society. As long as their numbers were small and they could be controlled, they were not seen as a real threat. Ultimately, a group of Visigoths (a Germanic tribe) who had been allowed to migrate into the empire revolted against the government. They defeated the Roman emperor in 378 at Adrianople. Although they were confined for the time being to the Balkan region (an area of southern

Europe between Italy and the Black Sea), they still were a "nation" within the boundaries of the empire that could not be managed by the central government.

The death of Theodosius left the empire without effective leadership, resulting in rebellions, assassinations, and power struggles. The eastern empire remained stable, but the government was unable to stop the western advance of the Germans and other barbarians. Groups of Germanic tribes attacked the empire during the fifth century. A group of Visigoths sacked Rome in 410, and then formed a large kingdom in southern Gaul and Spain. In 455 the Germanic Vandals pillaged Rome.

Other groups, including the Burgundians, Sueves, Alains, Alemanni, and Huns, captured large sections of Roman Europe. Angles, Saxons, and Jukes attacked Roman outposts in Britain and established small kingdoms. In the late fifth century, the Franks, led by their brilliant king, Clovis (481–511), drove out other tribes and established a large realm in northern Gaul and along the Rhine River. While most of these tribes were content to call themselves subjects of Rome, in reality the local areas were controlled by tribal kings.

As a result, by 500 the emperor in Constantinople had little authority in the western empire. The Germans were firmly established. The region was divided among competing tribes with little central control. Political chaos reigned. Thousands of large estates became isolated economic units having less contact with the outside world. The empire in the West had collapsed.[2]

Notes

1. From this point on, most of the dates in this book refer to times after the birth of Christ. As a result the label "C.E." is dropped. As with Tiberius, the dates after emperors' names will indicate the period of their rules, not their lifespans.

2. For a good discussion of the rise and fall of the Roman Empire, see John B. Harrison, Richard E. Sullivan, and Dennis Sherman. *A Short History of Western Civilization,* 6th ed. New York: Knopf, 1985, pp. 100–189.

BEGINNINGS

(6 B.C.E.–100 C.E.)

The Resurrection of Jesus

Jesus of Nazareth was born into a world dominated by Rome and filled with Jewish expectations of a Messiah. It was in this world that the new religion developing around him found a place for itself. This chapter briefly reviews the life, teachings, and ministry of the person who millions claim was the Messiah. The importance of the Resurrection for the early church and later Christian teaching is noted. Two approaches to Christianity that played a part in the creation of the new faith are discussed. Finally, we trace the development of the church at the end of the first century.

THE LIFE, TEACHINGS, AND MINISTRY OF JESUS

Stories about Jesus and his teachings were shared by word of mouth for many years before they were written down. Bits and pieces of very early information about Jesus have survived in the letters, or the Epistles, of Paul. Yet almost everything that is accepted as fact about Jesus is contained in the first four books of the New Testament: Matthew, Mark, Luke, and John.

These four books, which present the life and teachings of Jesus, are called the *Gospels*. In fact, since the first century, the term *Gospel* has been given to any of several writings that tell the story of Jesus' life. To produce the Gospels, the authors wrote down traditional, word-of-mouth stories about Jesus and used several older works, now lost, that told parts of Jesus' life and teachings. These stories were put together in readable life histories of Jesus. Mark was written ca. 70 C.E.; Matthew and Luke were composed ca. 80 C.E.; and John was authored ca. 80–100 C.E. (**C.E.** means "common era," referring to the time since the coming of Jesus, which is shared by Jews and Christians.)

Each of the Gospels was written for a different audience and presents a somewhat different understanding of Jesus. Matthew, Mark, and Luke contain much of the same material and paint a similar picture of Jesus. Because of this, they are called the **Synoptic Gospels.** The word *synoptic* means "giving an account from the same viewpoint."

Because they are the oldest of the Gospels, and because John presents a more highly developed theology, the synoptics are usually seen as containing the most accurate historical information about Jesus. We must realize, however, that even the synoptics are not intended to be simply factual accounts of Jesus' life. They are works written by people who believed that Jesus was the Messiah. They were intended to present the story of Jesus so that the people reading them would convert to the new faith.[1] Each Gospel is also meant to make certain points with its audience. Because of these characteristics, historical information must sometimes be separated from interpretation in these sources, as in any other historical document.

The Synoptic Problem

Scholars who research historical material often use existing documents to try to uncover actual events. As a rule, the sooner a document was written after an event, the better it records what occurred. Yet stories about events may be told for many years before they are written down. Moreover, earlier writings may be lost altogether or may appear in later documents in whole or partial form. Sometimes several documents exist that tell about the same event. These may contain the same or similar material, but they may also have different "tellings" of an event. From such a "puzzle" scholars must try to understand what actually happened.

One biblical puzzle is called the synoptic problem. The synoptic problem is to explain why Matthew, Mark, and Luke contain so much material that is the same and so much that is different. Scholars offer a number of theories, one of which is the four-source theory. It holds that Matthew and Luke wrote independently, drawing upon four different sources.

The four-source theory goes something like this. Because most of Mark is contained in Matthew and Luke, it must have been the earliest of the Gospels and must have been used by the other two writers in preparing their works. Matthew and Luke also contain an identical body of material that does not appear in Mark. They must have been using another source that has since been lost. Scholars call this source "Q" from the German word *Quelle*, which means *source*. Matthew also contains material that is not found in Mark, Luke, or Q. This is labeled "M." Luke contains material that is not found in Mark, Matthew, or Q. This is designated "L." The way the authors used this material to produce their Gospels is diagrammed on the next page.

The Life of Jesus

Jesus was born sometime between 6 and 4 B.C.E. and died sometime between 28 and 33 C.E.[2] He was born in the town of Bethlehem during the reign of Herod the Great, the son of a young woman named Mary. Some accounts say Mary was a virgin and that Jesus was conceived by the Holy Spirit. Jesus' family could be traced to King David.

Very little is known of Jesus' childhood. The Gospels relate only a few stories about his birth and infancy and provide details about a trip to the temple when he was around twelve. It is thought that Jesus was reared in Nazareth by Mary

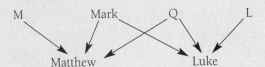

Scholars have also re-created the content of M, Q, and L, which must have been earlier than either Matthew or Luke. By looking at these and at Mark, they can gain insight into how some of the earliest Christian communities must have understood Jesus. This type of careful research helps us uncover the events of Jesus' life and teachings.

Because they are the oldest of the Gospels, and because John presents a more highly developed theology, the synoptics are usually seen as containing the most accurate historical information about Jesus. We must realize, however, that even the synoptics are not intended to be factual accounts of Jesus' life. They are works were written by people who believed that Jesus was the Messiah, and were intended to present the story of Jesus so that readers would convert to the new faith. Each Gospel is also meant to make certain points with its audience. For instance, Matthew was written for a Jewish audience and stresses how Jesus fulfilled many Old Testament prophecies. Luke was written for Gentiles, and therefore, does not stress the prophetic significance of Jesus' coming. Because of these characteristics, historical information must sometimes be separated from interpretation in these sources, as in any other historical document.

and her husband Joseph and that he probably became a carpenter like Joseph. Joseph seems to have died before Jesus began his ministry. Jesus received much the same education and religious training as other poor Jewish children of his day. He undoubtedly knew the Law and the Prophets well and had deep religious insight at an early age.

When Jesus was about thirty, he was attracted to the preaching of John the Baptist, who was his second cousin. John is portrayed as the last of the Old Testament Prophets in the Gospels and was possibly an Essene. His mission was to prepare the way for the coming Messiah. John lived in the desert and gathered

Important Events Related to First-Century Christianity

DATES	EVENTS	ROMAN EMPERORS	NEW TESTAMENT WORKS
37–4 B.C.E.	Palestine ruled by Herod the Great		
27 B.C.E.		Augustus	
6(?) B.C.E. to 4(?) B.C.E.	Birth of Jesus		
4–39 C.E.	Rule of Herod's sons: Archelaus, Antipas, Philip		
14 C.E.		Tiberius	
26–36	Pilate procurator of Judea; John the Baptist and Jesus minister		
24–29	Jesus' crucifixion		
35(?)	Stephen martyred		
37		Caligula	
41–44	Agrippa I, king of Judea; Jews expelled from Rome	Claudius	
48–54	Paul visits Thessalonica, Corinth, Ephesus		1 & (?) 2 Thessalonians
54		Nero	1 & 2 Corinthians, Galatians, Romans
56–64	Paul arrested in Jerusalem, tried, taken to Rome		Philippians, Philemon, Colossians (?)
66–73	Jews rebel against Rome; Jerusalem and temple destroyed	Galba, Otho, Vilellius, Vespasian	Mark, Ephesians (?)
79		Titus	Matthew, Luke–Acts
81–96		Domitian	Hebrews, 1 Peter, Revelation (?)
96		Nerva	John
98		Trajan	Letters of John, James
117–138	Bar Cochba revolt of Jews against Rome	Hadrian	Jude, 2 Peter, Pastoral Epistles*

*The date of the writing of many of the New Testament books is debatable, especially these. Some scholars date them in the first century.

Source: Adapted with modifications from Edwin D. Freed, *The New Testament: A Critical Introduction*, 2nd ed. Belmont, CA: Wadsworth, 1991, pp. xvi–xvii. © 1991 by Wadsworth, Inc.

a group of disciples (students, followers) around him. He preached a message calling for **repentance** (turning away from sin) and **baptism** (submerging in water), which was a sign that sin had been washed away. John taught that people were to repent and be baptized because the kingdom of God was near.

Jesus' ministry probably began with his baptism in the Jordan River by John. The synoptic Gospels report that after the baptism, the heavens opened and the spirit of God in the form of a dove descended on Jesus. A voice then said, "This is my beloved Son, with whom I am well pleased" (Matt. 3:16; also see Mark 1:10, Luke 3:22). This passage is very important because it shows how the early church (and perhaps Jesus himself) understood Jesus' messiahship. It combines an Old Testament passage from Psalms 2:7 about the Anointed One (Messiah) with another from one of the suffering servant sections of Isaiah (42:1). The teaching here is that the Messiah was to be a religious person who would suffer for his people, not an earthly king. This understanding of the Messiah is upheld in a temptation experience in the desert following Jesus' baptism.

After the temptation, Jesus collected a group of twelve disciples and began to minister in Galilee and Judea. Scholars disagree on how long Jesus' ministry lasted. Some claim it lasted for one year, while others hold that it was as long as three years. Whatever its duration, it had a period of initiation, followed by a time of popularity, and finally, a stage of increasing opposition.

Jesus' mission involved teaching, healing, and concern for the impoverished of society. These attributes and his extraordinary personality drew people to his work and allowed him to speak with authority. People were filled with expectations about the coming Messiah, and many ordinary people were probably attracted to Jesus by rumors of his miracles. The Pharisees and the Sadducees felt it was necessary to investigate this "new prophet." They were baffled by the depth of his answers to their questions and the manner in which he escaped their verbal traps. Few, if any, understood the nature of his mission and teaching. Even his closest followers failed to see. Opposition to Jesus increased.

Although Jesus' friends warned him of his disfavor with the authorities in Jerusalem, Jesus became determined to preach there during the Passover season.[3] Jesus' final week in Jerusalem before his crucifixion is the basis for what Christians call the *Passion Week*. It began with Jesus' entry into the city on Sunday where the crowds greeted him as the Messiah and waved palm branches and shouted greetings. The rest of the week he taught in the temple. His conflict with Jewish leaders in the temple made them finally decide to kill him.

The Gospels also report that Jesus began a meal with wine and bread that was to be the sign of a new covenant with his followers. This supper took place with his twelve disciples on Thursday night during the Passover celebration. After the supper, Jesus was betrayed and arrested, tried before the Sanhedrin for **blaspheming** God (cursing God), and tried by Pontius Pilate, the Roman governor, for plotting rebellion. Pilate sentenced him to death even though he could find no wrongdoing. Jesus was **crucified** (nailed to a wooden cross) on Friday by Roman soldiers on a hill outside Jerusalem and died before sundown that day.

The Teachings of Jesus

Most of what Jesus taught was drawn from his Jewish background. To many people he was just another wandering rabbi. The founding of Christianity rested more on who Jesus was and what he did than on what he said.

As did many other rabbis, Jesus taught about the kingdom of God and what it was like to be a citizen of that kingdom. Yet Jesus also sensed that God was working through him in a very powerful way. He did not merely say that the kingdom was "at hand." He said that the kingdom was already among or within God's children.

Jesus often called himself the Son of man. He may have chosen this term because it has different meanings. In the earlier parts of the Hebrew Scriptures, it often indicates nothing more than "a man." In later writings the Son of man is a figure who played a part in the coming of God's rule and the Day of the Lord. If Jesus used the term in this later meaning, then the presence of the kingdom and the Son of man meant that God's rule had broken into history as a changing power. Sin was being conquered and the world was being judged. People were living in the last days before history would be brought to an end. God would be revealed as the ruler of all.

Jesus taught that this power could be experienced in a very personal way. It was so personal that God's children could call him *Abba* (Hebrew for Daddy, Papa). They no longer had to see God just as an all-powerful king and stern lawmaker.

Jesus taught about ethics (ideas of right and wrong), particularly ethics of the kingdom. The center of these ethics was an intense love of God. God's children were to love God with all their hearts. Then they were to love their neighbors as themselves. This stress on love of God, one's neighbor, and one's self allowed people to live by the real spirit of the Law. If people were acting out of sincere love, they would automatically live according to the Law of God. Jesus taught that God's children were to keep their lives focused on God. They were not to become overly concerned with day-to-day matters. They were not to pursue worldly power, wealth, or position. They were to think little about clothing, shelter, or even their daily food. God knew what they needed. They were to seek first the kingdom of God and these material things would be given to them.

They were not to demand their "rights" at the expense of others. In fact, they were to go out of their way to do good for others. Jesus taught a radical departure from what was usually thought of as moral behavior. People living according to the principles of the Kingdom of God were to "resist not evil." If someone stole their coats, they were to give the thief their shirts as well. If a person struck them on the cheek, they were to offer the offender the other cheek to strike. They were to pray for their enemies, not despise them. They were to live honestly, humbly, and simply before God and at peace with others. When they failed or strayed, God would forgive. Like a loving parent, God would seek to bring them back to the right path. Jesus taught that these were the requirements and benefits of life in the kingdom of God.[4]

The Miracles and Ministry of Jesus

Jesus' ministry was mainly to the impoverished as well as to others in need. The Gospels report that Jesus' response to the needs of others around him often resulted in a miracle. **Miracle** is a relatively modern word. It indicates some occurrence in which natural laws are violated or set aside. Jesus' miracles took many forms, from turning water into wine, to healing the sick, to producing food from almost nothing, to casting out demons, to reviving the dead.

The nature of miracles has produced much debate in the Christian community, especially in the last four centuries. Since the eighteenth century, many people have come to believe that the universe runs according to natural laws. These laws cannot or would not be suspended by God or anyone else. Miracles simply do not occur. For example, a crooked leg that leaves a person unable to walk may result from a disease such as polio or a genetic defect. The ability to walk might be restored by a surgeon using medical skills and the body's natural healing process. However, no holy figure, not even the Son of God, can heal the lame by saying, "Take up your bed and walk" (Matt. 9:5–6). It may have been that miracles were natural happenings misunderstood by the superstitious people who saw them. Or miracles could be legends deliberately created by the writers of the Gospels to convince people that Jesus was divine.

Some people firmly believe in the miracles of Jesus and others found in the Bible. They argue that the miracles not only could occur but also did occur: if miracles involve the setting aside of natural laws, then God has the power to suspend them. Yet miracles may not mean that the laws of nature were changed. It is possible that God worked through these natural laws. So it is that the same power that created the universe is active in maintaining it. If a leg was made crooked, it can be "remade" straight. The same self-healing powers present in a patient's body that help a surgeon mend a crooked leg could be used by God to mend the leg without a knife!

Perhaps it is important not so much to settle this debate as to understand the role of miracles in the synoptic Gospels. As a rule, they seem to be used as signs of the divine. A **sign** is something that happens "naturally" when the divine is present. This idea is seen in Jesus' reply to John the Baptist found in Matthew 11:2–6.

> **Now when John heard in prison about the deeds of the Christ, he sent word by his disciples and said unto him, "Are you he who is to come, or shall we look for another?" And Jesus answered them, "Go and tell John what you hear and see: the blind receive their sight and the lame walk, lepers are cleansed and the deaf hear, and the dead are raised up, and the poor have good news preached to them.**

The total ministry of Jesus, including the miracles, is seen as showing the presence of the power of God in him. Following biblical tradition, the miracles are seen as the works of the Messiah—the deeds that no one else does. We must be careful at this point. Miracles are *not used to prove* Jesus is the Christ. In fact, Jesus refused to use them in this way. Rather, they are pictured as naturally "flowing out of" him as he responded to the needs of those he met. In short, the healing ministry and other miracles are signs of the presence of God in history. They show that in Jesus the kingdom of God has entered the human scene. The healing, wholeness, and peace promised in that kingdom are active in the world.[5]

THE POST-RESURRECTION CHURCH

After Jesus died, it seemed that his mission was a failure. His followers were disheartened and believed that their faith in him was in vain. They disbanded and scattered, fearing for their lives. Several returned to their former jobs.

But something happened in the early Christian community that turned the group around. The Gospels report that around dawn on the Sunday morning after Jesus' death one of his followers, Mary Magdalene, and a group of other women went to his tomb to put spices on the body. Jesus had been buried in a cave with a large stone covering the entrance. When the women got to the cave they noticed the stone had been rolled away. They looked in the cave and found that the body of Jesus had disappeared. They then saw one or perhaps two "young men" dressed in "shining clothing" who proclaimed that Jesus was not in the tomb but had risen from the dead. This rising from the dead is called the **Resurrection.** The Resurrection turned the early church around. It forced a rethinking of Jesus and his mission and became a cornerstone of the Christian faith.

Several appearances of the "risen Lord" to groups of followers are mentioned in the Gospels and other New Testament writings. During one appearance the disciples were commissioned (ordered) to preach about Jesus to the ends of the earth, to baptize those who believe, and to make disciples of all nations by teaching them "to observe all that I have commanded you (Matt. 28:19)." The book of Acts indicates that these appearances continued for forty days and ceased when Jesus was "carried up into heaven." This ascension of Jesus into heaven was accompanied by a promise that he would return to earth again in the same way.

The Question and the Power of the Resurrection

Debate about the nature of the Resurrection began very early in the church. Some denied that a physical raising of the body of Jesus from the dead had occurred. Others argued that a belief in the rising was vital to the Christian faith. This debate has continued over the centuries. Some contemporary scholars say that the New Testament stories are a way of talking about a change in thinking that happened among Jesus' early followers. The believers suddenly grasped the real nature of Jesus' teaching. He was not to be an earthly Messiah, and the kingdom was a spiritual kingdom not a political one. Another contemporary explanation is that Jesus was not really dead but had merely fainted from the pain and stress of the crucifixion. He revived in the coolness of the tomb and then was taken away by his disciples. Another popular approach holds that Jesus' "conscious personality" was freed from the body. In its new "spiritual form," it made several visible and audible appearances. Still others strongly defend the physical resurrection of Jesus from the dead.

Whatever the actual nature of the Resurrection, two things are undeniable. First, a belief in the physical resurrection became one of the most important teachings of orthodox Christianity. The Resurrection became the key for understanding the life, teachings, mission, and person of Jesus. It transformed a dead Jewish rabbi into the Christian living Lord who was God in the flesh.

Second, a very powerful event occurred in the early Christian community. The band of followers who were at first thrown into complete confusion by the crucifixion were soon roaming the empire, preaching the death and resurrection of Jesus as God's means of saving the world. Many of them boldly faced rejection, imprisonment, and death to proclaim that Jesus was the Christ.

The Church at Jerusalem

The earliest Christian church was at Jerusalem. This community began the process of understanding Jesus' mission and living in relationship with their "living Lord." Almost all that is known about the church at Jerusalem is found in the Acts of the Apostles, a New Testament book. Acts is a continuation of the Gospel of Luke, and both books were written by the same author. Luke tells of the birth, life, death, and resurrection of Jesus. Acts tells about the church in Jerusalem and the expansion of the church into the **Greco-Roman world** (the part of the world controlled by Rome). This church would remain an important center for the young Christian faith until the destruction of Jerusalem by the Romans in 70 C.E.

The church at Jerusalem was dominated by Simon Peter and the other eleven **apostles** (the people chosen by Jesus to be his students and most intimate friends).[6] The church met in homes for simple services involving prayer, singing, preaching, and, often, the celebration of a love feast remembering Jesus' last meal with his disciples. At first, the Christians saw themselves as a Jewish group. In addition to holding their own services, they worshiped at the temple and followed the Jewish Law.

The Church Spreads

The Scriptures tell of an extraordinary event that occurred fifty days after the Passover, and some scholars say this event marks the beginning of the church. Acts 2 reports that the group of believers had gathered with Jews from all over the world to celebrate the Jewish feast of Pentecost. Suddenly, a sound "came from heaven like the rush of a mighty wind and . . . filled . . . the house where they were sitting." Tongues of fire touched each believer. "They were all filled with the Holy Spirit and began to speak in other tongues, as the Spirit gave them utterance." The ruckus attracted the attention of a number of devout Jews, and Peter then preached to this group. According to Acts, about 3000 people became believers in Jesus Christ that day.

This passage is important for two reasons. First, it shows how much the early church emphasized the activity of the Holy Spirit. Although a complete understanding of the Trinity (Father, Son, Holy Spirit) had not yet been developed, the believers felt that God's Spirit rested on them in a very special way. He energized them, burning within their hearts. He empowered them to preach, to perform miracles, and to endure suffering for Jesus' sake. He guided their decisions and inspired them to spread the Gospel. His presence assured them that their faith in Jesus was correct and helped them live in the belief that Jesus' promise to return might be fulfilled at any moment.[7]

Second, the passage relates ways in which Christianity began to spread. The band of disillusioned followers began to boldly proclaim that Jesus was the Christ. When the converts (those who had changed to Christianity) from the Pentecost feast returned to their native lands, they carried the Gospel with them. They talked to friends and neighbors and preached Jesus as the Christ in Jewish synagogues throughout the Greco-Roman world.

Persecution actually aided the spreading of the Gospel. While the Christians in Jerusalem saw themselves as loyal Jews who were fulfilling the Law, the Jewish leaders took a different view. They regarded the believers as rebels who were teaching about a false Messiah. Persecution of the young church thus began. It resulted in the stoning death of Stephen, a Jew who had converted to Christianity and had become a leader in the Jerusalem church. Many fled the Jewish leaders, preaching about Jesus the Christ as they went. Christianity spread throughout Judea, to Samaria, and to Cyprus. Unknown believers took the message of Jesus to the city of Antioch in Syria. It was in Antioch that the first **Gentiles** (non-Jews) were converted to Christianity and the followers of Jesus were first called *Christians*. Antioch became an important center of Christianity in the first century.

Acts 2:43–47 paints an idealistic picture of life in the early Christian community. It says that the believers **held all things in common** (did not own their own property), sold their possessions and gave their money to the needy, had glad and generous hearts, and lived in favor with all people. A careful reading of Acts, however, reveals that this picture of perfect harmony is not entirely correct. Disagreements arose very early in the church over four issues:

1. Who can hear the Gospel?
2. Who is in charge?
3. What does it mean to be free?
4. Where can the story of Jesus be found?[8]

The first question concerns the universality of the Gospel. The second deals with the problem of authority. The next stems from different views among believers about the meaning of law and of grace. The last question leads to the eventual formation of the New Testament.

The most important question in the early community concerned the universality of the Gospel. The church had to decide if the Gospel was intended for Jews alone or for *all people*. In the beginning, Peter took the position that the Gospel was for Jews alone. Eventually he was led to see that the message of Jesus was for all people. Peter's chief opponent in the argument about the universality of the Gospel was Paul of Tarsus. It was with Paul, not Peter, that the future of the young church lay. It was Paul who became the great missionary spreading the message of Jesus Christ to the Gentiles. More than any other figure, Paul formed the theology of the Christian church. (Theology refers to the ways in which people understand and explain their faith.) In fact, Paul is second in importance only to Jesus in the history of Christianity.[9]

PAULINE CHRISTIANITY

Paul (died ca. 65 C.E.) was born to Jewish parents in the Cilicia (now in Turkey) city of Tarsus. Paul also had Roman citizenship because at least one of his parents was a Roman citizen. He was reared a strict Pharisee and went to Jerusalem to study under one of the greatest rabbis of his day, Gamaliel. His strong orthodox Jewish beliefs helped him to become a leader in the persecution of the early church, and he was present at the stoning of Stephen.

Paul, who was called Saul before he became a Christian, experienced a dramatic conversion while traveling to Damascus, where he was to arrest some Christians and bring them to Jerusalem for trial. According to Acts 9:1–31, on the road to Damascus, Paul was blinded by a light and a vision of the living Christ. In this vision, Paul became convinced that Jesus was the Christ and converted to Christianity. He was baptized, then retired to Arabia for a three-year period of meditation and preparation. Afterward, he returned to Jerusalem, where he was received with suspicion.

Paul as Missionary and Pastor

Paul eventually came to see himself as the Apostle to the Gentiles. His unique background in both Judaism and Hellenistic culture equipped him well. Acts reports that Paul undertook three missionary journeys around the eastern lands of the Mediterranean Sea. He began churches throughout Asia Minor and preached in Athens. The Christian communities in Galatia, Macedonia, Philippi, Thessalonica, Beroea, Corinth, Ephesus, Colossae, Philadelphia, Hierapolis, and Laodicea, among others, probably had their origins in the work of Paul.

Upon completion of his third journey, Paul went to Jerusalem to bring donations from the churches in Asia Minor to the mother church. In Jerusalem Paul was arrested by the Jewish temple leaders, but he invoked his right as a Roman citizen to have his case heard by the Roman emperor. Paul was shipwrecked during the trip to Rome, but he had many opportunities to minister. The book of Acts ends with Paul under house arrest in Rome awaiting trial. Tradition says he was freed and then preached the Gospel in Spain, though most scholars dispute this. Little is known about his death. Very early traditions claim he was martyred (killed for the faith) in Rome during persecutions of Christians by the emperor Nero.[10]

Paul not only founded many churches in his role as a missionary but also served as a "pastor advisor" to a number of first-century congregations. He wrote often to these communities to provide encouragement, to give guidance on questions of how believers should behave, and to offer opinions on theological disputes. He also had opponents who seemed to have followed him throughout his life. One group, the "Judaizers," wanted to place the Christian faith under the laws of the Jewish covenant.

Paul wrote a number of letters, or Epistles, to these early churches, which became the documents that orthodox Christianity would use as its basis for correct Christian morals and theology. A good portion of the New Testament is made up of Paul's letters. Because of the influence of his letters, it can be said that Paul created the basic framework for the type of Christianity that is practiced by most Christians today.

Pauline Theology

Paul began to write some ten to fifteen years after Jesus' crucifixion. His was not the first attempt to express the Christian faith. In fact, the effort to understand and explain the meaning of the life, teachings, and ministry of Jesus began shortly after the Resurrection. With Pentecost, a "fire" had been ignited in the church. People felt the power of God and found their lives completely changed. They experienced forgiveness and cleansing. They knew **reconciliation** (coming together) with God, with others, and within themselves.

The first attempt by Christians to explain who Jesus was and what was happening in the new community is found in what scholars call the **Kerygma,** which refers to the preaching or proclamation of the early church. Examples of the *Kerygma* are found in several places in the New Testament, including Peter's sermon at Pentecost (Acts 2:14–40). This sermon can be summarized as follows:

1. Jesus came in fulfillment of Old Testament promises.
2. He lived among us doing many mighty works.
3. According to God's plan, he was delivered to lawless men and crucified.
4. He died, was raised from the dead, and sits at the right hand of God.
5. God has made him both Lord and Christ.
6. Because of this you should repent, be baptized in the name of Jesus Christ, and receive the gift of the Holy Spirit.

These ideas made sense to many Jews. As Christianity spread into the Greco-Roman world, however, these ideas had little meaning. Hellenic culture had no cultural or religious basis for understanding a Jewish Messiah. Paul and others thus used ideas from other religions and philosophies as well as events in the everyday lives of the Gentiles to try to explain who Jesus was and what he did for people.

Paul's powerful mind produced a great expansion of the simple teachings of the early church. To Paul Jesus was more than the Jewish Messiah. He was the Son of God who existed before the world was created. Because of his death on the cross, he now sits at the right hand of God where all of creation worships him. Christ is pictured as the head of a new humanity—a new Israel—which is made of people who are saved by belief in Jesus. God has established with these believers a new covenant that includes both Jews and Gentiles. It ensures that Christians are the true "sons of Abraham" who will inherit the good things that were once intended for Jews alone.

Jesus the Christ is also presented as the head of the church. The church serves as the "body" that does his work and completes his suffering in the world. Completing the suffering of Christ means that the church is involved in bearing the burdens of those in need and taking on injustice aimed at the weak. Completing

vincetian

the suffering of Christ also means that the church is involved in restoring humanity to the proper relationship with God and assisting in bringing God's salvation.

Salvation was needed because humankind's sin had removed them from their proper relationship with God. All of creation was wrecked as a result. Humans rebelled against God and God's laws. They could not relate as they should to one another. Their natural drives and instincts were perverted, and even when they wanted to do good, they could not.

Paul taught that salvation was by grace through faith. **Grace** is God's unearned favor or unmerited love toward people. It was God's grace that sent Jesus the Christ to redeem sinful humans. God's grace produces faith in believers. Through faith people accept God's action in Christ and try to live as Christ lived. **Faith** for Paul is not a matter of a person deciding to "be better." It is a response to God that is produced by the Holy Spirit, which allows the believer to "put on Christ" (to become more like Christ). Paul pictured the life of grace as one that brought about a radical change in humans. He described Christians as people "in Christ" who no longer lived for themselves. They no longer lived according to the **flesh** (their sinful state) but **lived according to the Spirit** (their newfound relationship to God).

Paul also had some significant thoughts on the relation of the (Jewish) Law to the true Law of God. The Law was imposed from the outside and could not bring about the type of drastic change needed for a person to live as Christ. Humans by their good works could not earn salvation. To Paul, Jewish Law was a teacher to point up human shortcomings to drive humans to rely on the grace of God. Whether one chose to follow the Jewish Law was not very important to Paul. This Law might change people's behavior but not their hearts. In Christ, the true Law of God had been "written on the hearts" of believers. That is, it had been made a part of their very characters. Doing good, obeying God, becoming like Christ were seen as the natural results of the work of the Holy Spirit in the lives of believers. Good works were not efforts to win salvation; they "flowed out" from the power active in the hearts of Christians.

The sign of the activity of the Spirit in the community was the way Christians loved one another and those around them. This activity would be complete when Jesus returned to establish the new heaven and the new earth where humans would live in proper relationship to God, fellow humans, and nature. Peace and harmony would be restored. Reflecting Jesus' ideas about God's kingdom, Paul's writings teach a radical equality of members of the church. For Paul, there are no males or females, rich or poor, master or slave. Everyone is equal before God. Early on, these and other teachings of Paul were accepted by parts of the church as correct understandings of Christ and his work. By the end of the first century, many Christians held that Paul's epistles were Scripture much like the Old Testament writings. Paul's writings continue today to be a powerful force in the church.

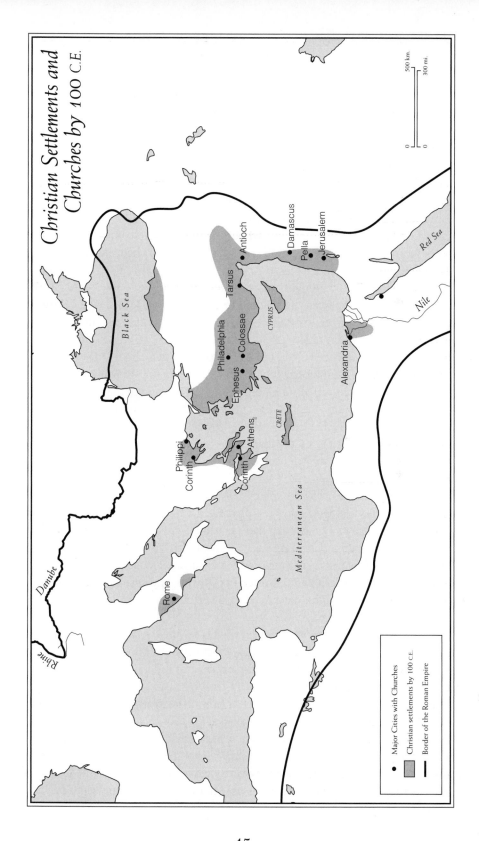

Christian Settlements and
Churches by 100 C.E.

500 km.
300 mi.

Red Sea

Nile

Damascus
Pella
Jerusalem
Antioch
Tarsus

Black Sea

CYPRUS

Philadelphia
Colossae
Ephesus

Alexandria

CRETE

Athens

Philippi
Corinth

Mediterranean Sea

Danube

Rome

Rhine

Major Cities with Churches
Christian settlements by 100 C.E.
Border of the Roman Empire

JOHANNINE CHRISTIANITY

Another important development in the early church is Johannine Christianity, which is the school of thought that appears in the Gospel of John, 1, 2, and 3 John, and, possibly, the Revelation of John. These books were written in the late first century, probably after 90 C.E. This material seems to have been written to Gentile Christians who were separated from the larger church and did not join that body until the second century.[11]

Modern scholars disagree over who actually wrote these books. Some agree with the ancient Christian tradition that John the son of Zebedee was the author. Together with Peter and James this John was one of the most important of Jesus' original twelve disciples. He may have been the one referred to in the Gospel of John as "beloved disciple" and the "one whom Jesus loved." If this is the case, his very special relationship to Jesus could have inspired the deep insight into the mission of Jesus that is in the Johannine writings. Other scholars believe the son of Zebedee could not have produced these books. They attribute the works to some "unknown John" who was a disciple of Jesus. Still others believe that the books were by a follower or followers of John the son of Zebedee who wrote down and expanded John's ideas. Another group contends the author was a Christian of Hellenistic or Hellenistic-Jewish tradition who may have lived several generations after Jesus.

The Johannine writings reflect a battle with two groups: the Gnostics, who rejected the idea that Jesus was divine, and those Jews who rejected Jesus as the Christ. As we saw in Chapter 1, the Gnostics kept a rigid separation between the spiritual world and the physical, material world. Spirit was good; matter was evil. As a result, they had great difficulty with any belief that had God, who was spirit, appearing in a physical body in Jesus. Some Gnostics believed Jesus was just a man who had special knowledge from God. Others thought that Jesus was a divine being (a god) who *only appeared* to be human. Against this thinking, John developed a powerful **incarnational theology** that taught that Jesus was indeed *God made flesh*.

John also disagrees with those Jews who rejected Jesus. For him the real enemies of Jesus were those Jewish leaders who were blind to the "light and life" Jesus brought, who rejected God's salvation found in Jesus, and who were the "children of Satan" who crucified Jesus. This strong teaching against "the Jews" is found in the Gospel of John but not in the synoptic Gospels or other New Testament writings. It probably reflects the poor relations that had existed from the beginning between the church and those Jews who did not accept Jesus. It may be also indicate resentment over the persecution of Christians by some Jews, which was common in the early years of the church. John's teachings are not intended to be applied to all Jews. After all, Jesus was a Jew and perhaps

John was, too. Jews who rejected Jesus were used by John as a symbol for all "people of the world" who refused to accept the light Jesus brought. Still, these writings have been interpreted in such a way that they have been the ground for much of the **anti-Semitism** (hatred of Jews) and the persecution of Jews by Christians in later centuries.

John's teachings about Christ had broad impact on the church. According to John, everything about Jesus was a revelation of God. Jesus is shown as the **Divine Word** (Logos) who was with God before creation. This Word made the universe and everything in it. The Word became flesh in Jesus and lived among humans to be their "light and life." To see him was to see God. In Jesus it is revealed that "God is love." The Word works with the Spirit to make sure that this love fills the Christian community. Love is the main trait of the person and of the community which is "in God." Christians take over Jesus' role as the revealer of God's love. For John, Jesus is God but also depends on God as a child depends on a parent. This conflict between equality and dependency was the source of many controversies that challenged the church in the years to come. John's "Logos" theology was readily understood by many Greco-Roman Christians who were familiar with the Logos from Stoicism and other philosophies. It has provided one of the bridges between Scripture and philosophy throughout Christian history.

John also extended Christian thought in another direction. According to John, Jesus not only reveals God but also is the Savior of the world. He has the role of giving life to the world. To know Jesus is to know God and to have eternal life. He is the source of life for Christians who can thrive and "bear fruit" only when they have the right relation to him. Being faithful to Jesus ensures that believers will receive the Holy Spirit as helper and counselor. Jesus' presence in the Christian community ensures its victory because he overcame the world. His death and Resurrection fulfilled the mission of God, and he returned to God and to the glory he had before creation. This high **Christology** (doctrine of Christ) contributed much to the church's developing understanding of the person and the work of Jesus.

THE CHURCH AT THE CLOSE
OF THE FIRST CENTURY

By the end of the first century, the Christian church was firmly established at the eastern end of the Mediterranean Sea, particularly in Palestine and Asia Minor. There were five churches in Greece. Two each were found in Cyprus, Italy, and North Africa. One of the Italian churches was located in Rome. The church had little overall impact on the empire at this point because Christians

Ignatius of Antioch: An Apostolic Father

The **Apostolic Fathers** were a group of second generation Christian leaders who were believed to have been taught by the twelve inner core of disciples who were the closest friends of Jesus. St. Paul was later added as the thirteenth apostle. The apostles were valued so highly because they had seen and learned directly from Jesus. The second-generation Apostolic Fathers were believed to have preserved true teachings of the Lord. They also are important because they indicate how the theology and structure of the church was developing. Some of these writers bridge the period from the late first century to the early second century.

Ignatius, Bishop of Antioch, (ca. 35–ca. 107) was one of the more important of these writers. Ignatius and his death at the hands of the Romans are discussed in Chapter 3. At this point, let us mention a few of his ideas. Ignatius is believed to be a student of John, Jesus' "beloved disciple." His ideas are important because they provide the basis for later teachings and they give some idea about what was controversial and what was beginning to be accepted by "mainstream" Christians at the end of the first century.

Ignatius strongly defended the idea that Jesus was born of the Virgin Mary and was truly God made flesh. Often when a writer takes a position for or against a particular issue, this means that the issue is a topic of controversy. Certainly, Ignatius' writings indicate the incarnation was controversial. However, he also seems to have believed that the Jesus-is-God-made-flesh position was "traditional" and should be accepted. (Despite this stance, Jesus' humanity, God-nature, and his relation to the Holy Spirit remained major areas of conflict in Christianity for the next 500 years—see Chapter 4).

Ignatius also taught a three-fold division of church leadership into bishops, priests, and deacons; loyalty to a Christian's bishop; the superiority of bishops to priests; the holiness of the Catholic Church (He is the first known writer to use the term "Catholic"—meaning universal church.); importance of the sacrament of communion—the ritual of taking bread and wine as part of the salvation process; (he is the first to refer to the sacrament as the Eucharist or "holy gifts"); the infallibility of the Church; the leading position of the church at Rome among other churches; the importance of remaining a virgin as a way to serve God; and the religious nature of marriage. For many generations, Christians have looked to Ignatius of Antioch as a source of inspiration as well as a powerful source of Christian theology.

were a very small minority. Its impact also was limited by the fact that the vast majority of believers were from the lower classes, though some middle- and upper-class people did belong to congregations.[12]

The Church and the World

The new faith did not completely escape the notice of government officials. The emperor Claudius Nero (37–68 C.E.) began a persecution of Christians at Rome in 64 C.E. Believers were tortured, thrown to beasts in the arena, and used as human torches to light parties in the royal gardens. These persecutions, the first of many that played an important role in early Christian history, will be discussed in greater detail in Chapter 3.

Persecution by the Roman government caused the new religion to reexamine its understanding of church–state relations. In its early years, Roman officials identified the Christian faith with Judaism. Because Judaism was an officially recognized religion, the new sect enjoyed government protection. During this time, Christian writers were favorable toward the authorities. Paul said that government was ordained of God to maintain good order and officials were ministers of God working for the good of all people. Christians were urged to submit themselves to government authorities as they would to God. When persecution began and Roman emperors began to call themselves gods, Christian writers then viewed government as evil. It was presented in the Scriptures in the Revelation of John as the embodiment of the **Antichrist** (a representative of Satan who is Christ's great enemy). The problem of church–state relations will occur again and again in Christian history. It still remains a source of on-going controversy.

The first century was a time in which the new religion struggled to understand itself and its relation to the world. The close association with Judaism gave way to a complete break between the two faiths, in part because of their conflict over the issue of whether Jesus was the true Messiah. In the beginning, Christians worshiped and preached in Jewish synagogues. Eventually they both withdrew from the synagogues and were barred by the Jews from them. Judaism also was abandoned by many because the majority of Christians ended up as Gentiles. They preferred to adapt ideas from Greek philosophy and other religions, rather than from Judaism, for understanding Jesus' mission and the Christian life. This separation from Judaism had several results. One was that the majority of Christians quit following the Jewish Law.

Worship was held on Sunday (the first day of the week) instead of Saturday (the Jewish Sabbath) to emphasize the break with Judaism. The fact that the Resurrection occurred on Sunday also encouraged early Christians to change their day of worship. Although Gentile Christians were beginning to dominate, groups who believed that Christians should follow the Jewish Law still existed at the close of the first century. Groups of "Judaizers," such as the Nazareans,

Ebionites, and the Clementines, would continue for some time. They would influence what eventually became orthodoxy, but the future of the young religion was not with them.

Another issue forced the church to decide how it was to live in its world. After the Resurrection and Pentecost, Christians, who experienced their faith directly, expected Christ to return at any moment. Tremendous excitement filled the small group of believers and the Spirit roamed free. Converts sold all that they had, gave the money they received to the church, and waited breathlessly for the coming of the Lord. Many left homes, possessions, families, and jobs to wait! In such a situation, little thought was given to the future and to dealing with such everyday matters as marriage and death, creating guidelines for church discipline, defining Christian beliefs, and establishing church officers. Yet the Lord did not return, and these practical issues had to be dealt with. Much New Testament writing is concerned with these problems.

Emerging Orthodoxy

As the church neared the end of the first century, the emotional, free-flowing religion that operated without forms or guidance had largely given way to a faith operating in more regular channels. Christians still met in homes but worship services followed more set rituals. Many churches had developed established officers such as bishops, priests, deacons, and elders. The basic qualifications for holding these offices had been identified. The pattern that made all Christians (males and females, masters and slaves) equal was beginning to break down. The move was toward a hierarchical arrangement in which some persons had higher rank than others. Thus men had higher rank than women and priests and members of the clergy had higher rank than other Christians. The bishop was no longer just another pastor but was increasingly seen as a person with the authority to decide questions of theology and church morals. He also presided over special ceremonies such as baptisms and the Lord's Supper.

A concern for sound doctrine was also obvious. While Gnostic Christians, Judaizers, and others were still present, Paul's teachings were widely accepted. Incarnational ideas, such as those of Johannine Christianity, were having their effects, too. The baptism and the Lord's Supper were seen as sacraments, not just as a ritual for admission into the church and a symbolic remembrance of Jesus the Christ's sacrifice. A **sacrament** is a physical act that somehow leads to participation in the supernatural. When Christians were baptized, their sins were forgiven, they experienced the grace of God, and their salvation was assured. In the same way, eating the bread and drinking the wine (eating the flesh and drinking the blood of Christ) at the Lord's Supper transferred the grace of God and assured continued participation in the divine life.

CONCLUSIONS

This chapter has presented a discussion of the emergence of Christianity in the first century. We looked briefly at the life and teachings of Jesus. From ideas about messiahship, the kingdom of God, and obedience to God, an elaborate theology began to take shape in which Jesus was presented as the eternal Logos, God incarnate, the Savior of the world, and the being who would come at the end of time to create a new heaven and new earth.

Day-to-day realities, such as dealing with the Jews and facing the fact that Jesus did not return, forced the church to come to terms with a number of important problems. By the end of the first century, a more unified, sound doctrine was appearing, patterns of worship had begun to be more standardized, a hierarchy of church leaders was being formed, and sacramental theology was being established. These trends are the roots of the catholic (universal) faith, which would take form in the following centuries.

Despite these new standards, a number of other patterns for worship, doctrine, and governing the church were still operating. Some of these would be the source of strong conflict within the Christian community and between the church and outsiders as the young faith struggled to establish orthodox beliefs and to win acceptance in the world.

Notes

1. For a discussion of the nature of the Gospels, see Mary Jo Weaver, *Introduction to Christianity*. Belmont, CA: Wadsworth, 1984, pp. 26–28.

2. Some scholars believe Jesus was born in 6 B.C.E. and others in 4 B.C.E. No one argues that Jesus was born at the start of the year 1 C.E. Jesus' birth was misdated when Dionysius Exiguus suggested the date for the incarnation in Rome in the sixth century C.E. Exiguus' date was eventually accepted throughout all Christianity, though it was soon discovered by Church officials to be incorrect.

3. Passover is the Jewish holiday that celebrates the deliverance of the Hebrews from Egypt.

4. For a discussion of the kingdom, especially in Mark, see David L. Barr, *The New Testament Story: An Introduction*. Belmont, CA: Wadsworth, 1987, pp. 151–171.

5. For a discussion of the teaching style and miracles of Jesus, see Edwin D. Freed, *The New Testament: A Critical Introduction*. Belmont, CA.: Wadsworth, 1986, pp. 167–188.

6. Jesus chose twelve people to be his closest students and disciples. One of these, Judas, betrayed him to the Sanhedrin and later hanged himself. The church at Jerusalem selected another follower to replace Judas.

7. For a discussion of the Resurrection, Holy Spirit, and spread of the church in the first century, see Kenneth Scott Latourette, *A History of Christianity*, vol. 1, *Beginnings to 1500,* rev. ed. New York: Harper & Row, 1975, pp. 57–75.

8. For a good discussion of the importance of these questions in the early church, see Weaver, *Christianity*, pp. 36–42.

9. For a discussion of Paul and his role in Christianity, see Roland H. Bainton, *Christendom: A Short History of Christianity and Its Impact on Western Civilization,* vol. 1, *From the Birth of Christ to the Reformation.* New York: Harper Torchbooks, 1966, pp. 43–50.

10. Early Christian tradition also indicates that Peter was martyred in Rome. The association of Rome with the two great figures of first-century Christianity was an argument for making the city the center of the religion.

11. For a discussion of the content and contribution of the Johannine tradition, see John Carmody, Denise Lardner Carmody, and Gregory A. Robbins, *Exploring the New Testament.* Englewood Cliffs, N.J.: Prentice-Hall, 1986, pp. 265–344.

12. For a good discussion of the social structure of the early church, see Kurt Aland, *A History of Christianity,* vol. 1, *From the Beginnings to the Threshold of the Reformation,* trans. by James L. Schaaf. Philadelphia: Fortress, 1985, pp. 56–64.

Additional Readings

Brown, Raymond E. *Antioch and Rome.* New York: Paulist, 1983.

———. *The Birth of the Messiah.* Garden City, NY: Doubleday, 1977.

Brown, Raymond E. et al. *John and the Dead Sea Scrolls.* New York: Crossroad, 1990.

Bultman, Rudolf. *History of the Synoptic Tradition.* New York: Harper & Row, 1968.

———. *The Gospel of John: A Commentary.* Philadelphia: Westminster, 1971.

———. *The Johannine Epistles.* Philadelphia: Fortress, 1973.

Cullmann, Oscar. *The Christology of the New Testament.* Philadelphia: Westminster, 1963.

———. *Early Christian Worship.* London: SCM, 1953.

Crossan, John Dominic. *The Historical Jesus: The Life of a Mediterranian Peasant.* San Francisco: HarperSanFrancisco, 1993.

_____. *The Birth of Christianity: Discovering What Happened in the Years Immediately after the Execution of Jesus.* San Francisco: HarperSanFrancisco, 1998.

Danielou, Jean. *The Theology of Jewish Christianity.* Vol. 1, *The Development of Christian Doctrine Before the Council of Nicea.* Translated by John A. Baker. Chicago: Regnery, 1964.

Davis, Stephen C. and Daniel Kendall.eds. *The Resurrection* New York: Oxford University Press, 1997.

Dodd, C. H. *The Apostolic Preaching and Its Developments.* London: Hodder and Stoughton, 1936.

Doran, Robert. *Birth of a Worldview: Early Christianity in Its Jewish and Pagan Context.* San Francisco: Harper, 1995.

Funk, Robert W. *Honest to Jesus: Jesus for a New Millennium. San Francisco: Harper,* 1997.

Harding, Mark. *Early Christian Life and Thought in Social Context: A Reader.* London: T. and T. Clark, 2003.

Hays, Richard B. *The Moral Vision of the New Testament: A Contemporary Introduction to New Testament Ethics.* San Francisco: Harper, 1996.

Kee, Howard C. *Jesus in History: An Approach to the Study of the Gospels.* 2nd ed. New York: Harcourt Brace Jovanovich, 1977.

MacDonald, Dennis R. *The Legend and the Apostle: The Battle for Paul in Story and Canon.* Philadelphia: Westminster, 1982.

Nolan, Albert. *Jesus Before Christianity.* Maryknoll, NY: Orbis, 1992.

Pagels, Elaine H. *The Gnostic Paul: Gnostic Exegesis of the Pauline Letters.* Philadelphia: Fortress, 1975.

Richardson, Alan. *An Introduction to the Theology of the New Testament.* New York: Harper, 1958.

Shorto, Russell. *Gospel Truth: The New Image of Jesus Emerging from Science and Why It Matters.* New York: Riverhead, 1997.

Stark, Rodney. *The Rise of Christianity: A Sociologist Reconsiders History.* Princeton, NJ: Princeton University Press, 1996.

Stowers, Stanley. K. *A Rereading of Romans: Justice, Jews, and Gentiles.* New Haven, CT: Yale University Press, 1996.

Torjesen, Karen Jo. *When Women Were Priests: Women's Leadership in the Early Church and the Scandal of Their Subordination in the Rise of Christianity.* San Francisco: Harper, 1995.

White, Michael. *From Jesus to Christianity.* San Francisco: HarperSanFrancisco, 2004.

Wicker, Kathleen, Musa Dube, and Althea Spencer Miller. *Feminist New Testament Studies: Global and Future Perspectives.* New York: Palgrave Macmillan, 2005.

Wilson, R. M. *Gnosis and the New Testament.* Philadelphia: Fortress, 1968.

Websites

http://catholic-resource.org/Reciprocal-links.htm. [Site provides links to Roman Catholic and Protestant sources.]

http://faculty.bbc.edu/RDecker/NT_gospe.htm. [Site provides a number of articles on New Testament books and scholarship.]

www.questia.com/library/religion/christianity/the-bible. [Site provides links to articles and books on relevant topics.]

www.religiousstudies.uncc.edu/JDTABOR/indexb.html. [Site provides links to a host of materials on the Jewish and Roman worlds of Jesus.]

THE FAITH OF THE FATHERS
Persecution to Establishment (100–500 C.E.)

Saint Lucy, an early martyr

The patristic period in Christian history ranged from ca. 100 to about 500 C.E.[1] The term *patristic* comes from the Latin word meaning *father.* During this period creative thinkers hammered out most of the basic doctrines (teachings) of Christianity in response to controversies within the church, persecution and threats from without, and other historical developments. As a group, these early writers are referred to as "the fathers of the church" or simply "the Fathers."

The patristic period also saw Christianity grow from a small, vulnerable, often persecuted sect in the first century to become the official religion of the Roman Empire. Other important changes also came about. Orthodox doctrines became firmly rooted. A hierarchy of church offices was clearly established. Higher officials increasingly sought to control the actions and teachings of lower-ranking Christians, including government officers. The beginnings of a fateful split between Western (Roman Catholic) and Eastern (Orthodox) Christianity emerged. Overall, the church developed in this period into an institution that was in a strong position to influence spiritual and political matters throughout Europe. The changing position of the church was in part due to drastic changes in the Roman Empire itself.

The patristic period was one of the most important eras in Christian history. This chapter begins by looking at developments in the Roman Empire that are important in the life of the church. We then look at church-state relations as the faith moves from persecution to domination of the Roman world and at theological developments and controversies created by changes in these church-state relations.

Chapter 4 continues to examine the patristic period. It reviews problems of authority and other major controversies within the Christian community, notes some important theologians, and discusses the condition of the church at the beginning of the sixth century.

CHURCH-STATE RELATIONS

From the first century onward, Christianity experienced dramatic growth. Beginning with the second century, the numbers of Christians had increased to the point that they could not be ignored. Yet the official Roman reaction to Christians varied considerably, ranging from toleration to persecution to acceptance to **establishment** (making Christianity the official religion). The treatment of the church was tied closely to the economic, social, and political conditions of the empire. More often than not, the faith was used as a pawn in larger political games. In this section, we look at church-state relations during the patristic period as the church gradually moved from persecution to establishment.

Important Events of the Patristic Period

DATES	EVENTS	ROMAN EMPERORS	CHURCH PERSONS	WRITINGS
64 C.E.	Burning of Rome, persecution of Christians, death of Peter and perhaps Paul	Nero	Peter, Paul	
81–96	Persecution of Christians	Domitian		The Revelation of John (?)
96–180	Height of Roman Empire	Nerva, Trajan, Hadrian, Antoninus, Marcus Aurelius		
107	Death of Ignatius		Ignatius of Antioch	Letters
111	Policy on persecution	Trajan		Correspondence with Pliny the Younger
150–254	Writings of apologists		Justin, Minucius Felix, Antenagoras, Tertullian, Melito of Sordis, Aristides, Origen, others	
193–211	Persecution of Christians	Septimius Severus		
250–251	Empire-wide persecution	Decius	Cyprian, Novatian	
251?–356	Beginnings of monasticism		Anthony of Egypt	

Persecution and Conflict

The first few hundred years of church history is commonly considered to be a time of constant conflict with Roman authorities, and some claim that "the church was built upon the blood of martyrs." The believers who gave their lives for their faith did place an unforgettable stamp on the church. Martyrdom was seen by them as a sure sign of the saving grace of God. It was regarded as the "highest calling" of a Christian and even was actively sought by some.

Important Events of the Patristic Period

DATES	EVENTS	ROMAN EMPERORS	CHURCH PERSONS	WRITINGS
257–258	Empire-wide persecution	Valerian		
295	Persecution begins again	Diocletian		
311	Beginning of Donatist Controversy	Constantine	Caecilian, Felix of Aptunga, Donatus	
313	Toleration granted to Christians	Constantine, Licinius		Edict of Milan
324	Sole emperor	Constantine		
330	Constantinople dedicated as new capital	Constantine		
330–379	Eastern monasticism founded		Basil the Great	Rule of St. Basil
361–363	Persecution of Christians	Julian the Apostate		
363	Persecution ends			
380	Christianity established	Theodosius I		Edict of Theodosius
410	Visigoths sack Rome			
455	Vandals sack Rome			
480–550	Western monasticism		Benedict of Nursia	Rule St. Benedict

Throughout Christian history these martyrs have been praised as shining examples of the Christian faith. Moreover, their steadfast beliefs and the peace with which they faced death often served as forceful witness to Christ to **pagans** (non-Christians). More than one pagan was converted to Christianity by witnessing an execution of a believer, which was supposed to discourage people from following the religion!

Early Patristic Period. For the most part, however, Christians were left alone during the early patristic period. Although the faith was declared "illegal" in the first century, actual persecution of the Christians was sporadic. It usually was limited to situations where an individual local official or emperor would attack the church. Even more common were cases of persecution where the "crime" of an individual Christian or a group of Christians was brought to the attention of authorities. Seldom did one find empire-wide abuse.

The average Christians probably lived quiet lives, mostly in cities. There they minded their businesses or practiced their crafts, married, had families, participated in most of the duties of a Roman citizen, and spread throughout all levels of Roman society. Their ethics required them to lead moral lives, to work hard, and to help others. They were challenged to dress plainly without ornaments or signs of office. They often would not attend pagan festivals, serve in the army, hold the office of judge, or give sacrifices to Roman gods.

At times the Christians' sacramental meals (where "blood" was drunk and "flesh" was eaten), their practice of baptizing both males and females, and their **love feasts** (a meal held in the early church along with the Eucharist) led to charges of cannibalism or sexual misconduct. But on the whole, most Christians were probably viewed by other citizens of the empire as "good neighbors." When there were periods of persecution, not all Christians chose martyrdom. Many fled, others denied their faith, and some performed sacrifices to the emperor or Roman gods while still regarding themselves as Christians.

The first known persecution of Christians began with the emperor Nero in 64, when large sections of Rome burned. Apparently to remove suspicion from himself, Nero decided to blame the fire on Christians. The Roman historian Tacitus says the Christians were persecuted because of "abominations" and their "hatred of humankind." While the exact nature of the charges against Christians is unclear, many did suffer cruel deaths because of their faith. It is possible that both Peter and Paul died in Rome during this era. These persecutions seem to have occurred only in Rome and ended when Nero was removed from the throne in 68.

Neither Vespasian nor Titus bothered the church. This situation changed when Domitian came to power. He did not take notice of the Christians at first, but for some unknown reason he later launched attacks on them. These attacks possibly occurred because he had begun to persecute Jews, and Roman authorities still did not make a clear distinction between Christians and Jews at this point. After Domitian's death Christians had another time of peace.

Reasons for Persecution. Early writings help clarify the reasons for the persecutions and the attitudes toward martyrdom. Some of the most important documents are the letters exchanged between Pliny and Trajan. In 111, Pliny the Younger was appointed governor of Bithynia on the northern coast of modern

Tertullian

There were many important theologians who contributed to developing Christian theology during the patristic period. Tertullian (ca. 160–225) was one. He was born and raised in Carthage in a pagan family and converted to Christianity before 197. After his conversion he became a strong defender of the Christian faith. He stressed strict morality, which was one factor that led him to become a Montanist later in life. The **Montanists** were a group that looked for Christ's immediate return and that practiced **asceticism** (strict discipline of the body). They flourished in North Africa in the early third century.

Tertullian's famous question, "What has Athens to do with Jerusalem?" implies a rejection of pagan philosophy as a ground for Christian theology. Yet he wrote several works that drew heavily upon pagan philosophy. Tertullian was a prolific writer and was the first major theologian to write in Latin (earlier thinkers wrote in Greek). His writings not only advanced Christian theology but also now serve as resources for historians studying the controversies, patterns of worship, and Christian morality of the early third century.

Tertullian's *Apology* is his most famous work. It argued that Christianity should be tolerated by the pagans. His *Against Marcion* defended the use of the Old Testament by Christians as well as the oneness of God. *Against Praxeas* developed a doctrine of the Trinity. His *On the Soul* was the first Christian psychology, and *On Baptism* was the earliest surviving document on that subject.[2]

Turkey. There were so many Christians in Bithynia that the pagan temples were abandoned. Someone sent Pliny a list of Christians, and, because the religion was illegal, he sought out those on the list. Those who denied the faith, made sacrifices to the Roman gods, and cursed Christ were freed. Those who did not deny Christianity suffered other fates. Non-Romans were executed for their "obstinacy" while Roman citizens were sent to Rome for trial. Pliny was uncertain how to handle the situation. He also had doubts about the legal grounds for executing the Christians. Outside of obstinacy, what was their crime? Should they be punished just because of "the Name" (Christian) or only if they had committed a specific crime?

Pliny wrote the emperor for guidance. Trajan's reply is important for three reasons. First, it does not seem to establish a new policy but instead expresses the practices that had been used for some time. Second, it became the "official" policy toward Christians followed throughout the empire. With a few exceptions this policy directed officials until the rule of Constantine. Third, it gives some idea why the government found Christians threatening.

Trajan said that there was no general rule as to when to punish Christians. Their crime of faith was so insignificant that government officials were not to waste time hunting them down. If Christians were accused, they were to be given the opportunity to deny their faith and to perform sacrifices to the pagan gods. The accusation could not be made by people who were unwilling to give their names. Should the accused refuse to worship the gods, they were to be punished. The reason for punishment is equally interesting. Christians were not to be punished for crimes they had committed before being brought to trial. Instead, they were punished for their lack of respect for Roman courts during their trials. In addition, their refusal to sacrifice to the gods and the emperor seemed to question the emperor's right to rule.

This last point is key to understanding pagan suspicion of Christians. It was not their supposed abominations (cannibalism, sexual immorality, and so on) that got them in trouble; rather, it was their "hatred of humankind" that led to their abuse. In other words, when the Christians failed to sacrifice to the gods, they were showing their disrespect for Roman tradition and civilization. Because the religious system was so intertwined with the civic duties of a citizen, refusal to perform acts of worship to the pagan gods meant that a person was disloyal to the empire.

This same idea is behind the charge of "atheism" that was sometimes leveled against Christians. We usually think of atheists as people who do not believe in a god or gods. Yet, Christians believed in God (although some Romans had trouble with the invisible God they followed). The problem was that they refused to submit to the "right" gods. The emperor himself was viewed as a god and a savior by the Roman people. If people sacrificed to the emperor and other Roman gods, thus performing the *proper* religious duties as well as indicating loyalty to the state, they were free to worship whatever other gods (or no other gods) they wished. The commitment of Christians to the empire was further questioned because they refused to attend Roman festivals and games and to serve in the army. No matter how much Christians proclaimed their loyalty to the empire, they could not overcome the suspicions of the obviously loyal pagans.

The Christian Reaction. Second-century writings also show the Christian attitude toward martyrdom. Among the more important writings are the seven letters of Ignatius of Antioch (ca. 35–107). Ignatius, bishop of Antioch, was a man so respected for his faith that he was known by the title "Bearer of God." The elderly bishop was condemned to death by imperial officials for his faith around 107 C.E. He was sent to Rome to have the sentence carried out, and on the way Ignatius and the soldiers guarding him traveled through Asia Minor. En route, he entertained other Christians and even dictated letters to Christian secretaries. Some scholars believe this would have been impossible had there been a general persecution in the empire.

As Ignatius approached Rome, he heard that Christians there were plotting to free him. He urged his fellow Christians not to prevent the execution as it was clearly God's plan for him. He desired to behave as a true Christian, to take part in the sacrifice of Christ, to be "God's wheat" ground in the teeth of beasts so he could be offered as the "pure bread" of Christ. This sacrifice would allow him to be the witness to the faith he desired. Apparently Ignatius was granted his request and died in a Roman game.

Other important figures who died at the hands of the Romans during these second-century persecutions include Polycarp (ca. 69–155), Justin Martyr (ca. 100–165), and the widow Felicity and her seven sons. Attacks against Christians also were carried out under Marcus Aurelius and Septimius Severus (193–211).

Most second-century persecutions were limited and local; however, the situation changed in the third century. As the empire began to decline, more and more Christians were persecuted. Sometimes they were used as convenient scapegoats by government officials for various problems. Other times emperors came into power who believed that only by returning to the "old ways" could the glory of Rome be restored. These emperors launched widespread persecution of the "new faith" in order to rebuild pagan religion. Septimius Severus carried on his persecutions into the third century but they lessened under the emperors who followed. During most of the first half of the third century, Christianity enjoyed relative peace and growth.

When Decius came to power in 249, a systematic, empire-wide attack on Christianity began. Decius was convinced that the empire was in trouble because the old gods were being neglected. He decreed that everyone must perform sacrifices to the Roman gods. Those who did not were arrested and tortured into submission. Decius did not want to kill Christians but rather make them turn from their faith. As a result, not many died during his period of persecution. Many Christians were faithful to their beliefs even when being tortured. These people earned the honor of being called "confessors" by their fellow Christians. Others performed the required sacrifices and received an official certificate saying they had obeyed the decree. Others bought fake certificates saying they had sacrificed.

The Question of the Lapsed. Those who received the certificates in one way or another were considered "lapsed" and outside of the Christian community.

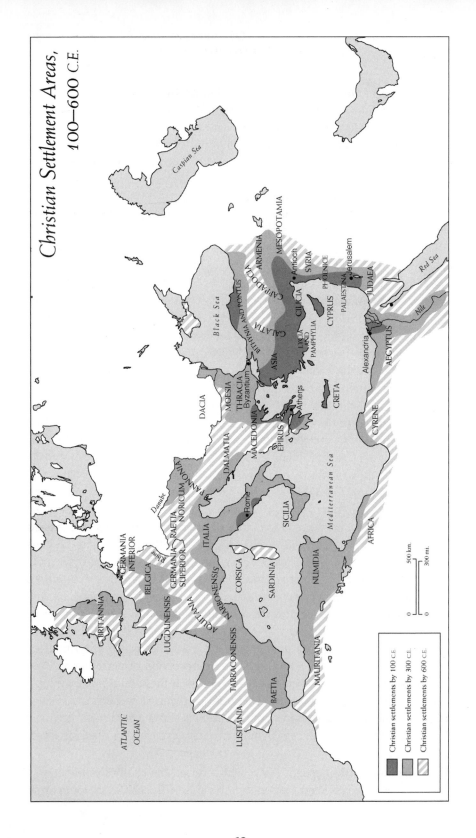

Christian Settlement Areas, 100–600 C.E.

ATLANTIC OCEAN

BRITANNIA

GERMANIA INFERIOR
GERMANIA SUPERIOR
BELGICA
Rhine
LUGDUNENSIS
AQUITANIA
NARBONENSIS
RAETIA
NORICUM
PANNONIA
Danube

LUSITANIA
TARRACONENSIS
BAETIA

CORSICA
SARDINIA
ITALIA
• Rome
SICILIA

DALMATIA
MACEDONIA
EPIRUS
MOESIA
THRACIA
Byzantium
Athens •

DACIA

Black Sea

BITHYNIA AND PONTUS
GALATIA
CAPPADOCIA
ARMENIA
MESOPOTAMIA

ASIA
LYCIA AND PAMPHYLIA
CILICIA
• Antioch
SYRIA
PHOENICE
PALAESTINA • Jerusalem
IUDAEA

CYPRUS
CRETA

Mediterranean Sea

CYRENE

AFRICA
NUMIDIA
MAURITANIA

Alexandria
AEGYPTUS
Nile
Red Sea

Caspian Sea

500 km.
300 mi.
0

Christian settlements by 100 CE
Christian settlements by 300 CE
Christian settlements by 600 CE

Questions arose when many of these lapsed Christians sought to be restored to the church. For example, should those who rushed to perform the sacrifices, those who performed them only under torture, and those who bought fake certificates all be treated in the same way? Who should decide how the lapsed were to be readmitted? The confessors felt their special status in the church gave them the right to decide. Many of the bishops believed that only *they* should decide under what conditions the lapsed could reenter the church. The bishops held this was necessary to maintain their authority, to uphold the unity of the church, and to ensure uniform treatment for those who were being judged.

The controversies about the lapsed produced two important figures: Cyprian (d. 258) and Novatian (d. ca. 257–258). Cyprian was the bishop of Carthage when the persecution under Decius broke out. He fled the city rather than face Roman authorities, and, from exile, he continued to direct the Carthage church by letters. When he returned to the city after the persecution, his authority was challenged by the confessors and others. Cyprian clashed with the confessors because they readmitted the lapsed on very easy terms, whereas he felt their reinstatement should be more difficult because their "crime" was so great. This controversy resulted in the development of a system of **penance**, which consisted of acts of repentance dictated by church officials to sinners based on the seriousness of their offense. These acts had to be performed before sinners could receive **absolution** (forgiveness for sins) and could be readmitted into the church. Cyprian's system was accepted throughout North Africa and eventually by the church in Rome.

Novatian and Cyprian. Another phase in the controversy was activated by Novatian, an official in the church in Rome who opposed the election of Cornelius (d. 253) as bishop of Rome. His opposition was partly because Cornelius was too lenient with the lapsed who sought to be readmitted to the church. Novatian was joined by other rigorists who felt the policies toward the lapsed should be stricter. He was elected as a rival bishop of Rome, but he and his followers were eventually driven out of the church. Novatian founded strict churches that survived into the fifth century.

Rome and Carthage sided together on following a more moderate policy than Novatian concerning the lapsed. However, the peace between the two cities was broken over the issue of accepting those who had been baptized in Novatian congregations. The bishop Stephen (d. 257), a successor to Cornelius, held that baptism performed by Novatian clergy was valid and people desiring admission to Orthodox congregations did not have to be rebaptized.

Cyprian and the North African church strongly opposed this acceptance of Novatian baptism. He argued that because there was "no salvation outside of the church," baptism performed outside the orthodox fellowship could not be legitimate. Therefore, Novatian converts had to be rebaptized. The controversy was complicated, however, because Stephen based his arguments on the demand that all churches should follow the practices approved by the bishop of Rome (the pope), whose authority could be traced to Saint Peter. Not all churches accepted the **primacy** (supremacy) of the bishop of Rome at this time But Stephen's position eventually won out.

Results of Conflicts. These conflicts had important implications for the church and its operations. One issue was the nature of the church. If the church was an organization comprising only those who were "pure," then only the pure could be members and administer its sacraments. On the other hand, the church might be seen as an institution that relied on the divine love of God for salvation. If that were the case, then those who were not totally pure might be members, hold office, and administer the sacraments without changing the rituals' effectiveness in conveying divine grace. That was not a new issue in the church. The questions of the lapsed and rebaptism of Novatians helped gain acceptance for the idea that the church was made up of "impure" people and officials who depended on the divine love of God. The problem of the "purity" of the church would often reappear in different forms.

The conflicts also established that only the bishop had the right to forgive or not forgive **mortal sins** (serious sins that could result in damning the sinner to hell). The "penance system" begun by Cyprian would emerge as a major issue in the church in the Middle Ages and would be one of the roots of the Reformation. Bishop Stephen's assertion of the primacy of Rome was another step in establishing the authority of the pope in Western Christianity.[3]

Fourth-Century Persecution

The church experienced sporadic persecution after Decius but enjoyed relative peace until Emperor Diocletian came to power in 284. At first Decius was busy with reorganizing the empire and did not take much notice of Christians. Around 295 he issued an edict expelling Christians from the army.[4] This edict was followed in 303 with a general edict ordering the removal of Christians from positions of responsibility in the empire as well as the burning of their books and churches. Further decrees were issued against church officials and, finally, one decree condemned all Christians to death. The persecution was the most widespread and severe the church had experienced. It was so drastic that Christians came to call it "the Great Persecution." The persecution continued under Diocletian's successors when he retired from public life. While many Christians fled and others gave up their faith, the list of early fourth-century martyrs is long indeed.

CHRIST AND CULTURE: THE APOLOGISTS

Physical persecution was not the only problem faced by the early church. Many pagan writers attacked Christian morality and beliefs. Despite the threat of persecution, the Christian community was not without its defenders. An important group of writers who sought to defend the early church against pagan attacks are known as the **apologists.**

Arguments against Christianity were diverse. Some attacked the supposed sexual immorality and cannibalism of the Christians. Others tried to show the futility of a belief in the Christian God, Jesus, or the Resurrection. Still others tried to show that Christian beliefs were too simple to compare favorably with pagan philosophy. Yet others questioned the loyalty of Christians as citizens of the empire.

Efforts to defend the faith against these criticisms actually began in the second century and continued long after that. The list of apologists includes Aristides (ca. 138), Justin Martyr, Theophilus (late second century), Minucius Felix (second or third century), Tertullian (ca. 160–225), and Origen (ca. 185–ca. 254).

The apologists followed several lines of defense. They defended Christians against charges of immorality and claimed it was the pagans who were immoral. The apologists also claimed the Christians were not atheists. They pointed out that even some great pagan philosophers believed in an unseen God. Christians were not disloyal citizens just because they did not believe in or sacrifice to pagan gods. Most Christians performed other civic duties well and they prayed for the emperor and the empire.

A major, and controversial, issue for Christian writers was how Christians were to relate to pagan culture and philosophy. Christians generally would not participate in pagan games and festivals because many, but not all, considered them immoral. More important issues centered around the achievements of Greco-Roman culture. Greeks and Romans had created great cultures with noteworthy art, literature, architecture, law, and philosophy, in which many pagans took pride. Should these achievements be ignored or denied? Should they be seen as anti-Christian? Or could they somehow be incorporated into the faith? Christian apologists took vastly different positions.

Christ against Culture

Some apologists claimed that pagan culture and ideas should be rejected outright. The attempt to appreciate Greco-Roman culture was a threat to the faith. One important theologian who took this position was Tertullian. He believed that many of the heresies of his day were caused by efforts to combine pagan philosophy with Christian doctrine. A **heresy** is a teaching that departs from accepted (orthodox) doctrine. In his *Prescription Against Heretics,* Tertullian raised the chilling challenge, "What does Athens have to do with Jerusalem? What does the Academy have to do with the Church?"

Christ in Dialogue with Culture

The opposite position was taken by Justin Martyr, who became the first Christian writer to attempt to reconcile his faith and philosophy. Justin was born to pagan parents. He converted to Christianity after a lengthy consideration of the various philosophical schools of his day, but his conversion did not mean that he ceased being a philosopher. He was convinced that Christianity and philosophy were not inconsistent. In fact, he found many points of contact between Christian beliefs and the teachings of great Greek philosophers such as Socrates and Plato, who had some insight into truth.

Justin found the explanation for this partial grasping of truth in the doctrine of the Logos that appeared both in the Gospel of John and in pagan thought. The Greek term *logos* may mean either *word* or *reason.* Pagan thinkers such as Socrates and Plato believed that the human mind could grasp truth only because there is a universal reason (*logos*) that underlies all reality. Some New Testament writers such as John also taught that this "true light" gives light to everyone. Justin held that the pagan philosophers had received light from the true Logos (Christ), which gave them insight into truth. Thus, they were "Christians" in their wisdom. This did not mean that pagan philosophy had a complete understanding of truth. What the philosophers had understood in part was revealed fully in Christ's incarnation.[5]

Beginnings of an Age-Old Dispute

These struggles to understand the relation of the faith to Greco-Roman culture point to issues of Christ and culture that are found in the church today. In the narrow sense the question is, What is the relation of theology to philosophy? Through the ages the two have been closely linked. This relation started in the New Testament. Its high point came in the Middle Ages, when philosophy and theology were very close indeed. Moreover, **philosophical schools** (lines of thought often associated with a certain philosopher) have often had a strong impact on Christian thinking. For instance, beginning with the second century (and some would say with Paul), the ideas of Plato started to underlie most Christian thinking. For a thousand years the beliefs of the Western church were built upon Plato's philosophy. In the twelfth century, Aristotle was rediscovered, which brought about a sweeping change in Christian theology (discussed in

Chapter 6). Each age has its own philosophies, and Christian theology must respond to them in one way or another.

Not only have Christian thinkers had to respond to the philosophies of the day, but they also have had to speak to other questions presented by the cultures in which they live. One position on how to respond to their cultures is taken by "fortress building" theologians. Like Tertullian, they believe their task is to proclaim the truth to the world outside of the church and the world can accept or reject these truths as it chooses. In part this is the stance today of the Roman Catholic church on such issues as the use of "artificial" birth control, abortion, and the ordination of women to the priesthood.

Still others are "bridge-building" theologians, who respond to the problems raised by their cultures by "entering into dialogue" with their cultures. Like Justin, these theologians speak to questions being raised by an entire culture, not just by the Christian community. A modern example of this approach is the liberation theologians, who have helped with the problems of the poor in Latin America by combining Christian thinking with the teachings of Karl Marx (who developed the theory of socialism). Each of these positions has its advantages and problems.

The issues of Christ and culture faced by the early Christians also reflect the same practical concerns that have confronted Christians throughout history. Just how are Christians to live in their culture on a daily basis? What is moral and immoral? Can Christians enjoy "pagan" art, literature, music, or theater? What about sporting events and movies? How can people be good citizens and good Christians?

The apologists dealt with these concerns in a time when the church was being persecuted. However, the situation was soon to change, which raised another set of issues.

TRIUMPH AND NEW CHALLENGES

After Diocletian retired, there was a power struggle for control of the empire. At one point six men fought to gain the right to rule. After much struggle Constantine emerged victorious in the western empire. This conquest was "aided" by a significant event during Constantine's attack on Maxentius, another contender. The definitive battle between the two was fought at the Milvian Bridge over the Tiber River in 312. Shortly before the battle, Constantine had a vision (or perhaps a dream) in which he was told to paint a Christian symbol (☧) on his army's shields and battle standards.[6] He was assured "in this sign you shall conquer." Constantine ordered his army to paint this symbol on their equipment, and he was indeed victorious.

The Conversion of Constantine?

One question that historians have debated throughout the ages is whether Constantine really converted to Christianity. Some Christian writers of his time believed he was Christian and that his conversion was the result of the working out of the kingdom of God on earth. Other historians have argued that he was a sincere convert, but because of his position of emperor he could not appear "too" Christian. For example, he could not suppress pagan worship because paganism was still a strong force in the empire. Still other historians believe that he was simply a smart politician who used Christianity for political ends.

On the positive side, Constantine considered himself a "bishop" who occasionally tried to guide and assist the church through important disputes. He also had Christians and Christian bishops attached to his royal court. He took many steps to favor the church, and there is little doubt that the situation of the faith improved under his rule. He was finally baptized on his deathbed, which was not unusual as late-life baptisms were a common practice at the time.

On the other hand, Constantine did not go through the normal process of becoming a Christian. He neither received instruction in the faith nor placed himself under the direction of Christian teachers and bishops. He determined his own religious practices until his death. The fact that he was not baptized until shortly before his death means that technically he was not a Christian. In addition, he had continued to serve as the pagan high priest and to take part in pagan rituals. After his death, the senate declared him a pagan god.

The question still remains: Did Constantine convert to Christianity?[7]

After securing the West, Constantine turned to the East. At first he entered into an alliance with Licinius, who was gaining control in the East. Together they issued the Edict of Milan in 313, which called for the end of persecution of Christians. It also required that churches, cemeteries, and other properties taken in earlier persecutions be returned to the church. This edict is usually considered the end of Christian persecution, although persecution continued in the East until Constantine took control of that area in 324. At this point, Christianity became an officially recognized religion that was equal to other legal religions in the empire.

Constantine and the Donatists

Constantine is often called the first Christian emperor. Although there is debate about how sincere his conversion was, he probably considered himself a believer. Yet he may not have had the same understanding of his faith that many held. It is clear, though, that with his rule, the fate of the church was changed and Christianity was now in favor. People who had previously been persecuted for their faith could participate in ruling the empire and could even take part in the splendors of the emperor's court. Laws were passed that favored the church. Its clergy were given the same privileges as pagan priests. Augustus' laws penalizing the unmarried were repealed. This ruling was significant because of the high value placed on **celibacy** (remaining unmarried and having no sex) by Christians. The first day of the week, the Sun's Day, was made a holiday.

Constantine called himself "a bishop, ordained by God to oversee whatever is external to the church." However, he was not beyond becoming involved in church matters, as we shall see in Chapter 4. More important, he regarded the church as a means to advance the aims of the state. Pagans were still the majority of the population in the empire. Constantine did not require them to become Christians and did not attack most parts of traditional Roman civilization. Yet he saw Christianity as a force to restore peace among the warring elements in the empire. In promoting Christianity, he believed he was promoting a stronger and more peaceful empire.

Constantine's plans for peace were threatened by several controversies within the church. One of these, the Donatist controversy, concerned the issue of the purity of the church. A group in Carthage refused to recognize Caecilian (consecrated 311) as bishop because he was **consecrated** (a ceremony to make one a bishop) by Felix of Aptunga. Felix had been a traitor to the faith under the Diocletian persecution. The situation was made more complex by native groups in North Africa who resented Roman occupation and who used the theological debate as an opportunity to loosen the government's control. Those who rejected Felix soon elected Donatus as an alternative bishop. Donatus would lead the Donatist movement for several decades. The **Donatists** continued to believe that the church must be holy (pure) and that sacraments administered by impure bishops were ineffective.

The bishop in Rome investigated the controversy and decided against the Donatists, who then appealed to the emperor. Constantine first referred the matter to a **synod** (meeting) of western bishops in 314. When this synod ruled against the Donatists, Constantine heard the case and also decided against them. Because they refused to obey his ruling, he tried to end the controversy with force in 316 but abandoned this policy in 321. The Donatists persisted and won many converts. In fact, by the fifth century the majority of Christians in North Africa probably were Donatists. Donatism was finally wiped out when the Muslims destroyed the African church in the seventh and eighth centuries.

Triumph and Establishment

Upon Constantine's death in 337, the empire was divided among his three sons: Constantine II, Constans, and Constantius. The death of his two brothers left Constantius in control of the whole empire in 350. When he died, the empire briefly returned to paganism under the rule of his cousin Julian the Apostate, who reigned from 361 to 363. After his death, Theodosius I took control. Theodosius then established Christianity as the official religion of the empire.

The place of Christianity in the empire changed significantly. From the time of Constantine onward, emperors helped construct Christian church buildings. Worship became more elaborate, with congregations participating less in the services. Christians were favored and pagans often were persecuted. Most Christians welcomed these changes. They believed Constantine and his successors were the instruments of God showing God's power to win victory in history. They were happy that they could be faithful to one empire, one emperor, and one church.

These changes were not without their dangers, however. Because it was fashionable to be a Christian, many converts had little commitment to Christian ideas. They were quite different from the early followers who held their beliefs with passion or the martyrs who gave their lives for their faith. Immoral behavior became more acceptable. It appeared to many that the church had become weak and corrupt.

Another danger was the new relation of the church to the state. Religion and politics were becoming closely connected. The power of the state was used to enforce Christian doctrines. In turn the church was expected to support the state. In the West, the pope would come to control much political power. In the East, the church came to be dominated by the emperor. The church was seen as an instrument to serve the purposes of the state. The problem of church–state relations would cause many conflicts throughout Christian history.[8]

The Rise of Monasticism

Not all were pleased with the changes in the church and many reacted negatively. One movement that grew as the church became more accepted in society was monasticism. **Monastics** are people who seek to live pure Christian lives by withdrawing from society. In the early stages, these individuals would withdraw into the desert where they would dedicate themselves to becoming more Christ-like. Males in this group came to be called **monks** and females came to be called **nuns**.

Although the word *monk* means *alone,* most monks and nuns lived in communities. At first many lived in desert caves. They tried to control their flesh completely so they could dedicate themselves to God, which meant practicing celibacy, living in simple **cells** (rooms with little comforts), and possessing only the clothing necessary to protect the body. They dedicated themselves to prayer, **fasting** (going without food), and worship. Many waited for the rapid return of Christ and the establishment of the kingdom of God on earth. To control the flesh some took drastic measures, such as starving or castrating themselves. They often felt they were involved in a life-and-death struggle with the devil and demons.

Although it is impossible to know who was the first monk or nun, Anthony of Egypt (251?–356) is called the father of the movement. Anthony introduced to monasticism an ordered plan for living. Pachomius (ca. 290–346) was another important figure in early monasticism. He founded a **monastery** (where monks live) at Tabennisi, which inspired the founding of eight other monasteries. The rule he developed to guide his monks influenced both Basil and Benedict.

Basil the Great (ca. 330–379) was a well-educated man who withdrew into the desert for a period of time. Even though he would eventually leave the desert to become bishop of Caesarea, he left his mark on monasticism by the creation of a rule (laws) to guide monks in their lives. The Rule of Saint Basil is very strict but was not as extreme as the practices followed by many monks at the time. It is the basic rule followed by eastern monks to this day.

Benedict of Nursia (ca. 480–ca. 550) was another key person in the monastic movement. Benedict was educated in Rome where the low moral quality of society led him to withdraw. Eventually a community of followers grew around him. He founded other monasateries, each presided over by an **abbot** (head, overseer). In later life, he lived in the monastery at Monte Cassino. There he wrote a rule that carefully explained how a monastery was to be administered and the nature of the monastic life.

According to the Rule of Saint Benedict, monks were to elect an abbot who would direct operation of the monastery and who also would be a spiritual guide and counselor to the monks. The abbot was to be obeyed without question. The monks were to dedicate themselves to the **Divine Office** (series of prayers and readings to be said at appointed hours of the day and night). Saying the Divine Office required that monks have books from which to read. Monks consequently became very good at copying books by hand, a skill that came to be very important in preserving learning and literature in the early Middle Ages. They also were to dedicate themselves to private prayer and hard work. The Rule of Saint Benedict was disciplined and austere but not unduly harsh. It spread throughout the Western church and was also the basis for later reform movements in church history. Saint Benedict is referred to as the father of western monasticism.

The monastic movement had several significant effects on the church. Many dedicated Christians imitated monastic ways even though they did not join monasteries. Temporary retreats into lonely places or monasteries became common for those seeking to renew or deepen their spiritual lives. There was an effort to enforce celibacy on all clergy in the Western church. This effort was not successful for centuries in the West. (Celibacy has never been required for the lower-level clergy in the East.) Because of the respect paid to monks, they were frequently called from their monasteries to serve in church offices. The monks were often viewed as superior to other Christians. This view increased the growing tendency to separate Christians into spiritual classes. There developed "ordinary" and special, or "extraordinary," categories of Christians.

CONCLUSIONS

A major factor in the first 500 years of the church was its changing relations to the state. Early in the patristic period, the Christian community was subject to periodic persecution. This persecution was often initiated by emperors or officials who were trying to reverse the declining empire. Christians became convenient scapegoats for the problems of the empire. Doing away with the Christians was seen as a means of restoring Rome to its ancient glory.

As a result of the persecutions, martyrs assumed a strong role in the early church. At the same time, issues raised by the movement to restore the lapsed led to an understanding of the church as a body of "sinful" people who depended on the grace of God rather than on their own purity. The role of the bishop increased and the church in Rome tried to assert its leadership of the Christian world. The apologists attempted to defend Christians against pagan attacks. They took positions of "Christ against culture" (fortress building) and "Christ in dialogue with culture" (bridge building). These positions have continued throughout church history to the present day.

As the church became established, new problems arose. One set of issues centered on the church's use of political power. Other problems resulted from Christianity's sudden popularity, which brought into the church "social Christians," who joined for reasons of social and political advancement. Certainly many lacked the passionate commitment of the faith of the martyrs. Other Christians were dissatisfied with the low levels of commitment found in the church, which increased the trend for some Christians to seek a deeper and more meaningful faith than was practiced by the average church member. This trend, in turn, strengthened the role of monastics in the Christian community.

Church–state relations was not the only factor that led to changes in the church. Other controversies *within* the community also produced changes in Christian theology and church structure. We will examine these changes in Chapter 4.

Notes

1.   Choosing the beginning and end of historical periods is always difficult. History is something of a continuous line, with events from the past feeding into those in the future. The historian is often without clear-cut "signposts" that tell exactly when one period ended and another began. The year 500 was chosen as the end of the patristic period because the church fathers were dead, the most important of the early councils of the church had been held, and the Roman Empire had experienced invasions in the West from "barbarians."

The term *barbarian invasions* is used in this text to emphasize the replacement of one order with another. To many Romans it may have seemed that hordes of uncivilized Germans suddenly swept into the empire, destroying the old ways. Many contemporary historians argue that the Germans were neither "barbarians" nor "invaders." The Germans had a civilization that included all the basic structures of culture, such as family, religion, politics, and economics. The "invasions" may have been more of a gradual movement into the empire. The invading Germans considered themselves good Romans for centuries. Some historians say that calling the coming of the Germans "barbarian invasions" is a way for Romans to transfer the blame for the collapse of the empire from themselves to others.

The movements of German tribes during the early fifth century are particularly important because they marked the beginning of the end of effective political control in the West. Although the emperor in Constantinople continued to claim western Europe, he had limited control over the region, which opened the way for the church to assert more influence. The sixth century was still a time of change from the old empire to the new situation where the church would be the dominant political as well as spiritual force in the West. After 500 the emperor relied more upon bishops to assert political control in the West. After 600 it was obvious that a new order was emerging in western Europe.

2.   For a good discussion of Tertullian, see Justo L. González. *A History of Christian Thought,* vol. 1, *From the Beginnings to the Council of Chalcedon.* New York: Abingdon, 1970, pp. 175–190.

3.   For a good discussion of Cyprian, Novatian, and Stephen, see Kurt Arland, *A History of Christianity,* vol. 1, *From the Beginnings to the Threshold of the Reformation,* trans. James L. Schaaf. Philadelphia: Fortress, 1980, pp. 156–161.

4.   The question of military service always has been a problem for Christians. Early on, most Christians apparently would not serve because of teachings against the use of force and the taking of human life. They are taught by Jesus in the Gospels against taking oaths and taking up the sword. They were warned about hating their brothers and sisters. They were required to love their enemies. These admonitions were taken seriously by the earliest believers. By this time, however, the situation had changed. Although church leaders continued to teach against military service, many "ordinary" Christians were in the army.

5.   For a good discussion of the apologists, see Justo L. González. *The Story of Christianity,* vol. 1, *The Early Church to the Dawn of the Reformation.* San Francisco: Harper & Row, 1984, pp. 50–57. A classic study on the church's relation to the world is H. Richard Niebuhr, *Christ and Culture.* New York: Harper & Row, 1975. He identifies several different basic positions the church has assumed, including Christ against culture, the Christ of culture, Christ above culture, and Christ in paradox with culture.

6. This is a combination of *Chi* and *Rho,* the first two Greek letters in the name *Christ.* Although it may not have been used by the earliest Christians, since Constantine it has been used as a monogram for Christ.

7. For a good discussion of the conversion of Constantine, see González. *Story.* vol. 1, pp. 120–123.

8. The problem of the relation of church to state is not exclusive to Christianity. For instance, Islam, Shinto, Hinduism, and Buddhism also have had similar relations to the states where they dominate.

Additional Readings

Athanasius. *On the Incarnation.* Translated and edited by Penelope Lawson. New York: Macmillan, 1981.

————. *The Life of St. Anthony the Great.* Willits, CA: Eastern Orthodox Books, 1976.

————. *Select Treatises of St. Athanasius in Controversy with the Arians.* 5th ed. Translated by John H. Newman. 2 vols. 1890. Reprint. New York: A M S, 1978.

Bainton, R. H. *Christian Attitudes Toward War and Peace.* New York: Abingdon, 1960.

Benedict. *The Rule of St. Benedict.* Edited and translated by Justin McCann. London: Sheed and Ward, 1972.

Bowersock, G. W., Peter Brown, and Oleg Grabot. *Late Antiquity: A Guide to the Postclassical World.* Cambridge, MA: Belknap, 1999.

Burton-Christie, Douglas. *The Word in the Desert: Scripture and the Quest for Holiness in Early Christian Monasticism.* New York: Oxford University Press. 1993.

Dodds, E. R. *Pagan and Christian in an Age of Anxiety.* Cambridge, England: Cambridge University Press, 1968.

Doerries, Hermann. *Constantine the Great.* New York: Harper & Row, 1972.

Dudley, D. R. *Civilization of Rome.* New York: New American Library, 1960.

Elm, Susanna. *"Virgins of God": The Making of Asceticism in Late Antiquity.* New York: Oxford University Press. 1994.

Fergeson, John. *The Religions of the Roman Empire.* Ithaca, NY: Cornell University Press, 1970.

Frend, W. H. C. *The Donatist Church: A Movement of Protest in Roman North Africa.* Oxford: Clarendon, 1952.

————. *Martyrdom and Persecution in the Early Church.* Garden City, NJ: Anchor, 1967.

————. *The Rise of Christianity.* Minneapolis, MN: Augsburg Fortress, 1986.

Grimal, Pierre. *The Civilization of Rome.* Translated by W. S. Marquinness. New York: Simon and Schuster, 1963.

Harnack, Adolf von. *The Mission and Expansion of Christianity in the First Three Centuries.* New York: Harper & Row, 1962.

Hinson, E. Glenn. *The Evangelization of the Roman Empire: Identity and Adaptability.* Macon, GA: Mercer University Press, 1981.

MacMullen, Ramsay. *Paganism in the Roman Empire.* New Haven, CT: Yale University Press, 1981.

Nardo, Don, ed. *The Rise of Christianity.* Turning Points in World History series. San Diego: Greenhaven, 1999.

Pelikan, Jaroslav. *The Christian Tradition: A History of the Development of Doctrine, Vol. 1: The Emergence of Catholic Tradition.* Chicago: University of Chicago, 1975.

Stark, Rodney. *The Rise of Christianity: A Sociologist Reconsiders History.* Princeton, NJ: Princeton University Press, 1996.

Tertullian. *Apologetical Works. Fathers of the Church,* vol. 10. Washington, D.C.: Catholic University Press, 1963.

———. *Disciplinary, Moral and Ascetical Works. Fathers of the Church,* vol. 40. Washington, D.C.: Catholic University Press, 1959.

Waddell, Helen. *The Desert Fathers.* Ann Arbor: University of Michigan Press, 1957.

Workman, Robert B. *Persecution in the Early Church.* Reprint. London: Epworth, 1960.

Websites

www.earlychristianwritings.com [Site provides access to a number of authors for 30 C.E.–250 C.E.]

www.ccel.org [Site provides access to a number of scanned electronic books by and about the church fathers.]

www.questia.com/library/religion/Christinaty/history/early-church [Site provides access to online books and articles about the church fathers.]

THE FAITH OF THE FATHERS
Controversies and Councils (100–500 C.E.)

Saint Augustine

The Christian faith did not emerge as a fully formed body of ideas during New Testament times. It took hundreds of years to settle many issues and, indeed, many have not been settled to this day. The previous chapter showed how conflict with the Roman Empire helped shape the church. Chapter 4 looks at several major controversies within the church that formed its basic theology during the patristic period.

The church that emerged from the first century was still very flexible. Different ideas about what it meant to be a Christian continued to exist. At one extreme were the **Ebionites,** a **sect** (group) of Christian Judaizers who instructed Christians to follow the strict practices of the Jewish Law. At the other extreme were the **Antinomians,** who held that because Christians were saved by faith alone they should have to submit to no rules to control their behavior. Orthodox teachings about such ideas as the nature of Christ had not been settled. No **canon** (officially accepted list) of Scripture existed. The role of officials such as the bishop had not yet been settled.

THE QUEST FOR AUTHORITY

The competing ideas and groups found within the second-century Christian community raised two burning questions: Who is a true Christian? What group holds the true faith? Controversies concerning Gnostic Christianity and Marcion (d. ca. 160) forced Christians to address these issues.

Gnostic Christianity

Gnosticism was a set of philosophical and religious ideas that had wide influence both in and outside the church. Some of its basic teachings, such as matter being evil, the creation of the world by the Demiurge, salvation by releasing the "good" spirit from "evil" matter, and salvation by obtaining secret knowledge, were discussed in Chapter I. When these teachings were applied to Christianity, many new issues were raised. The world and matter were evil instead of good as they had been in Hebrew thought. Because the world was evil, salvation involved total release from physical existence. There could be no hope for the creation of a new heaven and new earth or the resurrection of the body as first-century writers such as Paul had taught.

Christ was sent by God to give the secret knowledge necessary for salvation. However, because matter was evil, he could not have truly been incarnate and only appeared to have a body. Those Christians who believed Jesus was a spirit that only appeared to have a body were known as **Docetics.** (It is interesting that modern people have trouble accepting the divinity of Christ, but the early church had to struggle to accept his humanity.) Moreover, salvation through knowledge was not available for all; it was possessed by few and was received in secret ceremonies.

Some Gnostics followed an ethic that said that because the real self was the spirit, they could do anything they wanted with body without contaminating their spirit. These Gnostics felt free to engage in all sorts of immoral activity. However, most Gnostics believed in severely disciplining the body and its needs, avoiding all sorts of pleasures. Sex in particular was to be avoided since it carried the possibility of pregnancy. According to Gnostic thought, pregnancy meant that another spirit had been trapped in sinful, material flesh.

The New Testament has some indication that Gnostic ideas existed in the early church during the first century. Gnosticism became very widespread in second century Christianity. In fact, some historians believe that the majority of second century Christians were Gnostics. Even at its height, Gnosticism was not an organized movement, but centered around several important teachers such as Basilides (2nd. century), Valentinus (2nd. century), and, perhaps, Marcion (d. 160). These men shared some common ideas, but also had unique emphases in their systems. These writers were opposed by some of the brightest Christian minds of the first three centuries, including Irenaeus (ca. 130–200), Tertullian (ca. 160–ca. 225), and Hippolytus (ca. 170–ca. 236). By the end of the second century, Gnostics were beginning to be labeled as heretics and driven out of orthodox Christian congregations. Although orthodoxy moved in another direction, Gnostic Christian communities survived for centuries.

The Establishment of an Official Canon

Another challenge for the poorly organized Christian community was presented by Marcion. Marcion grew up in a Christian home, but he developed a hatred of both the material world and the Jews. As a result he could not see how the evil world in which he lived was created by the good God of the Christians. His solution was to separate the loving God seen in Christ from the vindictive, petty **Yahweh** (an Old Testament name for God) of the Jews. If the world was evil, then it could not have been created by the God of Christ; it must have been created by Yahweh. This Yahweh was inferior to the supreme God revealed in Christ. Marcion also rejected the incarnation, the birth of Jesus to the virgin Mary, and final judgment (the judgment of people by God at the end of time).

Based on his ideas, Marcion developed a distinctive view of Scripture. For him, the Old Testament revealed only the petty god Yahweh and, therefore, it should not be read by Christians. Christians also used first-century writings to guide them. Some of these writings, however, seemed to reflect the Old Testament God of justice rather than the compassionate God of Christ. As a result, Marcion accepted only some of the first-century writings commonly used by the church. Even in those writings he accepted, he would have nothing that reflected Old Testament ideas. He put together what he considered a list of true Christian Scripture. His canon consisted of ten of Paul's letters and parts of the Gospel of Luke.

Because of the challenges of Gnostics and Marcionites, the church had to create ways to define who was a true Christian and who possessed the truth of Christ. These efforts led to three developments: canon, creed, and bishop.

One effort was to develop an official canon. The true believer was one who accepted the true Scriptures. Yet what was Scripture and what was not? For the most part, when the early church spoke of Scripture it was referring to the Hebrew Scriptures or Old Testament. One mark of the true believer came to be the acceptance of these works as canon.

This acceptance still did not solve the problem because there were many writings created in the Christian community that were used in the various churches for worship and instruction. The letters of Paul were rapidly accepted as Scripture as were the synoptic Gospels (Matthew, Mark, and Luke). Even in this form, the Christian canon made up of the Old Testament, the synoptic Gospels, and Paul's Epistles could be used to separate true Christians from Gnostics and Marcionites. Eventually, the Gospel of John, James, 1, 2, and 3 John, Hebrews, 1 and 2 Peter, and the Revelation of John would be accepted. The first list to contain the twenty-seven books of what Christians now call the New Testament was the Easter Epistle of Athanasius in 367.[1]

The Development of Creeds

The need to determine true Christians also led to the development of creeds. A **creed** is a statement of beliefs, and a true believer was a person who accepted the correct creed. The earliest known one is the Apostles' Creed, a short statement most likely written in Rome about 150. It was probably based on a series of three questions that were asked of people being baptized. Its parts center around the nature of the Father, the person and work of Christ, and the Holy Spirit. All of its beliefs are carefully stated in such a way that they could not be accepted by Gnostics or Marcionites. From this simple beginning, creeds came to play an important role in the history of Christianity. They tended to become more complicated as new creeds were developed to address new issues. Although they were effective in defining orthodox beliefs, they also raised some key issues: What is the relation between faith and beliefs? Are commitment and saving experience more important than holding certain beliefs in determining who is a true Christian? If commitment is most important, what beliefs may be eliminated and what must be kept? These issues have been and continue to be the source of endless debate among groups of Christians holding opposing views.

Important Events of the Patristic Period

DATES	EVENTS	ROMAN EMPERORS	CHURCH PERSONS	WRITINGS
ca.140 C.E.	Growth of Gnosticism	Hadrian		
	Debate over canon begins		Marcion	
ca. 150		Antonius Pius		Old Roman Symbol (start of Apostles' Creed)
190	Begin Monarchian controversy			
306–337	First "Christian" Emperor	Constantine		
ca. 319	Begin Arian controversy		Arius, Alexander of Alexandria	
325	Council of Nicaea (condemns Monarchians and Arius)		Eusebius, Athanasius	Creed of Nicaea
330–395	Life of Cappadocians		Basil the Great, Gregory of Nyssa, Gregory of Nazianzus	
367	27 books of NT canon		Athanasius	Easter Epistle

The Establishment of Bishops

The final effort to establish who was a true Christian led to an increase in the importance of bishops. True Christians were those who could claim their bishop was a true bishop of Christ. This issue concerned the question of who held the authority to define the proper teachings of the church. Gnostics, Marcionites, and Orthodox Christians all held that their truth could be traced directly to Christ. How then was one to decide which group represented the true teachings of the Savior?

Important Events of the Patristic Period

DATES	EVENTS	ROMAN EMPERORS	CHURCH PERSONS	WRITINGS
381	Council of Constantinople (condemns Apollinarius; end of Arian controversy)	Theodosius	Apollinarius	Nicene Creed
354–430	Life of Augustine		Augustine of Hippo	*Confessions, City of God,* others
400	End Manichaean controversy; begin Donatist controversy		Augustine	
410	Fall of Rome; begin pagan controversy		Augustine	
411	Begin Pelagian controversy		Augustine	
429	Begin Theotokos controversy		Nestorius	
431	Council of Ephesus (upholds Theotokos)			
451	Council of Chalcedon (upholds Theotokos and Nicene faith; Christ fully God and fully man); begin Monophysite controversy			Nicene Creed (final form plus definition)

At this point, the idea of apostolic succession came into play. **Apostolic succession** is the idea that a bishop could establish that he was orthodox by tracing his lineage back to a bishop who learned from the apostles. Church leaders argued that if Christ had some secret knowledge as the Gnostics claimed, he would have passed it on to his disciples. These were the same apostles to whom he gave over the direction of the church. The apostles would have turned this knowledge over to their disciples who would have turned it over to their disciples, the bishops. Therefore, true knowledge about the teachings of Christ would be found among those bishops who could trace their lines directly back to the apostles.

The Apostles' Creed

The early creeds developed from a series of questions asked of persons who were being baptized. One of the most important of these is the Apostles' Creed, which legend says was written by the Apostles themselves. In reality, it is a variation of a baptismal confession used by the Roman church called the Old Roman Symbol (Creed). Here is an early version:

> I believe in God almighty
> And in Christ Jesus, his son, our Lord
> Who was born of the Holy Spirit
>   and the Virgin Mary
> Who was crucified under Pontius Pilate
>   and was buried
> And the third day rose from the dead
> Who ascended into heaven
> And sits on the right hand of the Father
> Whence he comes to judge the living and
>   the dead
> And in the Holy Spirit
> The holy church
> The remission of sins
> The resurrection of the flesh
> The life everlasting.

This creed was later expanded into the Apostles' Creed, which is used by the Roman Catholic church at baptisms. This creed was never widely accepted in the Eastern Orthodox church.

A comparison of this creed with the Nicene Creed (p. 88) gives us some idea how controversies led to the development of Christian theology.

The establishment of apostolic succession was not difficult for many of the older congregations as they had lists of bishops that traced them back to the New Testament period. Many orthodox churches could show their connections to apostolic times while Gnostics and Marcionites could not. A congregation unable to trace its origins back to the apostles was not considered heretical. It was only necessary that the teachings of a congregation agree with those ideas shown to be the "apostolic faith." The idea of apostolic succession would eventually take on different meanings. However, in the second century it was used only to show who had the true faith. The true bishop was one who defended the apostolic faith.

At this point, orthodoxy was taking shape around those who held to a certain canon, an accepted creed, and bishops. Those who held to these ideas were considered part of the catholic, or universal, church. Those who did not were considered heterodox or outside the true church.

THE NATURE OF CHRIST AND THE TRINITY

The problem of authority was not the only one faced by the early Christian community. Major controversies also centered around the nature of the incarnate Christ and the Trinity. The church had always wrestled with the problem of who Jesus was. Many Christians came to believe he was the Son of God. But when did he become the Son? And exactly what does it mean to say he is the Son of God?

Early Christians seem to have held an **adoptionist** position: Because Jesus was such a good man, at some point in his life he was adopted to be God's Son and to bear his message to the world. This idea is present in the Gospel of Mark where there is no mention of Jesus' divinity until he is "adopted" by God at his baptism by John.

By the time of the writing of the other Gospels, there was the feeling that God sent his Son from "heaven" to be born of the Virgin Mary. His purpose was to redeem humankind. John goes so far as to say that this was the Logos made flesh. But if Jesus was the Son of God sent from the Father, what was the relation of the Son to the Father? Had they always existed as Father and Son or was there a "time" when the Father created the Son? Was the Son equal to or less than the Father? What was the relationship of the Son of God to the human Jesus? Could Jesus be fully God and fully human? If Jesus was really God, what happened to God the Father when he took on flesh in the earthly life of Jesus? Did he stop being the God who ruled the universe? Was it really God the Father who suffered and died on the cross?

Even if these difficult questions were answered, what about the Holy Spirit? From early times, Christians had baptized in the name of the Trinity (Father, Son, and Holy Spirit). But how does the Spirit relate to the other two? What is the Spirit's purpose? Is the Spirit equal to or less than the Father and Son? Has the Spirit always existed with them?

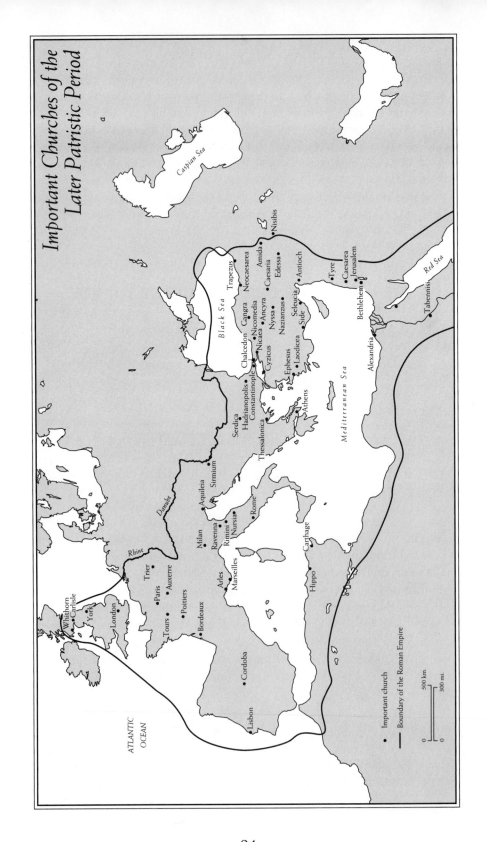

Important Churches of the Later Patristic Period

ATLANTIC OCEAN

Whithorn
Carlisle
York
London
Trier
Paris
Auxerre
Poitiers
Tours
Bordeaux
Lisbon
Cordoba
Arles
Marseilles
Milan
Ravenna
Rimini
Nursia
Aquileia
Sirmium
Rome
Carthage
Hippo

Rhine
Danube

Black Sea

Serdica
Hadrianopolis
Constantinople
Thessalonica
Chalcedon
Gangra
Nicaea
Nicomedia
Cyzicus
Ephesus
Athens
Laodicea
Side
Nyssa
Ancyra
Nazianzus
Caesarea
Seleucia
Neocaesarea
Amida
Trapezus
Nisibis
Edessa
Antioch
Tyre
Caesarea
Jerusalem
Bethlehem
Alexandria
Tabennisi

Caspian Sea

Mediterranean Sea

Red Sea

• Important church
— Boundary of the Roman Empire

500 km.
300 mi.

One God: Monarchianism

One attempt to deal with these questions was presented by Monarchianism in the second and third centuries. The **Monarchians** were concerned with defending the unity (monarchy), or oneness, of God against the criticism that the Christians were not monotheists, but instead were worshiping three gods.

Monarchians were divided into two groups. **Adoptionist or Dynamic Monarchians** felt that Jesus was God only in the sense that the power of God rested upon him in a special way during his earthly life. The **Modalistic Monarchians** taught that *Father, Son,* and *Holy Spirit* were simply convenient labels for how people had known God in history. God had existed in the mode or temporary expression of the Father (Creator), Son (Savior/Redeemer), and Holy Spirit (Sustainer). These three modes were really temporary expressions of the same God. They showed nothing essential about the nature of God.

In contrast to the Monarchians, other Christians thought that such an approach did not do justice to the nature of God. The Trinity was not superficial to God but somehow spoke about something essential in God's character. Moreover, many believed Monarchist ideas lowered the place of Christ because Jesus and the Christ event were not essential to God. Monarchian ideas also meant that Jesus was not really God or, at least, not the full revelation of God. As a result, something less than the total God had been involved on the cross. Because God was not involved how could the cross be the central event in history? How could the salvation of humanity and this world be complete?

The Equality of Christ: The Arian Controversy

Another debate started as a disagreement between a priest, Arius (ca. 250–336), and his bishop, Alexander of Alexandria (d. 328). Arius began teaching that Christ was not eternal but rather had been created by God. He held that "There was [a time] when he was not" and that he was the first among creatures (beings created by God). This interpretation made Christ less than God. Alexander strongly held that Christ was God, he had existed with God from eternity, and he was not created. Alexander ordered Arius to stop his teachings, and when Arius refused, he was sent into exile. Arius received considerable support for his position from other Christians and bishops who demanded that Alexander restore him to his church. A tremendous conflict resulted, primarily in the Eastern church.

This controversy threatened the peace that Constantine hoped to bring to the empire. After trying other means to settle the dispute, the emperor called a council of the church to try to resolve problems facing both the church and the empire. Bishops and other clergy were brought to the council at government expense. Most of the bishops were from the East, though a few came from the West. They met in Nicaea, located near Constantinople, in 325. This meeting is referred to as the First **Ecumenical** (universal) **Council** of the church, or the Council of Nicaea.

The council undertook a number of administrative tasks such as who had the right to restore the lapsed. The biggest issue faced by the council, however, was the dispute between Arius and Alexander. There were three major positions. The Arian (pro-Arius) position was defended by Eusebius of Nicomedia (d. ca. 342) and his followers. The opposing side was presented by Alexander and his supporters, one of the most important of whom was Athanasius (ca. 296–373). In between the extremes was a large group represented by Eusebius of Caesarea (ca. 260–340).[2] These people initially hoped to reach some compromise between Arius and Alexander.

In the course of the debate, the tide turned to favor Alexander. Efforts were then made to create a creed that would define the orthodox faith. Eusebius of Caesarea offered a creed used for baptism in his congregation as a means of resolving the dispute, which was eventually adopted after considerable changes. Constantine presented the critical Greek word **homoousios** ("of the same substance") to define the relation between God and Christ. In the end, Arians and Modalistic Monarchians were condemned. The Creed of Nicaea confirmed that God and Christ were of the same substance (*homoousios*), Christ was begotten not made, and there was not a time when he was not. It also stated that the Holy Spirit was to be worshiped with the Father and Son. Anyone who could not affirm these beliefs was considered outside the true faith. This creed was revised in 381 and then in 451 and is now known as the Nicene Creed.[3]

Coeternal and Coequal: Father, Son, and Holy Spirit

While the Creed of Nicaea may have been offered to settle the dispute, it did not. The Arians were numerous and powerful and had many friends in high places. For many years the battle between the Arians and Nicenes continued. The death of Alexander left Athanasius, his successor as bishop of Alexandria, the leader of the Nicene party. His leadership was so powerful that he is called the great defender of the Nicene faith. His death left the defense to the Great Cappadocians: Basil the Great, Gregory of Nyssa (ca. 330–ca. 395), and Gregory of Nazianzus (328–389).[4]

Although the Nicene faith had able defenders, it did not immediately win out. The popularity of the Arian position, along with their political influence, almost gave the victory to them. In fact, Constantius, one of the sons of Constantine, was Arian. When he came to be sole emperor, he pursued a pro-Arian policy throughout the empire. This policy led Jerome (ca. 342–420) to exclaim, "the entire world woke from a slumber and discovered that it had become Arian." Even when the Nicene position did gain the upper hand, Arianism remained a powerful force for some time. The Germanic tribes were converted by Arian missionaries. These churches remained Arian well into the Middle Ages.

The Creed of Nicaea left many unanswered questions. The term *homoousios* made a number of Christians uncomfortable. They were concerned that it made the link between Father and Son so close that they could not be seen as separate. These believers preferred to say that the Father and Son were **homoiousios** ("of a similar substance"). This view made Christ like God but not the same.

Saying that Jesus was both human and divine presented another problem. Exactly how did the human nature and the divine nature relate? One solution was given by Apollinarius (ca. 310–390), who wanted to defend the oneness of God and the humanity of Christ. He taught that humans were composed of body, soul, and spirit. In the incarnation, Jesus had a human body and soul, but the human spirit was replaced by the Divine Logos. Orthodox thinkers believed that this portrayal did not leave Jesus fully human, however. Another approach was taken by Nestorius (d. ca. 451), who taught that in Jesus there were two persons (natures)—one human and one divine. This idea led him to object to the term *Theotokos,* commonly used by Christians in referring to Mary in worship. *Theotokos* means "God-bearer" or "the mother of God." Nestorius believed that Mary may have given birth to the human Jesus but did not bear the divine Christ.

The teachings of Apollinarius were condemned at the Council of Constantinople (381)—the same council that produced the Nicene Creed, the updated version of the Creed of Nicaea. The ideas of Nestorius were condemned at the Council of Ephesus in 431. This council also reaffirmed the faith as defined by the Nicaea and the Constantinople councils.

The nature of Christ, his relation to the Father, and the role of the Holy Spirit continued to produce conflict. Another council was called to try to produce harmony within Christianity. When the Council of Chalcedon met in 451 it accepted the Nicene Creed and added a more extensive definition of orthodox teaching. The definition affirmed that Mary had the right to be called *Theotokos*. It made clear that Jesus was of the same substance as both God and humans. The two natures existed "inconfusedly, immutably, indivisibly, inseparately", but were distinct. This distinction, however, could not be understood in any way that saw the two natures as separate. The definition further affirmed that this was the tradition of the prophets, taught by the Lord Jesus Christ, and transmitted by the holy fathers of the church.

When all was said and done, orthodox Christianity came to teach that there was one God who existed in three persons: Father, Son, and Holy Spirit. These

The Nicene Creed

The Nicene Creed is actually not the creed presented at Nicaea in 325 (which was called the Creed of Nicaea). Rather, it is a version of the Creed of Nicaea that was updated to deal with ongoing issues. The Nicene Creed was given its final form at the Council of Chalcedon in 451, and it gives the basic understanding of church doctrine and the Trinity for both Western and Eastern Christianity.

> We believe in one God the
> Father All-sovereign, maker of
> heaven and earth, and of all
> things visible and invisible;
>
> And in one Lord Jesus Christ,
> the only-begotten Son of God,
> Begotten of the Father before all
> the ages, Light of Light, true God
> of true God, begotten not made,
> of one substance with the Father,
> through whom all things were made;
> who for us men and our salvation
> came down from the heavens, and was
> made flesh of the Holy Spirit and the
> Virgin Mary, and became man,
> and was crucified for us under

three were **coeternal** (had always existed) and **coequal** (completely equal). The Son was "begotten," not made. Jesus was fully God and fully man. The human and divine natures existed in him in such a way as to avoid any confusion. The Son was born of Mary, who had the right to be called the Mother of God. The Holy Spirit "proceeded" from the Father and was to be worshiped also. The orthodox affirmed "one holy catholic and apostolic church," baptism for the remission of sins, the resurrection of the dead, and the hope for life in "the age to come."

These formulas still leave room for much interpretation and debate. They did not win complete acceptance. For instance, Monophysitism came into being soon after Chalcedon. **Monophysitism** teaches that in Jesus there was but one divine nature and no human nature. Monophysites eventually broke

Pontius Pilate, and suffered and
was buried, and rose again on
the third day according to the
Scriptures, and ascended into
the heavens, and sits on the right
hand of the Father, and comes
again with glory to judge living
and dead, of whose kingdom
there shall be no end:

And in the Holy Spirit, the Lord
and the Life-giver, that proceeds
from the Father, who with Father
and Son is worshipped together
and glorified together, who
spoke through the prophets:

In one holy catholic and
apostolic church:

We acknowledge one baptism unto
remission of sins. We look
for a resurrection of the dead,
and the life of the age to come.

with orthodox Christianity, and Monophysite churches continue into the present time. Yet with the Nicene Creed and the definition of Chalcedon, the heart of Christian theology had been presented.

AUGUSTINE: THE THEOLOGIAN OF THE WEST

The list of contributors to the development of Christian thought in the patristic period is long. Irenaeus, Clement of Alexandria (ca. 150–ca. 215), Justin, Tertullian, Origen, Cyprian, Athanasius, the Cappadocians, Ambrose of Milan (ca. 337–397), John Chrysostom (ca. 347–407), Jerome, and others could be called doctors (teachers) and fathers of the church. No other thinker of the time is greater than Augustine of Hippo (354–430). His teachings are the foundation for much of the Western church and Western civilization.

Augustine's Life

Augustine's theology was shaped by his keen mind as he drew upon many philosophies and thought about the pains of his personal struggles. Like other theologians, his ideas were formed in the context of controversies in which he was involved. He came to see the relationship of a person to God as intensely personal. He also reached a profound understanding of the depth of human sin and the extent of God's grace. He was the greatest theologian on grace since Paul of Tarsus.

Augustine was born to a pagan father and Christian mother in Tagaste in North Africa. He received a Christian education but abandoned most of it as he moved to Carthage to complete his studies. Later in life, Augustine would reflect on his childhood experiences in his famous *Confessions,* the first known psychological autobiography. In it Augustine detailed his torturous journey to faith. In a particularly troubling childhood experience, Augustine and several boys had stolen some pears from an orchard. The boys had stolen fruit they did not need and even had fed the fruit to pigs. Augustine later concluded that the only motivation for such an act was the joy of evil itself and that humans were evil indeed.

In Carthage he not only studied but also took on a mistress with whom he had a son. Augustine studied **rhetoric** (public speaking) with the idea of becoming a lawyer. He became involved in the study of philosophy along with its search for truth. His mother tried to use the spiritual turmoil produced by his studies to direct him into the church. Instead his search for peace and truth led him to explore Manicheism.

Manicheism was a religion based on the teachings of Mani that developed in Persia in the third century. It saw the world as a mixture of light and dark. Light was spiritual and good while dark was material and evil. God created the light, but the evil darkness was created by Satan. Satan was an evil force that was eternally opposed to God. Every part of the visible world, including humans, contained both light and dark. God sent a number of teachers, including Jesus, to help free humans from evil. Salvation was found by freeing oneself from the mixture of light and dark. This freedom prepared believers for a return to pure light. After nine years of seeking in this faith, Augustine could not find the answers he sought. He became disillusioned with the Manichee's simple identification of evil with matter. Among other things, this allowed some followers to engage in sexual immorality while claiming to remain pure. Some claimed that only the evil material body was sinning while the real spiritual self remained untouched.

He moved to Rome and then to Milan where he became involved in **Neoplatonism,** which was a popular philosophy at the time. It called for a reunion with the One (God) who was the source of all that exists. This reunion may be accomplished by study, discipline, and contemplation. In this school, evil is not identified with matter. Instead, it means moving away from the One. The further people are from the One, the further they are from truth and good. While Augustine found much of value in Neoplatonism, he found neither the answers to some of his most important questions nor the power to free himself from sin.

In Milan, Augustine's mother persuaded him to hear Ambrose preach. Ambrose was one of the most remarkable figures in Christian history. He was one of the greatest speakers of the day. He also was a former Roman civil servant who became a bishop, a leading figure in the Arian controversy, and a noted composer of hymns. Augustine was impressed not only by how well Ambrose expressed himself but also with what he had to say. Ambrose's eloquent teachings resolved most of Augustine's intellectual objections to Christianity. Augustine could not be a half-way Christian. He knew he could not control his passions. He was put to shame by simple monks who were able to control their sexual and other desires when he, a learned teacher of rhetoric, could not. At this stage, Augustine would pray, "Lord, give me chastity and continence; but not too soon."

Augustine was pushed further toward Christianity by the staunch example of Ambrose and the conversion of a noted Neoplatonist. Augustine felt deep spiritual turmoil and began to study the New Testament earnestly. One day, when pacing around a garden in despair, he heard a child's voice from over the wall saying, "Take up and read." He picked up a scroll of the New Testament lying on a bench. It was opened to Romans 13 where he read, "Not in reveling and drunkenness, not in debauchery and licentiousness, not in quarreling and jealousy. But put on the Lord Jesus Christ and make no provision for the flesh to gratify its desires." This event led to a powerful conversion experience in which Augustine finally began to find the peace he had so long sought. He and his son were both baptized by Ambrose.

Augustine resolved to put his old life behind him. His mother convinced him to send away his mistress. He, his son, his mother, and friends started to North Africa to take up life in a Christian monastery. His mother died en route and his son died soon after they arrived. Augustine and his friends settled into a life of contemplation until he went to the town of Hippo. There the bishop and other Christians ordained him a priest. Soon afterward he became bishop of Hippo and served in this post until his death.

Controversy with the Manichees

Augustine's thought was shaped by his long, painful spiritual journey. It also was influenced by four major controversies. The first of these was with the Manichees. He fought them over the authority of the Scriptures, the concept of free will, and the origin of evil. Augustine rejected the Gnostic elements in

Manicheism including the simple division between good spirit and evil matter. He also rejected the idea that God could not have taken on flesh in Jesus Christ as taught in Christian tradition. Augustine believed that God created the world as good. Even as darkness is the absence of light, evil is the absence of good.

To some extent then, in creating good and light, God is responsible for the development of evil and darkness. Still, angels and humans had the primary roles to play. Evil came about by the exercise of free will by these creatures. Evil was the result of the exercise of the will. The good God of the Christians did not create evil. He created the will. The origin of evil is the bad decisions made by both humans and angels as they used their will.

Controversy with the Donatists

The Donatist controversy also played an important part in Augustine's thought. The Donatists insisted that the church must be pure and the sacraments were effective only when they were administered by a pure priest. Augustine held that the true church was made of people who are pure, but that the earthly church as we know it is made up of those who are pure and those who are not. According to the teachings of Jesus, this condition must be tolerated. To insist that the sacraments work only when they are administered by a priest who is pure is not practical. How is one to know whether a priest is really pure?

Even more important, calling for a pure priest makes the sacraments and salvation depend on human effort. It leads away from depending solely on the grace of God. Augustine saw the sacraments as signs or occasions for the invisible grace of God to operate. Because the sacraments depend on God's grace and not on the efforts of humans, they operate even if the person who administers them is not pure. According to Augustine, it was only necessary that the sacraments have the proper matter (water for baptism, bread and wine for the Eucharist) and correct form (consecration by the priest) for them to operate. That did not mean that there was no place for the true church in the sacraments. Baptism washes away sin, but what that means to a person's life is realized only in the catholic, or universal, church.

Although Augustine did not question whether their sacraments were valid, he did see the Donatists destroying the unity of the church. He also doubted that the fullness of the Christian life could be realized outside the universal church. These things led him to consider if force should be used to bring Donatists back into the catholic church. This resulted in his Theory of Just War. According to him, a war is just if it: (1) is fought under the leadership of proper authorities, (2) has as its goal restoring peace or upholding justice, (3) is motivated by love, not greed or the desire for power, (4) has a reasonable chance to succeed, and (5) is fought to benefit society. This theory has had widespread impact in later

Christian history. It formed one of the justifications for the Crusades. It was used to justify the use of force against the powerless by proper authorities (the powerful). It was even used by the church as a reason to persecute, torture, and kill those who disagreed with church teachings. (The church rationalized that these actions were alright if they were motivated by love. In Christian love, it was better that the body of a heretic died if the soul were saved!)

Controversy with Pelagius

The controversy with Pelagius (d. ca. 420) was also important in the development of Augustine's teachings. Pelagius was a monk from Britain known for his zeal and strict discipline. He believed that humans had the free will to keep from sinning. The fall of Adam (his sin against God in the Garden of Eden) set a bad example but did not doom the race to continue sinning. At any given moment, people still had the power to choose sin or not. In part, God's grace consisted of sending Jesus to give humans a new example to follow. There were no sinful people, just sinful acts.

Augustine felt that Pelagius failed to understand the power of evil and the destructive nature of sin. The fall of Adam had distorted the whole human race and the entire universe. Something deep within people and their world had changed. Even when people were exercising their free will, they did not have the choice of doing something that was entirely good. Every act, every decision was a mixture of good and evil. People were genuinely sinful. It was not just that they commit sinful acts.

Because he was convinced that people were so bound to sin, Augustine was driven to accept **predestination** (some are chosen by God to be saved, others are not), irresistible grace (a person can not choose to reject the grace of God), and the absolute control of God over all that happens. To him, salvation depended entirely on the grace of God breaking into the human to change the heart of that person. With this assistance from grace, a person can improve his or her behavior and attitudes, but will never be able to choose to turn completely to the good. Augustine's position was debated for about a century. Eventually Pelagianism was rejected. The church officially accepted salvation by grace alone, but rejected Augustine's more radical ideas on predestination and irresistible grace. The issues of free will, grace, and predestination would continue to be sources of conflict.

Controversy with the Pagans

The final controversy that influenced Augustine's writings was with the pagans, which was brought about by the fall of Rome in 410. The Roman Empire had been Christian for almost a century. Pagans blamed Christian influence for the fall of Rome to barbarians. To combat this, Augustine wrote the *City of God,* a massive work begun in 412 and completed in 426. In it Augustine contrasted the earthly city (the state) with the city of God (the church). The earthly city was built on the love of self while the city of God was built on the love of God. The two would always coexist. Yet earthly cities came and went as greed for power led to a cycle of conquest and decline. Only the city of God, where people lived in submission to God, would endure.

Augustine was aware of corruption in the church but still felt that it was superior to the state. Even though the state was to be endured for the good of society, the church was to instruct it in the "ways of the heavenly city." These ideas were the basis for the church's involvement in politics, an involvement that would be an important part of life in the Middle Ages.

Augustine's *City of God* was completed near the end of his life as the Vandals were besieging Hippo. In many ways his work is the final contribution of a dying age to the empire. Still, his ideas were powerful enough to make him the teacher of the new, emerging age.

THE CHURCH AT THE CLOSE OF THE PATRISTIC PERIOD

The patristic period ended around 500 C.E. Historians agree that the church was in a vastly different situation after the collapse of the empire in the West. The issue they debate is exactly when the empire collapsed. Here we will regard the onset of the barbarian invasions as the end of one era and the start of a new one. These invasions sent shock waves throughout the Roman world. Invincible Rome, eternal Rome had fallen. The world as it had been known for a thousand years was becoming a new place.

Although religious, political, cultural, and economic ties still linked Constantinople with Rome, the emperor had little control in the West. At the same time, the East would remain fairly stable for several centuries. This caused the Western and Eastern branches of Christianity to have vastly different experiences. In the West, the church entered the chaos created by the lack of political power to become a major player in European politics. In the East, the church was dominated by a powerful state. We will examine these situations in Chapter 5.

During the patristic period, the church underwent dramatic changes. From humble beginnings in Palestine, Christianity spread throughout the empire and even into some tribes outside Roman control. By 500, Christianity was ready to spread beyond the old empire to additional barbarian groups. In the early patristic period Christianity spread despite persecution. By the close of the period, the church was in a position of power. It found itself in a situation where the power of the state supported Christianity. Force now was often used to try to settle disputes among Christians and to persecute non-Christians. Early in the patristic period, Christians often found themselves opposing pagan culture. By the end of the period, culture was officially Christian. This mixing of religion and politics and Christ and culture would present many new problems.

Theology also changed dramatically. At the start of the second century, there was little uniformity within the church and Christians still drew heavily on a variety of sources to explain their faith. Controversies with Gnostics and Marcionites forced Christians to begin to define an acceptable faith. Orthodox Christianity started to unite around a certain canon of Scripture, apostolic bishops, and creeds that set out what true Christians must believe.

Creeds played an important role in the controversies about the Trinity. Debates with the Arians, Apollinarians, and others forced the church to define its beliefs more carefully. These debates concerned the very heart of the Christian message. Orthodox thinkers came to realize that ideas about the Trinity were essential to understanding the nature of God. To say that God was not always Father, Son, and Holy Spirit or that the three were not coeternal and coequal would mean God was less than the God of the Scriptures and less than the God the church had experienced in history. To say that Jesus was not fully God would mean that God had not entered into history to redeem humans. To say that Jesus was not fully human would mean that he did not completely save humanity and the world in which he lived.

The Nicene Creed, with the addition of the definitions of Chalcedon, presented some of the church's basic beliefs. These documents were not intended to say everything there was to say about the Trinity nor were they intended to prevent people from thinking more about the nature of God, Christ, and the Holy Spirit. But they did set some limits on what ideas could be questioned.

People continued to disagree with these formulas. Arian congregations existed throughout the empire. Monophysite groups spread to form the Coptic church in Egypt and Ethiopia and the Jacobite church in Syria. Nestorian groups moved into Persia. Their descendants are still found in modern Iran and India.

The framework for orthodox thought on the work of Christ, the role of grace in salvation, and the place of the church in redemption was worked out. Sacraments as signs of grace played an increasingly important role. Because the church administered the sacraments, the church had a significant place in administering God's grace to sinners. The idea was slowly forming that there was no salvation outside the church.

The division between extraordinary and ordinary Christians had several consequences. A system of saints developed in the church. **Saints** were men and women noted for their spiritual contributions to the life of the church. Early saints were largely martyrs, but later other extraordinary persons were added.

Feast days were established to honor these special people and ordinary Christians were urged to follow their example. By the end of the patristic period, the **veneration** (worship) of saints had become a part of Christian worship. The concept that the saints could **intercede** (plead) with God in heaven for ordinary Christians gained acceptance. Praying to the saints became more common.

The division between extraordinary and ordinary Christians also led to the development of a "storehouse of merit." Ordinary Christians had some merit and were "good" enough to be saved, but extraordinary Christians had more than enough **merit** (good) to be saved. Eventually this storehouse, or bank of merit, could be drawn upon by the church to help make up for the shortcomings of ordinary believers.

In the first century, worship took place in homes and even catacombs (caves/graveyards) hidden from public view. The practice of worshiping in homes did not disappear altogether, but as the faith became more respectable church buildings were constructed. Early worship had been spontaneous and free-flowing, with limited set ritual. In the later patristic period, the form of Christian worship became much more set.

Baptisms were performed once a year at Easter after those seeking baptism had received proper instruction. The Eucharist, hymn singing, set prayers, Scripture reading, and preaching were parts of many worship services. When Christianity became an accepted religion, worship ceremonies became more ritualistic and formal. More and more ordinary believers were kept from active participation in the services. Bishops began to be treated like earthly princes. A calendar guiding Christian worship throughout the year began to appear and Christian holidays were formed. Christmas (celebrating the birth of Christ) and Easter (celebrating the Resurrection) were particularly important.

The bishop came to be seen as a central figure in Christian life. In the first century, the term *bishop* probably had simply meant *pastor*. In the patristic period, the bishops became overseers of congregations in particular towns or regions. They were the guardians of orthodoxy with some right to decide matters of morals and theology in their areas. One result was that traveling preachers who were not under the control of a bishop were discouraged. Women also came to play a much less active part in worship. Reflecting the views prevailing in society, they came to be seen as second-class citizens in a church progressively dominated by male officials.

The relation of the bishops to one another presented a problem. For the most part during the patristic period, bishops were seen as equals. One bishop could not assert his authority over other bishops. Only ecumenical councils had authority over the whole church. Yet, the bishops of certain important cities such as Rome, Constantinople, Ephesus, and Alexandria had great influence and they competed with one another.

From time to time, the **pope** (papa, father, bishop) of Rome would try to claim special authority because of the importance of the ancient capital and because the Roman church was associated with both Peter and Paul. To a degree during this period, the authority of the bishop of Rome was accepted in the Western church but not in the Eastern church. As the church moved into the Middle Ages, the Roman pope was able to claim greater authority over all of the churches in the West. In the East, the older pattern of the equality of bishops was retained. The *patriarch* (bishop) of Constantinople was given more respect than other bishops, but he never gained the high position of the Roman pope. To a large degree he remained "first among equals."

CONCLUSIONS

In the patristic period, the basic theology of the church was established. Many recurring issues were confronted. The faith grew from a small, persecuted sect into the official religion of the Roman Empire. This growth had a strong impact not only on church-state relations but also on the spiritual life of the church. Much of the zeal of the early Christians was lost as the religion became more fashionable. The spiritual life declined as more people came into the faith who were only slightly committed or "cultural" Christians. Monasticism was a powerful force for combating the low spiritual state of many Christians. The church was poised to take the lead in spreading the gospel beyond the bounds of the old empire into new barbarian territories.

The church at the close of the patristic period had experienced significant institutional development. It was a much "tighter" organization with a recognized structure of authority and means of disciplining its members. The institutional nature of the church allowed it to bring some order to the chaos that developed in the West as the Roman Empire declined.

Differences in theology and institutional structures were always apparent in Eastern and Western Christianity. These differences were heightened by the establishment of Constantinople, which left the empire with two political capitals and with two competing centers of faith. This schism within the Christian faith, combined with western political chaos and eastern stability, was to make the experiences of the church in these regions much different during the Middle Ages.

For better or worse, this was the state of the church as it faced the new world that was emerging.

Notes

1. The process of canonization was long. Just because Athanasius listed the twenty-seven books of the New Testament does not mean that all churches accepted them. Other works, such as the *Epistle of Barnabas* and the *Shepherd of Hermas*, continued to be used as "scripture" well into the Middle Ages.

The issue of the canon was not settled until the Reformation. At that time the Council of Trent fixed the canon for the Roman Catholic church. It accepted the traditional books of the Old Testament and the twenty-seven books of the New Testament. (The Orthodox church accepts the same canon as the Roman Catholics.)

Martin Luther set the Protestant canon. He accepted the same twenty-seven books as the Catholics for the New Testament. However, he removed some books that the Catholics accepted from the Old Testament. These are called *Apocrypha,* or hidden writings. Traditionally these books have been placed between the Old and New Testaments in the Protestant Bible. In twentieth-century versions of the Protestant Bible they often are omitted altogether.

Another interesting note is why the books of the New Testament were in fact accepted. There were many writings from the first two centuries that at one time were used for worship and instruction. Some of these were rejected because of their Gnostic content. For example, there were several Gnostic gospels that were not accepted by orthodox Christians. Others were eventually rejected because they were regarded as "inferior."

Those writings that became New Testament canon were accepted because they were seen to be self-validating, which means that the Christian community felt that God was speaking through these writings in a way not found in other writings. This validation is illustrated by a comment of the twentieth-century theologian Karl Barth. It was pointed out to Barth that many books have contained truth and insight into God. He then was asked why Christians believe the Bible is so special. Barth replied simply, "This book like no other book leads men to God!"

2.   Eusebius also is known as the "father of church history." His influential *Ecclesiastical History* chronicles the development of Christianity to his time. While it is not "historically accurate" in the modern sense, it still provides valuable information about the early church.

3.   For a good discussion of the councils of the church and their creeds, see David F. Wright. "Councils and Creeds," in *Eerdmans' Handbook to the History of Christianity,* ed. Tim Dowley. Grand Rapids, MI: Eerdmans, 1982, pp. 156–178.

4.   As history is often written by men, the role of women is often not recognized. Basil and Gregory of Nyssa were heavily influenced by their sister Macrina, a remarkable Christian whose life, devotion, and insight led many of her time to call her "the teacher." For a discussion of Macrina and the Cappadocians, see Justo L. González. *The Story of Christianity,* vol. 1, *The Early Church to the Dawn of the Reformation.* San Francisco: Harper & Row, 1984, pp. 181–188.

Additional Readings

Augustine, St. *Augustine: The Greatness of the Soul. Ancient Christian Writers,* vol. 9. Edited by J. Quasten and J. Plumpe and translated by Joseph M. Colleran. Mahwah, NJ: Paulist, 1950.

———. *Christian Instruction, Admonition and Grace, the Christian Combat, Faith, Hope, and Charity. Fathers of the Church,* vol. 16. Translated by John J. Gavin. Washington, D.C.: Catholic University Press, 1952.

———. *City of God. Fathers of the Church,* vol. 24. Washington, D.C.: Catholic University Press, 1954.

———. *The Confessions of Saint Augustine.* Translated by Edward B. Pusey. London: Collier-Macmillan, 1961.

———. *Treatises on Various Subjects. Fathers of the Church,* vol. 16. Washington, D.C.: Catholic University Press, 1952.

———. *The Trinity. Fathers of the Church*, vol. 45. Translated by Stephen McKenna. Washington, D.C.: Catholic University Press, 1963.

Baur, Walter. *Orthodoxy and Heresy in Earliest Christianity*. Philadelphia: Fortress, 1971.

Blackman, E. C. *Marcion and His Influence*. London: S.P.C.K., 1948.

Bonner, Gerald. *St. Augustine of Hippo: Life and Controversies*. London: SCM, 1963.

Brown, Peter. *Augustine of Hippo*. Berkeley and Los Angeles: University of California Press, 1967.

Campenhausen, Hans von. *The Fathers of the Greek Church*. New York: Pantheon, 1959.

———. *Men Who Shaped the Western Church*. New York: Harper & Row, 1964.

Carrol, James. *Constantine's Sword: The Church and the Jews: A History*. New York: Houghton Mifflin, 2003.

Clark, Gillian. *Women in Late Antiquity: Pagan and Christian Lifestyles*. New York: Oxford University Press, 1993.

Eusebius. *History of the Church (From Christ to Constantine)*. Translated by G. A. Williamson. New York: Hippocrene, 1985.

Gambero, Luigi. *Mary and the Fathers of the Church*. San Francisco: Ignatius, 1999.

Grant, R. M. *Gnosticism and Early Christianity*. New York: Columbia University Press, 1959.

Jonas, Hans. *The Gnostic Religion*. Boston: Beacon, 1958.

Jungman, Josef A. *The Early Liturgy to the Time of Gregory the Great*. London: Darton, Longman and Todd, 1959.

Payne, Robert. *The Holy Fire: The Story of the Fathers of the Eastern Church*. London: Skeffington, 1958.

Robinson, James M., ed. *The Nag Hammadi Library*. Revised Edition. San Francisco: Harper & Row, 1988.

TeSelle, Eugene. *Augustine, The Theologian*. New York: Herder and Herder, 1970.

Waddams, H. M. *The Struggle for Christian Unity*. New York: Walker, 1968.

White, L. Michael. *From Jesus to Christianity*. San Francisco: HarperSanFrancisco, 2004.

Websites

www.annettereed.com/Christian.html. [Provides a strong source with links to New Testament as well as materials on early and late antique Christians.]

www.dailycatholic.org/history/councils.htm. [Provides the history and documents of all major councils.]

www.2.evansville.edu/ecoleweb/. [Provides hypertext encyclopedia of early church documents, articles, images, and links.]

www.fordham.edu/hatsallsbook2.htm. [Provides full-text writings of fathers and church councils along with links to other sites.]

www.newadvent.org/fathers/. [Provides collected writings of the Church Fathers to about 800 C.E.]

CHRISTIANITY IN THE MIDDLE AGES

INTRODUCTION: THE MIDDLE AGES

The thousand years following the Patristic Period are called the "Middle Ages." They stand between the collapse of the Roman Empire and the emergence of the modern period which started with the Protestant Reformation in the sixteenth century. The Middle Ages in western Europe played out much differently than they did in the eastern section of the old Roman Empire. The Middle Ages are divided by historians into the Early Middle Ages and High Middle Ages. Each of these periods had its distinctive social, political, and religious developments. In this section, we set the stage for studying the religious developments by looking at the worlds of the Early Middle Ages and of the High Middle Ages.

THE WORLD IN THE EARLY MIDDLE AGES

The fifth-century barbarian invasions shattered the old Roman Empire. The emperor in Constantinople still claimed to be the rightful ruler of Rome and the West. Many in that region continued to recognize his rule, although from the fifth century onward he did not have effective control in the area. The real power was in the hands of the leaders of various Germanic groups. In the seventh and eighth centuries, the Muslims took control of Persia, Palestine, North Africa, and portions of southern Europe. These conquests divided the old Roman Empire into three large sections: the Byzantine Empire, western Europe, and the Islamic Empire. The history of each is briefly discussed below.

The Byzantine Empire

The distinctive empire and culture that emerged in the East is often referred to as *Byzantine* by modern scholars. This term helps distinguish it from the Greco-Roman culture it replaced. The name comes from Byzantium, the ancient city that became the site for Constantinople. Justinian I (527–565) was one of the people who was responsible for the creation of Byzantine culture. When he became emperor in 527, he set out to restore the failing Roman Empire.

Justinian undertook to re-conquer the lands lost to the Germanic tribes. He was only partially successful despite the valiant efforts of his armies. He regained North Africa from the Vandals, Italy from the Ostrogoths and Lombards, and a small part of southeastern Spain from the Visigoths. The rest of western Europe remained under control of the Germans. To make matters worse, Justinian was attacked on the east by Sassaian Persians who were trying to wrestle Persia from his control. By the end of his reign, it had become clear that the emperor would have to concentrate on holding the East. The West would have to be abandoned.

Another contribution of Justinian was the famous **Justinian Code,** a set of laws that gave shape to the legal system and government of the emerging society. It summarized the heart of ancient Roman laws and sought to define the principles on which the law operated. The code also created the centralized government holding absolute authority that characterized Byzantine civilization.

The Byzantine culture that emerged in Justinian's time drew heavily on the ideas of Greek Christianity, but it was influenced by the Near East, too. Byzantine civilization produced great cities and architecture. One of its finest achievements was the magnificent Santa Sophia, a church built by Justinian in Constantinople. The society was also deeply religious. There was a very close relation between the state and the church, which we will examine in Chapter 5.

The Byzantine Empire was under tremendous pressure of invasion from the reign of Justinian on. In the sixth century, most of northern Italy was lost to a Germanic tribe, the Lombards. Only a strip of land from Ravenna to Rome along with southern Italy was left in the hands of Constantinople. In the late sixth century, an even more serious threat by the Avars to the north and the Persians to the south was resisted successfully. In the eighth century the Muslims gained control of North Africa, Egypt, Palestine, Syria, and Asia Minor. By 717–718 they placed Constantinople under siege. Even when this siege was broken, the Muslim threat was not totally eliminated.

Although the Byzantines eventually regained some of the lands they had lost, they were left with an empire consisting of parts of Asia Minor and the Balkan peninsula. The Franks, who had become the major power in western Europe, continued to chip away at Byzantine control in Italy. By the ninth century, the empire was threatened by the emergence of the Bulgar state in the Balkans. The Bulgars were eventually destroyed. Byzantine influence was extended throughout central Europe and into Russia. Some progress was made in the East against the Muslims. By the eleventh century, however, the Byzantine state was considerably weakened at a time it was facing new challenges from a variety of enemies, most significantly the Turks. The Turkish invasion finally led the Byzantine state to call on western Europe for assistance. This appeal to Europe was one factor that gave rise to the Crusades, which are discussed in Chapter 6.

The State and the Church in Western Europe

The history of the West after the fall of the Roman Empire is much different. For most of the early Middle Ages, there was no strong central power. This lack of a central power, along with the emergence of **feudalism** (a system of economic, social and political organization centered in large self-sufficient manors), led to a number of struggles in which the church was a major player. Violence and disorder characterized much of the West. Some scholars believe this age was one of Europe's darkest times.

The Merovingian Dynasty. One of the most important tribal groups in the West was the Franks. The Franks began to carve out a widespread kingdom for themselves in the fifth century under their great leader Clovis (481–511). Eventually western Europe was dominated by the Lombards in the south and southeast, the Franks in the central area, and the Anglo-Saxons in England.

By far the largest area was controlled by the Franks. Clovis was a powerful warrior who successfully conquered many of the neighboring peoples. He founded the Merovingian dynasty, which ruled until 751. It declined steadily from the time of Clovis' death. Merovingian kings relied heavily on force, which caused them to be viewed as bloodthirsty. They seemed to have little concern for common people.

The kings found themselves relying on well-to-do landowners to support their causes and fight their wars. Ownership of land gave both laypeople and church officials great power. A system emerged in which a person's status depended on his ability to give land to those who served him. These "noble" landowners controlled their regions and often stood between the king and the people. The rules governing relations between the king and the nobles were unclear and constant strife resulted. The feudal system thus emerged as a way of coping with this situation.

The elite in this society were not "cultured" Romans but instead often crude and uneducated. They were concerned with drinking, gambling, fighting, and increasing their power. Family connections were especially important as a means of gaining land and control. Several powerful families would eventually control and influence much of western Europe. For peasants, life was difficult and short and characterized by hard work, ignorance, and isolation.

The church played an important role in the chaotic Merovingian world. Many of the Franks were Christian and looked to the church for spiritual direction. Unfortunately, the religious and moral life of many laypersons and clergy was at a very low level. Church officials did play important **secular** (nonreligious) roles. Because some church officials were educated and their political leaders were not, the clergy assisted in preparing documents and administering affairs of state.

The urban centers so important in the Roman Empire became relatively unimportant. Trade declined and people moved to the countryside to work the land. Local cathedrals dominated by bishops became the focus of regional life. In addition, the church itself was one of the largest landowners on the Continent, which gave it tremendous power. Bishops and other church officials came to act more as feudal lords than as spiritual leaders. The pope in Rome finally claimed he was the head of the church. Because he had a hierarchy of power and some influence over local affairs through his bishops, he came to provide a degree of central control that the political powers could not.

The Carolingian Dynasty. The later Merovingian rulers were so ineffective that the last few are sometimes referred to as "do-nothing" kings. This dynasty was replaced by the Carolingians, so named after their greatest ruler, Carolus (or Charles). Two able early leaders of this family were Charles Martel (714–741) and Pepin the Short (741–751).[1] Charles Martel is best remembered for his defeat of invading Muslims at Tours in 732, which prevented the Muslims from conquering western Europe.

Both men initially served as high officials under Merovingian kings. They were capable warriors who also effectively administered the realm. They built loyalty among the nobles in the society by giving large grants of land called **benefices,** or **fiefs,** for service to the state. Often this land was taken from property that belonged to the church. Despite this seizure of property, both men took actions that gained them favor with the church. They dispensed justice fairly, cared for the weak, and guarded church rights. They became the real power in the kingdom.

Pepin finally decided to seize power formally in the realm by removing the last of the Merovingian kings from the throne and transferring the crown to himself. Pepin sought and received the blessing of the pope for these actions. The pope was encouraged to bless the change because he was under pressure from the Lombards in northern Italy, and he needed Frankish protection for his properties there. This arrangement started a long history of Frankish involvement in the affairs of the papacy. Frankish kings came to see themselves as protectors of Rome and the pope. They also came to feel that they had the right to interfere in such church matters as the appointment of a new pope.

Pepin gave lands taken from the Lombards in central Italy to the pope. He did so despite the fact that these lands legally belonged to the Byzantine Empire. Pope Stephen II (d. 757) persuaded Pepin to give the land to him with the aid of a document known as the "Donation of Constantine." This document was a forgery, possibly prepared at that very time. In it Constantine supposedly gave the pope the control of the western empire, Italy, and Rome. The "Donation of Constantine" was widely accepted during much of the Middle Ages and was used as a basis for later papal claims to authority.

Charlemagne. Pepin's successor, Charlemagne (768–814), was the greatest of the Carolingian rulers as well as the first of the great European kings. Charlemagne (literally, Charles the Great) was an extremely successful military leader and diplomat who carved out a large, stable Frankish Empire. His able administration of the empire was fueled by his deep belief in the duties of a Christian king, based on his readings of the Old Testament and Augustine's *City of God.*

To Charlemagne the king was an agent of God anointed to carry out God's commands. He was to command his subjects to do good as well as to resist evil. Society was to function according to Christian ideas of right order, justice, and harmony. Charlemagne undertook a vigorous reform of the church through such steps as encouraging Christian missions, asserting the authority of bishops, improving the moral and educational standards for clergy, reforming monasteries through strict observance of the Rule of Saint Benedict, and ensuring financial support for religious causes by imposing a 10 percent tax on all Christians.

This reform was aided by the papacy. The pope's role in reform helped improve his position throughout Europe. Possibly in gratitude for this improved status, Pope Leo III crowned Charlemagne "Emperor of the Romans" on Christmas Day in 800. Historians still debate many of the details as well as the importance of this event. It is unclear how Charlemagne, his subjects, or the papacy understood the title of emperor. Yet Charlemagne did reign as emperor until his death and successfully forced the Byzantines to recognize his right to the title.

The Carolingian Renaissance. Another important achievement of Charlemagne's reign was the Carolingian Renaissance, which did much to preserve Western civilization. Charlemagne developed an appreciation for learning. He saw education of the leadership, especially the clergy, as one of the keys to providing a better quality of life. This idea was revolutionary in an age that had almost forgotten the value of education.

The stress on learning helped to produce a **renaissance,** or rebirth, of culture that brought together trends from earlier small revivals that had occurred in other places in Europe. Charlemagne invited Irish monks to teach in his realm. Ireland had not suffered the cultural and educational breakdown that the Continent had experienced after the collapse of Rome. Other scholars came from Italy, Spain, and England. Charlemagne established a court school at his new capital, Aachen (in what is today Germany), in the 790s. The noted scholar and monk Alcuin of York (735–804) was made head of the school.

Alcuin and other scholars developed a method of instruction that became the foundation for all education in the Middle Ages. It emphasized the study of subjects such as Scripture, church fathers, and literature *in the original texts*. This emphasis aided the development of historical studies and renewed an appreciation for literature. Art flourished. A standard form of Latin began to spread throughout Europe. Monasteries and cathedrals began to enhance their libraries and to copy texts, which was particularly important in the creation of the cathedral schools of the later Middle Ages.

Declining Empire and the Developing Feudal System. In the ninth century the Carolingian Empire declined from its high point under Charlemagne. Outside pressures aggravated internal problems. Muslims from North Africa, called Saracens, attacked Italy and southern France by sea. New invaders from Asia called Magyars, or Hungarians, attacked the eastern empire on horseback. But the most severe threat came from northern Vikings, or Norsemen. These Norsemen were the ancestors of Danes, Swedes, and Norwegians.

The Vikings were barbarians who were still pagan in their religion. In the ninth century they began to expand. They traveled by boat in small bands and attacked the entire Atlantic coast of Europe, the Baltic Sea region, Russia, Ireland, England, Iceland, Greenland, and North America. The rivers of Europe became highways, allowing them to attack far inland. They burned, pillaged, and looted everywhere they went, instilling such fear that ninth-century English Christians put a prayer in their liturgy that contains the desperate plea, "Lord protect us from the wrath of the Norsemen." Royal armies of the empire were ineffective against this northern threat. Local nobles with their own armies were more effective. This served to further diminish the control of the empire by leaving powerful lords with their own military forces that the emperor could not command. By 900, Europe again was fragmented.

Around 900, the feudal system became the dominant form of political and social organization in much of western Europe. The system grew out of German customs and the great self-sufficient manors that were a part of life in the late stages of the Roman Empire. In the feudal system, lesser lords swore alliance to greater lords in return for protection. The lesser lords gave their military service and that of their **vassals** (even lesser lords who had sworn allegiance to them) to the greater lord. In return, the greater lords granted others the right to rule fiefs (estates). Ideally, this system would create a grand hierarchy with the king at the top and many levels of lesser nobles under him. In reality, it led to a complicated system in which any one person might have a number of fiefs and allegiances. The feudal structure divided much of western central Europe into a patchwork of local domains over which central authorities had little control.

Peasants technically were not part of the feudal system. However, most of the peasants had become economically attached to large, self-sufficient agricultural estates known as **manors.** Other persons were obliged to serve their lords as **serfs** (people bound for life to their lord), tending the fields and performing other services. Because their position was hereditary, serfs could not leave the manor or the service of their lord. Serfs were bound to the soil but could not be bought or sold. Some lords also owned slaves, who were property and could be bought and sold.

The church was deeply involved in the feudal system because it was such a large landholder. Bishops and abbots were often the managers of extensive benefices (fiefs). They in turn were expected to give the same service to greater lords as any other vassal. Churchmen became as entrapped as laypeople in this world of war and intrigue where power involved holding and extending one's lands. Even the pope was seen as just another "earthly" noble to be controlled or to control. Many popes were appointed by powerful lords for political purposes, not for religious reasons.

On the whole, life was nasty, lacking in creature comforts, and full of dangers from war and disease. Lords were largely indifferent to peasants' needs. The vast majority of people remained uneducated. The church played a significant role in people's lives, and it was a very religious age. The church was the one institution where the common person could find compassion and a sense of meaning. The religion of the day was often simple, however, and not very thoughtful. The great debates of the patristic period had little meaning for most people. In many cases, the Christian faith amounted to little more than superstition. Morality among laypeople and clergy alike was at a low level, and the church was badly in need of reform.[2] By 1000, "winds of change" would begin to be felt.

The Rise of Islam

The third group that took over a part of the old Roman Empire was guided by Islam. In the early seventh century, a new prophet arose out of the Arabian desert. Muhammad (570–632) claimed that **Allah** (Arabic for *God*) had spoken directly to him through the angel Gabriel revealing the truth about himself and what he required of humans. In turn, Muhammad recited this to his followers who wrote these thoughts down in an inspired holy book called the ***Koran*** (***Qu'ran***) in which the laws of Allah were presented. After initial setbacks, Muhammad won followers who came to be known as **Moslems** or **Muslims** (literally those who submit to God). The religion he founded is **Islam** (making submission to God).

Islam is a monotheistic religion. It recognizes that Allah spoke in both the Old Testament and the New Testament. Christians and Jews are seen as brothers in the true faith as they too are "people of the Book." Islam regards Christ as a prophet, but Muslims do not believe he was divine. Muhammad is the final prophet of God with the mission of bringing Allah's full revelation to humans.

Islam is a highly ethical religion that teaches that commitment to God must be accompanied by a strong commitment to treating others correctly. Love, charity, justice, and mercy are characteristics to be cultivated by true believers. The new faith did much to improve the quality of life and notions of morality in the lands it came to dominate.

By the time of Muhammad's death, his followers had control of the holy cities of Mecca and Medina (in present-day Saudi Arabia) and much of the surrounding desert areas. After his death, Muslim warriors conquered numerous lands in the name of Allah, his prophet Muhammad, and the true faith of Islam. By 750 they had taken Persia, Arabia, parts of Asia Minor, North Africa, and Spain.

The impact of Islam was widespread. For the most part, North Africa and sections of Asia Minor, which had played an important part in early church history, were lost to Christianity. Although Spain was dominated by the Muslims during the early Middle Ages, it still kept a strong Christian community. The Holy Land around Jerusalem was under Muslim control.

In most of western Europe, the Muslims were not a serious threat to the empire after 732 and that region was relatively free to develop on its own. However, the West did become isolated from North Africa, the Holy Land, and the Far East, which cut it off from trade and limited its cultural development. In the Byzantine Empire, the government was a strong central authority, but the Muslims continued to be a constant external threat to both the empire and the church.

WESTERN EUROPE IN THE HIGH MIDDLE AGES

By the year 1000 significant change was afoot. Religious and social energy was ready to explode. New forms of religious, social, and political structures were in the making. Between 1000 and 1500 a new Christian society emerged in western Europe. These centuries are called the "High Middle Ages." The High Middle Ages reached its peak in the thirteenth century and then began a slow decline. This section looks at some of the important trends of the era. These trends were the foundations for developments in Christianity and the Christian church.

Nation Building, Trade, and New Rights

During the High Middle Ages, western Europe was relatively secure from external invasions. The foundations were laid for the emergence of modern nations in England, France, and Germany as separate monarchs came to rule in these regions. The Holy Roman Empire came to power in Germany. This heightened political presence was challenged by the papacy, leading to newly defined roles for both pope and emperor. By the end of the era, France and England resembled modern nation-states. To a lesser degree, this process of nation building was under way in Spain, Portugal, and the Netherlands. In a series of steps, the Muslims were driven from Spain and Portugal. The European continent, with its emerging nations, was under Christian control.

Agricultural improvements led to an increase in the population of western Europe. Improved trade resulted in the rise of a new rich, the merchant class, which would vie with the traditional nobility and clergy for power. The merchant class revitalized town life. Manufacturing and trade gave urban centers a new position of importance. As monarchs sought to assert their control over "nations," national assemblies and parliaments formed to defend the rights of nobles, clergy, and townspeople. Documents such as the Magna Carta (1215) helped maintain the balance of power between people and kings. In turn, these documents became the basis for later recognition of human rights.

Towns became a new source of freedom as the nobility was forced to recognize their power and grant them a measure of independence. The wealth of towns was based on manufacturing and trade, both of which were furthered by the reopening of contacts with sections of the world closed since the days of the Roman Empire. The religious Crusades brought Europe back into contact with the Muslim world and also created new opportunities for commerce. Merchants from western Europe opened trading posts on the Black Sea and began to expand into Asia. These endeavors were stimulated by accounts of travels such as those written in the late thirteenth century by the Venetian Marco Polo. Increased trade generated more exploration of distant lands for new markets and products that could be sold in Europe. This cycle of trade and exploration resulted in the European discovery of the New World by Christopher Columbus in the late fifteenth century.

Manufacturing and trade meant an increased importance for money. The necessity to accumulate funds for trade resulted in the creation of a banking system. It also made money, not land, the basis of the European economy. This change to a money-based economy radically altered the whole European social system. It shifted control of the region away from feudal lords to those who were able to accumulate forms of wealth other than land.

A money-based economy also meant that kings and others were now able to pay mercenaries to fight for them. They did not have to depend on the services of their vassals. Taxation became an important issue for any lord who sought to assert control or fight a war. The control of money gave the townspeople additional power. Towns, especially the Italian city-states, began to assert tremendous power in European affairs. The land owned by the church became less important. The church also began to depend on money to defend its interests and extend its influence. Fundraising became a prime concern for church officials. All these trends led to a slow decline in the feudal system and to a reordering of European society.

Black Death and Rebirth

Around 1300 the population growth, which had continued since 1000, was beginning to strain the food supply and other resources of western Europe. A devastating plague began in the mid-fourteenth century. The **Black Death** (bubonic plague) swept through the Continent between 1347 and 1350. All classes of people were affected. As much as one-third of the total population may have died in three years. Outbreaks of the Black Death would continue throughout the century, disrupting the social and economic order.

The Black Death had a strong impact on the religion of the time. Because the plague struck apparently at will, there seemed to be no way to protect against it. Life was very uncertain. Death, misery, and decay were everywhere. Belief in sorcery and witchcraft grew as people sought explanations for the Death and ways to prevent it. Traditional religion also benefited. While many gave themselves over to wine, sexual excess, and other worldly pleasures, many others flocked to the church. The tendency in Christianity to play down the importance of life in this world was heightened. Many believed that because life in this world was so uncertain and full of misery, the only hope must be in the next. Life on earth was but to prepare for the hereafter. By the early fifteenth century conditions had improved somewhat. People became tired of the nastiness of life and were ready to find beauty again in this world. This was also accompanied by a new appreciation for human abilities. Greco-Roman art, philosophy, and law, with their focus on living in this world, were rediscovered. This Renaissance caused a questioning of many of the values and practices of "traditional," other-worldly Christianity.[3]

Notes

1. The dates in this case are when the two men served as mayors of the palace. The mayor of the palace technically served the king but ended up administering the kingdom.

2. For a good discussion of the early Middle Ages, see John B. Harrison, Richard E. Sullivan, and Dennis Sherman, *A Short History of Western Civilization,* 6th ed. New York: Knopf, 1985, pp. 175–225. Also see Donald Kagan, Steven Ozment, and Frank M. Turner, *The Western Heritage,* 3d ed. New York: Macmillan, 1987, pp. 201–236.

3. For a more detailed discussion of developments in the High Middle Ages, see Donald Kagan, Steven Ozment, and Frank M. Turner, *The Western Heritage,* 3d ed. New York: Macmillan, 1987, pp. 237–351.

5

THE CHURCH IN THE EARLY MIDDLE AGES

Chaos, Darkness, and Emerging Order (500–1000 C.E.)

Pope Gregory I

Differences had emerged in New Testament times between the two main branches of orthodox Christianity—the Eastern and Western churches—that began to lead to a split between them. A major difference between the branches was that they spoke different languages. The preferred language of the East was Greek while that of the West was Latin.

Differences in preferred language in turn helped to create vast differences in the Greek and Latin "minds." It is not far from the truth to say that the Greeks were more philosophical, artistic, and mystical (stressing direct contact with God) and the Latins were more practical and legalistic. When these attributes were applied to Christianity, different concerns in the faith were obvious. For example, the questions of the basic problem of humans and the work of Christ was seen differently in the two halves of the church. In the East the basic problem of humanity was that sin had caused people to lose their divinity. The work of Christ was to restore that lost divinity. In the West, the basic problem of humans was understood to be sin itself. The work of Christ was to pay the price for that sin. As a result, the East's most important symbol was the Resurrection, which indicated a return of the lost divinity. The West's most important symbol was the cross, which showed the price paid for sin.[1]

These differences were heightened in the patristic period by the rivalry between Rome and Constantinople. They were highlighted even more by the unrest over barbarian invasions in the West and the relative stability of the East. They were further aggravated by the varying impact of the rise of Islam on the two halves of the old Roman Empire. All of these situations contributed to a growing schism between Greek and Latin Christianity.

This chapter looks at the cultural and political world in which Christianity existed during the early Middle Ages. Then it presents some major developments in the Eastern and Western branches of the faith. It also reviews the state of the church at the beginning of the eleventh century.

THE EASTERN CHURCH

The Eastern church remained in union with the Western church, although it developed along rather different lines during the early Middle Ages. In this section we look at several developments in the Eastern church: church–state relations, monasticism, expansion, and some major controversies in the East.

Symphonia

The church played an important role in the politics and culture of the East as it did in the West. Yet the stable eastern Byzantine Empire was in sharp contrast to the western situation. This stability helped to maintain and strengthen ancient patterns of church-state relations in Greek Christianity that disappeared in Latin Christianity. Emperors had been deeply involved with matters of the church ever since the time of Constantine. They would call councils, appoint church officials, and attempt to solve theological debates.

These church-state relations continued in Eastern Christianity. The emperor was not a priest and could be excommunicated by a **patriarch** (the head of the church in a major city like Constantinople). The emperor and other officials remained so active in affairs of the church, however, that western scholars usually say the church was dominated by the state in the East. The East calls the relation between church and state **symphonia,** or harmony. In this *symphonia,* the spiritual and civil authorities supported one another. State administration was left to political officials. Spiritual matters, such as theology, liturgy, and contemplation of the divine, were the domain of the church.

The whole society believed itself to be under the protection of God and Mary, the Mother of God. The emperor was God's anointed, much like David and Solomon in the Old Testament. The accomplishments of the empire were seen as signs of God's favor. The emperor used his power to persecute pagans and people who disagreed with official positions. Efforts were made—with varying degrees of force—to bring Jews into the Christian community. This effort was only partially successful and many Jews would not convert. Jews began a long, troubled stay on the edges of Christian society.

Despite the understandings between church and state, perfect *symphonia* was far from realized. Theological controversy continued, especially during the early Middle Ages. There was occasional conflict between the two, but the state generally dominated the church. In many ways secular officials used the church to accomplish their political purposes.

Monastics

Another important characteristic in the Eastern church was the role of monastics. Monasticism developed somewhat differently in the East than in the West. In the West, monks and their abbots tended to be more involved in the daily activities of society and politics in addition to their church duties. In the East, the monastics were much more dedicated to the **"contemplative life,"** which means they tended to withdraw and dedicate themselves to prayer and devotion. The goal of the contemplative life was mystical union with God. Eastern monasteries were often located in isolated spots that were difficult to reach.

This isolation does not mean that monks had no role in Byzantine culture. They were seen as ideal Christians who were to pray for society. The lower clergy (parish priests) were allowed to marry in the East, but monks were not. Because of their deeper dedication to religious life, monks were often called

Important Events of the Early Middle Ages

DATES	EVENTS	SECULAR PERSONS	RELIGIOUS PERSONS	WRITINGS
431 C.E.	Conversion of Ireland begins		Patrick	
440–467	Assertion of papal authority		Leo I	
492–496	More development of papal authority		Gelasius I	
511	Merovingian Dynasty	Clovis		
527–565	Byzantium rises	Justinian I		Justinian Code
529	Monastery at Monte Cassino founded		Benedict of Nursia	Rule of St. Benedict
553	Council of Constantinople			
570–629	Rise of Islam; new claims of papal authority, liturgy, rule for medieval life		Muhammad, Gregory I	Koran, *Pastoral Rule*
597	Mission to England begins		Augustine of Canterbury	
650–754	Theology of Orthodoxy compiled		John of Damascus	*Fount of Wisdom*
664	Celtic and Roman churches joined (Whitby)			
719–754	Mission in Germany		Boniface	
726	Iconoclast controversy begins			
732	Muslims defeated at Tours	Charles Martel		
751–752	Carolingian dynasty founded	Pepin the Short		
768–814	Reign of Charlemagne	Charlemagne		
844	Transubstantiation controversy begins		Paschasius, Radbertus, Ratramus, Gottschalk	*Body and Blood of the Lord*
847	Filioque controversy begins			
863	Conversion of Moravia begins		Cyril, Methodius	
858–867	Successful assertion of papal independence		Nicholas I	

from their monasteries to assume positions as bishops and patriarchs. Married clergy were not allowed to reach these higher positions. Monks also played important roles in the development of theology and liturgy, and they often led the expansion of Christianity into pagan lands.

The Expansion of Eastern Christianity

The story of the expansion of Eastern Christianity is a long one indeed. The faith probably was spread mainly by countless ordinary Christians living in pagan lands. Established missionaries did expand Christianity, however, and one of the earliest recorded stories occurred in the last days of the Roman Empire when Emperor Constantius sent missionaries to the Germanic tribes outside the empire's borders. The most important of these missionaries was Ulfilas (ca. 311–383). Ulfilas' grandparents were taken prisoner by the Goths on one of their campaigns in Cappadocia. His mother, who was probably a Christian, married a Goth. Ulfilas was baptized as an infant. He later was forced by persecution to move into areas protected by the empire. He became a monk and eventually was sent by the emperor as a missionary to the Goths.

Ulfilas translated a Greek Bible into the Gothic language, and in so doing he invented a Gothic alphabet. He also translated liturgy into the Gothic language. His work allowed missionaries to communicate and worship in the language of the people, and by the time the Goths invaded the Roman Empire many of them were converted to the faith.

Constantius was Arian. The form of Christianity that spread among the Germans also was Arian, which allowed it to survive and compete with the Nicene faith for a long time after the Germanic invasions.[2] Arian Christianity survived among the Germanic groups for several centuries. It was an alternative to the Nicene faith that was now orthodox.

Even with these beginnings, the greatest success of Eastern Christianity was not among the Germans but was among the Slavs of Eastern Europe and Russia. The most important missionaries to these groups were two brothers, Cyril (826–869) and Methodius (ca. 815–885). In 863, Rostilav, the ruler of Moravia, requested missionaries to preach and conduct worship services in his people's language. The patriarch of Constantinople sent Cyril and Methodius. The two brothers developed the first usable Slavic (Cyrillic) alphabet and translated the Bible and other liturgical books into Slavonic.

In Moravia the mission met with some success, but the Eastern Christians soon clashed with German Latin Christians also working there. One area of conflict was what language to use in worship. The Germans conducted services in Latin, while the Greeks used the language of the people. As conditions worsened, Cyril and Methodius went to Rome to place their mission under the protection

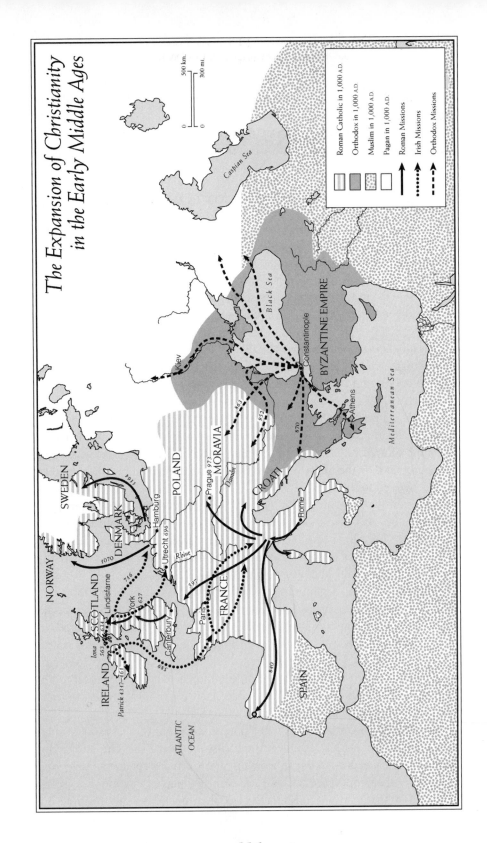

The Expansion of Christianity in the Early Middle Ages

500 km.
300 mi.

Roman Catholic in 1,000 A.D.
Orthodox in 1,000 A.D.
Muslim in 1,000 A.D.
Pagan in 1,000 A.D.
Roman Missions
Irish Missions
Orthodox Missions

Caspian Sea

Black Sea

BYZANTINE EMPIRE

Constantinople

Athens

Mediterranean Sea

861

952

870

Kiev

SWEDEN

NORWAY

1911

DENMARK

Hamburg

1070

POLAND

MORAVIA

Prague 973

Danube

CROATI

Rome

Utrecht 696

Rhine

746

SCOTLAND

Lindisfarne

York 627

563 635

Iona

IRELAND

Patrick 431? 461

685

Canterbury 597

Paris

FRANCE

840

SPAIN

ATLANTIC OCEAN

of the pope. The pope did grant recognition for the mission, although the permission was later withdrawn.

Cyril died in Rome, but Methodius returned to his work. Upon arrival in Moravia, he was again persecuted by the Germans. He was imprisoned and eventually died and his followers were driven from Moravia. The country ended up firmly in the camp of the Latins. The followers of Methodius and Cyril were driven into Bulgaria, where Eastern Orthodoxy took over. Because of Methodius' followers, Eastern Christianity gained a firm hold in Serbia. Eventually it would dominate Latin influence. Another country in the region, Romania, was originally Latin but was heavily influenced by the Eastern churches on its borders. Its present-day religion identifies with Eastern Christianity, but to some extent it is a blend of Greek and Latin characteristics.

By far the greatest conquest of Eastern Christianity was Russia. Conversion from paganism to Eastern Christianity began in the late tenth century and was completed in the late Middle Ages. Russia is discussed in greater detail in Chapter 6.

Controversies and the Seven Councils

The Eastern Orthodox church was deeply involved in the controversies over the Trinity, the lapsed, and the Donatists in the patristic period. However, even in the Byzantine Empire the harmony desired by both church and state did not always occur. For one thing, the church continued to be involved in theological controversies.

The Monophysites, who believed Christ had only a divine nature, never accepted the definition of Chalcedon, which held that Christ had both human and divine natures, and continued to resist it. Efforts to reconcile them to the church by popes, the patriarchs of Constantinople, and assorted emperors failed. Emperor Justinian, who thought he had discovered a way to create peace in the church without abandoning Chalcedon, called an additional council in 553. The council met in Constantinople but only succeeded in making matters worse. The conflict continued.

At the urging of the emperor, Patriarch Sergius of Constantinople (d. 638) tried to find a way of explaining the nature of Christ that would be acceptable to both Monophysites and supporters of Chalcedon. He held that Christ had two natures (human and divine) but only one will. This idea came to be called *monothelitism*, from the Greek words for "one will." What he meant by "one will" is unclear, but people interpreted him to mean that the divine will took the place of the human will. Opponents raised the same arguments against his position as were raised against Apollinaris earlier. Sergius' teachings gained the support of

Pope Honorius (d. 638). A long and bitter debate resulted. However, the Muslim conquest of Egypt and Syria where the Monophysites were strongest left the emperor without reason for trying to bring those who disagreed back into the church. The Council of Constantinople (680–681) condemned monothelitism and labeled Pope Honorius a **heretic** (one who rejects the true faith).[3]

Another controversy started in the eighth century that was particularly important in the East. It concerned the use of **icons** (drawings or paintings of Christ, the Virgin Mary, or saints) as aids to worship in churches. The early church had no problem with the use of these images. They had become very popular among average Christians. Through the ages some leading bishops had expressed concern that icons could lead the masses into idolatry but had not forbade their use.

Several eighth-century Byzantine emperors moved against the use of icons. In 754 Constantine V called a council that outlawed their use. The West generally ignored the law forbidding images. The East was torn apart and for years conflict raged between *iconoclasts* (destroyers of images) and *iconodules* (worshipers of images). One defender of images was the monk Saint John of Damascus (ca. 675–749). John argued that images were found in the Bible. Even more important, the incarnation and the Eucharist were physical means through which the divine was made present. If that were the case, then the images used in the church could not be bad. The icons were thus "books" for the uneducated, who were lifted by the images to the invisible world for which they stood.

Eventually the iconodules won out in the East. A council meeting at Nicaea in 787 restored the use of images, although they had to be painted in low relief with no features standing out. Icons have remained a very important part of worship in the Eastern church and are considered "windows into heaven" through which the faithful may experience contact with the divine. The Western church allowed statues of religious persons as part of its worship practices, which was unacceptable to the East. The problem of possible idolatry with the use of icons or statues in worship would reappear during the Reformation.

John of Damascus made another significant contribution to the Eastern church in his well-regarded *Fount of Wisdom*. The *Fount* is not a work of original theology but rather a summary of Christian theology until the time of John of Damascus. It presents the teachings of the Greek fathers on major doctrines such as the Trinity, creation, the incarnation, the Virgin Mary, angels, and the Eucharist. The book was used extensively in the Eastern church without comment. The East believed there was no need to elaborate beyond what John had said. In the West it also would influence a number of thinkers.

An important conflict occurred in the ninth century between East and West over the *Filioque*. The original Nicene Creed had said that the Spirit came from the Father. The *Filioque* adds "and the Son" to this. The indication is that the Spirit came from both the Father and the Son. This idea seems to have originated in Spain and made its way to the royal court of Charlemagne. When some Frankish Benedictine monks recited the creed with the *Filioque* in their monastery on the Mount of Olives in Jerusalem, the Orthodox were outraged. They demanded to know who had given the Franks the right to alter the creed. The theologians associated with Charlemagne's court took up the battle. The situation worsened because of the rivalry between the Byzantine Empire and the Franks.

In the long run, the West kept the *Filioque* in its version of the Nicene Creed, but the East rejected the new addition. The pope then started using the Apostles' Creed to avoid offending either the Byzantines or the Franks. The Apostles' Creed thus became the most commonly used creed in the West. The conflict also heightened the schism that had been developing in the church. The East and the West stood farther apart than ever.

After the iconoclast controversy, the Eastern church experienced very little internal conflict. As far as the Orthodox church was concerned, the first seven councils of the church had defined Christian doctrine and presented a workable church structure. These are called the *Seven Ecumenical Councils* and are the only ones recognized in the East.[4] Saint John had given an adequate summary of the teachings of the fathers in the *Fount of Wisdom*. Nothing else needed to be said. External pressure on the Byzantine Empire also contributed to a trend to resist theological changes. Some scholars argue that the Orthodox church did not continue to develop its theology after the eighth century. Instead, its energy went into creating a rich, deep, and meaningful liturgy.[5]

THE WESTERN CHURCH

The relative instability in the West created a power vacuum that many groups sought to fill. One of these competing groups was the church. In this section we look at the successful rise of the pope in this power struggle. We then review the expansion of the church. Finally, we examine briefly some of the theological controversies of the time.

The Rise of the Papacy

The barbarian invasions of the late patristic period created chaos in the western empire. It was in this cultural and political vacuum that the papacy began to ascend to real power. During the early Middle Ages the papacy became the one enduring institution with links to the past that could give some stability.

Life on the Manor

Feudal lords and their manors were supported by a large number of peasants who labored in their fields. The manors usually were large enough to be self-sufficient. They often consisted of cleared areas used as fields for crops and animals. One-third to one-half of the cleared land was dedicated to the lord's use and the rest provided a living for the peasants. In addition to areas for planting, the typical manor also contained meadows for hay and grazing, woodlands to gather fuel and building supplies, and wetland areas. The manor had its own government, laws, and court.

The center of the manor was a village with the lord's house, surrounding buildings such as barns and a mill, peasants' huts, and a church built by the lord.

Peasants were slaves, serfs, freemen who owned small plots of land, or cottars who owned their own huts but no land. Although there were some legal differences in these statuses, in reality most peasants were bound as "serfs" to their lord. Some serfs escaped if they had an especially difficult lord. They would roam the countryside looking for a kinder lord to serve.

Three days a week the peasants worked the lord's land. They also had to work extra days during planting and harvest seasons and to maintain estate roads, buildings, and fortifications. Female peasants frequently had to provide domestic labor for the lord's household.

Peasants paid a tithe to the church that, at times, ended up in the lord's pocket. They were taxed by the lord if their daughters married off the estate. They paid additional fees to use the lord's mills and wine presses. A death tax was collected when a son inherited property. The feudal system kept the lords rich and the serfs poor. At best the manor life provided serfs barely enough to get by. There was little left to save for difficult times. Yet it did offer some security and survival in a chaotic time.

Early in Christian history bishops were considered equals. The title *pope* was applied to any bishop. It was only in the late Middle Ages that the West used it exclusively for the bishop of Rome. The churches at Antioch and Alexandria were originally more important than Rome. Theological leadership in the western, Latin-speaking church was in North Africa.

Papal Primacy. Despite the importance of Eastern church leadership, a tradition began to develop that considered the bishop in Rome as the most important Christian leader. Eventually this tradition led to the idea that the bishop of Rome was the supreme Christian leader. All other Christians were to be submissive to him. This idea is known as **papal primacy.**

Papal primacy is based on several factors. Rome was the capital. It was natural to look to the city for both religious and political leadership. The founding of the church in Rome also was associated with the two great figures of early Christianity—Peter and Paul. Finally, those holding to the primacy of the Roman pope could cite Matthew 16:18–19, where, because of Peter's confession that Jesus was the Christ, Jesus says:

> **You are Peter, and on this rock I**
> **will build my church, and the powers of**
> **death shall not prevail against it.**

> **I will give you the keys of the kingdom**
> **of heaven, and whatever you bind on**
> **earth should be bound in heaven, and**
> **whatever you loose of earth shall be**
> **loosed in heaven.**

The argument based on this scripture reasons that because Peter was the first "bishop" of Rome, the powers given to him were transferred to all other bishops of Rome. As a result, the pope was the "rock" upon which the church was built. Holding "the keys of the kingdom" meant those he forgave on earth would be forgiven in heaven; those who were condemned (excommunicated) on earth would be condemned in heaven. This reasoning eventually gave the pope tremendous power in matters of faith and morals and in practical concerns such as appointing or removing church officials and dealing with political leaders. This tradition was even used to assert the supremacy of the pope to councils at later times.

The argument for papal primacy developed over many centuries. For example, the Matthew text was not taken seriously as a ground for papal primacy until the reign of Pope Damasus (366–384). Even though the pope and his supporters claimed primacy, that did not mean he was recognized as supreme. The Eastern church has always given a special place to the bishop of Rome, but it refuses to this day to recognize that he has much greater authority than any other patriarch. Since the time of the Reformation, Protestant denominations have rejected the claims to papal primacy.

In addition, the pope has had difficulty in establishing his right to supremacy even within the Roman Catholic church itself. All through the Middle Ages, church people and secular leaders alike defied papal authority. The pope has always had just as much authority as he has had the power to enforce.

Leo the Great. At any rate, during the first four centuries of church history there was a growing trend to recognize a special place for the pope and some recognition of his primacy. It was Pope Leo I (440–461) who first asserted papal primacy in its full sense. Leo was convinced that he was the successor to Peter and that the Lord had given to him the care of the whole church. To resist him was a sure way to hell. Anyone who did not recognize his authority was outside of the "body of Christ" (the church).

Leo's claims were given some support by the Romans because of the political chaos in the West. The western emperor was weak and made little effort to resist various invaders. Leo came to the rescue. In 452 he successfully negotiated with Attila the Hun to prevent the capture of the city of Rome. Legend says that great fear was created in Attila by a vision of Saint Peter and Saint Paul marching with the pope as he went to confront the Hun. Leo then negotiated in 455 with the Vandals. This time he was not successful in saving Rome from capture but did prevent the city from being burned. His achievements have led him to be referred to as Leo the Great.

Gelasius I. One of Leo's successors, Pope Gelasius I (492–496), advanced the claims to papal primacy further when he declared that priestly power was above kingly power. The chair of Saint Peter (the pope) is supreme. There can be no appeals for its decision. Church authorities must submit to the emperor in secular matters. But in things concerning the church, the emperor must submit to the pope. With Leo and Gelasius, the foundation was laid for asserting papal authority in the Middle Ages.

Chaos continued to engulf Italy. Barbarian invaders competed with established residents for control. The schism between East and West over theological questions lasted for years. Rival popes supported by the Germans and the Byzantines appeared in Rome. Armed conflict between their supporters caused extensive damage to the city.

Gregory the Great. It was in this dangerous situation that one of the ablest popes of the Middle Ages came to be bishop of Rome. Gregory I (590–604) was the son of a Roman government official and he may have been a government officer himself. Later he sold his land and possessions. He gave the money to the poor and became a Benedictine monk. He was appointed by Pope Pelagius II as an ambassador to the royal court in Constantinople. After serving six years, he returned to his monastery in Rome where he became abbot.

At that time the city of Rome was in a state of decay: aqueducts were unrepaired; city walls were falling down; public buildings were not maintained. To make matters worse, the city was experiencing floods, food shortages, and plague. The Lombards were threatening to destroy the ancient capital. Little help could be expected from the East. Pope Pelagius, with the aid of the monks, worked tirelessly to feed the hungry, care for the sick, and bury the dead. After Pelagius became ill and died, Gregory was elected pope.

Gregory: The Politician and Reformer. Though Gregory initially resisted taking office, he finally turned his talents and energy to performing its duties. He took Augustine's *City of God* seriously. He set out to show that the church was the successor to ancient Rome's political power and dedicated himself to repairing the city, providing a food supply, and dealing with the plague. Through Gregory's efforts, the control of the Lombards was broken. He became the real ruler of much of Italy. The lands possessed by the pope in Italy came to be known as the **Patrimony of Saint Peter.** They became an important source of papal revenue and often had to be defended. With the reign of Gregory, the pope became the most powerful force in Italy.

Gregory saw himself mainly as a religious leader. He preached often, calling people to renew their commitment to the faith. He promoted clerical celibacy, which was slowly becoming the norm in Italy. He did not claim for himself the papal primacy of Leo but did see himself as the patriarch of the West. He took steps to tighten his control over other bishops in Europe through a new administrative process. In this role, he also wrote letters to the bishops in Africa dealing with the Donatist schism and tried to defend church interests against Frankish rulers, but he was not very successful in either of these efforts.

Gregory was successful in expanding Christianity through missionaries. Monks were his chief instruments, and their contributions are discussed later. Monks also were useful in expanding the pope's influence. Gregory granted them a degree of freedom from the control of local church authorities. This freedom was later expanded so that monks and others in religious **orders** (monks, nuns, and friars who live in religious communities) were responsible only to the pope. These orders have been a source of tremendous power for the pope.

Gregory: The Theologian. It was not for any of these achievements that Gregory is called *the Great* in Christian history. He was also a theologian who wrote extensively. Gregory was not a particularly original theologian. He drew on the writings of Saint Augustine and applied them to his times. Augustine was a lively, creative thinker who engaged in much speculation. Gregory turned many of Augustine's speculations into unquestionable doctrines. For example, Augustine had speculated that there might exist a place where the dead could stay for a while to cleanse themselves from sin before they were ready to go to heaven. Gregory believed the **Mass** (the ceremony in which the Eucharist is performed) repeated the sacrifice of Christ. It benefited the living and the dead. These ideas were turned into a firm doctrine of **purgatory** (a place where the dead await to be cleansed of their sins). Gregory recommended the saying of the Mass and other acts for the dead in order to release them sooner from purgatory.

Gregory also taught that original sin was washed away by baptism. Later sins could be forgiven by meritorious (good) works if these were accompanied by penance (confession, repentance, and doing penalties given by a priest). He also followed earlier Christian traditions and advocated the effective, almost magical power of religious relics (such as the heel bone of Saint Peter or a piece of the cross) to heal or accomplish tasks for someone who owned them. Likewise, he was quite willing to accept legends and stories no matter how strange or questionable they were as long as they promoted the Christian faith. As a result, misguided information, superstition, and supposed miracles were accepted uncritically into the faith. In most of these tendencies, Gregory was just following the popular religious traditions of his time. Nevertheless, his support contributed to trends that would come to characterize the mind of the Middle Ages. Such traditions as purgatory, penance, masses for the dead, and relics would be strongly challenged in the Reformation.

Gregory: Life and Worship in the Middle Ages. Gregory wrote his *Pastoral Rule,* which would set the standard of behavior for bishops throughout the Middle Ages. The rule also affected secular leaders. Gregory held that either a bishop or a king could rule only if his actions conformed to the conduct demanded by Christ, which became an accepted idea in the Middle Ages. Popes would later use the rule as a tool to subdue their opponents in that the pope claimed the right to determine what conformed to Christ's expectations. Some historians argue that the *Pastoral Rule* was one of the foundations of medieval society.

Gregory's various writings on Scripture promote the allegorical method as the standard for interpreting Scripture in the Middle Ages. The **allegorical method** interprets the stories and teachings of the Bible as though they have hidden, symbolic meanings. As a result, interpreters and theologians stayed away from simple, straightforward meanings of the Scripture. Even the simplest biblical story was thought to have deep moral and spiritual meaning. Some interpretations of biblical passages departed radically from the simplest, most straightforward meanings of the Scripture. Gregory was also involved with work on the liturgy. He was credited traditionally with arranging the Gregorian chant, which was so important to church music in the Middle Ages, and the Gregorian sacramentary, an early form of the Latin liturgy that became standard in the Frankish kingdom. Modern scholars debate exactly what were his contributions in these areas. Gregory the Great's achievements were so widespread that he was considered one of the four

Latin doctors of the church.[6] The word *doctor* means teacher. Gregory is one of the great teachers of the church.

The Decline of the Papacy

After the death of Gregory, the papacy began an even closer alliance with the Franks. The Lombards were still a threat in Italy. The Byzantines were unwilling and unable to assist the Romans in their defense. Pope Zacharias (741–752) sought Frankish help to repel the Lombards. In turn, he supported the crowning of Pepin, who had taken the place of the ruling Merovingian king. This alliance was further strengthened when Pope Leo III (795–816) crowned Charlemagne as emperor in 800. Interestingly, this act seemed to indicate that the pope had the right to "make" an emperor. Although it increased the prestige of the pope in the rest of Europe, it did very little for him at home. Most of the popes during the Carolingian dynasty were weak and ineffective. They were constantly engaged in the petty fights of Italian politics.

One exception was Nicholas I (858–867). Under Nicholas the papacy enjoyed a period of independence and supremacy. His claims to primacy were supported by the famous *Pseudo-Isodorian,* or *False Decretals.* These were a collection of writings including letters from early popes, rulings from councils, and the "Donation of Constantine." They established the pope as the successor to Peter, asserted the superiority of the church to the state, and held that priests were free from control by secular rulers. According to the *Decretals,* only God could remove a pope.

Although these documents were forgeries, they were nevertheless widely accepted for centuries. Certainly Nicholas believed them and came close to presenting a doctrine of **papal infallibility** (the pope makes no errors in deciding matters of faith or morals). His authority was increased by victories in controversies over secular authorities, the Byzantine emperor and the patriarch of Constantinople, and a German archbishop. In all of these controversies, the pope appeared to be the upholder of morality and the defender of right.

When Carolingian power collapsed, the papacy also experienced a decline. John VIII (872–882) was poisoned by a group of powerful Italian nobles. When the poison worked too slowly, the group broke into the pope's bedroom and bashed his head with a hammer. Another low moment occurred in 897, when Pope Stephen VII (896–897) presided over the "Cadaveric Council." He had Formosus, one of his predecessors, dug up from his grave. The corpse was dressed in his papal robes, paraded about the city, and tried before a council for numerous crimes. After being found "guilty," the body was mutilated and thrown in the Tiber River.

The tenth century proved even worse. Political and religious intrigue reigned. Pope followed pope. At times there were two or even three popes supported by various families or political groups, each claiming to be the successor to Saint Peter. One pope was the illegitimate son of an earlier pope and a wealthy married woman from an important Italian family. Another pope was said to have used the papal place as a brothel. Popes were strangled, died of starvation in prison, and murdered their rivals. At the close of the century, the papacy, like the rest of the church, was badly in need of reform.

Missionary Expansion

The history of the expansion of Christianity in western Europe during the early Middle Ages is one of the faith's brighter points. At times the faith was spread by force and used for political purposes. For instance, Charlemagne forced thousands of Frisians, a Germanic tribe from northern Holland, and Saxons to be baptized as an act of submission to him when he conquered them. Those who would not be baptized were killed. This forced baptism was used partly as a method of political control. As long as the Frisians and Saxons held to their pagan religion, they fought in the name of the pagan gods against Charlemagne. Once they were baptized, they seemed to have believed that their gods had forsaken them. They had no god to turn to but the emperor's Christian God.

Early Expansion on the Continent. On the whole, Christianity was spread with great courage by persons of deep conviction. Much of the spread of Western Christianity is owed to countless, unknown Christians as it was with Eastern Christianity. By the time of the barbarian invasions, the Nicene faith had spread to those parts of Europe controlled by the old Roman Empire. The barbarian invaders were largely Arian, though some were still pagan.

These barbarians admired the older culture they had replaced. They tended to want to adopt Roman ways rather than to destroy them. To its advantage, Nicene Christianity was associated with the older culture of Rome. This association led to the conversion of some barbarian groups. For instance, the Visigoths who took Spain around 415 were Arian. Almost two centuries later, their king Recared (586–601) came to believe that the only way to successfully rule the realm was to convert to Nicene Christianity. He and many of his nobles converted at a great assembly in Toledo in 589. Arianism soon disappeared. Catholic Christianity was deeply involved with running the kingdom. It became so entrenched that it was a strong source of resistance to the Muslims, who ruled the country for most of the Middle Ages.

The experience in Gaul was much the same. The Arian Burgundians ruled a part of the territory. They soon converted to the Catholic faith of the people they conquered. The Franks were pagan at the time of the invasion. Their great king, Clovis, was married to a Christian princess, Clothilde. On the eve of an important battle he promised he would become a Christian if Clothilde's God gave him the victory. Clovis won. On Christmas Day in 496, he and a number of his nobles were baptized. Soon the rest of the kingdom followed suit.[7]

Expansion in England and Ireland. Most of southeast England had been controlled by the Romans. In those areas, Christianity spread. When Roman legions were withdrawn to protect the Continent, the area was soon overrun by pagan Angles and Saxons. Many older residents left with the legions. Those who remained kept the Christian faith alive after the invasions of the Angles and Saxons. The form of Christianity that survived in the region is known as Celtic Christianity.

Ireland was never captured by the Romans, but the faith spread there before the collapse of the empire. Although many people spread the Christian faith, the conversion of Ireland is traditionally attributed to Saint Patrick (ca. 390–ca. 460). Patrick was born in England and was raised and educated in the Celtic church. When he was a young man, he was captured and taken to Ireland as a slave. After a dangerous escape, he returned to England. There he had a vision that God was calling him to convert his former captors. Sometime before 431, he returned to Ireland to begin his work. The struggle was difficult but he was able to convert large numbers. Legend says he drove a plague of snakes out of Ireland, which impressed so many of the Irish that they converted to the faith.

Monasteries were founded in Ireland that were dedicated to the study of ancient learning. Because Ireland was not affected by the successive invasions that hit the Continent, a great deal of the knowledge of Roman culture was preserved in these monasteries. Monks would later take this learning back to the Continent. Because it was isolated from much of the rest of Christianity, the faith developed along different lines in Ireland. To some degree, the Irish church preserved and built upon the old form of Celtic Christianity found in southern England.

Ireland was rural with very few major towns, and therefore monasteries became the focus of Irish religious life. The Irish church was structured around monasteries that were ruled by an abbot, rather than towns ruled by bishops. Worship practices also differed. For example, Irish Christianity had a different date for Easter than Roman Christianity and a different way of performing baptism. Irish monks had a very strong commitment to missions. Despite the impact of monasticism, Irish clergy did not have to practice celibacy.

About 563, the Irish missionary Columba (ca. 543–615) founded a monastery on Iona, an island off Scotland. This monastery became an important place for the preservation of knowledge and for mission activity. Efforts to evangelize both

Saint Patrick's Breastplate

One of the best ways to understand the religion of any age is to look at its hymns. "Saint Patrick's Breastplate" is an Irish hymn that came into existence before the ninth century. It is attributed to Saint Patrick, which is possible but unlikely.

> I bind unto myself today
> The strong name of the Trinity,
> By invocation of the same,
> The Three in One, and One in Three.

> I bind this day to be for ever,
> By power of faith, Christ's incarnation;
> His baptism in the Jordan river;
> His death on [the] cross for my salvation.
> His bursting of the spiced tomb;
> His riding up the heav'nly way;
> His coming at the day of doom;
> I bind unto myself today.

> I bind unto myself today
> The power of God to hold and lead,
> His eye to watch, his might to stay,
> His ear to harken to my need;
> The wisdom of my God to teach,
> His hand to guide, his shield to ward;
> The word of God to give me speech,
> His heav'nly host to be my guard.

Scotland and England were launched from Iona. About 589, Columbanus of Bangor (ca. 543–615) and twelve companions went to the Continent where they preached, built churches, and established monasteries in Burgundy, Switzerland, and northern Italy.

Gregory and Later Expansion. Gregory the Great was deeply involved in mission activity. One area he had been concerned with for a long time was the land of the Angles. Gregory commissioned Augustine, a Benedictine monk, to

Against all Satan's spells and wiles,
Against false words of heresy,
Against the knowledge that defiles,
Against the heart's idolatry,
Against the death-wound and the burning,
The choking wave, the poison'd shaft,
Protect me, Christ, till thy return.

Christ be with me, Christ within me,
Christ behind me, Christ before me,
Christ beside me, Christ to win me,
Christ to comfort and restore me,
Christ beneath me, Christ above me,
Christ in quiet, Christ in danger,
Christ in hearts of all that love me,
Christ in mouth of friend and stranger.

I bind unto myself the name,
The strong name of the Trinity,
By invocation of the Same,
The Three in One, and One in Three,
Of whom all nature hath creation,
Eternal Father, Spirit, Word.
Praise to the Lord of my salvation:
Salvation is of Christ the Lord.

Translated by Mrs. C. F. Alexander

reestablish the church in England. Augustine and forty monks arrived for this mission in 597. His first success was with King Ethelbert, who was influenced toward Christianity by his Frankish wife Bertha. Ethelbert required that his first meeting with Augustine be held in an open field. This meeting place was chosen to lessen the effects of the power a monk supposedly had that could cause tails to grow on the backs of his enemies! Ethelbert gave Augustine a residence at Canterbury. One year after he arrived, Augustine baptized Ethelbert and 10,000 of his subjects. Relics, prayer books, and instructions from Rome flowed to the new church. Augustine was made the first archbishop of Canterbury and since then Canterbury has been the main seat of English Christianity.

Missionaries from Rome worked their way northward and continued to have great success. They soon came into conflict with northern missionaries who represented Celtic Christianity. Religious and political differences heightened tensions. A synod meeting at Whitby in 664 decided to accept Roman Christianity. Within a short time, the Celtic missions on the Continent and the English, Irish, and Scottish churches conformed to Rome and recognized her authority.

Benedictine monks from Great Britain soon began to work among the unconverted tribes on the Continent. One of the earliest of these monks was Willibrord (658–739), who worked in Frisia and along the Rhine where he became the first bishop of Utrecht. The most famous Benedictine missionary was Boniface (680–754). He started his work in 716 but was successful only after gaining the support of Pope Gregory II (715–731) and Charles Martel. He founded numerous **dioceses** (districts under bishops) and eventually became archbishop of Mainz. Boniface was firmly committed to the purity of the universal church. His close work with the pope gave the papacy a strong influence in the churches of northern Europe. By the end of the eighth century, paganism and Arianism were defeated in France, Germany, and Great Britain. Monasticism and the papacy were well established in large sections of Europe.

The Body and Blood of Christ and Other Controversies

The early Middle Ages was not a period of great theological activity in the West. The greatest theologian of the era was John Scotus Erigena (ca. 810–ca. 877). He was a native of Ireland who was familiar with ancient learning preserved in the monasteries there. Scotus was a Neoplatonist and was invited to teach at the Carolingian court.

Neoplatonists drew heavily from the philosophies of Plato. Other early writers such as Augustine had been influenced by the ideas of Plato. Through the work of Scotus, Neoplatonism came to be so confused with Christian theology that the two could not be separated. During much of the Middle Ages, Christian theology was Platonism in a different package. The rediscovery of Aristotle in the later Middle Ages caused this trend to change. The impact of the change from Plato to Aristotle is discussed in Chapter 6.

Predestination and Transubstantiation. Several controversies occurred in the early Middle Ages. One of these, concerning the *Filioque,* was discussed earlier in this chapter. Two important and related conflicts involved predestination and **transubstantiation,** which is the doctrine that the bread and wine become the body and blood of Christ in the Eucharist. One person involved in these debates was Gottschalk (ca. 808–868). Gottschalk had thoroughly studied Augustine and was convinced that the church had distorted his teachings.

One area where this distortion was particularly important was Augustine's teachings on predestination. Augustine had speculated that God had chosen some people for salvation from before the world was created. Their selection depended entirely on God's grace. No human effort could cause a person to be saved or lost. When Gottschalk presented these views, he was quickly attacked, condemned as a heretic, severely beaten, and imprisoned in a monastery until his death. One of the reasons that the opposition to Gottschalk's understanding of Augustine was so strong was its impact on the church. If salvation depended entirely on the grace of God operating through predestination, the church would have no role in the salvation process. The authority of the church as the "dispenser" of grace would be undermined.

Another debate in which Gottschalk was also involved concerned what would later be called transubstantiation. The monk Paschasius Radbertus (ca. 790–865) wrote a book in 831 called *The Body and Blood of the Lord.* In it he claimed that when the priest spoke the **words of consecration** ("This is my body . . . this is my blood") in the Eucharist, the bread and wine *became* the actual body and blood of Christ. This transformation held true only for the believer who accepted the body and blood in faith. The elements remained bread and wine for nonbelievers who lacked the necessary faith. It was a miracle of God produced *through the priest.* To the eye, the elements remained bread and wine, but to the believer they really were the same flesh that was born to Mary and had suffered on the cross and the same blood spilled on the cross. When believers ate this flesh and drank this blood, they became a part of the mystical body of Christ, the church. Others opposed this view of transubstantiation. Some held to the teachings of Augustine that the bread and wine were symbols by which Christ was made present.

The debate that followed illustrates several points. For one, the idea of a real presence of Christ in the Eucharist was popular and had been gaining ground for some time. There were still many, however, who held to a symbolic presence of Christ. Transubstantiation would not become official doctrine until the Fourth Lateran Council in 1215, and it would be debated until the Reformation. Almost 200 years after Radbertus started the debate, transubstantiation would become a powerful tool in the hands of the church in its conflicts with secular rulers. Many held the belief in the real presence and a ruler who was denied the Eucharist was seen as outside the church. This rejection by the church had powerful implications for leaders in a Christian society, as will be seen in the next chapter. Finally, because so many believed they were eating the body and blood of Christ, the sense of magical awe of Christians increased. The status of the priest also was enhanced because he had the power to make this awesome change happen.

THE CHURCH AT THE CLOSE OF THE EARLY MIDDLE AGES

In some ways, the church at the close of the early Middle Ages was more divided than at the beginning of the period. Differences in thinking, styles of worship, and political situations had caused Eastern and Western Christianity to take different paths. In the East, older patterns of church organization and thought prevailed. The church tended to be dominated by the state and resisted changes in theology. The political power vacuum in the West caused the church to take on a different form. The papacy assumed a more active role in both secular and religious realms. Theological development continued as important doctrines emerged. All of these factors contributed to a growing schism within the Christian community. The Eastern and Western halves of Christianity were held together by a slim thread.

Missionary expansion brought such far-flung places as Ireland, Scotland, Moravia, Serbia, and Romania under Christian control. Headway had been made in converting Russia. Still, because of the Muslim conquests in North Africa and Asia Minor, the faith held less land than it had when the Roman Empire had first collapsed. The Muslims in the south, the Norse in the north, and assorted groups in the east were threats to the existence of Christian societies.

In the West, the feudal system divided Europe into numerous competing fiefdoms. The church's involvement with the feudal system corrupted its spirit. Bishops and popes acted like feudal warlords. Morals were at a low level and spiritual matters were often neglected. Almost no one, including priests, could read. Some of the knowledge of ancient Rome was lost. Religion often was simple, superstitious, and magical. Such trends as the worship of relics added to the shallow character of faith. As the year 1000 approached, many became convinced the Lord was returning soon. Some became involved in strange activities and movements intended to prepare for Jesus' return.

Yet there were positive signs. Many people were deeply religious. There was a real concern for being Christian. Secular leaders, church persons, and common people wanted a Christian society. Some scholars argue that common people were more dedicated than either their secular or religious leaders. This dedication is shown by the fact that some powerful individuals gave up their positions to become monks. Some dedicated people gave large sections of land to the church or to a monastery, which is one way the church came to hold so much land in western Europe.

The church itself did show signs of genuine spiritual vigor. Many local priests and monks were dedicated Christians. The church exhibited concern for the needs of society; it founded hospitals and orphanages and fed the poor. It often tried to halt the disorder and violence that characterized much of western Europe. Most of the art, literature, and music of the period rested on Christian themes. The parish church was the center of life for most medieval people.

The Latin Mass was becoming the standard liturgy in western Europe. The Christian calendar, prayer books, and hymns gave the faith a common basis. Many people looked to the pope as the spiritual head of the church. The pope was able to assert some central authority through his bishops and monks. Emerging doctrines such as transubstantiation gave the church new power.

CONCLUSIONS

In the West, the early Middle Ages were a time of chaos, which has led some scholars to call them the Dark Ages. Yet the struggles that occurred were the pains by which a new order came into being. Central political control collapsed, but in its place the feudal system developed. Despite its limits, the feudal system was remarkably good for the times. Much of the trade that had characterized the Roman Empire had disappeared, but the large manors associated with the feudal system supplied basic needs. Formal education was often lacking, but crafts and skills were abundant. Systems had been created to train new people in these skills. Life was nasty and often cut short by disease and war. Yet people survived. The population of western Europe actually increased significantly.

In some ways, the religious faith of popes and common people was shallow and superstitious. The commitment required of the martyrs was absent. The deep theological concerns of the patristic period were replaced by more practical problems. The morals of clergy and ordinary Christians often were questionable. Priests, bishops, and popes acted more as feudal lords than as spiritual leaders. At the same time, the church had many positive effects on society and missionary expansion did occur. Paganism, Arianism, and other forms of heterodox beliefs disappeared. The type of Latin Christianity taught by Rome came to be generally accepted in the West.

The papacy rose as a powerful spiritual and political force that helped unify the region. People in the West gradually began to conceive of themselves as distinct from other parts of the old Roman Empire. They had a common political and economic system in feudalism as well as a common faith in

Roman Christianity. Thus, it was during this period that Europe emerged as a separate cultural and political unit. Toward the late tenth century, reform movements were felt in the church, a new central political structure gained power, and a fresh, hopeful spirit began to spread in the West. The time was right for the flowering of medieval society.

Notes

1. It is important not to carry these distinctions too far. Remember the Eastern and the Western churches were united well into the Middle Ages. The Eastern church certainly recognizes the price of sin and the cross. The Western church believes in the "restoring of divinity" and the Resurrection. The point here is that the two halves of Christianity have somewhat different concerns in their common faith.

2. The story of the spread of Christianity is much more complicated than indicated here. For a good discussion of the early expansion, see Kurt Aland, *A History of Christianity,* vol. 1, *From the Beginnings to the Threshold of the Reformation,* trans. James L. Shaaf. Philadelphia: Fortress, 1980, pp. 216–251.

3. The fact that Honorius was found to be a heretic became an important argument against papal infallibility when it was debated in the nineteenth century.

4. The Seven Ecumenical Councils are Nicaea (325), Constantinople (381), Ephesus (449), Chalcedon (451), Constantinople (553), Constantinople (680–681), and Nicaea (787). The important council at Chalcedon established five major cities to lead Christianity: Rome, Constantinople, Alexandria, Antioch, and Jerusalem. The bishops of these cities were called *patriarchs.* Other bishops who exercised control over a province (state or region) were called *metropolitans.* Through the years, the cities have changed, but the Orthodox world is still led by patriarchs. Ideally, the patriarchs and metropolitans have no special authority over other bishops. Even the bishops of small cities are equal to the great patriarchs and metropolitans.

Belief in this structure has caused an ongoing conflict between the Orthodox and the Roman Catholics. In Orthodox thought, there is a special place for the pope (bishop) of Rome. He is "first among equals," but no more than that. He has no authority for the church at large.

Because of this definition of the pope's authority, the East rejected the growing trend for the pope of Rome to claim he was the leader of the church. The pope and the patriarch of Constantinople often were at odds. These conflicting understandings of the church were aggravated by the political rivalries between Rome and Constantinople and, later, by the troubles between the Byzantine Empire and western Europe.

5. For an excellent discussion of the history and character of the Orthodox church, see Timothy Ware, *The Orthodox Church,* reprint ed. Baltimore: Penguin, 1973.

6. The other three Latin doctors of the Church are Jerome, Ambrose, and Augustine.

7. These instances of mass conversion give some idea of religion at the time. People who converted in this way had a very limited understanding of Christianity. There is little wonder that there was a decline in the depth of the faith from the period of the martyrs to when Christianity became fashionable under Constantine to the era of the mass conversions of pagans.

It also is interesting that God was understood as a "warrior God" constantly doing battle for his causes. The battle between a Christian king and a pagan leader often was seen as a battle between their gods. If the Christians won, mass conversion would follow, which had many results. For one, the converts were still pagan in many of their ways and practices. In their religion, their pagan gods were replaced by an almost equally pagan Christ.

The "warrior God" of the Old Testament was better suited to the early Middle Ages than was the suffering God of the New Testament. Kings, nobles, bishops, and popes often did battle convinced that God was on their side. The warrior God found a place at all levels of life. For instance, a common way of proving one's innocence came to be trial by combat. A person accused of some crime would fight his accuser with religious and secular officials observing. If he won, he was innocent.

Additional Readings

Bede, [Venerable]. *The History of the English Church and People*. Translated by Leo Sherley-Price. New York: Dorsey Press, 1985.

Benedict, St. *Rule of St. Benedict. In Documents of the Christian Church*. Selected and edited by Henry Bettenson. 2d ed. Oxford: Oxford University Press, 1973.

Bloch, Marc. *Feudal Society*. Translated by L. A. Manyon. Vols. 1 and 2. Chicago: University of Chicago Press, 1964.

Boethius. *Consolation of Philosophy*. Translated by V. E. Watts. Classics series. New York: Penguin, 1976.

Brown, Peter. *The Rise of Western Christendom: Triumph and Diversity A.D. 200–1000*. Malden, MA: Blackwell, 1996.

Cohn, N. R. C. *The Pursuit of the Millennium*. New York: Oxford University Press, 1970.

Coulton, G. G. *Life in the Middle Ages*. Cambridge: Cambridge University Press, 1928–1930.

Daniel-Rops, Henry. *The Church in the Dark Ages*. New York: Dutton, 1959.

Davis, R. H. C. *A History of Medieval Europe: From Constantine to St. Louis*. 2d ed. London: Longman, 1988.

Decarreaux, Jean. *Monks and Civilization: From the Barbarian Invasions to Charlemagne*. Translated by C. Haldane. Garden City, NJ: Doubleday, 1964.

Fichteau, Heinrich. *Living in the Middle Ages: Mentalities and Social Orders*. Translated by Patrick J. Geary. Chicago: University of Chicago Press, 1991.

Gregory the Great. *Pastoral Care*. No. 11, *Ancient Christian Writers*. Translated by Henry Davis. Westminster, MD: Newman, 1950.

———. *Dialogues*. Translated by Myra L. Uhlfelder. Library of Liberal Arts Series. Indianapolis: Bobbs-Merrill, 1967.

Hodgson, Marshall G. S. *The Venture of Islam*. Vol. 1, *The Classical Age of Islam*. Chicago: University of Chicago Press, 1974.

Hollister, C. Warren and Judith M. Bennett. *Medieval History, A Short History*. 9th ed. New York: McGraw Hill, 2002.

John of Damascus. *Selected Works*. Vol. 37, Fathers of the Church Series. Washington, D.C.: Catholic University Press, 1958.

Leclercq, Jean. *The Love of Learning and the Desire for God: A Study of Monastic Culture*. Bronx, NY: Fordham, 1985.

———, Francois Vandendroucke, and Louis Bouyer. *The Spirituality of the Middle Ages*. Vol. 2, *A History of Christian Spirituality*. Reprint. New York: Harper, 1982.

Leff, Gordon. *Medieval Thought: St. Augustine to Ockham*. Baltimore: Penguin, 1958.

Le Goff, Jaques. *Medieval Civilization, 400–1500*. Translated by Julia Borrow. Cambridge, MA: Blackwell, 1990.

Lewis, Bernard. *The Arabs in History*. Rev. ed. San Bernardino, CA: Borgo, 1991.

Moss, H., St. L. B. *The Birth of the Middle Ages: 395–814.* Oxford: Oxford University Press, 1935.

Pirenne, Henri. *Mohammed and Charlemagne.* Translated by Bernard Maill. Reprint. Mineola, NY: Dover, 2001.

Richards, Jeffrey. *Consul of God: The Life and Times of Gregory the Great.* London: Routledge and Kegan Paul, 1980.

Runciman, Steven. *Byzantine Style and Civilization.* New York: Penguin, 1975.

———. *The Byzantine Theocracy.* Cambridge, England: Cambridge University Press, 1977.

Russell, James C. *The Germanization of Early Medieval Christianity.* New York: Oxford University Press, 1996.

Sawyer, Peter. *The Age of the Vikings.* 2d ed. New York: St. Martins, 1972.

Volz, C. A. *The Church of the Middle Ages.* St. Louis: Concordia,1970.

Websites

www.teacheroz.com/Middle_Ages. [Provides a multitude of links to an array of topics and resources on Middle Ages]

http://en.wikipedia.org/wiki/Middle_Ages. [Provides encyclopedia type articles with many links to topics associated with the early and later Middle Ages]

http://en.wikipedia.org/wiki/Byzantine_Empire. [Provides articles and links to a host of topics associated with Byzantium in the Middle Ages]

http://witcome.sbc.edu/ARTHmedieval.htm. [Provides links to Medieval art and art of other periods]

6

THE CHURCH IN THE HIGH MIDDLE AGES

Flowering of Christian Society (1000–1500 C.E.)

Pope Innocent III

As the year 1000 approached, a tremendous surge of pent-up energy was ready for release. In the East the church had begun its spread into the vast expanse of Russia. In the West new political structures were arising. Religious zeal was set to lead to church reform, holy pilgrimages, cathedral building, and the Crusades against the Muslims. The papacy moved to consolidate its control. New educational structures and a renewed vigor in theological and philosophical thought were about to burst on the scene.

This chapter and the next review one of the most creative periods in Christian history. We first look at the political and cultural background in which the rise and decline of medieval civilization occurred. We then examine the many trends that inspired the high Christian society of the West. The increasing power of the papacy, monastic reform, the Crusades, and Scholasticism are discussed. Finally we examine the effects of Aristotelian thought on the West.

EMPIRE AND CHURCH REVIVED

The early Middle Ages had been a period of struggle. Eventually a new order began to emerge as political and cultural institutions began to solidify and as the papacy developed as a powerful religious force. In this section we examine important changes in the political system, significant reforms in the monastic movement, a new role for the pope, and a significant clash between church and state.

The Holy Roman Empire

The original "Holy Roman" Empire was created under Charlemagne. Its decline in the early Middle Ages was marked by a lack of central political authority in western Europe. In the tenth century a new political system developed that would play a role in the history of Christianity. The Saxon duke Henry I (d. 936) became the first non-Frank to be king of Germany. Henry had consolidated his power by forcing other dukes who had been ruling the eastern regions of the old Carolingian Empire to submit to his rule. His death left his son Otto I (936–973) with a considerable empire.

Otto proved to be a capable ruler. He increased his power and developed a workable system for administering his realm. Part of this system involved an alliance between the emperor and the clergy. Otto tried to control church officials through a process called **lay investiture.** The emperor assumed the right to invest (to install) clergy in their offices and to grant them land for their support. The lands granted to the clergy became royal fiefs and the clergy themselves were vassals of the monarch. They not only attended to their religious duties but also took care of civil matters for the emperor.

Otto eventually entered Italy. He seized Rome in 962 and persuaded Pope John XII (955–964) to crown him emperor, thus reviving the Holy Roman Empire. This title was eventually recognized by the Byzantines, and the new empire became the most powerful force in western Europe. The five successors to Otto continued to use his policies to govern fairly effectively. Despite the strength of the empire, there was growing opposition from the Germans, Italians, French, and Slavs. The church also became one of the strongest sources of opposition. Strangely, this opposition originated in monastic reform.

Cluny and Monastic Reform

In the early Middle Ages there had been a decline in the quality of religious life in the church. Monastics were something of a spiritual high point. Their high principles and sacrifices were greatly admired. At the same time, the outside world had an impact on many of the sheltered monasteries. Some had been destroyed by the Norse and the Hungarians. Other monasteries were exploited by the princes and bishops sworn to protect them. The great abbeys themselves became a source of political and economic power. Abbey leadership often was obtained through **simony** (purchase of church offices) or through even more questionable means. The Rule of Saint Benedict often was ignored. Many who took their calling to a religious life seriously were aware of a real need for renewal in monasticism.

The much-needed reform had a simple beginning. In 909, Duke William III of Aquitaine founded a small monastery at Cluny, a common practice for nobles of his time. Several provisions in William's deed of land for the monastery freed Cluny from outside interference and the political corruption that characterized much of the church. William also established a reform-minded monk named Berno as head of the monastery.

Berno headed Cluny until 926.[1] After his death six able abbots ruled the monastery, ensuring continuing reform for 200 years. The most famous of these was Odo (926–944), whose aggressive promotion of renewal contributed greatly to the success of the reform movement centered in Cluny. Other monasteries began to accept the ideas initiated at Cluny. At the height of the movement, almost 1500 monasteries had a dependent relationship with Cluny.

The Cluniac reform seemed simple at first. Monastics were called back to a strict observance of Benedict's rule. Saying the Divine Office as required by the rule was to be the chief occupation of monks and nuns. One negative result of the reform was that as the ceremonies associated with the Divine Office became more complicated, the monks and nuns neglected the physical labor that was also required by the rule. However, the Cluniac's strict, simple devotion to religious duties inspired many at a time when there was so much corruption in the papacy and church.

Important Events of the High Middle Ages

DATES	EVENTS	SECULAR LEADERS	CHURCH PERSONS	WRITINGS
909	Cluny founded	William of Aquitaine	Berno, Odo	
936–973	Holy Roman Empire revived	Otto I		
988	Conversion of Russia begins	Vladimir of Kiev		
1000	Cathedral building begins			
1033–1109	Rise of Scholasticism		Anselm of Canterbury	*Monologion, Proslogion, Cur Deus Homo*
1054	Near fatal schism between East and West			
1077	Investiture controversy begins, reform from papacy	Henry IV	Gregory VII	
1079–1142			Peter Abelard	*Commentary on Romans, Ethics, Sic et Non*
1096	First Crusade		Urban II	
1122	Investiture controversy ends			*Concordat of Worms*
1137	Gothic cathedrals begin			
1198–1216	Peak of papal power, papal reforms, Cathari and Waldenese		Innocent III	
1204	Fourth Crusade captures Constantinople			

By the eleventh century, the success of the movement led the Cluniacs and their adherents to begin efforts to revitalize the whole church. They attempted to enforce the model of Cluny and its monastic practices throughout the Christian community. The reformers believed that the freedom granted to

Important Events of the High Middle Ages

DATES	EVENTS	SECULAR LEADERS	CHURCH PERSONS	WRITINGS
1210	Franciscans recognized		Francis of Assisi	
1215	Fourth Lateran Council, Inquisition founded			
1216	Dominicans recognized		Dominic	
1221–1274	Franciscans stabilized		Bonaventure	
1225–1274	Peak of Scholasticism		Thomas Aquinas	*Summa Contra Gentiles, Summa Theologica*
1270	End of Crusades			
1302	Highest claim of papal authority		Boniface VIII	*Unam Sanctam*
1309–1377	Avignon papacy		Clement V, Gregory IX	
1347	Black Death begins			
1320–1384	Defense of monarchy, attack on papacy		John Wycliffe	
1369–1415	Christ/Bible superior to pope		John Hus	
1414	Council of Constance, peak of conciliarism, Hus burned			
1441	*Devotio moderna*		Gerhard Grotte, Thomas à Kempis	*Imitation of Christ*
1449	Movable type applied to printing press	Johann Gutenberg		*Gutenberg Bible*

Cluny in William of Aquitaine's deed allowed for meaningful renewal. Other clergy, bishops, and popes needed to have similar freedom from interference from nobles and kings to perform spiritual functions properly. Simony had to be eliminated. Lay investiture also was questioned.

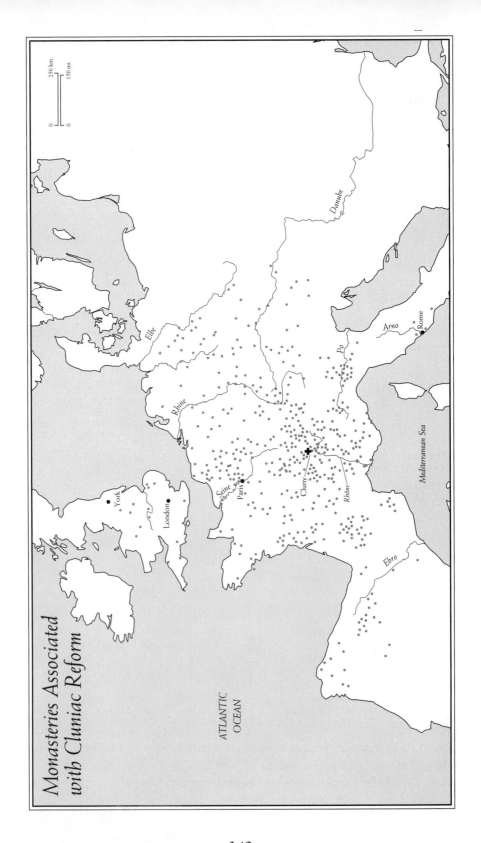

Monasteries Associated
with Cluniac Reform

ATLANTIC
OCEAN

Mediterranean Sea

York

London

Paris

Seine

Cluny

Rhône

Ebro

Rhine

Elbe

Danube

Po

Arno

Rome

250 km.

150 mi.

The extension of celibacy to all clergy was another goal of the reform movement. For centuries, many clergy in the West had practiced celibacy, but it had never been required. The Cluniacs wanted married clergy to give up their wives and demanded an end to concubinage.[2] Obedience also played a part in the Cluniac reform program. Even as monks and nuns are obedient to their superiors, so the church was to obey the pope. Despite the success of the reforms, wealth proved to be the undoing of the Cluniac movement as it did with other eleventh-century reforms.

The Papacy and the Investiture Controversy

The Cluniac reform first came to the papacy in the mid-eleventh century in the person of three remarkable men: Bruno (1002–1054), Humbert of Silva Candida (d. 1061), and Hildebrand (ca. 1021–1085). Humbert and Hildebrand accompanied Bruno to Rome where he had been appointed pope by the emperor, Henry III. All three would have leading roles in attempting to spread monastic reforms to the larger church. In appointing Bruno as Pope Leo IX in 1048, Henry III had hoped to have another pope he could easily dominate; however, he got something else. Acting upon advice from Hildebrand, Bruno refused to accept his new office from the hands of the emperor. He only accepted the position when it was confirmed through election by the people and clergy of Rome. This action questioned the emperor's authority to appoint a pope. As Pope Leo IX, Bruno placed Cluniacs in important administrative posts and held regional synods to combat simony, clerical concubinage, and other abuses.

The emperor's son, Henry IV (1056–1106), was still a child when he came to the throne after his father died. Several popes took advantage of the weakness of the child-emperor and continued to assert their independence. For instance, Pope Nicholas II (1059–1061) worked through the Second Lateran Council to establish the College of Cardinals in 1059, which would play a key role in electing the pope.[3] The Third Lateran Council (1179) placed the election of the pope entirely in the hands of the cardinals. Although political leaders still attempted to influence the election process, the college gave some protection from civil control of the papacy.

Gregory VII and Reform. Hildebrand became Pope Gregory VII in 1073. He proved to be one of the strongest advocates of reform and independence of the church from secular authorities. Gregory had visions of one world united under the authority of the pope. His attempts to extend this authority over the Western church met with limited success. In the West, Gregory's reforms attacked simony and clerical marriage. This twofold assault created alliances

Cathedral Building

Tremendous creative energy was building at the end of the early Middle Ages. This found expression in the great Christian civilization of the High Middle Ages. Cathedral building was one area where this creativity was expressed. The building of grand cathedrals became one of the characteristic features of late medieval life. Rich and poor alike found religious expression by taking part in the construction of these massive churches. Every town and parish wanted a great church as a way to express its devotion and understanding of the Christian faith. Politics also provided much motivation for the building of cathedrals. Bishops and cities could increase their status by erecting magnificent churches.

These structures required vast numbers of workers and artisans as well as quantities of stones and other materials. They often took generations to complete. A father could look forward to seeing his sons and grandsons work on the same cathedral he had started. Much of the work was carried out by volunteers. Yet many of the participants were paid workers. Skilled craftsmen such as stonemasons, carpenters, and smiths were in demand.

New engineering techniques in the late twelfth century enabled the creation of a Gothic style of architecture. Gothic cathedrals were vast

between those who benefited from the sale of clerical offices and the many dedicated married priests who hated simony but refused to put away their wives. The pope's efforts to have his authority recognized in the East were a failure.

Many reformers, including Gregory, came to see lay investiture as simony. Their reforms were based on writings by Humbert. Gregory decreed in 1075 that lay investiture for any level of clergy was forbidden. Any secular leader who continued the practice would be excommunicated. That was a blow to many secular authorities, but especially to Henry IV. Losing the right to invest bishops seriously undermined his ability to rule. It was a situation he could not tolerate.

Henry IV and the Investiture Controversy. Henry quickly acted on the challenge when he deposed the bishop of Milan and put another in his place. Gregory responded by demanding that Henry appear in Rome to account for his sins. If he did not, he would be removed as emperor and his soul condemned buildings with high vaulted ceilings that seemed to sweep up to heaven. Walls were made thinner and large sections were covered with stained-glass windows. The cathedrals served as the glorious setting for the miracle of the Eucharist. Christians regarded them as fitting places for the earthly appearance of Christ.

Cathedrals also were "open books" for the many persons who could not read. Scenes painted on the ceiling, walls, and stained-glass windows depicted biblical stories and the lives of the saints. Often these scenes were arranged in the grand hierarchy that was the basis for medieval social and religious structures. God's heavenly court was at the top. Beneath God at descending levels were depictions of the saints in heaven, the earthly Christ, the lives of saints, popes, and, finally, ordinary life. Through such images the uneducated could learn biblical stories and church history. More important, they could see the lesson that "God's in his heaven and all's right with his well-ordered world." Their daily lives were pictured as carefully integrated into the grand hierarchy, which stretched from heaven to earth. The great cathedrals still bear witness to the deep devotion, creative energy, and powerful ideas that drove the High Middle Ages.

to hell. Henry then called a meeting of the German bishops at Worms, where they declared Gregory a "false monk" and no longer pope. Gregory called his own synod at which he excommunicated Henry and declared that the loyalty oaths sworn by the emperor's vassals were invalid. He invited the German princes to elect a new emperor at a gathering in 1077 presided over by the pope.[4]

Henry was left in a difficult position but reacted with a brilliant move. He intercepted the pope on his way to the German election at Canossa. Dressed in the clothes of a penitent (one seeking forgiveness) he sought the pope's forgiveness. Gregory forced the emperor to stand barefoot in the snow for three days. In the end, Gregory had to forgive the repentant sinner. The ban against Henry was lifted. He was restored as emperor.

Gregory's actions seemed to be a great victory for the pope. He had asserted his right to judge the emperor and forced him to submit. In reality, it gave Henry time to deal with the unrest at home in Germany. After he defeated his political opposition, Henry returned to Italy with an army, drove Gregory from the papacy, and put a rival pope in his place.

Henry's victory did not end the controversy. The popes were determined to assert their independence and end lay investiture. Successive popes and emperors battled over the issue. Finally a settlement was reached in 1122 by the Concordat of Worms. The concordat gave church officials the right to invest bishops with the symbols of their ecclesiastical authority (the ring and the crosier, or bishop's staff), but civil authorities kept the right to give them fiefs and the symbols of their role as secular leaders. A degree of separation of church and state had been established. However, popes and civil authorities could not live together peacefully. They would continue to battle one another for power over several centuries.[5]

THE PEAK OF PAPAL POWER

Neither the Concordat of Worms nor the creation of the College of Cardinals as the body for the election of the pope put an end to the interference of political officers in papal business. In addition, the popes continued to be deeply involved in political intrigue, the goal of which was to establish papal control over western Europe. This control was expressed in the idea of "one flock under one shepherd." For a time a unified Europe under papal control was realized, especially during the reign of Innocent III (1160–1216). Innocent was elected pope in 1198 and rapidly became the most powerful pope in Christian history.

When Innocent came to the throne, Germany was in disarray because of the sudden death of Emperor Henry VI. Innocent exploited the situation in Germany by shifting his loyalty back and forth between those who would be emperor. Henry's wife placed her young son, Fredrick II, under the protection of the pope because she feared he would be killed by those vying for power in Germany. In the long run, Innocent supported Fredrick's claims to the throne and assisted him in becoming emperor.

Fredrick made several concessions to papal authority to gain Innocent's support. These amounted to recognizing the pope's right to determine who was the proper ruler. Innocent also forced the king of France to submit to papal authority by nullifying his marriage to a Danish princess. He caused the kings of England and Spain to submit their territories as papal fiefs through the powerful threat of excommunication. He also was successful in interfering in the politics of Leon, Castile, Portugal, Bohemia, Hungary, Denmark, Iceland, Bulgaria, and Armenia. When the Fourth Crusade captured

Constantinople and established a Latin kingdom there, Innocent's domination of the East was extended.

Innocent ensured papal power by making the papacy a powerful economic and trading force. He enacted extensive new taxes on the laity and clergy alike. The growing money-based economy was beginning to have an impact on the church. The church's wealth and its efforts at obtaining revenue would be issues for reformers over the centuries to come.

Innocent's achievements were not limited to politics. He also undertook important changes in church life. Innocent recognized the power of the sacraments to control behavior. He assumed it was the pope who had the power to forgive sins. The forgiveness of sins was delegated to priests who administered the sacraments. The priests were related in obedience to the pope through ordination and the rights of apostolic secession. The doctrine of transubstantiation greatly increased the position of the priest and, thus, the pope. It meant that the priest had the power not only to forgive sins but also to make present the actual body and blood of Christ. Although transubstantiation was still controversial, it became an official doctrine of the Catholic church at the Fourth Lateran Council (1215).

Innocent also used the Fourth Lateran Council to introduce other changes. The Council created a bishop's inquisition in each territory that was responsible for rooting out heresy in the region. The council declared that no new monastic orders could be created that adhered to new rules; each cathedral should have a school that was open to the poor; clergy could not attend games or the theater or participate in hunts; Muslims and Jews in Christian lands had to wear clothes that set them apart; and relics could not be used without papal approval. In addition, the council required bishops to see that regular preaching services were conducted. It mandated that all Christians attend services and engage in confession and penance at least once a year, usually at Easter.

Innocent saw himself standing between heaven and earth as the head of a grand hierarchy. He was the first to use the title **Vicar of Christ** (one who rules on earth at the representative of Christ). Most thirteenth-century popes tried to maintain Innocent's high standards. They met with limited success. The last of the thirteenth-century popes, Boniface VIII (ca. 1234–1303), made the greatest claim for papal power in history. In his **bull** (a serious written papal mandate) *Unam Sanctam* he contended that all temporal (earthly) powers must be subject to the pope. Secular rulers must be judged by the spiritual power, but no temporal power had the right to judge spiritual authorities. It was necessary for salvation for all creatures to be in submission to the Roman papacy. Despite such lofty claims, Boniface was unable to enforce his unchallenged authority. The power of the papacy already had begun to decline.

THE CRUSADES

The Crusades were a pivotal element of life in the late Middle Ages. The **Crusades** were military ventures against the Muslims to free the Holy Land from their dominance. While it is common to talk about several distinct Crusades, it is more accurate to say that a "crusading spirit" gripped much of the High Middle Ages. The Crusades mentioned below were the high points of a process in which many other religious adventures were undertaken against the Muslims and dissenters in the Christian church.

Participating in a Crusade came to be a principal way of expressing devotion and seeking forgiveness for sins. This crusading spirit resulted in many **visionaries** (persons who felt they had a call from God) leading poorly organized expeditions that ended in failure. One example was the Children's Crusade in 1212, which was started by a shepherd boy named Stephen who felt that God had called him to lead Christian children in a Crusade against the Muslims. The children were supposed to have special protection from the Lord because of their innocence. Most of the children who undertook the Crusade died en route or were captured by Mediterranean sea captains who sold them into slavery.

Reasons for the Crusades

Religious devotion and the desire for salvation stimulated the crusading spirit. It was rooted in two systems that had emerged in the church through the centuries: penance and indulgences. The word *penance* means *punishment*. The Latin "legalistic" mind of the Western church never quite got away from the idea that a price had to be paid for wrongdoing. Although people were forgiven by God, they still had to pay a price for sin in this world or in purgatory. In purgatory, the soul of a saved person "did time" to finish that portion of the punishment for sins not completed while living.

The system of penance developed as a means of ensuring that a person was properly punished for sin. It also was a means of directing a sinner into expected forms of behavior. Early on, severe acts of penance were required that could last a lifetime. Eventually these punishments were reduced to more manageable levels. The idea evolved so that pious acts, such as building a church or hospital or giving land for a monastery, could be substituted for the required penance. In time, the donation of money to the church was allowed in place of land. Because all Christians could not afford large donations, a sliding scale was created that allowed people to give according to the amount of wealth they possessed.

The reduction of temporal punishments or time in purgatory rested on the idea that Christ and the saints had built up a storehouse of excess merit. This merit could be transferred by the church to sinners to compensate for any inadequacy in their punishment. It was but a short step from the transfer of merit to the concept of indulgences. **Indulgences** are the waivers from temporal punishments for sins made possible through the church drawing upon its storehouse of merit. Initially popes and bishops permitted indulgences only for great acts of charity. By the twelfth century, granting general indulgences was fairly common. The sale of indulgences by professional "pardoners" became a favorite way of raising money for the papacy. Some of these "pardoners" even made the claim that the pope had the power to release souls from purgatory, for a fee of course. Anger over these practices was one of the causes of the Protestant Reformation. (See Chapter 8.)

Penance and indulgences were closely related to the Crusades. Pilgrimages to the Holy Land had long been one important way of doing penance. Christian pilgrims resented the fact that many of their holy shrines were held by Muslims. They were easily encouraged to fight against enemies of the faith and free the holy sites. In addition, the Crusades themselves came to be seen as "holy pilgrimages" that could serve as penance. Pope Urban II (ca. 1042–1099) reinforced this idea when he granted indulgences to all who would participate in a Crusade against the Muslims. Later popes would grant indulgences to those who contributed money to a Crusade or who outfitted a crusader.

Religious motives were not the only inspiration for the Crusades. Popes also used them to increase their own control of the West and to secure their political position. The pressure from increasing population in western Europe made the Crusades a good avenue to escape a worsening situation. The promise of new lands made the adventures especially attractive to the younger sons of noble families who would not inherit property from parents. Trade was increasing and several Italian cities gained new trading territories through the wars.

A Brief Overview of the Crusades

The First Crusade was the most successful. The Seljuk Turks had overrun the Near East, defeated a Byzantine army, and reached the outskirts of Constantinople. The Byzantine emperor appealed to the pope for assistance. At the Council of Clermont in 1095, Urban II delivered one of the most successful sermons in history. In it he called for a great Crusade to protect the Greeks and free the Holy Land from unbelievers. He promised land and indulgences to those who participated and eternal life to those who died in the adventure. At the end of the rousing sermon, the crowd responded, "God wills it!"

The First Crusade officially left in 1096 under the direction of several nobles. They captured Nicaea, Antioch, Tarsus, and Edessa. In 1099, they captured the holy city of Jerusalem. The slaughter along the way and in Jerusalem itself was devastating. Cities were pillaged, women were raped, and adults and children were killed without mercy. The crusaders divided Asia Minor and Palestine into a series of principalities. Jerusalem became the center of a Latin kingdom.

The fall of Edessa to the Muslims in 1144 prompted the Second Crusade. An army of 200,000 men under the leadership of the king of France and the German emperor marched toward the Holy Land. They were defeated and accomplished little. The recapture of Jerusalem in 1187 by the Muslims renewed the crusading spirit. The Third Crusade, led by the kings of England and France along with the German emperor, was also unsuccessful.

The Fourth Crusade fell under influence of the Venetians, who used it to increase their trade territory. They diverted the crusaders from their original task of battling Muslims to an attack on Constantinople, which was held by Eastern Christians! The city fell and was sacked by the crusaders in 1204. A Latin kingdom was established in the city that led to reuniting Western and Eastern Christianity for a time. The union was not permanent, however, and the attack produced much hatred between Eastern and Western Christians.

The Fifth Crusade was a failure, but the Sixth Crusade enjoyed some temporary success. The Seventh and Eighth Crusades, led by Louis IX of France (later named Saint Louis), were disasters. There were no more Crusades after 1270.

The crusading spirit was not limited to efforts to capture the Holy Land. Military "crusades" were undertaken against dissenters in the church. More important, Christians were driven to retake Spain and Sicily from the Muslims. The history of these efforts is complex. In short, Sicily was taken by the Normans in the eleventh century. By 1492, all of Spain was firmly under Catholic control.

The Results of the Crusades

The results of the Crusades were mixed. The church had completely reversed its traditional teaching against serving in the military and had caused much violence and death. The crusaders did not behave with "Christian charity." They often were more barbaric than the "unbelievers" they were fighting. The Crusades also failed to accomplish their major goal of freeing the Holy Land. They produced a long history of hatred and mistrust among Christians, Jews, and Muslims and between Latin and Greek believers. The legacy of this hatred is seen to this day. Some Muslims see the incursion of Western ideas and the intervention of Western armies into Muslim armies as a continuation of the Crusades. This belief, in turn, becomes the basis for calls for a "holy war" against Western Christian infidels.

On the other hand, the Crusades enhanced the power of the papacy in the West. Contact with the Holy Land stimulated a renewed focus on the Bible and a deeper appreciation for the humanity of Jesus. A new spirituality emerged based on the contemplation of the humanity of the Savior. The veneration of relics increased. Pieces of the "true cross," bones and teeth of saints, and other holy objects flooded western Europe.

Perhaps the greatest accomplishment of the Crusades was increased trade. Europe came to demand cloth, jewels, and other products of Muslim societies, and the trading power of independent cities in Europe increased significantly. The Muslims had created a very advanced culture. Science, mathematics, education, medicine, and philosophy were more highly developed in Islamic civilization than in western Europe. New ideas and inventions flowed into Europe.

These new ideas had the greatest impact on philosophy and theology. As early as the eleventh century, a dramatic change began to occur in Western thought. Increased contact with Jewish and Islamic philosophies caused philosopher-theologians in the West to adopt a new approach to their work.[6] Reason was elevated to a higher place of importance. A strong emphasis developed in using reason to examine doctrine. Some theologians attempted to demonstrate the validity of Christian concepts by reason alone, in part to try to convert the philosophically minded Jews and Muslims. Reason was one of the main criteria for judging truth in the non-Christian world.

The campaigns against Spain also introduced western Europe to the Jewish philosopher Maimonides (1135–1204) as well as the Muslim thinker Averroës (1126–1198). Spanish scholars had brought about a revival in the study of ancient philosophy. Particularly important was their study of Aristotle, who almost had been forgotten in Europe. Averroës had written a number of commentaries on Aristotle. These were so important that he was known simply as "the Commentator" in Medieval European universities. The rediscovery of Aristotle together with the emphasis on reason caused a flurry of theological and philosophical activity. In the long run, Aristotle and reason would produce the scientific revolution. In the short run, they gave rise to Scholasticism.

SCHOLASTICISM

Scholasticism refers to the theological-philosophical thought that dominated the twelfth and thirteenth centuries. The movement got its name from its association with the great cathedral schools and universities. The Schoolmen believed that reason could shed deeper light on the meaning of revealed truths in the Bible and Christian doctrine. Scholastics organized, systematized, and analyzed Christian ideas. They drew heavily on the philosophy of Plato and Aristotle in their search for greater insight. Early Scholastics were monks living in monasteries. Scholasticism later developed in the great cathedral schools that were so influential in the twelfth century. In the thirteenth century, however, the

Women's Life in the Middle Ages

Historians often produce contradictory images of the role of women in medieval society. On the one hand, beginning with the church fathers, most Christian writers portrayed women as morally and physically weaker. They were seen as tools of the devil who tempted and led men astray. As a result, the church and society justified controlling and even abusing women. They were dominated. Men had an obligation to protect and discipline them. Wife beating was considered acceptable. Marriage and childbearing was considered a lesser calling than the religious life.

On the other hand, virgins and widowed wives were glorified as having a particular place of service to God. Strong cults sprang up that focused on devotion to the Virgin Mary. In addition, women were sometimes portrayed as more sensitive and caring than men. At times they were even seen as morally superior to males. Practices of "courtly love" developed in the Middle Ages; women were idealized and were worshiped in poetry and song.

Carolingian and Germanic law viewed women as having certain rights but they were often considered second-class citizens. They were protected and had rights such as the ability to inherit property, but they did not have the same status as men.

Perhaps the main attitude toward women is best reflected in the writings of Peter Lombard (1100–1160). Peter was one of the forerunners of

center of scholastic activity shifted to the universities. This shift was related to the increasing importance of cities in medieval life, and universities were located in cities.

Anselm of Canterbury

Scholasticism had its roots deep in Christian history. Writers such as Augustine, Boethius, and John Scotus Erigena had pointed to the importance of using reason to better understand revealed truth. Saint Anselm of Canterbury (ca. 1033–1109) guided the program of many of the later Scholastics. He thought that reason could help people better understand what they believed. He did not attempt to use reason to prove the truths of faith. For him, faith always came first. He operated from the position, "I believe that I may understand."

Scholasticism. His writings, especially the *Sentences,* formed the basis for education in much of the Middle Ages. Peter said woman was created neither from the head of Adam so she could rule over man nor from the feet of Adam so she could be a slave to man. She was created from the rib of Adam so she could be loved by man and stand as a trusted companion at his side.

It is often incorrectly stated that two careers were open to women: they could be nuns or subjugated housewives. In fact, only a small portion of wealthy women had the option of becoming nuns. Those who did were often praised for their piety and admired for their spiritual leadership. They performed a number of important services such as caring for the sick and assisting the poor. In convents, they could rise to positions of leadership not available to them in society at large (though they were still ultimately subject to the authority of men).

Most women were not housewives in great manors but peasants or part of the working class. These women worked with their husbands in the fields and shops. While many also worked as domestic servants, others became skilled artisans in trades ranging from butchers to goldsmiths. They held positions in trade guilds, which were so important in medieval society. Even while working as craftswomen, they generally were paid less than men. It seems that many husbands treated their wives as loved and respected, if not totally equal, partners.[7]

Anselm wrote several important works including the *Monologion* and the *Proslogion,* which dealt with the existence of God. In the *Proslogion,* he presented his famous ontological argument for the existence of God. This argument is based on thinking of God as "that-than-which-no-greater-can-be-thought." If the idea of the greatest thing in existence occurred in the mind, then it must exist in reality. To him, this "greatest thing" was God. Moreover, reason demands that this Being be perfect and complete. Anselm's ontological argument had a strong impact on theology and philosophy and continues to be debated to this day. The key issue is whether just thinking something exists means that it really exists. For instance, just because people think God exists, does it mean that God actually exists?

Anselm also tackled the issue of the Atonement. For almost 1000 years, the dominant understanding in the West of the Atonement was the ransom theory, which is based on the rules of transactions in Roman society. It contends that God baited a trap for Satan. God sent Jesus into the world to be offered as a ransom for the human souls held in bondage. When Satan caused the unjust death of Christ on the cross, he overstepped his limits and thus gave up any claim he had to all those sinful souls in hell. The Resurrection of Jesus proved that the power of Satan had been broken.

Anselm set out to provide an explanation of the incarnation based on reason alone. In *Cur Deus Homo* ("why God became man," or, better, "why a God-man?"), he built an understanding of incarnation and atonement on feudal concepts. In feudal society, every lower had to honor (obey) his lord. If the lower failed to honor the lord, he would have to pay with his life or satisfy the lord by offering an equivalent payment, usually money or property.

Humans owed absolute obedience to God. When humans offended the honor of God by sin, they received death as just punishment. To avoid punishment, humans must offer satisfaction. But the offense against God's honor was infinite. Only God could offer the infinite satisfaction demanded by the offense against his honor. The solution to this problem was the God-man. In the incarnation, Jesus was able as man to live a life of perfect obedience to God, thus restoring God's honor. This obedience was only what was due to God. It did not satisfy the offense to God caused by human sinfulness. That was done when Jesus voluntarily chose to die on the cross for his fellow humans. His death was beyond the requirements for humans and earned Jesus a store of merit that could be transferred to humans to cover their sinfulness.

Anselm's approach came to be known as the satisfaction theory of atonement. It was so appealing to the people of his time that within a generation it became the "officially accepted" explanation of atonement. Different writers have changed elements of the theory, but Roman Catholics and many Protestant groups continue to teach some variation of it. The theory attained such control of Western thought that many Christians came to believe it was the only approach to atonement taught in the Bible.

Peter Abelard

Peter Abelard (1079–1142) was a younger contemporary of Anselm. He became a noted teacher and author whose ideas had a great deal of impact on medieval thought. His tragic love affair with Heloise is among the greatest love stories in history. While teaching in Paris, he met and fell in love with Heloise. The two became involved in a passionate affair, were secretly married, and had a son. Some of Heloise's relatives felt the family honor had been marred by the relation. They fell upon Abelard and castrated him. Heloise then became a nun and Abelard a monk. They continued to love each other and carried on a lengthy correspondence, although they resolved to turn their passion to devotion to God.

Abelard's writings also stressed reason, but from a more skeptical position than Anselm's. His position might be summarized as "Make me understand that I may believe." Abelard presented another view on atonement in his commentary on Romans. He started from the belief that God was love. Humans had gone astray, but God was not as interested in judging sin as in bringing humans back to the right path. For this reason, God sent Jesus to serve as our example. The sinless life of Christ, and especially his death on the cross, motivates people to follow his example. In this way, they are reconciled to God.

Abelard's position has come to be known as the moral influence theory of atonement. His view was soon attacked. One problem was that it had a weak view of sin. It assumes that humans have the ability to do good, if they just know what good is. Abelard was accused of Pelagianism. Despite its difficulties, the moral influence theory has continued to have followers. Its appeal seems to have increased in the twentieth century.

Abelard's greatest contribution to Scholasticism was his perfection of the use of dialectic. The dialectical method involves first producing contradictory opinions on topics and then encouraging students to resolve the conflicts. To this end, Abelard wrote *Sic et Non* ("Yes and No"). This book took 158 theological questions and showed how the Bible, church fathers, and other Christian authorities had differed on answering them. The goal was not to question authority, but to drive students to deeper insight by resolving the apparent contradictions. This method came to be widely used by the Schoolmen. Later Scholastics went beyond Abelard by presenting solutions that tried to show that it was possible all of the authorities were correct.

Thomas Aquinas

The thirteenth century witnessed the rise of the universities as major centers for study. Although the medieval universities were much different from our modern universities, they did organize students and scholars into guilds for study in particular disciplines. The rise of the universities was accompanied by the reintroduction of Aristotle to western Europe. Continental scholars soon divided into antagonistic groups who supported either Plato or Aristotle. A third group of theologian-philosophers sought to reconcile Plato, Aristotle, and Christian teaching. The best-known of these were Albert the Great (ca. 1200–1280) and his student Thomas Aquinas (ca. 1225–1274).

Saint Thomas represents the peak of Scholasticism and is one of the greatest theologians in history. His genius was not recognized early. As a young man he was so big and quiet that his fellow students called him the "dumb ox." Although he died when he was barely fifty, he wrote many works. The most famous of these are *Summa Contra Gentiles* (a summary of the true faith against the Gentiles) and *Summa Theologica* (a full summary of theology).

The *Summa Theologica* is a vast work that uses systematic arguments to uncover answers to a series of questions on Christian doctrine. Some have compared the work to the construction of a great medieval cathedral. Questions of faith-knowledge-truth, the existence of God, the relation of the Being of God and humans, faith-grace-works, creation, sin, salvation, and the sacraments all were explored in the *Summa*. It is the crown of Scholasticism.

It is impossible to summarize Thomas Aquinas' system here; we only mention a few of his ideas. Following Albert the Great, Thomas Aquinas distinguished between faith and reason. Reason was seen as the proper realm for philosophy while faith was the place for theology. Reason and faith both pointed toward one truth. They did not contradict each other. Reason could grasp certain forms of truth that were available through sense perception and the activity of the human intellect. Reason could prove much truth, but it could not come to those truths necessary for salvation. God must reveal these truths. Because these have been revealed by God, salvation is open to everyone, not just those skilled in intellectual matters. Truths such as the Trinity, purgatory, the Resurrection, original sin, and the incarnation have been revealed by God. Reason can show they are probably true, but can not demonstrate them beyond a shadow of a doubt. Faith and reason support each other.

With these limits in mind, Thomas Aquinas offered five ways to prove the existence of God.

1. *From movement:* Each movement depends on a movement that went before. Trace this line of movement back far enough and you come to the Unmoved Mover (God).
2. *From cause and effect:* In this world, people observe a series of cause-and-effect events. Something happens and causes other things to happen. If the chain of cause and effect is traced back far enough, the First Cause (God) is found.
3. *From contingency:* Everything that exists is contingent on (depends upon) other things that exist. Without those things that went before, a thing in the material world would not exist. For example, each person's existence depends upon his or her parents. Their existence depends upon the existence of their parents and so on. Nothing exists in the material universe that is not contingent. Yet there must be something that is non-contingent to begin the process. This Non-Contingent Being is God.
4. *From judgment:* People make judgments about good, better, and best. The Supreme Good in this chain is God.
5. *From purpose:* Nature moves toward certain ends. The idea of ends implies purpose. If there is purpose in nature, there must be a Purpose Giver, which people call God.

Thomas Aquinas taught that people could learn much from reason about God. But all reason is limited because it is based on concrete experiences. The language used to talk about God is finite and draws upon human experience. Yet God is infinite and is spirit. Experience in the material world and even the experiences of the human spirit can not be applied literally to God. The best humans can do is to speak of God by analogy (comparisons derived from human experience). For example, to say "God loves humans" is not a statement that can be taken literally. God's love is like the human experience of love, but it is greater than any human love. Still, Aquinas believed that human experience gave genuine insight into God, because the analogy between human experience and God was real. Human experience reflected God (no matter how imperfectly).

God provided internal aids to guide people toward good and right actions. God also provided external aids in the form of natural law seen in creation as well as pronouncements in the form of moral law such as the Ten Commandments. Still, humans are incapable of achieving actual righteousness for which they need grace. Grace not only brings forgiveness but also infuses a new nature in people. As a result of this new nature, people cooperate with God in doing meritorious works. These works can merit salvation. People can have more merit than necessary for eternal life. The excess can be transferred to others.

Thomas Aquinas taught that grace was brought to humans primarily through Christ. However, it was made available to sinners through the sacraments. His theory of the Atonement combined Anselm and Abelard. Christ was seen as humanity's sacrifice and moved people to love by his example. Aquinas also combined ideas from Plato and Aristotle, although his system is basically Aristotelian. For example, his arguments for God's existence all start with sense perceptions. In contrast, Anselm distrusted the senses. He started with ideas about God. Finally, Thomas produced the philosophical and theological justification for the social and political system that saw society as a grand hierarchy with the church on the top teaching the civil society. This approach was widely accepted from the time of Thomas and was especially favored by the popes. Saint Thomas' thought came to be known as *Thomism* and was the basis for Roman Catholic theology well into the twentieth century.[8]

Plato and Aristotle

For more than 1000 years, Western society and Christian doctrine were built on the ideas of Plato. Since the thirteenth century, the ideas of Aristotle have tended to dominate. Plato's concepts assume that reality exists in the eternal world of Ideas. It is in this higher realm that the Good and Perfection dwell. God as the Supreme Soul and Being also lives in the higher realm. On this plane, God created the Ideal Form of everything that exists in the material world. The things that inhabit the material world are only poor reflections of their Ideal Forms.

When Platonic ideas are applied to theology, life in this world is regarded as relatively unimportant. It is a preparation for the next world. The perfection of the soul is the significant thing. The body is not very significant and may hinder the spiritual process. This reasoning is **deductive.** That is, it starts from the top and reasons down. A theologian might start with a general principle, a revealed truth, or an assumption about the nature of God and try to understand what it might mean for the specific area under study. The senses can not be trusted, because the best they can do is give insight into the material world that reflects reality only imperfectly.

Aristotle was a pupil of Plato, but he took a much different approach. For Aristotle **universals,** or ideas or general conceptions, do not exist apart from the specific objects in which they dwell. General principles are reached by gathering information through observation of specific objects or happenings. This process is **inductive,** meaning that it starts at the bottom and reasons up. The material world is reality and the senses are invaluable tools for understanding this reality. Life in the material realm assumes importance. That does not mean that there is no spiritual realm, but it does change how an understanding of the spiritual is found. It is found by looking at life in the material world. The Aristotelian theologian looks at human experience and uses it to gain insight into God's workings.

Realism and Nominalism

For much of the High Middle Ages, the conflict between Plato and Aristotle took the form of lengthy debates over the nature of universals. Philosophers of a Platonic bent came to be known as **Realists** because they argued that universals had a real existence apart from the specific objects in which they dwelled. For example, we observe birds of many different shapes, sizes, and colors, but still recognize them as belonging to the species "bird." Realists argue that we recognize the species bird because all of the individual birds reflect a common "birdness" in which they participate. This "birdness" exists as a reality which is greater than and apart from any individual bird.

The Aristotelian opponents of the Realists are called "Nominalists" from the Latin word *nomina* which means "name." **Nominalists** argue that universals exist only because the human mind observes the natural world and creates categories (names) for the many individual objects it sees. None of these ideas, concepts, categories, or "names" exists apart from the specific objects to which they are attached. They are not a separate reality. They are only a creation of the human mind. Thus, when we observe birds we ignore the differences such as size, shape, color, or mating habits, and concentrate on what we *believe* are the similarities. We create the species "birds" which helps us bring order to our world. There is no separate "birdness" in which the variety of individual objects we label "birds" participate.

Another illustration may help clarify this difficult point. In the eighteenth century, scientists discovered dinosaur bones and realized that these were creatures which had not existed within recorded history. At the same time, techniques were developed which allowed them to date the bones as coming from animals living millions or hundreds of millions years ago. The question then arose, "what living species of animals most closely resembles ancient dinosaurs?" The answer to this question would help scientists understand the common ancestor from which both the modern species and dinosaurs evolved.

In the nineteenth and early twentieth centuries, most people believed that dinosaurs evolved from a cold-blooded ancestor that also resulted in modern reptiles such as snakes and lizards. In short, dinosaurs were "reptiles." New discoveries in the twentieth century changed this thinking. Most scientists now believe that dinosaurs evolved from the common ancestor of birds. In short, dinosaurs were "birds." This change is consistent with Nominalism in that the similarities that led some to label dinosaurs "reptiles" and others to name them "birds" were more in the mind of the observer than in reality. In fact, dinosaurs may have little in common with either reptiles or birds but may belong to an entirely different species yet to be identified and named by scientists. Or, the many animals we now place in the category called dinosaurs may be found to have nothing in common after all!

Implications of the Realists–Nominalist Debates

The debates between the Realists and Nominalists were not just so much "theological hair-splitting." They have critical implications for church doctrine, morality, political theory, and where truth is to be found, among many other areas. These differences become most obvious when the positions of the Realists and Nominalists are taken to the extremes.

If universals exist apart from the objects in which they dwell and this world reflects to some extent the realm of universals, the church may gain greater insight into these universals through revelation from God, study, prayer, and moral discipline. Because of this, the church may claim the right to be the teacher of the rest of society and to require adherence to the special truths of its doctrine.

If universals are merely the creation of finite human minds, then there is no real connection between the material world and spiritual realms. This earth along with its social and religious arrangements are human creations not

Veneration (Adoration) of the Blessed Virgin

Mary, the mother of Jesus, is the person called the "Blessed Virgin." According to accounts in the New Testament, the "virgin" Mary conceived a child by the Holy Spirit. The term used for virgin can also mean "young woman." Early in church thought it was widely accepted that Mary was, in fact, a virgin when Jesus was conceived and did not "know a man" until after Jesus' birth. The virginity of Mary was strongly defended by such early church fathers as Ignatius of Antioch. (See box in Chapter 2.)

The controversies involving the nature of God the Father, the Son, and the Holy Spirit contributed to the increasing status of Mary as she came to be seen as the Mother of God. She started to be regarded as worthy of special veneration because of her unique status as the Mother of God. Another factor that contributed to the special veneration of Mary was the idea that started emerging during the Patristic Period: that the model lives the saints lived left them with an excess of merit they could extend to earthly sinners to assist them in trials of day-to-day life. The saints also could intercede with God for sinners (plead with God for sinners). Since Mary came to be regarded as the greatest of the saints, she became one of the chief saints who could be requested to intercede with God for those in need. In fact, one of the titles she received is "lawyer for sinners." In addition, Mary is seen as being a messenger bringing God's word and mercy through appearances to selected people. Mary received a number of exalted titles including Queen of Heaven.

reflections of a greater "heavenly" reality. Because of this, the church has no right to claim special authority to teach and direct the rest of society. Its doctrines could be just as flawed as any other human creation. For instance, if there is no connection between doctrine and "heavenly" reality, there is little reason to believe in transubstantiation. In the communion service, it is obvious to the eye that the bread and wine physically stay bread and wine. They do not appear to be transformed into the body and blood of Christ. Church leaders could have "made up" this idea.

Similarly, if the Nominalists are correct, human ideas of morality, including our concepts of virtues and vices, are not anchored in the spiritual realm. They too are creations of the human mind. When observation teaches us that cultural standards vary among human societies, what is the basis for determining moral and

Although Mary had been venerated for some time, the High Middle Ages saw a significant increase in the cult (a group of worshipers) of Mary. In the twelfth century, the emphasis on veneration of Mary was promoted by the noted abbot, preacher, and theologian Bernard of Clairvaux (1090–1153). Bernard taught an intensely personal faith in which the Virgin was the intercessor. Some argue that the popularity of the Mary cult in the Middle Ages was a reaction against casting faith largely in terms of the logic of the scholastics. Still others say that Mary represents the "feminine side" of God. The "male side" of God portrays God as a demanding, punishing Judge ready to battle against evil. Mary as the "feminine side" of God presents an image of "God the Mother" who cares for, suffers with, and nurtures her children. In many ways, Mary, "God the Mother", is more approachable than is "God the Father" for ordinary people.

Whatever the reason, Mary has played a central role in Roman Catholicism and a very significant role in Orthodox Christianity. Most, though not all, Protestant groups have a much more limited role for Mary confining their interest mainly to Mary as she appears in the New Testament. The Blessed Virgin continues to play an active part in modern Catholic and Orthodox Christianity. She is especially important in understanding Latin American Christianity.

immoral behavior? According to the Nominalist position, we cannot really say that love, compassion, and gentleness are superior to hate, greed, and violence.

The Realist-Nominalist debates also had significant implications for the question of where government gets its authority to rule. If earthly institutions reflect the Divine heavenly realm, then governments are legitimate to the degree that they follow self-existing universal standards. This idea underlies the medieval contention that kings must be Christians who govern "according to the principles of Christ." To do otherwise undermines the authority of government. On the other hand, the Nominalist position means that any political arrangement that people consider legitimate is all right. Ultimately, this led to the rise of democracy, a system of politics in which the government derives its authority from the consent of the governed.

Finally, if Realists believe there is a connection between the material world and the realm of universals, then it is possible by revelation, reason, moral discipline, or other means to have insight into the truth found in the universals. The focus of the search for truth is the universals themselves. The senses cannot be trusted to gain insight into universals because their gaze is limited strictly to the material world. On the other hand, if the Nominalists are correct that universals do not exist apart from the particulars in which they reside, then truth is to be found in studying those particulars. The senses themselves are the instruments we use to observe the material world. Because of this, the senses become the source of truth.

Triumph of Aristotle and Nominalism

During the early Middle Ages most Western Christian philosophers and theologians were Platonic. The doctrines of the church were firmly grounded in Plato and Realism. The introduction of Aristotle into Europe in the twelfth century began a gradual shift in the basis for theology, church practice, society, and the quest for knowledge. To their credit, most medieval theologians were not radical Nominalists. While accepting many of the precepts of Nominalism, they still believed in the spiritual realm and revelation. Many, like St. Thomas, sought some kind of combination Plato and Aristotle. For instance, Thomas believed that reason and observation could teach us much about morality, truth, and God, but he also felt that saving knowledge of God and perfected truth could come only through the activity of God's grace. In other words, he taught that nature could be perfected only through grace.

However, the great synthesis which Thomas had created soon began to crumble. Through such Aristotelian theologians as Johannes Duns Scotus (c. 1265–1308), Nominalism began to carry the day. By the time of William of Ockham (also spelled Occam; c. 1285–1347), the Nominalist position had become dominant. In addition, Ockham's Nominalism was much more radical. In his thought faith and reason were completely separated. Even basic ideas like the existence of God and immortality of the soul had to be accepted because the Church taught them and they were found in the Bible. These tenets cannot be proven. They must be accepted in faith. With Ockham, there is a complete divorce between grace and nature. Nature alone became the focus of the search for truth. Although Platonic ideas have not completely disappeared, more and more religious, political, social, and philosophical systems emerged which are based on Aristotle.

The triumph of Aristotle and Nominalism had a profound impact across the board. In the short run, it spelled the end of Scholasticism. It undermined the whole goal of the Schoolmen to demonstrate by reason alone the validity of Christian doctrines. It also set the stage for the Renaissance, which focused on nature apart from faith or grace. In many ways, this shift was responsible for the Protestant Reformation. Many of the reformers were Nominalists. Nominalism is the foundation from which science emerged. Modern science arose out of Aristotelian inductive reasoning, not Platonic deductive thought. The new emphasis on the importance of the material world gave rise to the idea that humans should take control and make conditions better in this life. The eternal world became less important. In the long run, Aristotle contributed to **secularization** (the removal of human institutions from religious domination), which is characteristic of the modern world.

CONCLUSIONS

A new society dominated by Christianity emerged in western Europe out of the disarray caused by the decline of the Roman Empire. The papacy asserted great power in the political system. Religious fervor was widespread and found expression in the Crusades against the Muslims. The Crusades in turn brought about contact with the high civilization of the Muslims. New interest in intellectual activity developed and resulted in Scholasticism, which gave orderly expression to the aspirations of Christian society.

At the same time, the church hierarchy lost touch with the spiritual needs of people. Worldliness was widespread in the Christian community. Reform was needed, but the papacy and monastics were only mildly successful in producing long-range renewal in the church. The following chapter reviews some of the other reform movements that attempted to breathe new life into the church.

Notes

1. Berno not only headed Cluny but also founded or reformed several other monasteries. Some credit the spread of the Cluniac reform to his example. For a good discussion of Cluny's contribution see: Justo L. González, *The Story of Christianity,* vol. 1, *The Early Church to the Dawn of the Reformation.* San Francisco: Harper & Row, 1984, pp. 278–282.

2. While the marriage of clergy had not been forbidden in the church, the unmarried state had been preferred since the patristic period. In part, the Western church's preference for unmarried clergy is derived from Saint Paul's teachings on marriage in I Corinthians 2:8–9. Here Paul suggests that widows and the single remain unmarried. However, if they could not control their passion, it was better to marry than to burn in hell. Some interpreted this to mean that the most dedicated Christians like clergy should remain unmarried. Only the "less dedicated" laypeople were free to marry.

Many church officials avoided the marriage issue by taking a concubine—a permanent mate who is not technically married to a man. Often a clergyman would spend a lifetime with a concubine and raise a family with her. They reasoned that Saint Paul in the New

Testament had not suggested that Christians remain without families but that they only remain unmarried.

3. The title *cardinal* has a long history in the church. Its exact origins are unclear, although cardinal has been a "rank" in the church from early times. Eventually its use was restricted to those clergy (priests, bishops, deacons) directly associated with Rome. In the eighth century, cardinal-bishops were created to represent the pope and to assist him in church administration in outlying regions. During the Middle Ages, cardinals came to be viewed as princes of the church holding the same rank as princes of noble blood.

The current function of cardinals is largely administrative. Any priest may become a cardinal, but his appointment to this rank usually means he also is ordained a bishop. Unless they are bishops over some distant region, cardinals are expected to live in Rome where they hold offices in the central administration of the church.

4. In medieval society, excommunication was a particularly effective weapon. Because the society was a theocracy, the ruler held his position as a minister of God. To be outside the Christian community meant that his right to rule was no longer valid. Only Christians in fellowship with the church could rule legitimately in a Christian society.

5. For a more detailed discussion of the revival of the Holy Roman Empire and the investiture controversy, see Kurt Aland, *A History of Christianity,* vol. 1, *From the Beginnings to the Threshold of the Reformation,* trans. James L. Schaff. Philadelphia: Fortress, 1980, pp. 279–309.

6. A distinction was made between theology and philosophy. Theology was understood as dealing with truths revealed by God. Philosophy dealt with lower-order truths, which could be understood by reason. Theology was the foremost science. Some argued that the revealed truths of theology could not be investigated by reason. Most felt that reason had a role in understanding revealed truth. Some went so far as to say that a doctrine that was offensive to reason should be rejected. Despite the supposed differences between theology and philosophy, they were very closely related in the Middle Ages. Most of the great philosophers were also theologians.

7. For a good discussion of life in the Middle Ages, including the role of women and children, see Kagan et al., *Western Heritage,* pp. 263–282.

8. For a detailed discussion of Scholasticism, see Kenneth Scott Latourette, *A History of Christianity,* vol. 1, *Beginnings to 1500,* rev. ed. New York: Harper & Row, 1975, pp. 495–521.

Additional Readings

Anselm of Canterbury. *Why God Became Man.* Edited by Jasper Hopkins and Herbert Richardson. Lewistown, NY: Mellen, Edwin, 1980.

————. *Anselm of Canterbury.* Vol. 1, *Monologion, Proslogion, Debate with Gaunilo, Meditation on Human Redemption.* Edited by Jasper Hopkins and translated by Herbert Richardson. Lewistown, NY: Mellen, Edwin, 1974.

Aquinas, Thomas. *Summa Theologica.* Edited by William P. Baumgarth and Richard J. Regan. Indianapolis: Hackett, 1988.

Clancy, M. T. *Abelard: A Medieval Life.* Cambridge, MA: Blackwell, 1997.

Cohn, Norman. *The Pursuit of the Millennium.* Rev. ed. New York: Oxford University Press, 1970.

Duby, Georges. *The Age of the Cathedrals: Art and Society, 980–1420.* Translated by Eleanor Levieux and Barbara Thompson. Chicago: University of Chicago Press, 1985.

————. *Rural Economy and Country Life in the Medieval West.* Translated by Cynthia Postan. Reprint. Columbia: University of South Carolina Press, 1990.

————. *The Three Orders: Feudal Society Imagined.* Translated by Arthur Goldhammer. Chicago: University of Chicago Press, 1982.

Esposito, John L. *The Straight Path.* New York: Oxford University Press, 1990.

Gamber, Luigi. *Mary in the Middle Ages: The Blessed Virgin in the Thought of Medieval Latin Theologians.* San Francisco: Ignatius, 2005.

Gilson, Etienne. *Reason and Revelation in the Middle Ages.* New York: Scribners, 1966.

Kritzeck, James. *Peter the Venerable and Islam.* Princeton, NJ: Princeton University Press, 1964.

Oakley, Francis. *The Medieval Experience.* Cheektowaga, NY: University of Toronto, 1988.

————. *The Western Church in the Later Middle Ages.* Ithaca, NY: Cornell University Press, 1985.

Ozment, Steven, ed. *Religion and Culture in the Later Middle Ages.* Kirksville: Sixteenth Century Journal Publishers, 1988.

Shahar, Shulamith. *The Fourth Estate: A History of Women in the Middle Ages.* New York: Routledge, 1984.

Simpson, Otto von. *The Gothic Cathedral.* New York: Harper & Row, 1964.

Tuchman, Barbara W. *A Distant Mirror: The Calamitous Fourteenth Century.* New York: Ballantine, 1978.

Websites

http://dir.yahoo.com/Arts/Humanities/Philosophy/Scholasticism. [Provides access to links it sites associated with scholasticism; ALSO gives access to PHILOSOPHY SKIN CARE PRODUCTS!]

www.georgetown.edu/labyrith. [Provides assess to Labyrith – extensive resources for Medieval studies]

www.questia.cim/library/philosophy/medieval-and-renaissance-philosophy/scholosticism. JSP?CRID=Scholasticism. [Provides access to library of books and articles on scholasticism]

www.uca.edu/divisions/academic/history/hb4361.htm. [Provides extensive bibliography on wide range of medieval topics]

THE CHURCH IN THE HIGH
MIDDLE AGES

Reform and Decline (1000–1500 C.E.)

St. Francis of Assisi

The Cluniacs and popes made strong attempts at reform. Despite their efforts, problems continued in the church. Immorality remained common among clergy and laypeople alike. The wealth and power of the church seemed much different from the simple life required of believers in the New Testament. During the later Middle Ages several other reform movements appeared. Some remained within the church while others were persecuted as heretical. All of these reform movements tried to free the Christian community from worldliness.

This chapter examines some of these major reform movements. We also look at the decline of the papacy, the rebirth of civilization through humanism, major developments in the Eastern Orthodox church, and, finally, the state of Christianity at the close of the Middle Ages.

REFORM WITHIN THE CHURCH

An important event of the twelfth century was the rise of the **mendicant orders.** *Mendicant* means those who live by begging. In contrast to the older monastic orders who were housed in rural areas, the mendicants lived in cities. They took the New Testament seriously and were determined to live in **apostolic poverty** (poverty like the early apostles), applying the simple teachings of Jesus to their lives. Although the new **friars** (brothers) had houses in most major cities, they still roamed from place to place ministering and preaching as they went.

The Franciscans

Saint Francis of Assisi (1182–1226) was one of the first monks to live in poverty as a way to serve God. Francis was born into wealth; his father was part of the new capitalistic rich in Assisi. As a carefree young man, Francis threw great parties and liberally gave away his father's money. His conversion to the religious life was slow and was filled with impulsive but meaningful events such as embracing a rotting leper, exchanging clothes with a beggar, and stripping himself naked in front of the bishop and his court as a way of pursuing "lady poverty."[1] A reading of Matthew 10 caused Francis to turn his attention to preaching. He gave away everything except a long coarse dark robe tied together at the waist with a rope. He went about barefoot, preaching the Gospel. His desire to preach the Gospel even led to an unsuccessful mission to convert the Muslims in Egypt.

Guided by the Holy Spirit, Francis lived a spontaneous life in which he tried to rejoice in all creation. Even the sun, moon, wolves, and birds were his brothers. He so mystically identified with the suffering of Christ that he is said to have received the **stigmata** (wounds of Christ) in his own body shortly before his death. He practiced self-denial but was not an ascetic.

Disciples began to join him and follow his example. Eventually Francis formed a simple rule that he submitted to the pope. In about 1210, Innocent III recognized the Order of Friars Minor (lesser brothers), which is commonly known as the *Franciscans*. The order grew rapidly. New rules were created that departed further from the original simplicity and spontaneity of the founder. Strife resulted as friars fought over how rigidly they should hold to the true spirit of Francis, how to deal with the wealth accumulated by the order, and whether friars would have to leave the worldly church to remain pure. Saint Bonaventure (ca. 1217–1274), an able theologian and organizer, saved the order from destruction and stabilized it.

In many ways, Francis' ideas captured the religious desires of the age. Rich and poor alike were tired of the politics and immorality of the church. They wondered whether the earthly pomp of bishops and popes reflected the message of Jesus. They longed for a return to simple, meaningful religion. Saint Clare (1194–1253), one of those inspired by Francis, founded a sister order for women known as the "Clarisses," or "Poor Clares."

The Franciscans continued their preaching mission. Following Francis' example they tried to convert Muslims. Late in the thirteenth century, the Franciscan John of Montecorvino journied through Persia, Ethiopia, and India to Cambaluc (Beijing). There he converted thousands and was made archbishop of the region.

The Dominicans

Saint Dominic (1170–1221) founded the other great mendicant order. Dominic was a canon of the cathedral at Osma. While on a visit to southern France, he was impressed by forceful efforts to convert the Albigenses (Cathari), a heretical group discussed below. He became convinced that there was a better way to convert the Albigenses than to use force. He felt that heretical doctrines appealed to people because of the disgust many felt at the pomp and worldliness of the church. Dominic began a mission of preaching and teaching the orthodox faith. He combined this teaching with a rigorous, disciplined life and hard study designed to sharpen the mind for arguing against the **heterodox** (the unorthodox).

Dominic and his followers received approval for the Order of Preachers from Innocent III in 1215. They also adopted Franciscan poverty and mendicancy but set these aside as they were secondary to the mission of teaching and preaching. Dominic possessed a world vision. Missionaries were sent to a variety of countries where schools for training converts and preachers were established. The Dominicans soon became the main force in Innocent's Inquisition, which aimed to stamp out heresy.

The Dominicans found a home in the universities. Their order produced some great scholars, including Roger Bacon (ca. 1214–1292), Albert the Great, Thomas Aquinas, and Meister Eckhart (ca. 1260–1327). The early Franciscans avoided education, preferring the simple spiritual life. Eventually they also became enthusiastic about learning. A number of the best-known theologians of the Middle Ages were drawn from their ranks: Alexander of Hales (ca. 1186–1245), Bonaventure, Duns Scotus, and William of Occam.

REFORM MOVEMENTS OUTSIDE THE CHURCH

The Franciscans and Dominicans were a part of reform that stayed within the recognized church. Both orders grew out of a widespread sense of frustration with the wealth, political intrigues, and worldliness found everywhere in the established Christian community. Other movements that were driven by this same frustration ended up outside the orthodox church.

The Cathari and the Waldenses

The Cathari, or Albigenses, were a heretical group in France. Like the Gnostics, the Cathari stressed the difference between body and spirit. Humans were spirits trapped in evil flesh. The Cathari practiced asceticism (denial) and rejected marriage, war, property, and animal products. They believed the greatest sin was to have children because that would trap more spirits in flesh. The Roman Catholic church developed its position against birth control and abortion in response to these teachings. The Cathari avidly read the New Testament but rejected the cross, incarnation, and sacraments. They considered Catholics to be tools of the devil.

The Catholics ruthlessly suppressed the Cathari. Secular rulers acted for the church, torturing, maiming, and burning heretics at the stake. The Fourth Lateran Council allowed the punishment of heretics by secular authorities. It permitted the confiscation of their property and excommunicated those unwilling to move against heretics. Innocent III declared a Crusade against the Cathari, which led to widespread slaughter in France.

In 1220 the Inquisition was turned over to the Dominicans. The Inquisition recognized almost no rights for the accused; they had to prove their innocence. Witnesses favorable to the accused were charged with heresy. Witnesses and the accused were tortured. Because the Cathari used the Bible and translated it into their common language (the vernacular), the Synod of Toulouse (1229) condemned translation of the Scriptures into the vernacular and forbade laypeople to possess the Bible. The Inquisition continued until 1834, when it officially ended. It was an important tool against sixteenth-century Protestants.

The Waldenses were another reform group. Although they were quite different, they were persecuted along with Cathari. The Waldenses were named after Peter Waldo (d. 1218), a wealthy merchant from Lyon who was bothered by his fortune. He was inspired by the New Testament and Saint Alexis, who had renounced his wealth. Waldo provided for his family and then entered a life of preaching. His preaching attracted large crowds, which concerned local authorities. Rome rejected Waldo's request for official recognition for his preaching. Waldo and his disciples decided to follow God, not man. They lived in poverty and continued their preaching, soon spreading to northern Italy, the Alps, and Germany.

They believed in the New Testament, especially the Sermon on the Mount. Their emphasis on the Bible led them to reject oaths, war, property, veneration of saints, masses for the dead, relics, images, tithes, indulgences, death as a means of punishment, and purgatory. They accepted only baptism and communion. They attacked the clergy and papacy. Sacraments administered by unworthy priests were considered invalid. They ordained their own ministers.

The Waldenses wanted to purify the church by returning it to simplicity. Like the Cathari, the Waldenses were considered heretical and a threat to medieval society. Innocent III organized the Poor Catholics to combat their expansion. Dedicated to poverty and ministering among the needy, the Poor Catholics did much to limit the progress of the Waldenses. Persecution eliminated the Waldenses from France and Spain, but pockets of Waldenses still survive in the Alps and Piedmont, and Waldensian seminaries flourish in Rome and Florence.

Wycliffe and Hus

Reform efforts were not limited to the thirteenth century. By the fourteenth century, papal power had been weakened by scandal and schism. Increasing nationalism also galvanized strong opposition to the papacy especially in England, where laws were passed restricting the rights of the pope.

John Wycliffe (1328–1384) was a reformer who became an able defender of the English king. Wycliffe felt that the Scripture was superior to the pope. Everything belonged to God. People only used what was given to them. If priests and popes failed to use their positions properly or were immoral, they should be replaced. If church authorities would not replace them, secular leaders should. Wycliffe also pictured a national church ruled by the king. This national church was formed in sixteenth-century England under Henry VIII.

In addition to attacking the clergy, Wycliffe rejected transubstantiation. He believed Christ was spiritually, but not physically, present in the Eucharist.

This stance cost him some of his popularity. After Wycliffe's death, his followers came to be known as *Lollards*. In many ways the Lollards were the forerunners of the sixteenth-century reformers. Persecution forced them underground where they thrived among the poor until the Reformation.

John Hus (1373–1415) was a priest from Bohemia who held ideas similar to Wycliffe's. He condemned abuses and immorality. For Hus, Christ, not the pope, was the head of the church and the true church was composed of the **elect** (those chosen by God for salvation). The Bible was seen as the supreme authority in the church. Any pope who did not obey the Bible should not be obeyed. Hus became the head of the University of Prague and was a powerful preacher who used the pulpit at Bethlehem Chapel in Prague to present his ideas. Hus soon had the support of the Bohemian king and many of the local inhabitants. The pope excommunicated him because he refused to stop preaching.

The Council of Constance was called in 1414 to reform the church. The emperor invited Hus to the council to defend himself under the promise of safe conduct. Upon Hus' arrival, the pope arrested and tried him. The emperor refused to protect Hus when he realized the reformer's cause was unpopular. The council drove the pope out of the city and tried Hus itself. Because of a desire to appear orthodox, the council condemned Hus to burn at the stake. His ashes were spread on a lake to prevent his supporters from using his "relics" to further their cause.

The news of Hus' death caused rebellion in Bohemia. A long, complicated conflict emerged in which the Hussites were supported by Taborites, Horebites, and other groups opposed to Catholic policy. The Catholics launched several unsuccessful crusades against the Bohemians, but they were forced to negotiate. The Bohemian church was rejoined to the West under an agreement that allowed it to keep several distinctive features, including giving communion "in both kinds" (bread and wine) to laity. Some groups rejected this agreement. One of the most important of these was the *Unitas Fratrum* (Union of Brethren). Although they were severely persecuted, some of the *Unitas Fratrum* survived and came to be called *Moravians*. They would play a role in the Protestant Reformation.

DECLINE AND REBIRTH

The thirteenth century was one of the most remarkable periods in history. The papacy reached the height of its power under the rule of Innocent III. Papal efforts at reform and the energy produced by the mendicant orders promised new life for the church. Scholasticism, along with improved education, made the intellectual climate lively. For a time it seemed that Christendom (a Christian world), united under the pope with the state and the universities playing proper

To See God: The Mystics

Mysticism was an important force in both the Eastern and the Western churches. In the East, the mystical contemplation of God contributed to the rich theology, prayer, and liturgy of the Orthodox church. Even atonement had a mystical quality of absorption into God. Atonement was seen as a process of divinization where believers were progressively brought into a relationship with the Divine and became more like God.

In the West, mystical tendencies and movements were very strong throughout the Middle Ages. Ordinary Christians often had direct visions of God. Many of the greats of the age, such as Bernard of Clairvaux (1090–1153),[2] Francis of Assisi, and Thomas Aquinas, were mystics. By the fourteenth century, mystics abounded in England, Spain, and Italy. Areas bordering the Rhine were a hotbed for mysticism. Meister Eckhart (1260–1327) was the best-known German teacher of a form of mysticism based on Neoplatonic thought.

Eckhart believed God was beyond all being and non-being but was present in the world and in human souls as a divine spark. God was the only reality. People should seek a union with God in which the soul was completely absorbed into the Divine. External practices like good works could assist this union, although they did not produce true knowledge of the Divine. People must seek the ecstatic experience of oneness with God.

supporting roles, was a real possibility. After Innocent, however, the power of the papacy declined and the vision of a united Christendom faded. This section briefly examines that decline and the beginnings of a new order in the Renaissance.

Papal Decline

There were many reasons for the declining power of the papacy, including the rising money-based economy, the increased power of the merchant class, the growth of **nationalism** (where people see themselves as loyal to a nation-state), and the Black Death of 1347. Under these pressures the carefully constructed,

The Flemish mystics John of Ruysbroeck (1293–1381) and Gerhard Groote (1340–1384) became the fathers of the *devotio moderna* (modern devotion), which concentrated on contemplation of the life of Christ and imitation of him. They challenged church abuses, insisted that true religion must be experienced internally, and called for simple, undogmatic Christianity.

The best-known book from the modern devotion was *The Imitation of Christ* by Thomas à Kempis (1380–1471). *The Imitation* is considered one of the greatest works on spirituality in the history of Western Christianity. It is still used by many who seek to deepen their religious life. The efforts of Ruysbroeck and Groote resulted in the founding of the Brethren of the Common Life. The group followed the ways of the modern devotion but did not insist that its followers become monks. The Brethren founded a number of schools open to laypeople that stressed devotion, simple piety, and academic study and that were important sources for renewal in the church for many generations.

The mysticism of the Middle Ages contributed greatly to the life of the church. It was a source not only of deepened religious life but also of reform. On the whole, the church hierarchy accepted the mystics. Yet mysticism tended to undermine the hierarchical church by implicitly questioning the role of the church in salvation. If a person could have direct access to God, what was the need for the church and its sacraments?

rational hierarchy began to crumble. The decline began about the same time as the Hundred Years' War.

The Hundred Years' War (1337–1453) was a series of battles between the French and the British that occurred off and on for more than a century. The political result was that the British lost most of their possessions on the Continent. Papal involvement in the war caused it to lose much of its claim to be the universal head of Christendom. Pope Boniface VIII attempted to bring peace between England and France by forbidding clergy to make contributions to secular powers. He had hoped to make both kings submit to papal mediation.

The kings ignored the peace effort and responded by turning against the pope and his clergy. The French king, Philip, took particularly strong action.

Boniface issued the bull *Unam Sanctam* against him. When Philip continued to pursue his course, Boniface decided to excommunicate him. He called an assembly in Anagni to prepare the excommunication. While in Anagni, Boniface was captured and humiliated by armed supporters of Philip. Although the pope's allies eventually freed him, Boniface died shortly thereafter, probably from the rough treatment he had received.

The papacy never recovered from this humiliation. Boniface's successors were attacked on all sides. They eventually came to depend on the French for support. Pope Clement V (1264–1314) undertook actions to aid the French, including moving the papal residence to Avignon in southern France (even though he was still bishop of Rome). Thus began a period when popes lived in Avignon (1309–1377). This era is known as the Babylonian Captivity of the Church, during which time popes were viewed as puppets of the French.

Elaborate taxation systems were developed to finance the popes' wars against their enemies. One system that had dreadful consequences involved filling vacant church positions. When a position was vacant for some time, the funds collected to support it went to Avignon; therefore, it was to the advantage of the papacy to leave church positions unfilled. As a consequence, many areas had no pastors for long periods of time.

Simony also became common again. To make matters worse, people started purchasing church offices because they carried good incomes. As a result, one person might be the pastor or bishop of several places at one time, a practice called **pluralism.** A bishop or pastor could officially reside in only one place. Thus, absenteeism became usual and many localities found themselves without a spiritual leader.

Gregory XI (1329–1378) returned the papacy to Rome in 1377, but this return did not solve the problems of the pope. Conflict among the French, the Italians, and other parties continued. The intrigue finally resulted in two popes being elected by the same set of cardinals. One took up residence with his court in Avignon. The other continued to live in Rome. France supported the pope in Avignon; England identified with Rome. The Holy Roman emperor endorsed Rome but was opposed by a number of German nobles. Other countries switched sides repeatedly. Europe was so divided that this situation came to be called the Great Western Schism.

Many grew tired of the schism and its impact on the church. They started to call for a council to reform the church and restore unity, a movement called **conciliarism.** Early councils had been called by the Roman emperor. Later they were called by the pope, who generally was able to use them for his purposes. Conciliarism had two problems. First, there was the issue of whether the council was superior to the pope or the pope was superior to the council. The conciliarists held the former position, the pope the latter. Second, there was the issue of who could or would call a council. There were now two popes who refused to negotiate to heal the schism much less call a council. Cardinals supporting each pope called a council to resolve the schism, and it met in Pisa in 1409. The council was unable to decide which of the contenders was the legitimate pope, so it elected another. The situation was then worse than ever for there were three popes.

Finally the Council of Constance (1414) established a single successor to the seat of Saint Peter. This council also sought to end corruption and rid the church of heresy. It decreed that councils would be convened frequently by the pope to continue reform. It seemed that conciliarism had won a great victory. However, most fifteenth-century popes were worldly. They were greatly concerned about gaining wealth, luxury, and power but had little interest in guiding the spiritual life of the church. Conciliarism declined in the latter half of the century, although many hoped for a council to purge abuses. People throughout Christendom began to doubt that the pope was the true representative of Christ.

The Renaissance and Humanism

The *Renaissance* refers to the flourishing of thought, literature, and art that occurred in the fourteenth, fifteenth, and sixteenth centuries. In many ways the Renaissance grew out of trends that began in the Middle Ages. At the same time, it represented a break with the immediate past through a rediscovery of the classical culture of ancient Rome. This break further undermined the foundations of medieval society and prepared the way for a new age.

The Renaissance sprang up in Italy and spread to the rest of Europe. Many of the people who promoted it believed that medieval civilization was corrupt and pale when compared to the civilizations of ancient Rome and Greece. They believed that a reintroduction of the art, literature, and law of the ancients could produce a vital new society. The art and architecture of ancient Rome were studied and copied.

The literature of classical poets and writers was sought. Vast libraries were begun. In the process of uncovering old texts, corrupt versions of classical works were discovered. Interest grew in determining what writers had said in their original texts. The science of textual criticism developed in an effort to find those versions that were closest to the original writings. Textual analysis led to the conclusion that the "Donation of Constantine," which had been so important to papal claims of primacy, was a fake. Questions were raised about a number of Christian documents such as the *Apostles' Creed* and the Vulgate (the Latin version of the Bible used in the church). The quest for original sources would play an important role in the Reformation.

The rise of **humanism** accompanied the Renaissance. *Humanism* is a term with many meanings. Originally humanists were those who believed that the study of the humanities (art, literature, philosophy, and languages) could improve religion and society. Many humanists were (and are) dedicated Christians. Yet much of the art and literature of Greece and Rome focused on humans and their potential. It did not have the negative view of life or human nature that is implied in traditional Christian doctrines such as original sin.

Instead, humanism emphasized the possibility of good and beauty in this world as well as the responsibility of humans to improve life. An appreciation for beauty in art and literature grew. The human body became an object to be adored as it had been in the classical period. The focus shifted from the next world (the afterlife) to this one. On the positive side, humanism resulted in a new appreciation of human goodness and achievement even among the religious. On the negative side, some used humanism as a reason to abandon religion altogether. Humanism would have a strong impact on Western culture. It would eventually help change the view that life should be judged purely on religious terms. Humans were on their way to becoming the measure of all things.

The work of the humanists and other scholars was expanded in the mid-fifteenth century by one of the most important inventions in history. A goldsmith, Johann Gutenberg (1396–1468), invented movable type for a printing press. Gutenberg used the new invention to create the famous *Gutenberg Bible,* which was printed between 1450 and 1456. Soon printers were reproducing copies of other literature as well. Renaissance scholars circulated these copies among themselves. They did not try to use printed material to influence common people. It was during the Reformation that the power of the printing press was used to produce mass quantities of the Bible and other tracts that spread the ideas of the reformers.

During the Renaissance, Italy was divided into several independent city-states, including Milan, Genoa, Venice, Florence, and Naples. These city-states earned profits from increased trade and used their wealth to compete with one another. The emphasis on art, literature, and architecture gave them one more area for competition. Each city tried to enhance its own glory by commissioning artists and architects to create new works and buildings. Vast libraries were built. The inspired creations of fifteenth-century artists such as Raphael, Michelangelo, and Leonardo da Vinci have enriched the human experience ever since the Renaissance.

Most fifteenth-century popes were caught up in this Renaissance fever. They wanted Rome to rival other cities and they dedicated themselves to encouraging religious art. The Vatican library became one of the greatest in the world. Popes became patrons of artists and architects. The best were brought to Rome to work on churches, palaces, buildings, and monuments. One example is the Sistine

Chapel, constructed by Sixtus IV (1471–1484). Michelangelo painted the famous artwork on the chapel ceiling. The height of Renaissance fervor was reached when Julius II (1503–1513) realized the dream of those who went before and began building Saint Peter's Basilica in Rome. The new church was constructed on the site of one built by Constantine. When completed it was the largest church in the world. The building projects required tremendous funds, however. Resentment grew as the tax burden increased and people were even deprived of food to finance the popes' grand plans.

The late fifteenth-century and early sixteenth-century popes generally were not concerned with spiritual matters. Most dedicated themselves to the pursuit of power, luxury, and pleasure. Offices were bought and sold openly. Papal concubines and their children were accepted at court. Popes not only acknowledged their illegitimate children but also actively promoted their interests. Italy was bathed in the blood of papal wars. Alexander VI (1492–1503) and Julius II were among the worst of these decadent popes.

THE ORTHODOX CHURCH IN THE HIGH MIDDLE AGES

The High Middle Ages saw two significant changes in the life of the Eastern Orthodox church. The first was the decline of Byzantine Orthodoxy. The second was the rise of the Russian Orthodox church. These developments are discussed briefly in this section.

Byzantine Orthodoxy

As the year 1000 approached in the East, the Byzantine Empire was under pressure from the Muslims but would still maintain control over the remains of its empire for another four centuries. Orthodoxy had a generally comfortable relation to the state. The church's missions to the Slavs were well on their way to securing those regions for the Orthodox faith. Efforts to convert Russia finally were successful.

The relationship of Greek Orthodoxy to Western Christianity remained troubled. Papal claims to supremacy and differences in liturgy continued to be problems. The question of the *filioque* and its issue of the Holy Spirit was still debated. At the beginning of the eleventh century, the papacy officially adopted the *filioque* as an addition to the Nicene Creed. The patriarch of Constantinople quietly retaliated by removing the pope's name from the list of patriarchs regarded as orthodox. For various reasons, this caused little stir in the Western world.

The Churchwomen

Women have always been important in the life of the Christian community. Not only have women contributed through their devotion and example at the local level, but many also have taken active leadership roles on a larger scale. Some held official positions such as nuns, abbesses, or **anchoresses** (a devout woman living in seclusion and often attached to a parish church). Others were laywomen who possessed special spiritual gifts and wisdom. Many women, through teaching, advising influential churchmen, and writing, have asserted considerable influence on the church. Often these influential women were mystics. Three particularly noteworthy churchwomen of the Middle Ages were Hildegard of Bingen (1098–1179), Julian of Norwich (ca. 1342–1413), and Margery Kempe (ca. 1373–1433).

Saint Hildegard experienced profound religious experiences from early childhood. She was reared by Jutta, abbess of a local Benedictine monastery, and eventually was accepted into the Benedictine order. She succeeded Jutta as abbess of the monastery and moved her group of nuns to Rupertsberg where a large convent was built. From there she traveled widely and founded a daughter house. She was encouraged by her confessor to write down her visions. These writings became the influential *Scivias,* which condemned worldly evils and predicted pending disasters. She also wrote other important works. She seems to have exhibited

Early in the eleventh century, the rise of Hildebrand (Gregory VII) to a position of prominence not enjoyed by any previous pope caused additional tensions over papal primacy. Another fight between Eastern and Western Christians erupted because the Normans (French) insisted that Greek churches in sections of Italy still controlled by the Byzantines use Latin practices in worship. The patriarch in turn demanded that Latin churches in Constantinople conform to Greek customs. When they refused, he closed them in 1052. Attempts to resolve this issue had failed by 1054.

The year 1054 is often given as the time when the schism between East and West became final. However, friendly relations between the two branches of Christianity continued for some time. People on both sides still hoped that differences could be resolved. Another decisive event was in 1204 when the considerable influence on the Emperor Fredrick Barbarossa, various kings, church leaders, and saints. Numerous miracles were attributed to her during her life and others were attributed to her tomb. She was declared a saint in the fifteenth century.

Julian of Norwich was probably an anchoress who lived outside the walls of Saint Julian's Church. On May 8, 1373, she had a series of fifteen visions while in an ecstatic state that lasted five hours. The following day she had another vision. After twenty years of reflection, she composed *The Sixteen Revelations of Divine Love*. In this book she presents her visions and reflects on the mysteries of prayer, faith, and divine love. She felt that divine love held the clues to all the secrets of life.

Margery Kempe was a laywoman and English mystic who had fourteen children with her husband John. She became subject to visions after a bout with mental illness. She traveled widely, undertaking pilgrimages to Canterbury and the Holy Land. In 1413, she and her husband took vows of chastity to increase their devotion. Kempe was given to long periods when she experienced direct relations with Christ. Her condemnations of pleasure and worldliness led her into frequent conflict with religious authorities. Almost all that is known about Kempe is found in her work called the *Book of Margery Kempe*.

Fourth Crusade sacked Constantinople. For three days, crusaders pillaged the city. The crusaders ruthlessly desecrated holy sites. Pieces of the altar and the icon screen were torn from Santa Sophia. Prostitutes were placed on the throne of the patriarch. Such acts by their fellow Christians produced a lasting hatred in the Greeks. After 1204, Christianity was divided. Attempts to reconcile Eastern and Western Christianity were made at the Councils of Lyons (1274) and Florence (1438–1439). These were unsuccessful because many in the Eastern church refused to accept the unions proclaimed at the councils.

Another decisive event in the history of Greek Orthodoxy occurred in 1453 when the Turks captured Constantinople. The fall of the "God protected city" shocked the Orthodox world. Santa Sophia was turned into a **mosque** (a Muslim place of worship). Yet the Muslims regarded Christians as people of

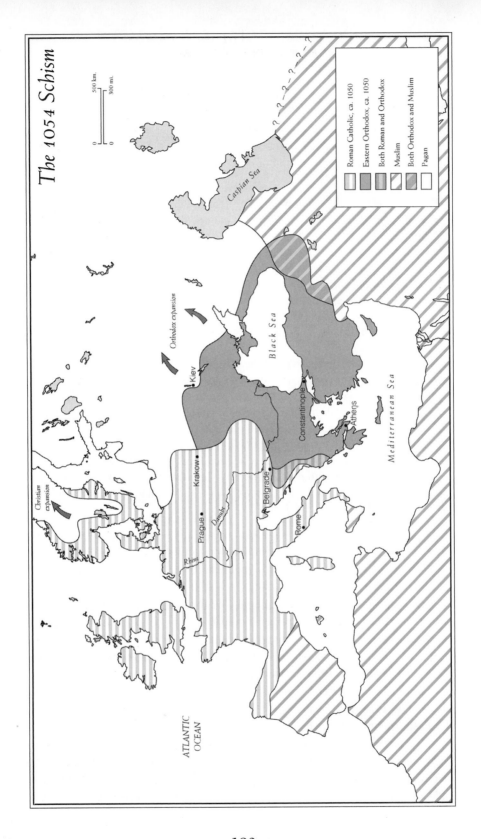

The 1054 Schism

500 km.
300 mi.

Roman Catholic, ca. 1050
Eastern Orthodox, ca. 1050
Both Roman and Orthodox
Muslim
Both Orthodox and Muslim
Pagan

Caspian Sea

Black Sea

Orthodox expansion

Kiev

Constantinople

Athens

Mediterranean Sea

Christian expansion

Krakow

Prague

Danube

Belgrade

Rome

Rhine

ATLANTIC
OCEAN

the Book and did not persecute them; they were allowed free expression of their religion.

The Turkish leader, the sultan, became the protector of the church in much the same way as the Roman and the Byzantine emperors. Moreover, the Islamic faith does not recognize a distinction between the laws of God and of humans. As a result, the leaders of the Greek church were also made civil authorities. The sultan relied on the church for administering matters of state such as law enforcement and social welfare. Even though the church was subject to Muslim rule, it became one with the state in Greece, eastern Europe, and many sections of the Mediterranean world. The close identification of the patriarchate of Constantinople with Turkish politics caused national churches in such regions as Greece, Romania, Bulgaria, and Serbia to assert their independence. The power of the patriarch of Constantinople was greatly reduced.

Russian Orthodoxy

Early efforts to convert the Russians had not been very successful. Something of a breakthrough occurred when the Russian princess Olga converted in 955. In 988 her grandson, Prince Vladimir of Kiev (980–1015), accepted Christianity. He then married the sister of the Byzantine emperor. Orthodoxy soon became the state religion of Russia. Idols of pagan gods were destroyed. The true faith was proclaimed throughout the land. Christian social services were organized. Monasteries sprang up. In this early era, Christianity likely had its greatest impact in the cities. Much of the countryside remained pagan.

Kievan Russia was brought to an abrupt end by the invasion of the Mongols in 1237. Kiev never recovered from the destruction brought by the conquerors. It was the church that gave unity to the country and helped preserve a sense of Russian identity during the Mongol occupation. The Russian metropolitan Peter (1308–1326) settled in Moscow. His presence helped raise the city to the position of importance it has had in Russian secular and religious history ever since.

The church continued its mission activity, expanding among the Mongols and the tribes in the northern and eastern reaches of the Asian continent. Monks seeking the solitude of the vast Russian forests spread out on the continent only to be followed by disciples who established religious communities. These colonists and monks spread the Gospels wherever they went. New areas came under Orthodox influence.

Sergius of Radonezh (ca. 1314–1392) was the greatest Orthodox saint of this era. As a young man, Sergius withdrew to the forest where he founded a **hermitage** (a place where a hermit lives) dedicated to the Holy Trinity. This grew into the Monastery of the Holy Trinity, which soon became the most important monastery in Russia. Sergius became a spiritual guide, or elder, to many. People from all over Russia sought his advice on both spiritual and political matters. His guidance encouraged Moscow to resist the Mongols and his mystical prayerfulness strengthened the Russian church.

After Constantinople fell to the Turks in 1453, Russia assumed a new place of leadership in the Orthodox world. This leadership was accompanied by the development of the **Third Rome Theory.** According to the theory, the original Rome was the seat of the church, but fell to the barbarians. Constantinople became the second Rome, but became apostate and was conquered by the Turks as punishment. Only Moscow remained pure. It was now seen as the center of all Orthodox Christianity, the third Rome.

The **tsar** (emperor of Russia literally, tsar is Russian for Caesar) took on the role of protector of the church and secular minister, similar to the Roman and Byzantine emperors. The tsar was quite willing to use his new "appointed by God" position for political ends. In theory, the Byzantine *symphonia* also applied to relations between church and state in Russia. In reality, the Russian church was almost completely dominated by the state. Eventually priests were required to report to government officials any information obtained in the confessional that might involve disloyalty to the state. The person making confession could be imprisoned or exiled. Such practices led Russian Christians to resent the close relation between church and state.

On the other hand, the spiritual life of the Russian church was deep and meaningful and noted for its strictness. It required charity toward the less fortunate as well as a liturgical and moral discipline that was often missing in other branches of Christianity. Orthodoxy and Russian life were closely intertwined.[3]

THE CHURCH AT THE CLOSE OF THE MIDDLE AGES

At the close of the Middle Ages, the church was split into two distinct halves— Eastern and Western Christianity. Most of the basic theology of both churches was formed before the division became permanent. This common theology is expressed in the Nicene Creed. The Orthodox church accepted only the first Seven Ecumenical Councils of the church and any theological ideas developed since then were rejected. For example, the Eastern church does not accept the *filioque,* purgatory, or papal infallibility.

Both the Eastern and Western churches agree on the basic nature of sacrament. They agree there are seven sacraments (baptism, confirmation, the Eucharist, confession, last rites, orders, matrimony), although there are slight differences in how Eastern and Western churches administer them. The Eastern church has never insisted on clerical celibacy. Their parish priests could marry, but higher officials were to remain celibate. The main differences concern liturgy. The forms of worship differ and the languages have diverged. Usually, the Orthodox church presents the liturgy in the vernacular while the Roman Catholic church has used Latin until recent times. The Orthodox church has never accepted the pope as the head of the church. It sees him as an important bishop (a first among equals), but no more. The Eastern church organizes itself into national churches presided over by a patriarch.

By the end of the Middle Ages, the Greek church had spread into eastern Europe and Russia. Constantinople had fallen. Moscow was on its way to becoming the "third Rome." Western Europe began to find new political order as nation-states struggled to develop. The political vacuum of the early Middle Ages was filled in part by the papacy. The pope started to claim he was both the spiritual and the political leader of Christendom.

In the thirteenth century, the popes came near to realizing the grand hierarchy they had visualized. This hierarchy presented a united Christendom with the pope at the top as the vicar of Christ. Under him were earthly rulers and cardinals (the princes of the church). Beneath them were the lower aristocracy, merchants, parish priests, craftspeople, and, finally, the peasants. The pope controlled this hierarchy by administering the sacraments and carrying prayer to God. He reserved the right to judge king, prince, merchant, bishop, priest, and peasant alike. This grand design was also seen in the great theological systems of the Scholastics and the vast medieval cathedrals.

After the thirteenth century, the power of the pope started to decline. The grand hierarchy began to unravel at all levels. Secular leaders, aided by rising nationalism, were successful in establishing a degree of independence. Scholasticism was challenged, especially by scholars with an Aristotelian viewpoint. Papal quality declined. Their constant warfare, their dedication to luxury and power, and their lack of concern for their role as pastor of the church led many to doubt if they were really the representatives of Christ on earth.

Various problems in the church went unaddressed by church authorities. Spiritual and mystical movements arose both in and outside the church. The call for a return to the simplicity of New Testament Christianity was in sharp contrast to the pomp of the church hierarchy. Despite its difficulties, the church retained the loyalty of the majority of the believers. In many ways, the church was still the most democratic of medieval institutions. Even the pope had to be elected by the cardinals. An individual of lowly origins could rise to a high church position.

Religion dominated the thought and life of many people. Salvation was actively sought. People went on pilgrimages and did severe penance to cleanse their souls in preparation for eternity. A powerful spirituality developed as mendicants, mystics, and ordinary people sought deep, abiding religious experience. Efforts were made to maintain consistent worship and to require all

Christians to participate. Absenteeism and pluralism limited the effectiveness of these requirements. Many regions found themselves without regular preaching and administering of the sacraments. The sacraments were held in high regard because they brought the grace of God to humans.

The Mass was venerated as it was during that ceremony when the great miracle of the bread and wine becoming the body and blood of Christ occurred. It is claimed that in the cities where Mass was said at noon daily crowds would rush from church to church hoping to receive a blessing by just seeing the bread lifted by the priest at the moment it became the body of Christ. Great care was taken so that a crumb of bread or a drop of wine would not fall to the floor where it might be eaten by a mouse who would thus gain entrance to heaven!

Fear dominated much of life in the Middle Ages—fear of God, fear of the devil, fear of death, fear of facing the Eternal Judge, fear of hell, fear of witchcraft. The Black Death increased this fear. Religion was a defense against the evil that surrounded people.

The Renaissance brought changes to this environment. The rebirth of study in classical culture produced a renewed interest in humanity. There was again appreciation for the beauty of this world and the abilities of humans. Art glorifying the human body flourished as did new inventions and architecture.

Renaissance popes generally were worldly with little concern for the spiritual needs of the Christian community. The sentiment grew that some avenue of reforming the church other than the papacy had to be found. People started putting faith in church councils as the only way to end abuses that were everywhere in the church.

CONCLUSIONS

The High Middle Ages saw a great increase in the power of the papacy. The grand hierarchy of the thirteenth century allowed the pope to exercise tremendous control throughout Europe. Yet the reforming popes and spiritual movements within the church failed to produce the needed renewal. As the power of the papacy declined, other changes occurred that undermined the institutions of feudal society. Nationalism, the money economy, the importance of the merchant class, and the significance of cities weakened the old order and marked the start of a new one. The Renaissance undermined many ideas on which medieval society had been built.

At the beginning of the sixteenth century, there was widespread desire for change in the church. The old institutions had been weakened but they still had life left, as the events surrounding the Protestant Reformation show.

Notes

1. Following the customs of the Middle Ages, Saint Francis and others often allegorized their ideas. The pursuit of "lady poverty" became a way of expressing a life of apostolic poverty.
2. One problem in writing a concise history is deciding who to discuss and who to leave out. Bernard was a very important twelfth-century figure not discussed above. He was not a creative theologian; however, he was very influential throughout Europe. Bernard was known as a man of deep devotion, an eloquent preacher who staunchly defended tradition. He took part in many of the important events of the era. For instance, he was the most memorable opponent of Abelard. He also helped to inspire the "fever" that resulted in the Second Crusade.
3. For a good discussion of Orthodoxy's history and theology in the Middle Ages, see Timothy Ware, *The Orthodox Church,* reprint ed. Baltimore: Penguin, 1973, pp. 87–119.

Additional Readings

Baker, Denise Nowakowski. *Julian of Norwich's Showings: From Vision to Book.* Princeton, NJ: Princeton University Press, 1997.

Capellanus, Andreas. *The Art of Courtly Love.* Translated by John J. Parry. Irwin-on-the-Hudson, NY: Columbia University Press, 1990.

Clark, James M. *The Great German Mystics: Eckhart, Tauler, and Suso.* Oxford, England: Oxford University Press, 1949.

Diehl, Peter D. and Scott L. Waugh, eds. *Christendom and Its Discontents: Exclusion, Persecution, and Rebellion, 1000–500.* New York: Cambridge University Press, 1995.

Dorcy, Mary J. *St. Dominic.* Reprint ed. Rockford, IL.: T A N Books, 1982.

Habig, Marion A., ed. *St. Francis of Assisi: Writings and Early Biographies. English Omnibus of the Sources for the Life of St. Francis.* Chicago: Franciscan Herald, 1973.

Hyma, Albert. *The Christian Renaissance: A History of the Devotio Moderna.* 2d ed. Hamden, CT: Archon, 1965.

à Kempis, Thomas. *The Imitation of Christ.* Translated by Michael Oakley and Ronald Knox. Rev. ed. South Bend, IN: Greenlawn, 1990.

Knowles, David. *The Monastic Order in England. A History of Its Development from the Times of St. Dunstan to the Fourth Lateran Council, 943–1216.* Cambridge, England: Cambridge University Press, 1940.

———. *The Religious Orders in England.* Cambridge, England: Cambridge University Press, 1948.

Moorman, John. *A History of the Franciscan Order.* Chicago: Franciscan Herald, 1988.

Morris, Colin. *The Papal Monarchy: The Western Church from 1050 to 1250.* New York: Oxford University Press, 1991.

Nicol, Donald M. *Byzantium and Venice.* New York: Cambridge University Press, 1989.

Noonan, John T. *Contraception: A History of Its Treatment by the Catholic Theologians and Canonists.* Cambridge, MA: Harvard University Press, 1986.

Petroff, Elizabeth Alvilda. *Body and Soul: Essays on Medieval Women and Mysticism.* New York: Oxford University Press, 1994.

Polizzotto, Lorenzo. *The Elect Nation: The Savonarolan Movement in Florence 1494–1545.* New York: Oxford University Press, 1995.

Powers, Eileen. *Jesus as Mother: Studies in the Spirituality of the High Middle Ages.* Berkeley: University of California Press, 1982.

Ross, Ellen M. *The Grief of God: Images of the Suffering Jesus in Late Medieval England*. New York: Oxford University Press, 1997.

Runciman, Steven. *The Byzantine Theocracy*. New Edition. Cambridge: Cambridge University Press, 2003.

Southern, R. W. *Scholastic Humanism and the Unification of Europe*. 3 volumes. Oxford: Blackwell, 1995, 2000, 2003.

Websites

http://en.wikipedia.org/wiki/Late_Middle_Ages [Provides article on Middle Ages along with links to other articles on related sources and other resources]

http://www.nmhschool.org/tthornton/mehistorydatabase/high_middle_ages.htm [Provides data base that relates events in Medieval Europe to those in Islamic countries]

www.fordham.edu/halsall/byzantium/index.html [Provides access to a number of sources and links on Byzantium]

www.georgetown.edu/labyrinth/ [Provides access to Labyrinth's resources for Medieval studies]

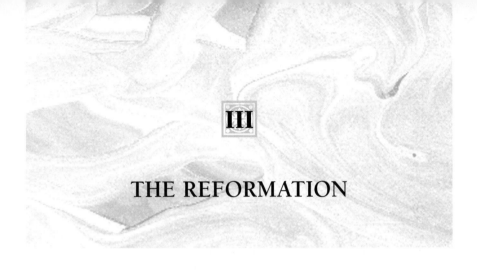

THE REFORMATION

THE WORLD OF THE REFORMATION

The Reformation occurred within the numerous social, economic, and political changes that were reshaping Europe and the rest of the world. The nation-state was becoming established as the dominant political force in the world. Capitalism had increased the desire for both stable nations and stable government policies to protect the interests of merchants and traders. However, the new capitalism also caused social unrest as peasants were removed from their lands. Feudal lords lost both economic and political power. Capitalism combined with the discovery of new lands to stimulate the desire for empires and led to the abuse of conquered peoples. This section briefly reviews the interplay of sixteenth-century religious movements with the nation-states, capitalism, and expanding empires.

The Nation-States

The great period of the nation-states began in the fifteenth century. What is now Spain struggled to free that region from domination by the Muslim Moors. The feudal landholdings were united gradually into four large regions: Castle, Aragon, Granada, and Navarre. The marriage of Ferdinand of Aragon and Isabella of Castile in 1469 united the largest portions of Spain under a single monarchy. By the end of their rule in 1516, the regions of Granada and Navarre had been conquered and Spain was at last united.[1]

Monies from the expanding Spanish empire in the New World gave Ferdinand and Isabella considerable power. They freed themselves from control by nobles. The "Catholic Sovereigns," as they were called, undertook an aggressive program of extinguishing heresy throughout their lands. With the help of the Spanish Inquisition led by Cardinal Ximénes (1436–1517), Jews, Muslims, and other dissenters were systematically persecuted. They were converted to Catholicism by force, killed, or driven into exile.

The Inquisition successfully kept Protestants out of the country. The Spanish Inquisition not only vigorously persecuted dissenters but also undertook programs of reform and education within the church. It left Spain "the most Catholic" of countries and became a model for reform used throughout the Roman Catholic church.

Portugal was one of the most powerful of the nation-states during the early sixteenth century. It had successfully freed itself from domination by Spain, had developed its own language as a source of unity, and had created a vast overseas empire as a base for its power. Portugal also successfully persecuted Jews, Muslims, and Protestants, thus remaining firmly in the Catholic faith.

Louis XI (1461–1483) is often considered the first ruler of the modern nation-state of France. He built upon the feelings of nationalism created by the expulsion of the English from the Continent in the Hundred Years' War. Using the middle class as a source of power, he successfully limited the control of the feudal nobility. He built roads, ports, and other waterways and promoted commerce and successfully extended the borders of his kingdom. He waged war to capture such regions as Burgundy, Picardy, and a portion of Flanders. At the same time, he did little to help the lower classes, which he taxed heavily to support his projects. That left the lower classes very dissatisfied.

The fifteenth century was a period of great turmoil in England. The Hundred Years' War weakened the country. To make matters worse, it was followed by the War of the Roses (1455–1484) between the Lancasters and the Yorks, which nearly ruined the country. Henry VII (1485–1509) of the house of Lancaster ended this bloody conflict when he defeated the York king, Richard III. Henry married Elizabeth of York and established the Tudor dynasty. He handed down a united and strong kingdom to his son Henry VIII (1509–1547), who would play an important role in the Reformation. His granddaughter Elizabeth (1558–1603) established England as a first-rate world power.

The situation was much different in Germany and Italy. Though these regions had supposedly been controlled by the Holy Roman emperor since Otto the Great, the reality was much different. While other rulers were extending control over their nations, the German ruler was losing control over much of his domain. The Holy Roman emperor was never successful in subduing the states in Italy. By the sixteenth century, Italy was divided into six kingdoms that claimed little allegiance to the emperor.

In Germany, the emperor was unsuccessful in controlling the local nobles. By the time of the Reformation, seven of the most important nobles had won the right to elect the emperor. He had little ability to demand taxes or command the loyalty of his army. The emperor during the early stages of the Reformation, Charles V (1519–1558), technically controlled vast expanses, including Germany, the Netherlands, Luxembourg, Spain, the Mediterranean, and Spain's overseas colonies. He had great trouble maintaining his reign, however. Even the German nobles resisted his control. To make matters worse, he was opposed by the king of France and was under constant pressure from the Muslim Ottoman Turks in the East.

Switzerland was far from unified. It was divided into several competing **cantons** (states). This patchwork of cantons would eventually leave the area divided between Protestant and Catholic interests after the Reformation.

Capitalism and World Expansion

Capitalism is an economic system that is based partly on the idea that industry, agriculture, and trade should be operated to create a profit. During most of the Middle Ages, social conditions and church teachings discouraged capitalism. Europe was isolated and trade was limited. Manors were organized around subsistence agriculture (producing enough goods to sustain life). The church discouraged capitalism through such requirements as charging a *fair* price for goods instead of allowing a *market* price. It also forbade **usury** (the lending of money for interest).[2] The church glorified "apostolic poverty." There always was some tendency during the Middle Ages to see the collecting of wealth as unchristian.

Despite these limits, trade eventually emerged in Europe as did manufacturing industries. Along with trade and manufacturing came an increase in growing **cash crops** (crops that were sold for money). For instance, English lords started converting their manors from subsistence farms to large pastures for raising sheep. The wool from these sheep was sold to Holland to make cloth. Trade was not limited to regions within Europe but extended to Africa, the Middle East, India, and China.

By the late Middle Ages, many sections of Europe were actively trading with distant lands. Much of this trade traveled overland in long, difficult caravans. Often these trade routes were disrupted by war. Passage along the routes was often controlled by Muslims and Christian powers, such as the Italian city-states. The immense profits possible from trade drove some countries such as Portugal and Spain to seek sea routes.

In the early fifteenth century, Prince Henry the Navigator (1394–1460) founded a school for navigators on the southern Portuguese coast. From this base, expeditions were sent farther and farther down the west coast of Africa. The Portuguese amassed great wealth from their African trade in gold, ivory, sugar, and slaves. In 1498, Vasco da Gama (d. 1524) rounded the Cape of Good Hope at the southern tip of Africa and successfully sailed to India. This route opened vast new possibilities for profit and exploitation. The Portuguese also moved into South America.

The Spanish soon became involved in the quest for trade, colonies, and empire, but they traveled in a different direction. They pinned their hopes on an Italian, Christopher Columbus (1451–1506). Most of the profitable routes to India and the East Indies were controlled by Portugal. Like most educated people of his day, Columbus believed the world was round. Queen Isabella of Castile supported his plan to sail west to reach the East Indies. On October 12, 1492, he landed on an island in the West Indies (Caribbean) thinking he had reached his goal. Later explorations proved he had not found the East Indies and he died a disappointed man.

The Spanish quickly established a vast empire in the southern United States, Mexico, Central America, and parts of South America not occupied by the Portuguese. Indigenous peoples were killed or enslaved. Incredible amounts of gold and silver flowed from these possessions into the Spanish treasury. The English, French, and Dutch founded colonies in the northern United States and Canada. In 1519, Ferdinand Magellan traveled around the southern tip of South America, resulting in the first voyage around the world by a sailing ship.

The world was effectively divided among the European nations. Their colonies were viewed as realms to be exploited. Little thought was given to the rights or needs of the indigenous peoples. Their colonies were sources of wealth and power. These new colonies also became sources of competition and warfare for the Europeans over the next several centuries. Everywhere the conquerors, traders, and colonists went, the church followed. The sixteenth century was a great period of Roman Catholic missionary expansion, which we will examine in Chapter 9.[3]

The Context of the Reformation

The Reformation occurred in this climate of political and economic change. During the Reformation religion was frequently used to justify political ends. Henry VIII found a religious motive to justify his break with Rome and to extend the national aims of England. The German princes defended Protestants against the emperor to undermine his control. Protestant ideas gave peasants and others without power a new focus for their frustrations with the powerful. They even found grounds for revolt against established institutions in the teachings of the Protestants. Many historians claim that the Reformation had more to do with political, social, and economic unrest than with religious revival.

There can be little doubt that religious unhappiness played an important role in the conflicts that emerged in the sixteenth century, however. Most of Europe was torn between a deep loyalty to the church and a profound awareness of its many faults. The Avignon papacy and the Great Western Schism had produced a heightened mistrust of the pope as a spiritual leader. Absenteeism, pluralism, and simony were common. Often the wealthy would buy positions for their children as bishops, abbots, and abbesses, resulting in children as young as five being placed in high offices. Popes and bishops could not be expected to reform these practices because they profited from them.

Marriage of clergy was forbidden, but many openly married or engaged in concubinage and displayed their illegitimate children. The quality of spiritual life in many monasteries declined. The local clergy had almost no educational requirements. Learning declined even in the monasteries. New methods of historical study caused many thoughtful people to realize that some documents on which the church based its authority and practices were corrupt. Many desired a return to the simple purity of early Christianity. Spiritual dissatisfaction combined with Renaissance and humanistic ideas along with cultural pressures to move Europe toward the sweeping changes of the sixteenth century. The Reformation eventually divided into four main branches: Lutheran, Reformed (Calvinism), Anglican, and Anabaptist (Radical). Some of the denominations traced to these branches are noted below.

Denominations from the Reformation

BRANCH	DENOMINATIONS	EARLY LEADERS
Lutheranism	Lutheran	Martin Luther, Philip Melanchthon
Reformed	Reformed church,	Ulrich Zwingli, John Calvin
(Calvinism)	Presbyterian Puritan Congregationalist United Church of Christ	John Knox
	Baptist	John Smyth, Thomas Helwys, Henry Jacobs
Anglican (Church of England)	Anglican Episcopal Methodist	Henry VIII, Elizabeth I John and Charles Wesley
Anabaptist	Swiss Brethren	Conrad Grebel, Felix Manz
(Radical)	Mennonite Amish Hutterite Quaker Moravian Brethren	Menno Simons Jacob Huter George Fox Count Zinzendorf

THE WORLD IN THE SEVENTEENTH AND EIGHTEENTH CENTURIES

European political and social structures changed during the seventeenth and eighteenth centuries. Because the European nations were involved in colonization and empire building, disagreements on the Continent had worldwide impact. In the same way, changes in the fortunes of European colonies had vast implications for their parent states in Europe. The rearrangement of political power among the big European nations was hastened by the emergence of new nations such as Russia and Prussia. In the following section we glance at some of these major social and political changes.

States and Empires

The sixteenth century had been the great period of empire building for Spain and Portugal. Spain spread into the southwestern United States, Mexico, Central America, and large portions of South America. Portugal colonized parts of South America, Africa, India, China, and the East Indies. The indigenous populations were subdued and enslaved in the New World, but elsewhere trading colonies were established. Vast wealth in gold and silver flowed from the New World. Trade in spices and silk from the Far East and slaves from Africa further enriched the Portuguese. Spain and Portugal's overseas possessions made them the richest and most powerful nations. By the end of the sixteenth century, most of the easy wealth had been removed from the New World. Colonists then began to establish plantations and grow products for export to Europe. These plantations depended on slave labor, which produced a thriving trade in African slaves.

In the seventeenth century, the balance of power began to shift as the French, English, and Dutch established colonies around the world. The Dutch moved into parts of Africa, Ceylon, and the East Indies. The French took parts of North Africa, the Middle East, India, and Southeast Asia. The British established trading colonies in India and looked to the New World.

In the New World the French moved into Canada and down the Mississippi River to New Orleans. They failed to find the riches in gold and silver that had rewarded the explorers in South America. However, they claimed a vast territory and established a thriving fur trade. The Dutch established trading colonies in and around New York, which they called *New Amsterdam*.

The English were the most successful in creating agricultural and trading communities in North America. These colonies grew through a steady flow of immigrants from England and other places in Europe. Some settlers desired religious freedom. Others were fleeing political persecution. All were hoping for a better life, and many found it in the British colonies, which operated with a remarkable degree of freedom from England. The colonies soon developed interests that were different from England's, although most colonists continued to consider themselves loyal subjects of the English Crown.

The British drove the Dutch out of North America in 1664. The Dutch then turned their attention to further developing their profitable colonies in the East Indies. The conflict between the English and the Dutch was one of a series of seventeenth- and eighteenth-century wars that involved the European powers and their colonies. The power of Spain, Portugal, France, and Holland were considerably reduced. Britain was left the undisputed leader of the colonial world.

Royal Absolutism

Most seventeenth- and eighteenth-century rulers operated on a theory of government known as **royal absolutism,** meaning that the monarch was placed on the throne by God with absolute powers to rule. No one could challenge or question the monarch's decisions. Despite this theory, only a few monarchs were able to exercise absolute authority. On the whole, however, it was a great period of royal power.

Royal absolutism was most nearly realized in France. At the end of the sixteenth century, Henry IV (1589–1610) became king of France. He undertook an extensive program of gaining control of France, improving conditions at home, and increasing France's power abroad. His son Louis XIII (1610–1643) was inept and fickle. Fortunately for the Crown, he was served by Cardinal Richelieu (1585–1642). While he was a cardinal in the Catholic church, Richelieu was totally dedicated to France and its glory. From 1624 to 1642 he was a virtual master of the country.

Richelieu boldly advanced the cause of the French Crown within the country and sought to make France supreme on the Continent. This devotion to the interests of France led him to a violent attack on the Huguenots, who had won a limited degree of freedom from the Crown. He even supported the Protestants against the Catholics in the Thirty Years' War, which was fought to diminish the power of the Austrian branch of the Catholic Habsburg family. The Habsburgs were an aristocratic family with claims to the throne in Austria, Spain, the Netherlands, and elsewhere. Because of their great power, Richelieu believed whatever was bad for the Habsburgs had to be good for France!

The high point of royal power was the reign of Louis XIV (1643–1715). Louis took effective control of France in 1661.[4] By then the king was absolute in France and France was the most powerful nation in Europe. Louis called himself the Sun King and built a fantastic palace at Versailles, a city southwest of Paris. Versailles became the center of an elaborate, gaudy court that was the envy of other European rulers. The court operated on a strictly enforced set of manners, yet it was the source of endless intrigue as people vied for influence and engaged in limitless love games. This intrigue led the French to be characterized as the most polite, but most immoral, people in the world.

Louis felt that he embodied France and is supposed to have said, "I am the state." He believed he ruled France as Christ's appointed deputy. The monarchy was directly accountable to God alone. No human could judge it. He formed a strong, effective government that used the middle class in key positions. Common people did not participate in government.

The absolute power of the French monarchy was envied by other European royalty; however, few rulers were as successful at establishing complete control. In England the monarchy was successfully resisted by a Puritan revolt and was restricted by Parliament. The British opted for a limited monarchy. The Dutch also had a monarchy that was limited by the interests of powerful merchants. The government remained very decentralized. The Dutch took advantage of their seafaring heritage to plunder Spanish and Portuguese colonies and their trading ships. They wrestled control of the very profitable East Indies from Portugal. For a time, the Dutch were the dominant traders of Europe.

New States

Two new powers emerged in the East during the seventeenth and eighteenth centuries. One was Prussia. The rise of Prussia took several centuries. Its fate was connected with the activities of the Hohenzollern family. This family eventually became the electors of the province of Brandenburg, which was centered in Berlin. Frederick William, the Great Elector (1640–1688), made important strides in centralizing the government of Brandenburg. He also extended his territory by participating in the Thirty Years' War. His son, Frederick I (1701–1713), obtained the title of king and renamed his area *Prussia*. This helped Prussia establish its independence from the Holy Roman Empire. Successive Hohenzollerns ruled Prussia until the end of World War I, creating an efficient, military state that eventually evolved into Germany. Prussia/Germany would be a major player in world politics into the twenty-first century.

Russia was the other country to become a great power. The rise of Russia also occurred over several centuries and culminated with the founding of the Romanov dynasty in 1613. (The Romanovs ruled Russia until the Communist revolution in 1917.) The most notable of the early Romanov rulers was Peter I (1689–1725), also known as Peter the Great. Peter opened Russia to the West. He imported Western technicians to help create new industry. He also extended the northern border of Russia at the expense of Sweden and the southern border at the expense of the Ottoman Turks. It was Peter who put the Orthodox church under the Holy Synod appointed by the tsar. In this form, the church became a powerful tool used by the government. Catherine the Great (1762–1796) further extended the empire and increased the control of the tsar. By the time of her death, Russia had become a major world power.

Power was increasingly concentrated in the hands of monarchs after the Reformation. Some monarchs considered themselves enlightened and felt they ruled fairly and their decisions benefited the people. Despite some good intentions, more often than not the policies of most monarchs did little to help average citizens. Other rulers ignored the needs of their people altogether.

The situation was little better in the colonies. The colonists had more opportunity to do well financially, but government policy usually extended few rights to them. Moreover, Europeans regarded the colonies as places to be exploited for the good of the homeland. The exploitation of the colonies, the disregard of monarchs for their citizens' needs, and the general population's growing awareness of human rights all set the stage for revolution. The first two revolutions occurred during the late eighteenth century. The French and American Revolutions radically changed politics and religion.[5]

Notes

1. Ferdinand and Isabella were married before they became rulers in their regions. Isabella ruled in Castile from 1474 to 1504. Ferdinand ruled in Aragon from 1479 to 1516.

2. This forbidding of usury during the Middle Ages gave Jews a unique status in Europe. Jews could engage in lending because they were outside the church. Some Jews lent money to Christians at a profit. Ordinary people, princes, and popes borrowed from them. Various Jewish families became the bankers of Europe and accumulated vast fortunes. This made the Jews, who were despised by many Christians, necessary to the functioning of medieval society. Christians got into the banking business relatively late.

3. For a discussion of the world of the Reformation, see John B. Harrison, Richard E. Sullivan, and Dennis Sherman, *A Short History of Western Civilization*, 6th ed. New York: Knopf, 1985, pp. 331–372.

4. Louis XIV was a five-year-old child when he came to the throne. During his youth he was served by Cardinal Mazarin, who had been an understudy of Richelieu. Mazarin "ruled" France in the name of the young king until his death in 1661. Louis XIV's effective reign began at Mazarin's death in 1661.

5. For a good discussion of developments during the seventeenth and eighteenth centuries, see John B. Harrison, Richard E. Sullivan, and Dennis Sherman, *A Short History of Western Civilization*, 6th ed. New York: Knopf, 1985, pp. 399–505.

8

THE PROTESTANT REFORMATION
A Watershed in History (1500–1600 C.E.)

Martin Luther, the Protestant Reformer

The Reformation of the sixteenth century was the high point of a series of changes that began in the fourteenth century and did not end until well into the seventeenth century. The forces that had been building in the late Middle Ages and the Renaissance brought forth tremendous creative energy and destructive conflicts in the sixteenth century. Many historians argue that the Reformation was one of the great **watersheds** (turning points) in history. Some historians claim that the Reformation was the beginning of the modern world.

The Reformation was a watershed for a number of reasons. The Roman Catholic Reformation, which occurred in the mid-sixteenth century, determined the evolution of the Roman Catholic church well into the twentieth century. Both the Protestant Reformation and Catholic Reformation destroyed the medieval ideal of a united Christendom. Western Christianity has been fragmented ever since. The idea that all disputes among Christians could be settled by the church hierarchy or by a council fell by the wayside.

Some scholars argue that contemporary notions of individualism and secularism had their origins in the sixteenth century. The church became less important as a community that directed salvation to people. Protestantism taught that believers could go directly to God. The individual conscience, not the dictates of the church, became the guide for behavior. The bitter warfare that arose during the Reformation left many in Europe feeling that they were better off without religion. After the Reformation the secular state became the primary source of authority over people's lives and the agent chiefly concerned with their welfare. The role of religion in most daily concerns of people decreased. These results of the Reformation, combined with the rise of rationalism, the Enlightenment, modern science, and industrialization, tended to move the modern world toward secularization. In many ways, Christianity and society were never the same after the Reformation.

We examine the Reformation in this chapter and the next. This chapter looks at the histories of two major branches of the Protestant Reformation—Lutheranism and Calvinism. The following chapter looks at two other branches of the Reformation—Anglicanism and Anabaptists—and then explores the aftermath of the Protestant revolt including the Catholic Reformation.

LUTHER AND LUTHERANISM

No single person symbolizes the Reformation like the German theologian Martin Luther (1483–1546). His spiritual struggle was similar to that of many of his day. The frustration he expressed was felt throughout Europe. The concepts he taught came to express the ideas of a new era. His teachings became the focus for the political desires of rich and poor alike. Yet the Reformation

came about because the age was ripe for change, not because Luther deliberately set out to create it.

Luther and Early Lutheranism

Luther was born in Eisleben, Germany. His father was a poor miner who had
risen to own several foundries. As was common for the time, discipline in
Luther's home was strict and severe. School was an unhappy experience for
young Luther and he was whipped for not learning his schoolwork. These early
experiences marked Luther's character and may explain much of his later struggle to free himself from guilt and the judgment of God.

Luther's father wanted him to study law. But at the age of twenty-two he
entered the Augustinian monastery at Erfurt following an incident where he
was trapped in a thunderstorm. He was overcome by fear of death and hell and
he promised Saint Anne he would become a monk if he survived. At Erfurt
Luther excelled in discipline and devotion because he was driven by overwhelming fear of God's judgment of his sinfulness. He practiced good works,
engaged in severe penance, and faithfully confessed his sins. Still he could not
free himself from his terrible fear. Even the acts that were intended to free him
from guilt left him in despair. He felt he could not even love God.

To overcome these problems Luther's confessor recommended that he
study the Bible. Biblical studies also prepared him to teach at the new
University of Wittenberg. In 1512 he received a doctorate in theology,
although he was still in a state of conflict. In 1513 he began lecturing on
Psalms. About this time he began a study of Romans, which led him to discover the Gospel in a tower room at the Augustinian house in Wittenberg. In
studying Romans 1:17, he suddenly realized that the justice of God and the
Gospel were inseparably linked. God does not judge sinners, but forgives
them. Salvation cannot be earned, it is freely promised and given by God. This
promise only has to be claimed by faith. The righteousness (justice) of God is
transferred to the sinner. Luther's understanding of God was transformed.
God's actions toward humans that he had seen as Law (judgment) now were
understood as Gospel (good news).

It was as if the gate of paradise had been opened for Luther. Instead of the
angry God who judges sinners, here was a God seeking to free sinners from
guilt through Christ. This righteousness of Christ must simply be accepted by
faith alone (*sola fides*). All that people had to do was to claim the joy that God
offered. The Scriptures were the source of authority through which the Word
of God (Logos) reached sinners. They were the sole source of authority (*sola
scriptura*) for the faith. "By faith alone" and "by Scripture alone" became the
watchwords of the Reformation.

After his great discovery, Luther went quietly back to teaching. He did not cause a stir. The Reformation was instigated more by the business of religion than by theological discoveries. Religion was big business in Wittenberg. The church at Wittenberg Castle housed 18,000 relics. The local ruler, Frederick of Saxony, charged admission to pilgrims who came to see them. Luther preached against this practice. An even more unprincipled plot was brewing concerning indulgences. Pope Leo X (1475–1521) was one of the most corrupt popes of the age. He was obsessed with earning money to complete the building of Saint Peter's Basilica in Rome. Pope Leo secretly agreed with the Bishop-Prince Albert of Brandenberg and bankers to sell indulgences around Wittenberg and to split the profits. He sent the Dominican Johann Tetzel (1465–1519) to head a group of preachers who would stimulate the sale of indulgences. Tetzel made outlandish claims about the effectiveness of indulgences for the living and the dead. One catchy marketing slogan claimed "as soon as the coin in the coffer rings, the soul from purgatory springs."

Luther and many others were furious at this perversion of church teaching. This anger led Luther to prepare his Ninety-five Theses, which covered issues related to the sale of indulgences. Luther argued that forgiveness came only through repentance. The pope had no power to forgive sins. He could only confirm what God already had done. The pope could free Christians from the penance placed on them by the church but could not free dead Christians from purgatory. Even if the pope had the power to free souls from purgatory, he should do so out of love, not for money. In short, the selling of indulgences undermined true religion and the papacy.

On October 31, 1517, Luther nailed these theses to the door of the castle church at Wittenberg.[1] This was not an unusual action: the church door served as the town bulletin board where announcements and topics for debate were frequently placed. Luther invited scholars and theologians to debate the ideas presented. He did not anticipate the stir that his action caused. The Ninety-five Theses struck at the heart of much of the religious frustration of the day. They cried out against the exploitation church officials placed on the people. They also became the focus for rising German nationalism because they pointed to interference in German life by outside forces, in this case the pope. Printers soon used the power of the new printing press to circulate copies in Latin and German throughout Europe. Emotions on both sides of the issues were so inflamed that October 31, 1517 is usually regarded as the beginning of the Protestant Reformation.

Europe was split. The Dominicans opposed Luther while the Augustinians supported him. The universities of Wittenberg and Paris also supported him, but other faculties were among the opposition. Various political leaders took sides. In all of this controversy, Luther did not see himself as breaking with the church.

The Ninety-Five Theses

Luther's Ninety-five Theses centered on the issue of indulgences. They argued that the pope had limited ability to release people from punishments and that the sale of indulgences hurt religion and the papacy. A few of the theses are listed by number below.

1. Our Lord and Master Jesus Christ, in saying, "Repent ye, etc." meant the whole life of the faithful to be an act of repentance.

2. This saying cannot be understood of the sacrament of penance (i.e., of confession and absolution) which is administered by the priesthood.

5. The pope has neither the wish nor the power to remit any penalties save those which he has imposed at his own will or according to the will of the canons.

6. The pope has no power to remit guilt, save by declaring and confirming that it has been remitted by God; or, to be sure, by remitting the cases reserved to himself. If he neglected to observe these limitations, the guilt would remain.

8. The canons of penance are imposed only on the living, and nothing ought to be imposed on the dying in accordance with them.

10. Those priests who, in the case of dying, reserve canonical penances for purgatory, act ignorantly and unrightly.

20. The pope by his plenary remission of all penalties does not understand the remission of all penalties absolutely, but only of those imposed by himself.

21. Therefore those preachers of indulgences are in error who allege that through the indulgences of the pope a man is freed from every penalty.

79. It is blasphemy to say that the cross adorned with the papal arms is as effectual as the cross of Christ.

80. Bishops, curates and theologians who allow such teaching to be preached to the people will have to render an account.

81. This wanton preaching of pardons makes it hard even for learned men to defend the honour of the pope against calumny, or at least against the shrewd questions of the laity.

Source: Quoted in Henry Bettenson, ed., *Documents of the Christian Church*, 2d ed. (New York: Oxford University Press, 1963), 186–190. Reprinted by permission of Oxford University Press.

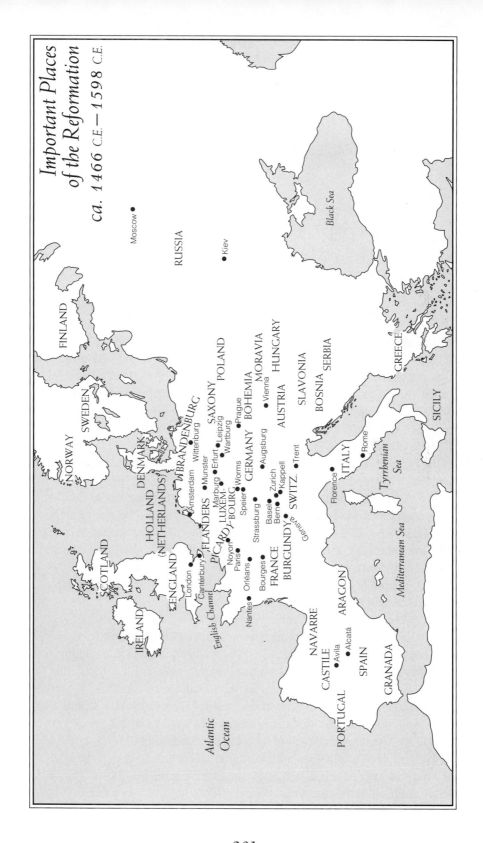

Important Places
of the Reformation
ca. 1466 C.E. – 1598 C.E.

Moscow

RUSSIA

Kiev

Black Sea

FINLAND

NORWAY

SWEDEN

DENMARK

BRANDENBURG

SAXONY   POLAND

Wittenberg

Munster   Erfurt   Leipzig

Marburg   Prague   BOHEMIA   MORAVIA

Amsterdam   Vienna   HUNGARY

HOLLAND   Worms   GERMANY   Augsburg   AUSTRIA

(NETHERLANDS)   Speier   SLAVONIA

FLANDERS   LUXEM-   Zurich   BOSNIA   SERBIA

SCOTLAND   PICARD BOURG   Strassburg   Basel Bern Kappell

                Noyon   SWITZ.   Trent   GREECE

ENGLAND   Paris   BURGUNDY   ITALY

London   Geneva   Rome

Canterbury   Florence   SICILY

IRELAND

English Channel   Bourges   FRANCE   Tyrrhenian
                                                          Sea

Nantes   Orléans   Mediterranean Sea

Atlantic
Ocean

NAVARRE   ARAGON

PORTUGAL   CASTILE   Avila   Alcatá

            SPAIN

            GRANADA

201

Luther welcomed his enemies' appeal to the pope to silence him. He was convinced that the pope did not know of the activities of Tetzel. Luther believed when the pope realized the abuses that were taking place, he would end them.

A series of events caused Luther to recognize the true character of the papacy and the radical nature of his own position. One important event was the Leipzig Disputation, held in June and July of 1519. Johann Eck (1486–1543), a professor at Ingolstadt, broke a temporary truce between Luther and his opponents by attacking a supporter of Luther, Andreas Bodenstein von Karlstadt (ca. 1480–1541). Luther took up the challenge and met Eck for a debate at Leipzig. Eck maneuvered Luther into both defending the teachings of Hus and questioning the council that condemned Hus. With this, Eck proved that Luther was a supporter of Hus and, thus, a heretic.

Leo X then moved against the errant monk. He issued the bull *Exsurge Domine* in which Luther was depicted as a wild boar running loose in the vineyard of the Lord. All copies of Luther's books throughout Europe were ordered burned. Luther was given sixty days to deny his teachings and to ask for forgiveness. Printed copies of *Exsurge Domine* were circulated throughout Europe. When Luther received a copy, he responded by publicly burning it along with other "papish" books on December 10, 1520. This was an open act of defiance of the pope. Leo excommunicated Luther in January 1521. The break was complete.

The recently elected Emperor Charles V was prevented from arresting Luther by the protection of Elector (ruler) Frederick the Wise. Charles used Luther as an instrument against the pope who he felt was favoring his rival, Francis I of France. After much political maneuvering, Luther was taken before the Diet of Worms, an empire-wide meeting, in 1521. Luther appeared before the emperor, was shown several of his books, and was asked to deny the teachings in them. After some wavering, Luther finally stood firm. Luther held that he could not violate his conscience, which was captive to the Word of God. If he could not be convinced from Scripture or reason, he would not deny his teachings. He proclaimed, "I cannot do otherwise, here I stand, so help me God!" In taking this position, Luther was now defying the emperor as well as the pope.

Luther's statement charged the atmosphere. The emperor was determined to have him condemned. The elector, Frederick, arranged to have Luther "kidnapped" and concealed at the castle of Wartburg. There Luther finished translating the New Testament into German. The Old Testament translation took another ten years. The German Bible was one of the great achievements of the Reformation. It not only was a source of religious instruction but also was a prime force in uniting the German language and focusing nationalistic energies.

While forming the German Bible, Luther was driven to answer the question of what was and what was not Scripture. The **Vulgate** was the version of the Scriptures used in the Roman Catholic church. It was a Latin translation based in part on a Greek Bible called the *Septuagint*. In comparing the Vulgate to earlier "original" texts, Luther came to question a number of books in the Scripture accepted by the Catholics. In the New Testament, he wanted to remove Hebrews. He believed it was not written by Paul and James because its emphasis on works seemed to contradict Paul's stress on grace. One of his most important supporters, Philip Melanchthon (1497–1560), convinced him to leave Hebrews and James in. However, Luther did remove several books from the Old Testament that were in the Septuagint but were not in the early Hebrew canon. These he called **Apocrypha** ("hidden [writings]"). They were placed between the Old Testament and New Testament in the Lutheran Bible. The books accepted in the German Bible were eventually accepted by all Protestant Bibles.[2]

After Luther's departure, Charles V issued an edict condemning him. He demanded that Luther be arrested and that all of his books be burned. He ordered that any of his subjects found supporting the "stiff-necked heretic" would be charged with treason and have their property confiscated. Nevertheless, the political situation prevented the emperor's orders from being carried out. In the 1520s, a new movement ultimately called *Lutheranism* gained momentum. In addition to the German New Testament, Luther prepared an *Order of Worship* and a *German Mass*. With Luther's blessing, Melanchthon published the first systematic theology of the new movement, called *Loci Communes*. With these publications, Lutheranism was well on its way.

Luther's Later Life

Luther's thought was also shaped by events in his later life. In a dispute with the humanist Erasmus Luther argued for the slavery of the will to sin. This disagreement lost the Lutherans the support of most Continental humanists, who defended human free will. An even more important event was the Peasants' War of 1524 and 1525, which was part of a series of revolts against peasant exploitation that dated back to the Middle Ages. Luther had taught that all Christians were equal. Each had the right to interpret the Scriptures when guided by reason. He refused to extend these ideas to the social realm. The peasants took the ideas of Luther to mean that all people were equal. On the basis of that idea and the Scripture, they demanded a release from serfdom as well as other rights.

Luther tried to reason with the peasants, asking them to suffer quietly. When they refused, he urged the princes to quash the rebellion. Protestant and Catholic princes united and viciously suppressed the revolt. At Frankhausen 50,000 peasants were mercilessly slaughtered. More than 100,000 serfs died in the revolt. Luther eventually regretted urging violence on the part of the princes.

In 1525 Luther married a former nun and started a large family. He also encouraged his followers who had left religious orders to marry. His practice would set the pattern for Protestant ministers. The story of Luther's marriage is interesting. He had come to believe that monastic vows and celibacy were not binding, although he vowed he would never be forced to take a wife. His teachings encouraged many monks and nuns to leave their monasteries and some sought marriage. A group of nuns escaped their monastery and arrived in Wittenberg in a cart. Luther decided to find them husbands lest a worse fate befall them. He arranged marriages for all but one—Katharina von Bora—who indicated she would consider Luther. Luther reasoned that marriage would please his father and displease the pope, and because Christ was coming again soon, it seemed to be a good idea. Luther did not marry for love, but out of a sense of duty. He did develop an affection for his wife, however, and often referred to her as *Herr Kathe* ("Lord Katie").

A short-lived peace between the opposing religious groups in Germany was established at the Diet of Speier (Spire) in 1526. Charles V was under pressure from both the French and the Turks, and he needed peace at home to deal with foreign threats. At the diet, he decreed a truce between Evangelicals and their opponents. (Christians in the reform tradition, especially Lutherans, came to be called **Evangelicals** in Europe.) Each prince would be responsible for religion in his territory. An individual would be allowed to follow his or her conscience until the religious issue could be settled. By 1529 Charles V felt that he could turn his attention to religious matters. At another Diet of Speier, he revoked the concessions to the Evangelicals. That led the Reformers to protest. It was this protest that gave Evangelicals the name **Protestants.**

Divisions were apparent among people in the reform movement. Different branches of religious groups had developed in Germany and other places in Europe. One branch in Switzerland centered around the ministry of Ulrich Zwingli (1484–1531). Zwingli was a founder of what became the Reformed church movement. Many of his teachings were similar to Luther's, but some of his ideas differed. He and Luther disagreed on the issue of the Eucharist. Zwingli taught that the Lord's Supper was but a symbol of Christ's sacrificial death. Christ was only symbolically present in the bread and wine of the meal. For Luther, the Eucharist was more than a symbol. In it the grace of God was brought to humans. As a result, Christ was really present in the bread and wine.

A German Lutheran prince, Philip of Hesse, called a meeting at Marburg in 1529 to try to unite the two main branches of the reform. He hoped such a union would strengthen his political position. At the Colloquy of Marburg, Luther and Melanchthon represented the Germans and Zwingli, John Oecolampadius (1482–1531), and Martin Bucer (1491–1551) represented the Swiss. Fifteen articles were prepared for discussion and the two branches agreed on fourteen. The fifteenth, concerning the Eucharist, proved to be a sticking point. Both Luther and Zwingli made some concessions but were unable to agree. Each side denounced the other and left convinced the other was the tool of the devil. Although Protestants of different shades continued to cooperate, unity of the reform movement proved impossible.

Charles V had successfully defeated the Turks by 1530. He called for a diet at Augsburg in July 1530 to settle religious differences. He requested that all parties prepare documents clearly stating their positions so orderly discussions could be held. The Lutheran position was prepared by Melanchthon. This document, known as the Augsburg Confession, was signed by most of the German Protestant princes and reform leaders. The Augsburg Confession so carefully states the Reformers' position that it not only became the most important Lutheran confession but also the foundation of most other Protestant creeds. Position papers also were presented by Zwingli and other reform leaders. The Catholic statement was prepared by Johann Eck and other theologians.

Although all parties had their say, the diet had little effect. In the end the different sides were unable to agree. Charles V took the Catholic position and issued an edict giving the Protestants until April 1531 to submit. The Lutheran princes formed the Schmalkald League to defend themselves. Both Protestants and Catholics prepared for war. An actual war was prevented when Francis I and the Turks reasserted themselves. Charles V was forced again to seek the help of the Lutherans to defend against foreigners. External threats and careful political maneuvering by the Schmalkald League resulted in sixteen years of peace. Protestantism expanded in Germany and Scandinavia.

Luther died in 1546. His death and other events weakened the Schmalkald League. On April 25, 1547, the forces of the league, which had been betrayed by one of its leaders, were defeated by imperial armies. That left Charles V and the Catholics in control of Germany. However, Catholics could not rule Protestant subjects effectively. Political maneuvering and rebellions were common. Efforts were made to reach workable agreements.

In 1555 Protestants and Catholics finally agreed to the Peace of Augsburg, which would ensure tranquility for some time. The Peace of Augsburg allowed the religion of the ruler to be the established religion of a region. Lutherans and Catholics living in areas where their religion was not recognized could emigrate. The peace did not extend to members of Zwingli's Reformed church or the Anabaptists (another branch of the Reformation discussed below).

Luther's Theology

A key to understanding Luther's theology is the idea of the Word of God, which for Luther was the final authority in the Christian community. Modern Christians sometimes use the phrase "Word of God" to mean the Bible. For Luther, the Word of God was nothing less than the Eternal Logos or Jesus Christ himself. The Bible was important because it is where the Word speaks to people. Luther rejected anything that was opposed to the Scriptures. On that ground, he rejected much of late medieval Christianity, including the strong stress on the papacy.

Luther also would not accept complicated approaches to understanding Scripture, such as the allegorical method. The Scriptures should be taken in their most simple and straightforward meanings. That does not mean that he believed in a strict **literalism.** Literalism is an approach to interpreting the Bible that insists that all passages must be seen as literally true. This implies that all passages are equally important, God speaks directly through Scripture, and there is no need for interpreting passages. Instead, Luther believed that people must interpret Scripture and that the key to understanding the Bible was the Gospel. The Gospel was the good news seen in the cross that God's words and acts in history were for humanity's salvation, not its judgment. It was God's "yes" on humans that was totally undeserved. According to Luther both the Old and New Testaments contain Gospel, although there is more of it in the New Testament. Because passages do not necessarily contain Gospel, some have little usefulness for Christians. For instance, some express only the Law, which is God's judgment on humans. These passages have only limited or no meaning for people living under the grace of God.

Justification by faith was another important idea for Luther. **Justification** has to do with how sinners "get right" with God. Luther believed that sin is much more than bad acts. It is a condition of the human soul in which even the will is held in bondage to sin. All people can do is to will evil. They cannot even will to do good. No human act is truly good. That is why good works are ineffective in trying to get sinners right with God. Justification comes in the activity of Jesus Christ, who releases sinners from their bondage to sin, death, and the devil. Because of Christ, God declares people justified despite their sin. This concept has been called **imputed justice.**

According to Luther, all humans can do is accept God's justification in faith. Faith is not a "work" that people can produce. It is a free gift of God's grace through the Holy Spirit acting on the human heart. Faith means that sinners are accepting the fact that God has declared they are just. They are not actually changed, but remain sinners. That is why Luther could claim that Christians were sinners and justified at the same time. Nevertheless, he believed Christians were in a process of becoming more like Christ. This process would be completed at the end of life.

The priesthood of believers was another important idea for Luther. He thought that each person was his or her own priest. People did not need priests to take their prayers to God or to speak God's forgiveness. Christians could go directly to the Lord. All Christians were capable of interpreting the Scriptures for themselves. The Bible was placed in the hand of the laity who could understand its message and make moral decisions.

Yet for Luther this emphasis on a person's conscience did not result in a complete individualism. The priesthood was not just for individuals but was for the community of believers. All Christians were to be priests to one another. Each Christian had the duty to pray for, care for, and give guidance to others. No believer could claim to be Christian without assuming the duties of the priest. That also meant that there were no special categories of Christians. All were equal in the work of the Lord. Each person had a special calling to carry out for the glory of God. Ministers were called to duties such as preaching or administering the sacraments that other Christians did not perform. But every human "job" was a special calling from God. Thus Luther could say, "The scrub maid on her knees is as much in the will of God as the pope on the throne!"

The church as a community of priests had a very special place for Luther. It was also the place where the tradition of the Fathers was preserved where the Word of God (Christ) came to people through Scripture, preaching, and the sacraments. Preaching had a special place for Luther but not as high a place as sacraments. The sacraments were physical acts that God had chosen as signs of his promise. In other words, they are the channels through which the grace of God comes to humans. Because they bring the grace of God, the sacraments have a central place in Lutheran worship. To be a sacrament, an act had to be instituted in the Bible by Christ and connected with a Gospel promise. That meant that there were only two sacraments—baptism and the Eucharist.

Luther regarded baptism as a sign of justification. In it God's Word comes to sinners. It is the beginning of the Christian life and is the sign of death and resurrection under which the whole believer's life takes place. Baptism is connected with faith, but it does not require that a person has to be old enough to make a personal decision to receive it. If personal decision were the basis for receiving baptism, then people would be depending on the work of their own will and not on the grace of God. For this reason, Luther accepted baptism of infants and rejected "believer's baptism" as practiced by other Reformers like the Anabaptists.

Luther tried to take a middle ground between the Catholics and more radical Reformers on the Eucharist. He could not accept transubstantiation and could not agree with Zwingli's concept of the symbolic presence. He felt that the clear, simple meaning of the Scripture had to be accepted when Christ said "This is my body . . . this is my blood." For Luther, Christ was clearly present in the Eucharist, although the bread and wine did not actually become his flesh and blood. Instead, the bread and wine existed in the same time and same place as the flesh and blood. Later theologians have called this doctrine **consubstantiation.** The nature of the Eucharist was a major problem that continued to divide the Christian community.

Luther also taught a doctrine of two kingdoms, which had implications for later Lutheranism. The kingdom of law is the state with its civic responsibilities.

It operates on the concept of justice. Its responsibility is to control the sinful impulses of people by seeking justice, maintaining order, and punishing wrong. The church operates under the kingdom of Gospel. It has no civic function and operates on the grace of God. The church has no control over secular authorities and it is not subject to the laws of the state. As sinners Christians *are* subject to the state. Because both kingdoms are under God's rule, Christians may hold state offices, including military positions. State and church are to cooperate with one another. Although Luther tried to separate church and state, the division was difficult to maintain. The Lutheran church often found itself dominated by the state.

Several doctrines that developed from Luther's teachings became common to Protestant groups in general. Most Protestants accept faith alone as the basis for salvation. They reject penance, merit, and priests who make the grace of God available to sinners. Protestants also teach the "priesthood of the believer," meaning that each person can go directly to God without a mediator. Each Christian also has an obligation to be a "priest" to others by bearing another's burdens. Generally, Protestant clergy are known as ministers or pastors, not as priests. Protestant ministers also marry.

The Scriptures are the only (or at least the main) source of authority for Protestants. Tradition plays a less important role for them. Vernacular translations of the Scriptures are placed in the hands of laypeople. Worship services are conducted in the everyday language of the people. Finally, Protestants recognize two sacraments—baptism and communion.

CALVIN AND THE REFORMED TRADITION

The second main branch of the Reformation is called the *Reformed tradition*. The best known of its early leaders was Ulrich Zwingli. After Zwingli's death, leadership of the developing movement was taken on by John Calvin (1509–1564). Because of Calvin's powerful influence and sharp theological mind, the Reformed tradition is also known as *Calvinism*. Denominations that owe their origins to Calvinistic influences include the Reformed church, Presbyterians, Puritans (including the Congregationalists and the United Church of Christ), and Baptists. In this section we briefly review the beginnings of the Reformed tradition in the work of Zwingli, then we discuss the life of Calvin and his theology.

Ulrich Zwingli

Zwingli was born in 1484 in the small Swiss village of Wildhaus. He was educated in Basel, Bern, and Vienna. His studies were influenced by the humanists. He received his degree in 1506 and shortly became the priest at Glarus. His study of the Greek New Testament and the church fathers led him to criticize certain Catholic practices. While at Glarus, he started serving as chaplain for mercenary soldiers from his district. The Swiss frequently supplied soldiers for warring groups to the highest bidder. The pope often used their services. (Swiss soldiers in medieval uniforms, the so-called Swiss Guards are still the official guards of the pope.) While serving with the army, Zwingli came to believe the practice of supplying mercenaries was destroying the morals of society. He eventually opposed the practice.

Between 1516 and 1518 Zwingli was pastor at Einsiedeln, a major center for pilgrimages. He spoke against both pilgrimages and selling indulgences. In 1518 he was appointed a chaplain to the pope and was promoted to the pastorate of the largest church in Zurich. But his doubts about many church practices continued to grow and he reached conclusions similar to Luther's. By 1519 he had made the Bible his only source of authority. He started in Mark (the first New Testament book) and preached through the entire New Testament. His sermons drew huge crowds.

In 1522 Zwingli undertook a major set of reforms in Zurich. He persuaded the town council to forbid any religious custom that was not in accordance with the Bible. This action undermined the authority of the bishop and established the idea of civil government according to the Word of God as the principle for reform in Zurich. In 1523, he defended his Sixty-seven Articles against Johann Faber (1478–1541), who had been sent by the bishop to deal with the heresy in Zurich. The Sixty-seven Articles asserted the authority of the Bible over the church, held that the Mass was a remembrance not a sacrifice, taught salvation by faith alone, and defended the right of priests and nuns to marry. They denied good works, invoking the saints, the position of the priest as mediator between God and humans, monastic vows, and purgatory. They claimed Christians did not have to do anything that was not in the Bible.

The town council implemented Zwingli's teachings, thus sealing the break with the Catholics. The movement later forbade the use of images in churches and changed the Mass to a love feast. Images, **clerical vestments** (special clothing used in worship services), relics, crucifixes, and tapestries were removed. Bell ringing, chanting, and organ music were stopped. The great cathedral organ was taken apart. The town council also persecuted Anabaptists, a number of whom were executed.

Zwingli's reforms spread to other areas. Martin Bucer from Strassburg and Zwingli participated in the Marburg Colloquy and the Diet of Augsburg. In 1531, five Swiss Catholic cantons attacked Zurich. These were opposed by a small Protestant force at Kappel. Zwingli was killed while serving as a chaplain to the Protestants. The Protestants were defeated, but in November 1531 the Catholics signed the Peace of Kappel with the Reformers. The Peace of Kappel allowed each canton to follow its own conscience in matters of religion, which left Switzerland divided into staunchly Protestant and equally committed Catholic states.

Important Events of the Reformation

DATES	EVENTS	SECULAR LEADERS	CHURCH PERSONS	WRITINGS
1466–1535	Humanism advanced	Erasmus		*Handbook of the Christian Soldier, The Praise of Folly,* Greek New Testament
1492	European discovery of the New World	Columbus, Isabella, Ferdinand		
	Muslims expelled from Spain		Cardinal Ximénes	
1506	Construction begins on St. Peter's Basilica		Pope Julius II	
1509–1547	King Henry of England	Henry VIII		
1517	Selling of indulgences spurs Reformation		Pope Leo X, Luther	Ninety-five Theses
1519–1556	Holy Roman Emperor Charles V	Charles V		
1519	Leipzig Disputation Reform begun in Zurich		Luther, Eck Zwingli	*Exsurge Domine*
1521	Diet of Worms places Luther under imperial ban			German Bible begun
	Lutheran theology takes shape		Melanchthon	*Loci communes*
1524–1525	German Peasants' War, Luther recommends use of force			
1525	Beginning of Swiss Brethren		Grebel, Manz, Blaurock	
1529	Marburg Colloquy		Luther, Zwingli	
	Diet of Speier, Evangelicals called Protestants			

Important Events of the Reformation

DATES	EVENTS	SECULAR LEADERS	CHURCH PERSONS	WRITINGS
1530	Diet of Augsburg		Luther, Eck, Zwingli,	Augsburg Confession
1531	Battle of Kappel, Zwingli dies		Zwingli	
	King becomes head of church	King Henry VIII of England		
1534	England breaks with Rome			
1534–1535	Kingdom of Saints in Münster		Matthys, Bockelson	
1536	Calvin begins work in Geneva		Calvin	*Institutes of the Christian Religion*
1540	Jesuits recognized		Pope Paul III, Loyola	
1545–1563	Council of Trent			
1547–1553	Reform extended in England	Edward VI	Cranmer	*Book of Common Prayer*
1553–1558	Catholicism restored in England	Mary Tudor		
1555	Peace of Augsburg			
1558–1603	Elizabethan settlement	Elizabeth I		
1565	Religious wars in the Netherlands			
1572	St. Bartholomew's Day massacre of French Huguenots			
1598	Edict of Nantes temporarily ends persecution of Huguenots			

John Calvin

After Zwingli's death, a number of leaders continued to spread Evangelical ideas in Switzerland, Germany, and France. However, it was not until several years later that the Swiss movement would find its greatest leader in John Calvin. Calvin was born in 1509 in Noyon, France, where his father was secretary to the bishop. He studied for a career in law at Orleans, Bourges, and Paris. Like Zwingli, Calvin was also influenced by the humanists and he eventually turned his attention to religion.

In 1533 he had a religious conversion in which he became convinced of the glory of God and the sinfulness of humans. He felt he had been called by God to restore the church to its early purity. Calvin became involved in reform efforts in Paris and eventually had to escape the city hiding in a basket. He took up residence in Noyon. There he resigned the church position his father had gotten for him and possibly was imprisoned for a period. Francis I had been fairly tolerant of the French Reformers, but in 1535 he persecuted the Evangelicals. That forced Calvin to flee to Basel, Switzerland.

While there Calvin wrote the first edition of the *Institutes of the Christian Religion*. He sent a copy to Francis I as a defense of the reform movement. The first edition of the *Institutes* came out as a small "pocketbook" of Protestant ideas that could be easily carried and concealed. The book enjoyed widespread popularity. By 1559 Calvin had expanded the *Institutes* into a four-volume work that remains one of the great systematic theologies in Christian history. The *Institutes* did more than any other book to provide Protestants with a thoughtful theology.

Calvin was interested in returning to a life of scholarship. In July of 1536, he visited Geneva. There he met William Farel (1489–1565), who had introduced the reform movement to the city. Farel and his assistants were in control of the town council but needed help in implementing reform. Farel convinced Calvin to stay in the city. Later that year, Calvin produced a document that contained strict regulations on administering the Lord's Supper and that required all citizens to submit to a profession of faith prepared by the town council. Failure to submit to the profession would result in exile. Strong opposition forced Calvin himself into exile in 1538.

Calvin was pastor of the French Protestant church in Strassburg from 1539 to 1541. These were the most happy and peaceful years of his life. There he was influenced by Martin Bucer and he also became friends with Philip Melanchthon. He preached, engaged in various conferences on the faith, and taught at the local theological school. In 1541, the Geneva town government invited him to return to prevent a return to Catholicism. He regarded his return as an opportunity to establish a **theocracy** (a society ruled by the "principles of God") in the city along Old Testament lines. The town government was assisted by a council of ministers and lay elders who were primarily concerned with morals. The council came to have tremendous impact on the lives of citizens. Severe punishments were given even for strictly religious offenses, and all pleasure, including dancing and games, was forbidden.

Force was used on those who opposed the council and numerous people were tortured and killed. One person killed was Michael Servetus (1511–1553), a well-regarded physician who also wrote theological works. He felt the church had erred when it had allowed Constantine to combine church and state, an idea that got him into trouble with Calvin. Servetus also taught anti-Trinitarian views that Calvin strongly opposed. Servetus' slow death by burning at the stake became a symbol of the repressive effects of religious zeal gone astray. From 1555 until his death in 1564, Calvin was absolute master of Geneva.

Calvin's efforts were not limited to the theocracy in Geneva. He also established a theological school to continue his teachings. He supported French Protestants. Calvin attempted to have the reform introduced in England and protected English Protestant refugees. He extended his influence to other parts of Europe through his writing and through persons who sought his advice. One well-known person who sought his help was John Knox (ca. 1513–1572). Knox helped spread Calvinism to Scotland where it became Presbyterianism.

Calvin's Theology

There are two ways to develop theology. A theologian can start with human experience and work up to assumptions about God and God's activity. Or a theologian can begin with assumptions about God and then try to draw conclusions about humans and their situation. To some extent, Luther used the first approach. He started with his experiences of sin, guilt, grace, Gospel, and release. He then built his theology around these experiences. Calvin used the second approach. He started with assumptions about God and then drew from them conclusions about sinners and the saved.

The key to understanding Calvin's thought is the sovereignty of God. God was seen as the absolute ruler of the universe. Nothing happened without God's direct involvement. If that were the case, how could the sin of Adam and Eve be explained? Either they went against the will of God or God willed their sin. Calvin believed that God willed their sin. In fact, as strange as it seems to us, God willed all good and all evil. Good believers do the "revealed will" of God. Evil persons are doing the "hidden will" of God. All things work for the glory of God. Despite God's sovereignty in willing humans' sin, Calvin believed He was not to be blamed for sin. Humans are fully responsible for the evil they commit. Calvin did not resolve the great mystery of this paradox (apparent contradiction). Calvin was well aware of the limits of human reason. Some things would have to remain a mystery.

Calvin on Predestination

The *Institutes of the Christian Religion* is one of the great systematic theologies in church history. It begins with the assumption of the absolute sovereignty of God and carefully derives other doctrines from that. Calvin did not want to deal with predestination, but he felt compelled to because logic and Scripture demanded it. Some of his ideas are presented below.

> As Scripture, then, clearly shows, we say that God once established by His eternal and unchangeable plan those whom He long before determined once for all to receive into salvation, and those whom . . . He would devote to destruction. We assert that, with respect to the elect, this plan was founded upon His freely given mercy, without regard to human worth; but by His just and irreprehensible but incomprehensible judgment He has barred the door of life to those whom He has given over to damnation. Now among the elect we regard the call as a testimony of election. Then we hold justification another sign of its manifestation, until they come into the glory in which the fulfillment of that election lies. But as the Lord seals His elect by call and justification, so, by shutting off the reprobate from knowledge of His name or from the sanctification of His Spirit, He, as it were, reveals by these marks what sort of judgment awaits them.
>
> Some . . . falsely and wickedly accuse God of biased justice because in His predestination He does not maintain the same attitude

Humans are the greatest and most noble of God's creation, Calvin believed. They are created in the very image of God. This image continues to reside in the human soul. The human soul is endowed by God with intellect along the ability to tell the difference between good and evil and justice from injustice. Nevertheless, Adam chose to revolt against the authority of God. This "original sin" is transferred to and corrupts all his descendants. Humans became so totally depraved that they could commit no good act unless assisted by the grace of God. As a result, salvation depends entirely on God's grace. Yet, Calvin believed the intellect still sought truth. Humans retain the need for social order and can understanding the operation of the world. These are signs of the continued work of God's Spirit with fallen humans.

toward all. If, they say, He finds all guilty, let Him punish all equally; if innocent, let Him withhold the rigor of His judgment from all. But they so act toward Him as if either mercy were to be forbidden to Him or as if when He wills to show mercy He is compelled to renounce His judgment completely.

Augustine's statements most aptly accord with this: "Since in the first man the whole mass of the race fell under condemnation . . . those vessels of it which are made unto honor are vessels not of their own righteousness . . . but God's mercy, but that other vessels are made unto dishonor [cf. Rom. 9:21] is to be laid not to inquiry but to judgment." Because God metes out merited penalty to those whom He condemns but distributes unmerited grace to those whom He calls, He is freed to all accusation . . . "The Lord can therefore also give grace . . . to whom He will . . . because He is merciful, and not give to all because He is a just judge. For by giving to some what they do not deserve, . . . He can show His free grace . . . By not giving to all, He can manifest what all deserve."

Source: From Hans J. Hillerbrand, ed., *The Protestant Reformation*. New York: Harper & Row, 1968, pp. 189, 211–212. Copyright 1968 Hans Hillerbrand. Reprinted by permission of HarperCollins Publishers.

Calvin taught that although God hated sin, he continued to love humans. Out of his love and mercy God sent Christ to be the redeemer of those to be saved. In order to accomplish this task, Christ had to be fully God and fully man as the Nicene faith maintains. Christ not only conquered physical death, but also spiritual death. His resurrection demonstrates that conquest and is the base upon which believers' faith rests.

Like Luther, Calvin taught that one purpose of the Law was to point to the depraved condition of humans and drive them to depend upon the grace of God for salvation. However, Calvin did not contrast grace and Law as had Luther. For him, the Law revealed in the Old Testament also restrained evil persons. This produced social order, but also was an aid to those whom God had chosen to be saved.

They felt compelled by fear to obey the Law even before God had converted their hearts to inward obedience. Calvin also believed that the Law revealed the will of God to believers. As a result, the Law must be studied and obeyed.

Calvin developed a strong doctrine of *predestination*. Traditional predestination teaches that some were chosen "before the foundations of the earth were laid" for salvation. Calvin extended this even further by preaching a type of **double predestination,** which means some were chosen to be saved while others were chosen to be damned. According to Calvin, God's choices cannot be understood because the ways of God are a great mystery that cannot be grasped by humans. A mighty gulf separates God and humans. People's actions could not affect their fate. A person could live like a saint, attend church, forsake pleasure, help the needy, and engage in prayer, sacraments, and worship. In the end, God might arbitrarily choose to damn that person. Another person could live like the devil, pursue pleasure, greed, and lust, and hate the church. At death, God might choose to save that person.

Calvin regarded those chosen by God as the *elect*. The elect are those redeemed by Christ. Christ died for all people; yet, only the elect benefited from His saving death. (The sovereign God sending His Son to die for all, but only the elect benefited is another of those mysterious paradoxes that Calvin did not resolve). Calvin believed the benefits of Christ are made available to the elect through the inner, secret operations of the Holy Spirit in their hearts. The main activity of the Holy Spirit is to produce faith in Christ. This faith is firm and sure. It is the deep awareness of the love of God toward the saved. It is revealed to the mind and sealed on the heart by the Holy Spirit. In part, faith is what one believes in the mind; in part, it is the inner assurance of one's salvation. Calvin also taught justification by faith. Calvin believed Christ's justification is imputed to the sinner, but justification still results in a change in the character of the believer. Christ works in the heart of the believer to produce obedience to God. The image of God in humans that was deformed by sin is slowly restored.

Calvin held that there is both a visible and an invisible church. The *visible church* is the institution apparent to everyone in the world. However, it contains both the elect and non-elect. The *invisible church* is the real church that contains only the elect. It is impossible to separate the elect from the non-elect. That will only be revealed at the end of time. Preaching and administering the sacraments are signs of the invisible church. Personal holiness is not a sign of the real church as the Anabaptists taught. Christians still remain sinners despite their efforts to submit to God's rule. Calvin believed that the church must be restored to the conditions of primitive Christianity as found in the New Testament. However, Calvin did not believe that it was possible to return to the actual conditions of first-century Christianity. Instead, he felt that the patterns of church order and discipline of the early church should be restored.

Calvin held there were two sacraments—baptism and the Lord's Supper. He took a middle ground on the sacraments. They were not merely symbolic as in Zwingli's teaching, nor. did they "bring down" grace as Luther and the Catholics taught. Like Zwingli and the Anabaptists, Calvin believed that the sacraments bore witness to the sacrifice of Christ. However, their main purpose was to feed the faith of the believer who took them. The sacraments did that through the activity of the Holy Spirit who "lifted up" the faithful to participate in union with Christ and God's grace.

Baptism washes away sin and also sustains the elect throughout their lives. Not only is original and past sin washed away, but baptism also cleansed future sins. Baptism could do this because the believer was not only being washed in water, but also in the eternal blood of Christ. Infant baptism was acceptable. People could be baptized by immersion in water or by sprinkling water on them.

The Lord's Supper provides invisible food for the soul through partaking of the body and blood of Christ. The Supper integrates believers into the society of Christ's church and also makes the elect Christ's by providing the means for him adopting believers as his own. The Lord's Supper assures believers that Christ's sacrifice was once and for all, and his sacrifice continually provides food for Christian living. The Supper is a meal that produces spiritual union with Christ by the action of God's Spirit. Although the meal makes available the "body and blood of Christ," the elements do not literally become the flesh and blood of Christ. Rather, the faithful are "elevated" to heaven to partake of the heavenly body of Christ. Finally, the communion meal also is a foretaste of that great banquet at the end of time when Christ invites all of his elect to dine with him in the Kingdom of God.[3]

CONCLUSIONS

Abuses in the Catholic church spurred widespread recognition of the need to reform. The fifteenth-century conciliar movement was largely ineffective at producing the needed changes. Luther's opposition to common abuses of his day generated excitement throughout the Continent. Dissatisfied Christians rallied to his cause. Some of the German princes identified with his religious convictions and used his popularity to offset the power of the emperor.

Ulrich Zwingli and John Calvin capitalized on the same discontent to start reform in Switzerland. Zwingli's and Calvin' theology was similar to Luther's but it disagreed significantly on some points. Efforts to reconcile the two branches of the emerging Reformation failed. Luther and Calvin came to be recognized as the leaders of two separate movements in Protestantism. The following chapter examines two other branches of the Reformation and assesses the impact of the Reformation on the church at large and on Western society.

Notes

1. Some historians believe that the only posting done that day was Luther mailing the theses to his bishop. They feel the "church door" scene is just a dramatic legend.

2. Luther's arguments were based in part on the Renaissance idea of studying manuscripts in the original texts. The Vulgate as well as the Bible used in the Eastern church were based on the Septuagint, a Greek translation of the Hebrew Bible done in Alexandria for Jews living outside the Holy Land. This version contained several books not found in earlier Hebrew canons. Interestingly, when Saint Jerome (ca. 342–420) was compiling a new Latin Bible that became the Vulgate, he insisted that translations be made directly from the Hebrew. He completed part of this Bible. However, the Vulgate, which probably was compiled in the sixth century, contained his new translations as well as older translations from the Greek. This mixing left a corrupted text that was a source of controversy well into the Reformation. Luther was building on this age-old controversy, which had been heightened by the Renaissance. Many who stayed in the Catholic church disputed the same books as Luther. The "conservatives" won out at the Council of Trent, which confirmed the Vulgate as the official Catholic Bible. The Eastern church accepts those books found in the Septuagint.

3. For a good discussion of the theology of Luther and Calvin, see Justo L. González, *A History of Christian Thought*, vol. 3, *From the Protestant Reformation to the Twentieth Century*. New York: Abingdon, 1975. For Luther, see pp. 25–62; for Calvin, see pp. 120–161.

Additional Readings

Bainton, Roland H. *Here I Stand: A Life of Martin Luther*. Nashville: Abingdon, 1950.
———. *The Reformation of the Sixteenth Century*. Boston: Beacon, 1952.
———. *Women of the Reformation in Germany and Italy*. Minneapolis: Ausburg, 1971.
———. *Women of the Reformation in France and England*. Minneapolis: Ausburg, 1973.
Battles, Ford Lewis and John R. Walchen. *Analysis of the Institutes of the Christian Religion of Jesus Christ*. Reprint. Phillipsburg, NJ: P&R, 2002.
Becker, Reinhard P. ed. *German Humanist and Reformation: Selected Writings*. New York: Continuum, 1982.
Calvin, John. *Institutes of the Christian Religion*. Translated by J. T. McNeill. Philadelphia: Westminster, 1960.
Collinson, Partick. *The Reformation (Modern Library Chronicles Series): A History*. New York: Random House, 2004.
Erikson, Erik. *Young Man Luther*. New York: Norton, 1962.
Furcha, E. J. and H. Wayne Pipkin, eds. *Prophet, Pastor, Protestant: The Work of Huldrych Zwingli after Five Hundred Years*. Eugene, OR: WIPF and Stock, 1984.
Grant, Arthur James. *The Huguenots*. Hamden, CT: Archon, 1969.
Hendrix, Scott H. *Luther and the Papacy: Stages in a Reformation Conflict*. Philadelphia: Fortress, 1981.
Luther, Martin. *Luther's Works*. Edited by J. Pelikan and H. Lehman. 55 volumes. St. Louis: Concordia, 1955.
Manschreck, Clyde L. *Melanchthon: The Quiet Reformer*. New York: Abingdon, 1958.
Neill, Stephen. *Colonialism and Christian Missions*. London: Lutterworth, 1966.
Ridley, Jasper. *John Knox*. New York: Oxford University Press, 1968.
Rilliet, Jean H. *Zwingli: Third Man of the Reformation*. London: Lutterworth, 1964.

Stark, Rodney. *For the Glory of God: How Monotheism Led to Reformation, Science, Witch-Hunts, and the End of Slavery*. Princeton, NJ: Princeton University Press, 2004.
Wilson, Douglas and George Grand, eds. *For Kirk and Covenant: The Stalwart Courage of John Knox*. Nashville, TN: Cumberland, 2000.

Websites

http://en.wikipedia.org/widi/Protestant_Reformation [Provides articles on discussion of the Reformation and links to materials about specific topics regarding the Reformation]
http://www.msu.edu/homepages/laurence/reformation [Provides links to original writings as well as material about the reformers and different branches of the Reformation]
www.hanover.edu/early/prot.html [Provides links to original documents of the Reformation as well as articles about the reformers and the Reformation]

9

THE PROTESTANT REFORMATION

Further Reform and Reaction (1500–1600 C.E.)

The persecution of early Anabaptists

While followers of Luther and Calvin were reforming their faith in Germany and Switzerland, other groups on the Continent and in England were promoting renewals and redefinitions of Christianity. These groups fall into two broad branches of Protestantism—Anglicans and Anabaptists. In England, Protestantism took the form of the Anglican or English Reformation. In the end, the English church retained more of its Catholic traditions than did other Protestant denominations. At the other extreme are several diverse groups lumped together by scholars under the label *Anabaptists*. Because the Anabaptists represent the most significant departure from Catholic tradition, they also are referred to as the *Radical Reformation* or the *left wing* of the Reformation.

We first consider the English (Anglican) Reformation and then study the Anabaptists. We then review the Catholic reaction to Protestantism, known as the Catholic Reformation or the Counter-Reformation. We also examine the immediate aftermath of the Reformation, the Orthodox church during the period, and the state of Christianity at the close of the sixteenth century.

THE ENGLISH REFORMATION

Both Lutheranism and the Reformed church had strong theological bases, although political forces also played a role in their formation. The English Reformation was somewhat different. The movement was fueled by religious ideas from the Continent and earlier English reform traditions such as those changes advocated by Wycliffe and by nationalistic ideas. In many ways, the **Anglican** Reformation was a political movement with religious overtones. It was partly an excuse for the assertion of nationalism. The early Reformation in England was the result of the struggle between King Henry VIII and the pope concerning Henry's desire for a male heir.

Henry VIII and the Early Reformation

Henry VIII had no original intention of breaking with the Catholic church. He was not impressed with the Reformation. In fact, he had written an essay against the Lutherans that had won him the title "Defender of the Faith" from the pope. Henry's break was because of his marriage to Catherine of Aragon. Henry's father had initially married his oldest son Arthur to Catherine (a daughter of Ferdinand and Isabella) to seal an alliance between Spain and England. Arthur died four months after the wedding. The English and Spanish then agreed to have Catherine marry her husband's younger brother, Henry, who was then heir to the English throne. Because church law forbade the marriage of a man to his brother's widow, it was necessary to obtain a **dispensation** (an exception from church law) from the pope.

The pope granted the dispensation. Henry married Catherine as soon as he was old enough in 1509. The marriage was not happy. To make matters worse, five of their six children died. The surviving child and heir to the throne was a girl, Mary Tudor. A woman had never ruled England. Henry convinced himself that the failure to produce a male heir was a divine judgment on an illegitimate union. He requested an annulment of the marriage on the ground that the pope should not have granted a legal dispensation. The annulment would have left Henry free to marry another woman (and to produce more heirs). Catherine was the aunt of Charles V, the Holy Roman emperor. The pope could not risk offending Charles because imperial armies dominated Italy. So he refused to grant the annulment.

Acting on the advice of Thomas Cranmer (1489–1556), Henry submitted the case to the universities for their ruling. Henry argued that Leviticus 21:14 forbade a man from marrying his brother's widow. The pope could give dispensations from church law but not from the law of God. After many negotiations, most of the major universities came out in favor of Henry. Henry put away Catherine (1533) and shortly married Anne Boleyn. Henry then forced the clergy in England to submit to him. He had the pope name Cranmer the archbishop of Canterbury. Henry's efforts at change were supported by those who opposed papal interference in English life and by those who supported Wycliffe's vision of a national church under the king.

A series of laws was passed that established the church under the king's control and prevented appeals to Rome. The final break came in 1534 when the English Parliament passed the Supremacy Act, which made Henry the supreme head of the English church. Anyone who produced a schism or was a heretic was declared a traitor. Sir Thomas More, the lord chancellor of England and a humanistic scholar, refused to swear an oath to Henry as head of the church. More had been one of Henry's personal friends. He was executed in 1535 because of his convictions. In 1935 he was declared a saint in the Catholic church.

In 1534 Henry also took measures that would eventually lead to suppressing and seizing the property of monasteries. His instrument in this and many of his other changes was Thomas Cromwell (1485–1540). Most of the property taken from monasteries was sold to raise funds for the royal treasury. Parliament also decreed that Mary Tudor was illegitimate and that the infant daughter of Anne Boleyn, Elizabeth, was the heir to the throne. Anne soon fell out of favor and was beheaded. Henry went on to marry four other women. His third wife, Jane Seymour, finally produced a son, Edward. His sixth and last wife, Catherine Parr, was a supporter of reform who helped promote Protestant reform ideas.

Henry did little to produce real reform during his reign. In fact, he tried to keep the church closely aligned with Catholic practices except in its submission to the pope. Reform ideas did spread throughout the land. Some were supported by the Crown. Cranmer commissioned a new English translation of the Bible. Henry ordered the English Bible to be placed in every church so people could read it. Henry was fairly brutal in enforcing his religious policies. Hundreds were arrested and some died.

Edward VI and Mary Tudor

Henry's death in 1547 left his nine-year-old son Edward VI (1547–1553) on the throne. Edward was a sickly child who ruled for six years. He was directed by a sixteen-member council of regents composed of eight Catholics and eight Reformers. In reality, the young king and the policies of England were dominated by Cranmer and Edward Seymour, the duke of Somerset. Both were inclined to the Reformers' position. Cranmer and Somerset sponsored several bills that put reform principles in law. English instead of Latin was used in worship. Priests were permitted to marry. The laity received the cup during the Eucharist. Relics and images were removed. The Lutheran view on justification by faith was accepted.

Cranmer produced the *Book of Common Prayer,* which was the first comprehensive liturgy in English. In 1549, the first Act of Uniformity imposed the *Book of Common Prayer* as the worship book in all Anglican (English) churches. This book maintained a number of Catholic doctrines and practices. Protestant ideas incorporated in it followed Lutheran lines. However, Cranmer also invited a number of Continental scholars to England. Many were from the Reformed tradition. Soon these ideas began to have an impact. In 1552, a revised edition of the *Book of Common Prayer* came out that was more Zwinglian in its emphasis. It looked as if the Reformers would dominate.

The situation in England changed when Mary Tudor (1553–1558) succeeded to the throne upon Edward's death. Mary always had been a Catholic—partly because of religious commitment and partly because her claim to the throne depended upon it. The Catholics had always recognized the marriage of Catherine and Henry as legitimate. That made Mary the rightful heir to the Crown. Many English regarded her as the legitimate heir and supported her claim. Mary saw this support as a desire for a return of the country to Catholicism. She obtained additional assistance for returning to Catholicism from bishops who had been deposed under earlier regimes, from her cousin Charles V, and from her marriage to Philip of Spain, who later was king of Spain.

In 1554 Mary officially returned England's obedience to the pope. Most reforms undertaken by Henry and Edward were destroyed. She persecuted the

Social Sources of Denominationalism

This book has stressed institutional and theological developments within Christianity and has noted the important role of political and cultural elements in various theological debates. Ernest Troeltsch, Max Weber, H. Richard Niebuhr, and others have demonstrated that sociological factors influence theology and the religious structures that emerge.

For instance, Niebuhr believes that social structure profoundly affects the emergence of denominations. Denominations are a product of social class, racial/ethnic groupings, regional divisions within nations, and nationalism itself. Often these characteristics interact to create religious divisions. A look at a few of his ideas about the churches of the disinherited (the have-nots of society) should illustrate his argument.

Niebuhr holds that over time denominations become established and comfortable in society. That even happened to Christianity as the church gained acceptance in the Roman Empire. When a denomination becomes established, its membership tends to be drawn from relatively well-off people. As that happens religion becomes "comfortable." It departs from any radical interpretation of the Gospel. Ethics become very tolerant of the world. Morality becomes little more than doing what is respectable by the standards of the prevailing society. Life in the hereafter lessens in importance; living a good life in this world becomes more important. The religion becomes very accepting of the existing society. It seldom criticizes injustices or attacks the powerful. Educated clergy concentrate on the fine points of theology and liturgy. Much of the zeal leaves the faith.

Protestants and 300 Protestant leaders were burned. Many others were imprisoned or went into exile. These persecutions earned her the title "Bloody Mary."

One well-known martyr was Thomas Cranmer. Mary was determined to break him because of his central role in the previous reform efforts. She forced him to sign a document recanting his earlier views and planned to have him killed as an example to those who might follow in his steps. He was taken to a wooden platform to be burned and was given an opportunity to speak. He was expected to ask forgiveness for his errors. Instead, he denied his recantation and condemned the pope as the Antichrist. As flames blazed around him,

As faith becomes more comfortable, the denomination's religion loses its appeal to the disinherited. Life for them is difficult. They receive few benefits from the existing social system. The disinherited rebel against the religion of the affluent. They establish a faith that better meets their ethical, sociological, and psychological needs. To the disinherited, this world is evil. Stress is placed on the world that is to come where there will be plenty of material goods. Suffering will cease. The world to come will be inherited by the weak, meek, and poor. Those with wealth and position in the present world will have a lowly place in the hereafter, if they are not cast into eternal damnation. The disinherited of the present world will be elevated and rewarded for their faithfulness.

The faith of the disinheriteds emphasizes spiritual experience over orthodox beliefs. Its clergy are not formally educated. Worship services are emotional and spontaneous. Few set forms are followed. Ethics are rigid and stress being different from the world. Nonetheless, Niebuhr believes that hard work and avoidance of pleasure, which are part of these ethics, produces economic prosperity. As members become more established economically, the character of their religion changes. It becomes another comfortable faith of the middle class. New churches of the disinherited must arise to aid the needy and to present faithfully the radical demands of the Gospel.

Source: H. Richard Niebuhr, *The Social Sources of Denominationalism* (Hamden, CT: Shoe String, 1954).

the aging bishop held his hand that had signed the recantation in the fire until the flesh fell away. He became a great hero of the Protestant cause.

Elizabeth and the Elizabethan Settlement

When Mary died in 1558 she was succeeded by her half sister, Elizabeth I (1558–1603), the daughter of Henry and Anne Boleyn. Elizabeth reversed most of Mary's policies. She was a Protestant in part because her claim to the throne depended on the Reformers' position. Elizabeth chose a moderate position.

Her middle way (*via media*) condemned Catholic teachings and practices, but it also forbade extreme Protestantism. This middle way came to be called the **Elizabethan Settlement.** Elizabeth compiled a new *Book of Common Prayer,* which included as wide a range of positions as possible. For example, the teaching on the Eucharist was so broadly written that almost all Protestant groups could accept it. This "inclusiveness" has been an attribute of the Anglican church ever since.

Catholicism continued under Elizabeth, and the Catholics were the source of several plots against Elizabeth and the Protestants. Many of these plots centered around Mary Stuart (the queen of Scotland), whom they wanted to place on the English throne. Elizabeth persecuted those who opposed her politically. Because religion was such an integral part of the political situation, she was guilty of persecuting religious dissidents in the name of protecting her throne. The total number who died during Elizabeth's reign is close to the number who died during Bloody Mary's reign.

Toward the end of Elizabeth's reign, the Puritans began to emerge. The **Puritans** were a group who felt that the middle way of Elizabeth did not go far enough. They wanted to reject the Elizabethan Settlement and purify the church of all popish elements. They wanted to impose strict Calvinistic doctrines on the Church of England. The Puritans would play a major role in the seventeenth century.[1]

THE ANABAPTISTS

The Anabaptists were the fourth main branch of the Reformation. **Anabaptist** means rebaptize. It was a name given in the sixteenth century to Reformers who insisted on baptizing only those who were old enough to make a conscious decision to accept Christ. That was known as "believer's baptism." They rejected infant baptism and "rebaptized" those professing salvation by Christ. Later scholars would also call this branch the **Radical Reformation** and the **left wing of the Reformation.**

The Early Anabaptists

The Anabaptists belonged to a very diverse, widespread movement and may have had many sources. Some argue that the Anabaptists date back to the Waldenses and the Cathari, heretical groups discussed in Chapter 7. Still others see the origins of the movement in the work of Bodenstein von Karlstadt, who left Luther to participate in radical reforms among the peasants. Other scholars believe Anabaptists began as a peasants' movement headed by Thomas Muntzer (ca. 1490–1525).

The main body of the movement probably originated as a reaction against Zwingli's reforms in Zurich by Conrad Grebel (1498–1526) and Felix Manz (1498–1527). Grebel and Manz were at first attracted to Zwingli's work. They became convinced that Scripture alone was the basis for the true church and began study of the Greek and Hebrew testaments in private homes. Soon they decided the church must be purified of all popish trappings. Zwingli did not go far enough in his reforms. For instance, he taught that baptism was symbolic but continued to practice infant baptism. Zwingli was bothered by their criticisms and faced several of the dissenters in debate before the town council in 1525. The council ordered Grebel and Manz to cease their meetings and demanded that all adults have their infants baptized or leave town.

This action did not stop the efforts of the brethren. (Several of these Anabaptist groups chose to call themselves *brethren* to distinguish themselves from people who became Christians by being born in Christian lands.) George Blaurock, an early convert and leader, asked Grebel to baptize him at the fountain in the square at Zurich. He in turn baptized several others. Initially this believer's baptism was done by sprinkling or pouring water over the head. Later Anabaptists would insist on baptism by immersion in water, as was done in the Scriptures.

Anabaptist ideas became widespread. Soon there were followers throughout Switzerland and southern Germany. Severe persecution was carried out against the early Anabaptists. Most of their early leaders suffered martyrdom. Manz became the first of many Anabaptist martyrs when he was drowned by the order of the Zurich town council in 1527. Ordinary men, women, and children also met similar fates at the hands of Lutherans, Calvinists, and Catholics. Many were burned at the stake while others were drowned. Drowning was considered especially appropriate given the radicals' tendency to baptize by immersion. As many as 50,000 Anabaptists had died for their faith by 1535. The total number of martyrs was probably greater than all of the Christians who died in the first three centuries of Roman persecution. Despite persecution, the movement continued to grow.

On the whole, the early Anabaptists were a peaceful group. They practiced **pacifism** (refused to go to war or take up arms). They wanted to return to the simplicity of the early church, practiced a direct personal spirituality, and were content to live and let live as long as they were left alone to practice their faith. Some even withdrew from society into communes. Given these characteristics, it is difficult to understand why religious and secular leaders reacted so strongly against them. The leaders, however, saw the Anabaptists as undermining both religious and secular authority. Anabaptists refused to recognize the authority of the state. They were citizens of the kingdom of God. They would not serve in the army or swear oaths. They refused to accept the idea that society could be really Christian. They rejected the union of church and state that had existed since Constantine. Many of the groups practiced a radical **egalitarianism** in which all were equal.

Women were equal to men. The poor and uneducated were equal to the rich and well educated. Many of these ideas contradicted the "Christian societies" that Catholics, Lutherans, and Calvinists sought to build.

The Radical Anabaptists

As many of the early Anabaptist leaders were killed, the movement became more radical. Many became convinced that the Day of the Lord—when the second coming of Christ would occur—was near. Melchior Hoffman (1495–1543) was one of these believers. Hoffman was a former Lutheran pastor who drifted into the Anabaptist movement. He preached extensively in southern Germany and Holland. In Holland his followers came to be called **Melchiorites.** He became convinced that the Day of the Lord would happen in 1534. A German "prophet" had a vision that Hoffman would go to Strassburg, be arrested, and the second coming would happen. Hoffman hastened to Strassburg, was arrested, and placed in prison. However, Christ did not return and Hoffman probably died in prison.

One of his followers, Jan Matthys, broke with Hoffman to establish his own violent attempt to bring about the Day of the Lord. He was convinced that the kingdom of God would be established with its capital, the New Jerusalem, in Münster. There he established a dictatorial regime known as the kingdom of Saints. He had daily "revelations" by which he directed the city. Among other activities, he drove out the sick and old and killed his critics.

Soon the city was surrounded by an army composed of Protestants and Catholics raised by the local bishop and Matthys was killed. Jan Bockelson (also known as John of Leiden) took over leadership of the city. He too ruled by "revelations" from God. Many men were killed fighting against the bishop's army. This left an excess of women so Bockelson decreed that **polygyny** (the marriage of one man to several women) would be the rule as in parts of the Old Testament. He took fifteen wives and declared himself the new King David of the new Jerusalem.

In June of 1535, the city was betrayed and fell to the besieging army. Women and children were driven from the city, but all the men were massacred. Bockelson and two other leaders were captured and imprisoned. A year and a half later they were tortured to death. Their bodies were placed in iron cages to hang from the front of Saint Lambert's Church until they rotted. These cages still hang from the church.

Other Anabaptists: Moderate and Radical

The violent commune at Münster was short-lived, but it left Anabaptists labeled as dangerous revolutionaries in the minds of many. Fortunately, a group of more moderate Anabaptists were emerging who would restore the movement. One was Menno Simons (1496–1561). Simons was a Catholic priest who joined a Dutch Anabaptist group. He was a capable preacher and organizer who collected a large following; eventually his followers would be called *Mennonites*. Menno was persecuted but survived to preach in Holland and surrounding areas. His teachings were similar to the Swiss brethren. He was a pacifist who urged his followers to submit to civil authorities as long as they were not required to do anything that contradicted the Bible. Despite their moderation, the Mennonites were persecuted. They were driven out of Holland to Poland, then to Russia, and then to North America where they sought to practice their religion in freedom.

Even in Russia and North America, Mennonites encountered difficulties with authorities, mainly because of their refusal to serve in the military. In the nineteenth and twentieth centuries many moved to South America, seeking isolation from the rest of society. Today many people respect Mennonites because of their efforts at social service. The Mennonites have organized themselves to perform various kinds of relief services and rely on volunteers from their denomination. During natural disasters such as floods, the Mennonites are often the first to arrive and the last to leave, offering help to the needy regardless of their national origin, race, or religious beliefs.

Jacob Huter (d. 1536) became the leader of another group of Anabaptists. Huter was a Swiss pastor who fled to Moravia to join Anabaptists there. The groups settled at Bruderhofs and established a communal society where they lived simply and practiced the Gospel. Although the group was pacifistic, Huter was burned at the stake and the "Hutterites" were persecuted. The group survived, however, and eventually they spread to the New World in the quest for religious freedom.

The spiritualists were another cathegory of Anabaptists. They were so different in their views that it is difficult to make general comments about them. They tended to be mystical and several of their leaders were influenced by Erasmus. To them the work of the Spirit of Christ was more important than either the church or the Scriptures. The child of God was guided by direct revelations from the Spirit to the heart. This revelation was an "inner light" that gave direction and assurance of salvation. It challenged individuals to simple and strict, but loving, lifestyles. Many spiritualists, but not all, rejected the authority of both the church and the state. Most wanted to return to the true faith of the early church. Caspar Schwenckfeld (1489–1561), Sebastian Franck (ca. 1499–1542), and Juan de Valdés (ca. 1500–1541) were among the most influential of the spiritualists. In the seventeenth century, George Fox (1649– 1691) adapted spiritualist ideas and formed the Society of Friends of the Truth, or the Quakers, as they are better known.

A different approach was taken by a group of dissenters sometimes called the *rationalists*. The rationalists disagreed with traditional doctrines mainly because they thought certain teachings were unreasonable or contradicted Scripture.

An Anabaptist's Letter

The Anabaptists frequently faced martyrdom with great courage. They exhibited a patient love toward their enemies that often baffles modern people. At the same time, it is difficult for us to understand why the Anabaptists' opponents objected so fiercely to them. Nowhere is the courage and gentleness of the Anabaptists more apparent than in the following passages. These are excerpts from a moving letter from Elizabeth, a Dutch Anabaptist martyr, to her one-month-old daughter. Elizabeth was in prison for her faith and died soon after writing the letter.

> [Testament] written to Janneken my own dearest daughter, while I was (unworthily) confined for the Lord's sake, in prison, at Antwerp, a.d. 1573

> My dear little child, I commend you to the almighty, great and terrible God, who is wise, that He will keep you, and let you grow up in His fear, or that He will take you home in your youth, this is my heart's request of the Lord: you who are yet so young, and whom I must leave here in this wicked, evil, perverse world . . . I will commend you to the Lord; let Him do with you according to His holy will.

> Hence, my dear lamb, I who am imprisoned and bound here for the Lord's sake, can help you in no other way; I had to leave your father for the Lord's sake, and could keep him only a short time. We were permitted to live together only half a year, after which we were apprehended, because we sought the salvation of our souls.

> Since I am now delivered up to death, and must leave you here alone, I must through these lines cause you to remember, that when you have attained your understanding, you endeavor to fear God, and see and examine why and for whose name we both died: and be not ashamed to confess us before the world, for you must know that it is not for the sake of any evil. Hence be not ashamed of us; it is the way which the prophets and the apostles went, and the narrow way which leads into eternal life, for there shall no other way be found by which to be saved.

If you seek your salvation, it is easy to perceive which is the way that leads to life, or the way that leads into hell. Above all things seek the kingdom of heaven and His righteousness . . . conduct yourself well and honestly, so that no one need have cause to complain of you . . . see that you like to work.

Hence, my dear Janneken, do not accustom your mouth to filthy talk, nor to ugly words that are not proper, not to lies; for a liar has no part in the kingdom of heaven . . . run not in the street as other bad children do; rather take up a book, and learn to seek there that which concerns your salvation.

And where you have your home, obey those whose bread you eat. If they speak evil, do you speak well. And learn always to love to be doing something; and do not think yourself too good for anything, nor exalt yourself, but condescend to the lowly, and always honor the aged wherever you are.

My dear lamb, we can merit nothing, but must through grace inherit salvation; hence always endeavor to fear God, for the fear of the Lord is the beginning of wisdom, and he that fears the Lord will do good, and it will be well with him in this world and in that which is to come.

And now, Janneken, my dear lamb, who are yet very little and young, I leave you this letter . . . and this I leave you for a perpetual adieu, and for a testament; that you may remember me by it.

. . . And I herewith bid you adieu, my Dear Janneken Munstdorp, and kiss you heartily . . . with a perpetual kiss of peace. Follow me and your father, and be not ashamed to confess us before the world, for we were not ashamed to confess our faith, since it is the true evangelical faith, another than which shall never be found.

Some rationalists also had spiritualist traits. Several were convinced that the doctrine of the Trinity was not reasonable and was not found in the Bible. Michael Servetus was one of the most important rationalists. Even though Servetus was deeply religious, he still came to believe the doctrine of the Trinity was wrong. He was from Spain, where Trinitarian teachings were problematic for Jews and Muslims. This Moorish influence, combined with his humanism and Protestant efforts to return to original sources, led him to reject the Trinity. He fled the Spanish Inquisition only to be burned at the stake by Calvin in Geneva. Servetus' anti-Trinitarian concepts were embraced by other Anabaptists. The most important of these was Faustus Socinus (1539–1604), who took anti-Trinitarianism to Poland where he won a number of followers. After his death Socinus' disciples wrote down his ideas in the Rakovian Catechism. Socinus' ideas had a strong impact on the emergence of Unitarianism in seventeenth-century England.[2]

THE CATHOLIC REFORMATION

Some refer to the changes in the Catholic church during the sixteenth century as the Counter-Reformation. Much of what went on was a reaction against Protestantism. In some ways, the Catholic church came out of the century as a highly conservative institution. It would react negatively to almost every major change in religion and society over the next 400 years; however, a genuine renewal of the church did occur. The problems and abuses the Protestants rebelled against were widely recognized, and many who remained in the Catholic church sought to remedy them. Efforts to reform the church took several directions, a few of which we examine below.

Renewal Efforts and Spiritual Movements

One early reform effort was undertaken by Girolamo Savonarola (1452–1498) in Florence. Savonarola was active during the reign of one of the most corrupt Renaissance popes, Alexander VI (1492–1503). Conditions were so bad in Rome that they were a scandal throughout the church. Preachers commonly spoke against the corruption. Savonarola was a Dominican friar who settled in Florence. His fiery preaching became so popular that for a time he virtually controlled the city. He attempted to produce such a strong discipline that even marriage was discouraged. People were encouraged to burn such vanities as art, books, and elaborate clothing. Many did so. His activities produced anger among the local politicians and the papacy. He was burned as a heretic in

1498, but he remained a popular hero. The politicians and church officials disliked him so vehemently that the bell at Saint Mark's Church, which called people to hear his preaching, was removed, publicly flogged, and banished from the city forever!

A move toward lasting renewal was instigated in Spain by Cardinal Ximénes with the support of Queen Isabella. Ximénes was an austere Franciscan devoted to spiritual renewal. He eventually became the queen's confessor and was named a Spanish cardinal. Ximénes undertook a wide-ranging program of reform that increased discipline and education among the clergy. He founded the University of Alcalá, which advanced humanistic studies, theology, and medicine. He was a staunch conservative who hated anything that departed from orthodoxy or threatened the unity of the church. Ximénes led Crusades against Muslims, Jews, and Judaizers (converted Jews who continued to practice Judaism). He formed the Spanish Inquisition to abolish heresy. The Inquisition started a violent campaign against dissenters. As a result, 2500 were killed, 40,000 were imprisoned and tortured, and as many as 200,000 were sent into exile. The Spanish reform became a model for the rest of the church.

A less-violent renewal took the form of numerous spiritual movements in the Catholic church. A significant one was the Oratory of Divine Love founded in Rome in 1517. The Oratory was a group of sixty clergy and laypeople who committed themselves to reforming their lives and those around them. They dedicated themselves to discipline and met frequently for prayer, discussion, and preaching. They also dedicated themselves to almsgiving and care for the needy and founded orphanages and hospitals. The Oratory taught against simony, pluralism, worldly bishops, and lax living.

Their beliefs generated oratories throughout Europe. Several people from the Oratory became leaders in the church. Gasparo Contarini (1483–1542) attempted humanistic reforms and advocated reconciliation with the Protestants. He even met with Melanchthon and worked out a program for reuniting Lutherans and Catholics. The program was rejected by both sides. Giovanni Caraffa was another member of the Oratory who represented the opposite extreme. He became Pope Paul IV (1555–1559) and was noted for his staunch conservatism, his total rejection of Protestantism, and his support of the use of force against dissenters.

Mystics also were active in renewing spirituality throughout Europe. Saint Teresa of Avila (1515–1582) and Saint John of the Cross (1542–1591) were two well-known mystics. Teresa, a native of Avila, probably was the most important woman in Spanish history. She joined the Carmelite convent just outside Avila but was dissatisfied with the quality of the spiritual life there. She dedicated herself to study of devotional books to find a deeper spirituality but found little comfort there and received little assistance from her confessors. In her distress, she had the first of several visions of Jesus. She eventually experienced mystical union, or "spiritual marriage," with him. She undertook a significant reform of the Carmelites, which resulted in the founding of a stricter order. She also founded a male order of Carmelites, and, in so doing, was the only woman ever to form a monastic order for men. Her *Autobiography* and *The Way of Perfection* are two of the greatest mystical works.

Teresa was assisted in her work by Saint John of the Cross. John believed that for the soul to be filled with God it must first empty itself. With great insight into human nature, he detailed the painful process this fulfillment involved. John believed that only a few could reach the spiritual heights he thought were possible. Nevertheless, his works, including the *Ascent of Mount Carmel*, the *Dark Night of the Soul*, and the *Living Flame of Love*, served as profound guides to the mystical life for untold numbers. He and Teresa were made saints and doctors (teachers) of the church.

Loyola and the Jesuits

The new monastic orders founded by Saint Teresa and Saint John were but two of many that were created in the sixteenth century. The most important of these to the later history of the church was one founded by Ignatius of Loyola (1491–1556). Loyola was a Spanish noble who had dreamed of obtaining fame and fortune in the military. His leg was broken by a cannonball in 1521 during a fight against the French. His long, painful recovery was difficult because his leg had to be rebroken and reset. A piece of bone that was sticking through the skin had to be sawn off. These procedures were done without anesthesia.

Loyola experienced great turmoil during his recovery. He read a life of Christ by a Saxon Carthusian and a volume on the lives of the saints. These, along with his own meditations, led him to a fateful event. One night he had a vision of Mary and the Holy Christ Child in which all the torment of his soul temporarily was erased. He vowed that he would become such a soldier of Christ that he would surpass all of the deeds of the saints. He journeyed to the Benedictine abbey at Montserrat where he diligently confessed his sins, gave away his mule, clothes, dagger, and sword, and dressed in the sackcloth of a pilgrim. His spiritual struggle continued at the Dominican house in Manresa, where he prayed, took confession, and read spiritual works, including à Kempis' *Imitation of Christ*. This book would have a profound impact upon him. Eventually he felt God was leading him to Jerusalem to minister to the poor and convert the Muslims. The Franciscans who were already in Jerusalem feared the fiery newcomer and soon drove him out.

When he returned to France he studied theology so he could be better prepared for God's work. In only four years, he advanced from a boys' school to the University of Paris where he earned a master of arts degree. In Paris several men were attracted by his zeal and spiritual discipline, but others were suspicious. He was investigated three times by the Inquisition but that did not stop him. In 1534 he and a group of his followers took solemn vows of poverty and chastity. They resolved to go to the Holy Land to aid the poor. When ministry in the Holy Land proved impossible, they decided to form themselves into a new religious order at the disposal of the pope. After some hesitation the pope approved their new order, the Society of Jesus, in 1540. The order would become better known as the **Jesuits.** The new order's close relation to the pope made it a very useful tool.

Loyola's disciples used a set of spiritual exercises that he had created and that eventually became his well-known *Spiritual Exercises.* The exercises have been used extensively by Jesuits and laypeople alike to deepen their spiritual lives. The exercises are dedicated to the idea that the goal of life is completely to serve God and others. This life of service is a means to save the soul. The will is free to serve whomever it chooses. It may be disciplined into serving God and the church. Obedience is expected to the church hierarchy. Any doubts should be expressed in private. The exercises are intended to lead to an in-depth examination of the soul so that it may be brought into complete submission to the Lord. The exercises originally involved a rigorous four-week program, although shortened versions were developed later.

The Jesuits soon became a prime tool for combating heresy. As part of their program to combat heresy, they developed an extensive system of education that started in grade school and extended through the university level. Students were taught a carefully limited curriculum in Latin. Books used in class were thoroughly examined and any heretical ideas were removed. The Jesuits' system encouraged thinking, but it also was intended to bring conformity to orthodox Catholic doctrine. The Jesuits brought a new uniformity and discipline to international education. Their educational system spread throughout Europe, successfully preventing many areas from falling to the Protestants and even reclaimed some regions that had been lost.

The Jesuits also were active in world missions. Francis Xavier (1506–1552) became a successful missionary to India, the Malay Peninsula, and Japan. Matteo Ricci (1552–1610) realized Xavier's dream of evangelizing China. Missions also were established in Southeast Asia, the Philippines, and Africa as well as North and South America. Although the Jesuits were successful, they won a reputation for ruthlessness and lying that left them hated by many Protestants and Catholics. In 1773 the pope dissolved the Society of Jesus. It was not reinstated until 1814.

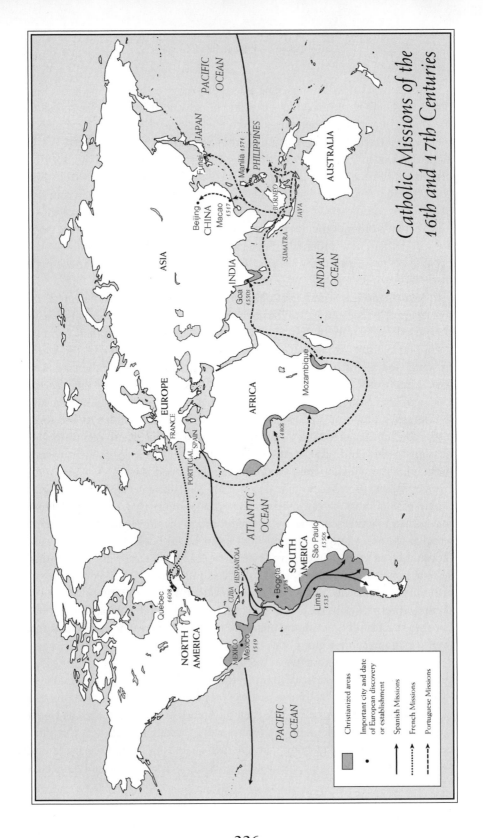

Catholic Missions of the 16th and 17th Centuries

PACIFIC OCEAN

JAPAN
Funai

Manila 1571

PHILIPPINES

Beijing
CHINA
Macao 1517

BORNEO

JAVA

SUMATRA

AUSTRALIA

ASIA

INDIA
Goa 1550s

INDIAN OCEAN

Mozambique

AFRICA

1480s

EUROPE
FRANCE
PORTUGAL SPAIN

ATLANTIC OCEAN

NORTH AMERICA

Quebec 1608

CUBA HISPANIOLA

MEXICO
Mexico 1519

PACIFIC OCEAN

Bogotá 1538
SOUTH AMERICA
São Paulo 1550s

Lima 1535

Christianized areas

Important city and date of European discovery or establishment

Spanish Missions

French Missions

Portuguese Missions

The Council of Trent

Devoted Catholics had been hoping for a council to deal with abuses in the church since the fifteenth century. The events of the sixteenth century exaggerated the calls for a council. Papal hesitancy and political intrigue delayed a council until midway through the century. Early in the century, moderates in the church seemed to dominate. If these moderates had been in charge of the council, the Protestants might have been won back. By the time the council was finally called, conservatives who took a hard line toward dissenters were in control. Their uncompromising stance left little hope that the church could be brought back together.

Pope Paul III (1534–1549) was finally forced to call a council in 1545 to deal with issues raised by Protestants and Reformers in the Catholic church. This council met off and on at Trent (and other places) until 1563. The Council of Trent was one of the most important in church history, and in many ways it marks the beginning of the modern Catholic church. The questions raised by the Protestants were so extensive that the council had to examine much of the church's theology and practices. Powerful efforts were made to ensure uniformity in doctrine and practice throughout the church. Clerical celibacy was enforced. Steps were taken to eliminate pluralism and simony. Seminaries were established to train priests. There had been no educational requirements for the priesthood until then.

The council responded negatively to almost all of the main objections of the Protestants. It affirmed justification by faith, but said that faith had to be supported by good works. It put tradition on the same level as the Bible as a source of authority. Christian tradition as established by the church fathers and the councils were a means of God's revelation, as was the Bible. It held that the Latin Vulgate with the Apocrypha was the official Scripture for the church. It upheld papal authority and the seven sacraments as the means of bringing grace to humans. It affirmed transubstantiation and the Mass as a sacrifice that benefited the living and the dead. The cup was withheld from the laity. Latin was to be the language of the Mass. Thomas Aquinas became the "official" theologian of the church.[3]

The Immediate Aftermath of the Reformation

The Council of Trent sealed the division between Protestants and Catholics. Many events helped widen the schism. The office of the Inquisition was revived in 1542 to become a powerful tool in the hands of papal forces, especially the Jesuits. Many would-be Reformers were imprisoned, tortured, or burned at the stake by inquisitors. Unfortunately, many innocent people also died simply by

Protestantism and Capitalism

This book has argued that the Protestant Reformation helped give rise to contemporary secular society. The sociologist Max Weber presented an argument that Protestantism contributed significantly to the creation of modern capitalism. Although Weber's ideas have been hotly debated, they deserve repeating.

Weber holds that Calvinism played a key role in the emergence of capitalistic society. Calvin's doctrine of predestination meant that God in his sovereignty chose who was to be saved and who was to be damned. Nothing a person could do would change his or her eternal destiny. But people still had a duty to work hard for the glory of God. Moreover, each person had a particular "calling." This calling meant that the primary place where a person was to work for God was in his or her occupation. People also were to help their neighbors and to faithfully carry out any task assigned. At the same time, pleasure and idleness were to be avoided.

Still, all of these acts did not ensure salvation. People were uncertain about their eternal state. While people could not be sure if they were to be saved or damned, they could have some idea whether they were among the elect should God seem to be working through their efforts. One expression of God's favor was in their work. If people prospered financially, then God must be blessing them and they must be among the chosen. This presented another difficulty. When the "chosen" became wealthy, what were they to do with their excess money? Certainly it should not be spent on expensive material goods or pleasure. Instead, it should be invested to produce more goods and more profits! In a reversal of the traditional Christian teachings of sharing, the accumulation of wealth became a religious duty.

Weber argues that this Protestant ethic (work ethic) is apparent in modern society. True, it has lost much of its religious meaning. Nevertheless, "it rattles around in the gilded cage of capitalism like the ghost of some long-dead canary."

Source: Max Weber, *The Protestant Ethic and the Spirit of Capitalism,* trans. Talcott Parsons (New York: Scribners, 1958).

being suspected of heresy. There was practically no way to prove one's innocence. In 1557, the Inquisition issued the *Index of Forbidden Books,* which was a list of books that could not be read by the faithful. The *Index* continued in one form or another until 1966.

The Reformation also resulted in extensive warfare between Protestants and Catholics. One example of this interfaith strife was the Schmalkaldic War (1546–1547) in Germany (see Chapter 8) that was ended by the Peace of Augsburg, which gave stability to Germany for some time. There was also warfare in the Netherlands, where Philip II of Spain (1556–1598) was ruler. The Netherlands were attracted to Protestantism, especially Calvinism. Philip hated Protestantism and was determined to stop its advance in his northern territories. A rebellion that began in 1565 over high taxes and Spanish interference in religious freedom resulted in a long, bloody conflict that did not end until 1609. The southern areas (Belgium) remained Catholic. The northern regions (Holland) were left in the Protestant camp. Philip also attacked Elizabeth I and Protestants in England. England defeated Spain and destroyed the Spanish Armada in 1588. Philip's defeat not only preserved Protestantism but also left England a major seafaring military power.

Although France was strongly Catholic, a significant Protestant minority existed there. These mainly Calvinistic Protestants were known as the *Huguenots* and were made up of nobles and common people alike. At times the Huguenots were persecuted. The fact that many nobles joined the Protestants made them a political threat. Queen Mother Catherine de' Medici plotted with Catholic leaders to suppress this threat in 1572. Protestant nobles were to attend an important wedding in Paris on Saint Bartholomew's Day (August 24).

When the group was assembled, a church bell rang and the Catholics attacked the unarmed Protestants. Mobs soon entered the action and men, women, children, and infants were slaughtered. Cartloads of bodies were dumped in the River Seine. The killings soon spread to the surrounding countryside. Huguenot homes and churches were attacked. About 8000 Reformers were killed in Paris and another 20,000 died in the surrounding regions. A civil war resulted and dragged on until 1593. In 1598 the king issued the Edict of Nantes, which called for forgetting the horrors of the past and guaranteed religious freedom for the Huguenots. Harassment of Protestants continued in the seventeenth century, however, and in 1685, the Edict of Nantes was revoked. The persecution that resulted caused thousands of Huguenots to flee to England, America, and Germany. Many of the Huguenots were merchants and artisans. This lack of skilled laborers and middle class persons put France at a competitive disadvantage compared to other countries and was a contributing cause of the French Revolution in the eighteenth century.

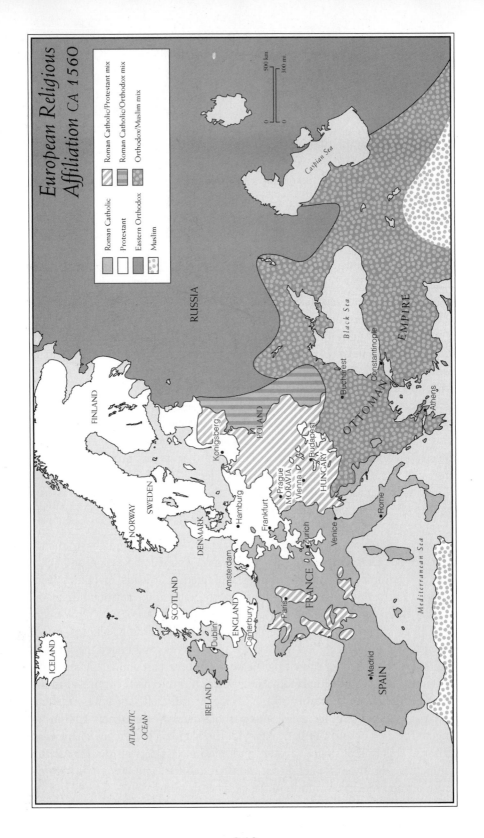

European Religious
Affiliation CA 1560

Roman Catholic
Protestant
Eastern Orthodox
Muslim

Roman Catholic/Protestant mix
Roman Catholic/Orthodox mix
Orthodox/Muslim mix

500 km
300 mi.

RUSSIA

FINLAND

SWEDEN

NORWAY

DENMARK

Königsberg

POLAND

Hamburg

Frankfurt

Prague

MORAVIA

Vienna

Budapest

HUNGARY

Caspian Sea

Black Sea

Constantinople

Bucharest

OTTOMAN

EMPIRE

Athens

Rome

Venice

Zurich

FRANCE

Amsterdam

Paris

SCOTLAND

ENGLAND

Canterbury

Dublin

IRELAND

ICELAND

ATLANTIC
OCEAN

Mediterranean Sea

Madrid

SPAIN

THE ORTHODOX CHURCH DURING
THE REFORMATION

During the Reformation, the part of the Orthodox church dominated by the Ottoman Turks languished. The Turks continued to use church officials as tools of their rule. Occasionally a church official would resist the Turks by opposing some immoral activity on the part of the rulers. But for the most part, the leaders were docile and the church marked time. Perhaps it is remarkable that Orthodoxy survived at all. Despite corruption in the upper levels of the church hierarchy, parish life was active. Many of the Orthodox faithfully continued their rich tradition. Most of the advancement in Orthodoxy during the sixteenth century occurred in the Russian church.

The Russian Church

The Third Rome Theory received great attention when Ivan IV (1530–1584), known as "Ivan the Terrible," came to power. Ivan busied himself with expanding his empire, which was centered in Moscow. Whenever he was successful, Orthodoxy also expanded. In 1547 he had himself proclaimed tsar and claimed to be the successor of the Christian emperors of Constantinople. Ivan saw himself as the protector of the church and, like the Byzantine emperors, expected support from it. Many Orthodox leaders willingly rallied to Ivan's cause. Partly because of religious conviction and partly because of political concerns, they strongly advanced the idea that Moscow was the third Rome. Moscow was granted the status of patriarchate in 1590. The new patriarchate of Moscow would soon become the most important in the Orthodox world.

The Russian church experienced some internal controversies during the sixteenth century, the most important of which was the split between the Possessors and the non-Possessors. It developed out of two trends that were at the heart of Orthodox monasticism—performing social work among the needy and retreating from the world for prayer and meditation. By the sixteenth century, monasteries owned about one-third of the land in Russia. At a church council in 1503, Nilus of Sora (ca. 1433–1508) challenged the practice. He argued that the duty of monks was to retreat from the world for mystical prayer and to set an example for society. The laity was to be concerned for charity; monks were not. Monasteries must detach themselves from landowning so they could perform their proper duty. Those who supported Nilus came to be known as *non-Possessors.*

Nilus was opposed by Joseph, abbot of Volokalamsk (1439–1515). Joseph argued that monks had social obligations to care for the poor, show hospitality, and teach. Monasteries needed money for these good purposes. They held their riches in trust for the poor. Those who supported him came to be called *Possessors,* or *Josephites.* The Josephites dominated the council and the non-Possessors were defeated. Moreover, because the Possessors generally supported the activity of the tsar, they were able to call upon the power of the state to persecute the non-Possessors.

The Reformation and Orthodoxy

The Protestant Reformation had little impact on the sixteenth-century Orthodox church. The Orthodox certainly were aware of the work of the Reformers. Ideas filtered through to Eastern Christianity by a variety of means. Many Orthodox went to the West to study. Western embassies from Protestant and Catholic countries not only represented their nations in the East but also spread religious concepts.

Still, the Orthodox showed little interest in Protestant thought. A good example of this disinterest was the dialogue between a group of Lutheran theologians and the patriarch of Constantinople, Jeremias II. The discussion began in 1573 when the Lutherans presented the patriarch with a copy of the Augsburg Confession translated into Greek. Jeremias responded with three sets of *Answers* in which he addressed the issues raised by the Protestants. All of his replies retained their Orthodox character and made few concessions to the Reformers. After the third set of replies, the patriarch ended the dialogue. He felt there was nothing else to say. Jeremias' *Answers* was the first systematic critique of Protestantism from the Orthodox perspective.

The Catholic Reformation had a greater impact on the Orthodox church. The Counter-Reformation produced a renewal of efforts to bring all Christians, including Eastern Christians, into submission to the pope. The Jesuits were especially active in this offensive. The main region where Catholics and Orthodox clashed was the Ukraine. After the Tartars captured Kiev, Russia lost the city and the rest of the Ukraine. It came under the domination of Poland and Lithuania. (These two countries had been united under a single crown in 1386.) This union left a Catholic majority in the region ruling over an Orthodox minority.

The Roman Catholic authorities made periodic efforts to force the Orthodox into obedience to the pope. This pressure heightened with the arrival of Jesuits in 1564. The Jesuits secretly negotiated with Orthodox leaders to reunify Orthodoxy with Catholicism. However, when a council was called in 1596 at Brest-Litovsk to finalize the union, the Orthodox hierarchy was divided and many delegates wanted to remain Orthodox. Despite opposition, a *Uniate* church was declared in Poland. The Uniate church officially submitted to the pope, but was allowed to keep the Orthodox liturgy and to maintain many Eastern practices. Most Greek Christians accepted the Uniate church at least outwardly.

Those who rejected the Uniate church and wished to remain strictly Orthodox were severely persecuted. The Eastern faith was kept vital by Orthodox brotherhoods that were composed of priests and laypeople who taught, published, and performed charitable activity. Interestingly, efforts to resist Catholic intrusion in Poland drove the Orthodox patriarch of Constantinople closer to Protestantism in the early seventeenth century.

THE CHURCH AT THE CLOSE
OF THE SIXTEENTH CENTURY

The sixteenth century was one of the most significant times in church history. The combination of widespread abuses within the church and political and social upheavals produced dramatic changes. The most obvious was the rift between Protestants and Catholics. This schism left the church divided into three main parts: Eastern Orthodox, Roman Catholic, and Protestant. No strong efforts were made to heal this division until the twentieth century.

Protestants and Catholics shared many beliefs and traditions. For instance, they generally looked to the Scripture as a base for Christian authority, taught justification by faith, and accepted the definitions of the Trinity established by the early church councils. They differed over such concerns as the nature of the Eucharist, the place of "works" in salvation, and the marriage of the clergy. However, the most important differences centered around the role of the church and its hierarchy in the Christian faith. The Catholics insisted that salvation occurs only in the church and comes to humans through the seven sacraments. Protestants held that humans have direct access to God, although some did not reject the sacraments altogether. The Catholics maintained that church tradition had equal authority with the Bible in directing Christian life. Protestants felt that Scriptures alone should be the authority for Christians. Catholics taught that Scriptures could be interpreted only by the church hierarchy, while Protestants believed that individual Christians had the ability to interpret the Bible.

After the sixteenth-century Reformation, Protestantism was divided into four main branches: Lutheranism, Calvinism, Anglicanism, and Anabaptists. There was a great deal of competition among these groups. Ever since its beginnings, Protestantism has tended to fragment into more and more denominations. There are sociological and psychological bases for this fragmentation but theology also plays a major role. If each Christian has the right to interpret the Scriptures, then there are potentially as many interpretations as there are Christians. When each interpreter is convinced that his or her understanding is the correct one as revealed by the Holy Spirit, there is little room for compromise. People break into groups and pursue their own definitions of truth. Early leaders such as Calvin and Luther recognized this problem and tried to guard against it.

The Catholic church evolved into a stronger faith at the end of the sixteenth century. There was a renewed spiritual vigor in the church. The Council of Trent clarified many issues. It produced a more unified liturgy and theology. It took steps to enforce a new uniformity in worship and other practices. Many abuses, such as simony and pluralism, were limited. Limits also were placed on indulgences and relics. Clerical marriage and concubinage were practically eliminated from the church.

On the other hand, Trent also helped to establish a Catholicism that would react negatively to many theological and social changes that would occur over the next four centuries. Catholicism would resist many forms of nationalism and capitalism and artificial birth control. This resistance would leave many faithful Catholics choosing between their societies and their religion. It would result in many feeling that the church hierarchy had little understanding of, or appreciation for, their daily needs. To some, religion would seem more and more irrelevant.

The warfare between Protestants and Catholics had a similar result. Neither side won. Many on both sides were disgusted by the bloodshed in the name of the Prince of Peace (Christ). The state, rather than the church, came to be seen as the legitimate authority in determining "morals" and dispensing justice. The real winner in the Reformation was the state!

Despite all the changes and upheaval, the church spread. It spread into places such as India, China, and Japan, and it followed explorers into entirely new territories. The sixteenth century was a great age of colonization. Portuguese and Spanish were busy establishing vast empires. New settlements were established by European powers in Africa, North and South America, and Southeast Asia, and many Jesuit, Franciscan, and Dominican missionaries went along to "evangelize" the indigenous peoples. Catholic missionaries established an especially powerful influence in the New World. Much of Canada, the southern United States, Mexico, Central America, and South America were converted to Catholicism. Sometimes conversion was done by force. Often the church sided with the European conquerors and assisted in exploiting the indigenous people. Other times church officials became their defenders and assisted in limiting their abuse. This rift between supporting the powerful and defending the weak has characterized the Latin and South American church to the present (see Chapter 12).[4]

CONCLUSIONS

The Reformation instigated trends that would reach fulfillment in the following centuries. In many ways, it laid the foundation for the modern world. While the Christendom of medieval society was built on Catholicism, the secularization of the last 400 years has part of its foundation in Protestantism. The individualism and mistrust of authority that characterizes modern life may well have a base in the Reformers. The dominance of the state, which started to be obvious in the sixteenth century, is now a main characteristic of contemporary life. We will see how some of these trends evolved in the following chapters.

Notes

1. For a good discussion of the English Reformation, see Kenneth Scott Latourette, *A History of Christianity,* vol. 2, *Reformation to the Present,* rev. ed. New York: Harper & Row, 1975, pp. 797–835.
2. For a good discussion of the Anabaptists, spiritualists, and rationalists, see Latourette, vol. 2, 778–796.
3. For a good discussion of the Catholic Reformation, see Latourette, vol. 2, 840–883, and Clyde L. Manschreck, *A History of Christianity in the World,* 2d ed. Englewood Cliffs, NJ: Prentice-Hall, 1985, pp. 194–209.
4. For a good discussion of the church in Latin and South America, see Justo L. González, *The Story of Christianity,* vol. 1, *The Early Church to the Dawn of the Reformation.* San Francisco: Harper & Row, 1984, 379–412.

Additional Readings

Arnold, Eberhard. *The Early Anabaptists.* 2d, rev. ed. Ulster, NY: Plough, 1984.
Bainton, Roland H. *The Travail of Religious Liberty: Nine Biographical Studies.* Philadelphia: Westminster, 1951.
Barthel, Manfred. *The Jesuits: History and Legend of the Society of Jesus.* Translated by Mark Howson. New York: Morrow, 1984.
Battles, Ford Lewis. *Interpreting John Calvin.* Edited by Robert Benedetto. Grand Rapids, MI: Baker, 1996.
Bender, H. S. *Menno Simons Life and Writings: A Quadricentennial Tribute 1536–1936.* Scottsdale, PA: Mennonite, 1936.
Bennett, John W. *Hutterian Brethren.* Palo Alto, CA: Stanford University Press, 1967.
Bernard, G. W. *The King's Reformation: Henry VIII and the Remaking of the English Church.* New Haven, CT: Yale University Press, 2005.
Burnes, E. M. *The Counter-Reformation.* Princeton, NJ: University Press, 1964.
Chemnitz, Martin. *Examination of the Council of Trent.* Fred Krammer, trans. St. Louis: Concordia, 1986.
Clissold, Stephen. *The Saints of South America.* London: Knight, 1972.
Daniel-Rops, Henry. *The Catholic Reformation.* New York: Dutton,1962.
Dickens, A. G. *The English Reformation.* 2d ed. University Park, PA: Pennsylvania State University Press, 1989.
Duffy, Eamon. *The Voices of Moreboth: Reformation and Rebellion.* New Haven, CT: Yale University Press, 2003.
Dunne, George H. *Generation of Giants: The Story of Jesuits in China in the Last Generations of the Ming Dynasty.* London: Burns and Oats, 1962.
Furcha, E. J., ed. and trans. *Selected Writings of Hans Denck.* Lewiston, NY: Mellen Press, 1989.

Hass, Guenther H. *The Concept of Equity in Calvin's Ethics*. Waterloo, ON: Wilfrid Laurier University Press, 1997.

Knappen, Marshall M. *Tudor Puritanism: A Chapter in the History of Idealism*. Chicago: University of Chicago Press, 1939.

Loyola, Ignatius. *The Spiritual Exercises*. Translated by Anthony Mottola. New York: Doubleday, 1964.

MacCulloh, Diarmaid. *The Reformation: A History*. New York: Penguin, 2005.

Mullett, Michael A. *Catholic Reformation*. London: Taylor & Francis, 1999.

Olin, John C. *The Catholic Reformation: Savonarola to Ignatius Loyola*. New York: Harper & Row, 1969.

Parkman, Francis. *The Jesuits in North America in the Seventeenth Century*. 1895 Reprint. Williamstown, MA: Corner House, 1970.

Ridley, Jasper. *Thomas Cranmer*. Oxford: Clarendon, 1962.

Stayer, James M. *Anabaptist and the Sword*. Lawrence, KS: Coronado, 1976.

Wenger, J. C. *The Complete Writings of Menno Simons*. Scottsdale, PA: Herald, 1956.

Wendel, Francois. *Calvin: Origins and Development of His Religious Thought*. Translated by Philip Mairet. Grand Rapids, MI: Baker, 1997.

Williams, George Huntston. *The Radical Reformation*. Kirksville, MO: Truman State University, 2000.

Wright, A. D. *Counter-Reformation: Catholic Europe and the Non-Christian World*. London: Ashgate, 2005

Websites

http://en.widipedia.org/wiki/Protestant_Reformation/ [Provides articles discussing the Reformation and links about specific topics regarding the Reformation]

http://fordham.edu/halsall.sbooks1y.htmlProtestant%20Reformation [Provides articles and documents about Protestant and Catholic Reformations]

http://www.msu.edu/homepages.laurence/reformation/ [Provides links to original writings as well as material about the reformers and different branches of the Reformation]

www.hanover.edu/early/prot.html [Provides links to original documents of the Reformation as well as articles about the Reformation]

10

THE AFTERMATH
OF THE REFORMATION

War, Piety, and Reason (1600–1800 C.E.)

Sir Isaac Newton

The sixteenth century set into motion forces that would radically change the world. France, England, and Holland would become deeply involved in empire building. In the seventeenth century, they would begin to replace Spain and Portugal as the great colonial powers. Exploitation of the colonies together with new ideas upholding individual rights and democracy ultimately led to the revolt of the thirteen colonies. The American Revolution in turn became the model for similar revolts in later centuries.

Changes in ideas accompanied social and political changes. A stress on reason came to dominate the thinking of the intellectual elite. The belief developed that if people could be freed from superstition and the misguided thinking of the past they could move into a glorious new age in which political decisions, morality, and religion would be based on reason. This enlightened thinking was closely related to the rise of science. The emerging scientific perspective promised to unravel all the mysteries of the universe and to provide humans with the tools to cure all their ills.

In this chapter we look at historical developments that occurred in the aftermath of the Reformation. We then consider some of the more important religious movements in the two centuries after the Reformation. Finally we look at the church at the close of the eighteenth century.

RELIGIOUS WARS

At the end of the sixteenth century an uneasy peace was established between Catholics and Protestants in Europe. This peace was not to continue in the seventeenth century. The Peace of Augsburg had left Germany terribly divided. There were numerous small states, each with its own religion. Political leaders exploited the religious tension for their own gains. Devout Catholics and Protestants resented each other's religion. Catholics had been encouraged to defend their faith by the Council of Trent. They began taking a harder position against the Evangelicals. The Jesuits especially struggled to regain lands lost to the Protestants. Such tensions would eventually result in the Thirty Years' War.

In France, Henry IV had produced peace by extending tolerance to the Huguenots in the Edict of Nantes. The Huguenots' freedom was guaranteed by being permitted to maintain a number of fortified cities. Richelieu considered the cities a threat to the Crown. He launched a series of vicious attacks against the Protestants. These attacks began a long period of persecution that continued under successive leaders.

In England tension continued between Protestants and Catholics. However, Puritans gained more power. They not only rejected the Elizabethan Settlement but also resisted the control of the king. This opposition eventually led to a revolt that established a brief period of Puritan rule. In the following sections we review the religious conflicts in Germany, France, and England.

The Thirty Years' War

Tensions between Protestants and Catholics in Germany resulted in occasional open conflicts. Anger built until some of the Protestant groups formed the Evangelical Union in 1608. The Catholics responded in 1609 by creating the powerful Catholic League. Open warfare was avoided until the situation worsened in nearby Bohemia, which is present-day Czechoslovakia.

Bohemia was the land of the Hussites, who aligned themselves with the Reformed tradition. Their ranks were swelled by Calvinists who had fled there from Germany to avoid persecution. Only Lutheranism and Catholicism were accepted in Germany by the Peace of Augsburg, and Calvinism was still illegal. The Calvinists had won the right to practice their religion with some degree of freedom in Bohemia. Because there were so many different faiths, Bohemia was a hotbed of unrest.

In 1617, Ferdinand of Styria, a Habsburg, became king of Bohemia. Ferdinand was a staunch Catholic educated by the Jesuits and had Jesuits as his counselors. He soon alienated his Protestant subjects by canceling the religious freedoms they had enjoyed. A group of armed Protestant nobles confronted the royal council in Prague in May 1618 and demanded a return of their liberties. When the council refused to hear their case, the nobles threw two of the king's counselors out a high window. Fortunately the counselors were not hurt because they landed in a pile of dung. This act became known as the "Defenestration of Prague," and it marked the beginning of the Thirty Years' War (1618–1648).

The war was marked by strange blendings of religion and politics. It was basically between Protestants and Catholics. Initially, however, the Lutheran Protestants would not support the Bohemians because they were of the Reformed (Calvinist) tradition. Moreover, the emperor was a Habsburg. Many, including the English, the French royal family (the Bourbons), and the Dutch, Danes, Swedes, and assorted German nobles, feared the power of the Habsburgs. As a result they were drawn into the conflict on the side of the Evangelicals partly to curb the influence of the Habsburg emperor. Even some Catholics sided with the Protestants for this reason!

In the early phases of the war, the Bohemian Calvinists enjoyed some advantage. They successfully defended their territory against imperial forces. They installed Frederick V of Palatinate as their king. Frederick was the son-in-law of James I of England. By this time Ferdinand II (1619–1637) had become the Holy Roman emperor. He had no intention of seeing parts of his

Important Events of the Seventeenth and Eighteenth Centuries

DATES	EVENTS	SECULAR LEADERS	CHURCH PERSONS	WRITINGS
1603–1625	Reign of James I in England	James I		
1608	First English Separatist congregation in Amsterdam		Brewster, Bradford, Robinson	
1609	First modern Baptist church		Smyth	
1611	New English version of the Bible	James I		King James Version
1612	First English Baptist church		Helwys	
1618–1619	Synod of Dort, TULIP Theology			Canons of Dort
1618–1648	Thirty Years' War			Treaty of Westphalia
1620	Puritans depart for America aboard Mayflower			Mayflower Compact
1624	Rationalism advanced	Descartes		*Discourse on Method*
1624–1642	Richelieu's government			
1625–1649	Reign of Charles I in England	Charles I		
1640	Long Parliament establishes Presbyterianism in England			
1642	Beginning of English Civil War	Cromwell		

empire fall to Protestantism. With the help of the Catholic League, Bohemia was invaded and Frederick V was driven from the throne. Much blood was shed as Catholicism was restored to the area under the direction of the Jesuits.

In 1625, England, the Netherlands, and Denmark formed the Protestant League for the purpose of invading Germany and restoring Frederick to his lands. The major part of the task fell to the Danish with only limited support coming from their allies. King Christian IV of Denmark invaded Germany. Fighting devastated large sections of the countryside. Christian's forces were

Important Events of the Seventeenth and Eighteenth Centuries

DATES	EVENTS	SECULAR LEADERS	CHURCH PERSONS	WRITINGS
1647–1649	Westminster Assembly			Westminster Confession
1649	Quakers begin		Fox	
1653	Protectorate established	Cromwell		
1670	Pietism begins		Spener	*Pia Desideria*
1687	Universe as machine	Newton		*Principia*
1689	Tolerance in England	William and Mary		Act of Toleration
1690	Humans learn through experience	Locke		*Essay Concerning Human Understanding*
	Deism advanced	Toland		*Christianity Not Mysterious*
1722	Herrnhut community founded (Moravians)		Zinzendorf	
1738	Aldersgate experience (Methodists)		Wesley	
1781	Reason undermined	Kant		*Critique of Pure Reason*
1784	First American Methodist bishop		Coke	
1787	Tolerance in France			

finally defeated by two Catholic armies. His army withdrew, having only increased the suffering of the German people. Emperor Ferdinand was now determined to restore the large sections he controlled to the Catholic faith. Many Protestants were converted to Catholicism at the point of the sword. Protestant areas were viciously looted and burned.

Another phase of the conflict began in 1630 when King Gustavus Adolphus (1594–1632) of Sweden launched an invasion of Germany. Gustavus, a strong Lutheran who also feared the Habsburgs, felt that he had a mission to save

Witch-Hunts

To the modern reader, one strange feature of Christian history is witch-hunts. The series of witch-hunts that occurred in the seventeenth-century New England colonies were only a small part of the total. An estimated 70,000 and 100,000 people worldwide were accused and killed as witches from 1400 to 1700. Beliefs about witches arose from popular culture as well as from the church itself.

Some villagers practiced magic as a way of coping with natural disasters and other problems of everyday life. Many villages had persons skilled in the practice of magic arts. These individuals held positions of respect, but often they were feared. The clergy practiced magic in the sacraments and in such procedures as exorcisms of demons.

In the thirteenth century, the church declared that only its priests had legitimate magical power. According to the church, because such power could come only from the devil or God, anyone outside the church who engaged in magic was in league with the devil. The witch-hunts were part of the larger struggle with Satan. They also may have been a way for Christianity to extend its control over non-Christian areas. A majority of witch-hunt victims were women, often aged forty-five or older.

Witch-hunts ended in the seventeenth century, perhaps partly because they tended to get out of control. Accused witches would often claim that important townspeople participated in satanic activities. The Reformation may have played a role in ending the witch-hunts. When the Protestants denied transubstantiation along with the sacrifice of the Mass, much of the magical element was removed from religion. Protestants also decreased the power and importance of the devil. For them, God was the all-powerful being. Rationalism and science reduced the importance of the supernatural and claimed that the material universe functioned according to natural laws, not at the whim of supernatural beings. Disease epidemics and natural disasters were shown to have their origins in the material world. People increasingly turned away from magic and religion to medicine and science to solve their problems.

Protestantism. He was aided by money from Cardinal Richelieu of France. Gustavus was a brilliant military commander. His campaign left him in control of major parts of southern and western Germany. He successfully defeated the opposing armies but was killed at Lutzen in 1632, depriving the Protestants of a great leader.

The French then openly joined the fight on the side of the Swedish in 1635. Neither side could win a clear victory. The war degenerated into a long stalemate, with raids, lootings, and killings on all sides. The troops seemed to have forgotten their original purpose, and war had become a way of life. Civilians of all faiths suffered. Finally everyone grew so tired of war that the only option was peace. The 1648 Treaty of Westphalia basically restored the conditions of the Peace of Augsburg. The one significant change was that toleration was extended to the Calvinists, though Anabaptists and other radical groups continued to be persecuted.

Germany was divided into more than 300 states. Habsburg power had been limited. People were to follow the religion of the ruler of the state, but many ceased to care. The folly of trying to enforce religion by force of arms was made clear on the Continent. The secular state was now supreme. Never again would the Continent go to war primarily for religious reasons; instead, its many wars were now openly for political purposes.[1]

The Church in the Desert

The French Protestants, or Huguenots, had grown steadily in the sixteenth century. They probably represented about one-ninth of the total French population. Many nobles and professionals were in their ranks, however, so they asserted a good bit of influence in French society. The monarchy feared their influence, which led to the persecution and warfare of the late sixteenth century. The Edict of Nantes finally ended the strife by guaranteeing religious and political privileges to the Protestants. To ensure these privileges, the Huguenots were permitted to keep a number of fortified cities that were almost self-governing as well as thousands of fortified castles.

This relative peace continued with only minor disturbances until Cardinal Richelieu came to power in the 1620s. Richelieu was not worried about the Protestants as heretics, but he was concerned about the potential threat to royal control that their fortified cities represented. As a result, in 1629 he had the French army attack the main Protestant stronghold at La Rochelle. The siege of the city was long and bloody and many who defended their city died valiantly. When La Rochelle finally fell, a Catholic mass was celebrated in all the churches there. This led other Protestant cities to take up arms against the Crown. The revolt was smashed and the fortifications of the Huguenot cities were destroyed. Because the Crown was no longer threatened by the Protestants and their fortified cities, Richelieu issued an edict that restored the political and religious rights of the Huguenots. Protestantism then grew among all social classes and was well accepted.

The fortunes of the Protestants again changed when Louis XIV came to power in 1661. The Sun King would not tolerate anyone who did not submit to him. He strongly defended the liberties of the Gallican church (ancient privileges granted to the French church) against the pope. He also attacked dissidents of all kinds, including the Huguenots. Measures were taken against the Protestants to force them to reunite with the Catholic church. In 1684 the army forced the reunion of tens of thousands of Protestants. A year later the king issued an edict that abolished the Edict of Nantes. It was now illegal to be a Protestant.

Thousands of Huguenots fled to Switzerland, Germany, England, the Netherlands, and North America. Many were skilled in crafts and business. Their talents contributed much to the economies in the countries where they settled. The loss of their talents in turn caused a great deal of damage to the French. Some historians claim the disruption that resulted from the flight of the Huguenots was one cause of the French Revolution.

Although it was illegal to be Protestant, many continued to practice their faith in private meetings. The meeting places were kept secret, but when officials uncovered them, the pastors were executed, the men were sent to slave galleys, and the women were imprisoned for life. Children of these prisoners were raised by Catholic foster parents. Torture was used to force the resistant Protestants to reunite. Under such conditions, the Protestants began calling themselves the "church in the desert."

As often happens, persecution generated apocalyptic movements. Many members of the desert church became convinced that the Lord would soon return. In turn, this belief created a rebellion that lasted for some time and resulted in much death. The rebellion was led by the lower classes because many of those who were better off had left the country. Persecution continued under Louis XIV's successors. These policies stopped in 1787, when Louis XVI declared tolerance of the Protestants. As many as 200,000 died in the persecutions from the time of Richelieu until toleration was extended in 1787. Despite the deaths, the church in the desert survived.

The Puritans and the Puritan Revolt

In England, Elizabeth I managed to maintain a high degree of religious peace during the latter part of her reign, but more trouble was brewing for her successor James I (1566–1625). James, the son of Mary Stuart, was already King James VI of Scotland when he was selected as heir to the English throne in 1603. Scotland already had gone over to the Presbyterians. James himself had a Presbyterian background. He wished to rule in the same absolute manner as the French kings but the Presbyterians hindered him from being an absolute monarch in Scotland.

James and the Puritans. When James assumed the throne in England, he was inclined not to support the Calvinistic Puritans because of his troubles with the Scottish Presbyterians. Instead he supported the Elizabethan Settlement and the episcopal structure of the church it established. An **episcopal structure** (episcopacy) is an organizational hierarchy in which bishops rule over the church. James regarded bishops as natural supports for a strong monarchy.

The Puritans had been gaining strength in England. They were not an organized group but a loosely knit movement comprising several groups whose common desire was to "purify" the church of Catholic influences. The Puritans also wished to force more disciplined living on society. They opposed frivolous games and heavy drinking and wanted to return to a biblically based faith. Their rejection of popish practices led them to attack the episcopacy; however, they disagreed on the pattern of church structure that should be adopted in its place.

Some opted for a presbytery. The word *presbyter* means elder. Presbyterian church congregations are presided over by a minister and several lay elders. They may also have a synodwide (districtwide) presbytery, consisting of ministers and lay presbyters who decide matters of theology and morals. Others believed a congregational structure was the biblical pattern. In the congregational pattern, the local congregation has final authority in matters of faith, morals, and practice. There is no hierarchy.[2]

Tensions grew between Puritans who dominated the House of Commons (the lower house of the British Parliament) and James I. James finally called the Hampton Court Conference in 1604 to resolve differences. Because James would not compromise his positions on the divine right of kings and the role of the episcopacy, the conference hopelessly deadlocked.

James did authorize a new translation of the Bible into English. This translation, done by scholars at Oxford, Cambridge, and Westminster, came to be known as the King James Version (KJV) of the Bible. The first edition containing the Apocrypha appeared in 1611. By 1629, the Puritans had the Apocrypha removed from those editions not used in Anglican churches. The KJV became one of the most important works in the English language. It helped form English culture from that point onward and was a significant influence throughout the English-speaking world.

Separatists and Baptists. As James put more pressure on the Puritans, a split began to develop. Some of them chose to create congregations not associated with the Anglican church. They felt the church was too corrupt to renew. These were called Separatist Puritans to distinguish them from those Puritans who stayed in the Church of England and continued to try to reform it. Some Separatists came to believe that they would have to leave England to find religious freedom.

One Separatist group led by William Brewster, William Bradford, and John Robinson established a religious community at Leyden in the Netherlands. Portions of the Leyden community came to believe that only in the New World could they practice their religion as they saw fit. They returned to England and departed from Plymouth on September 20, 1620 aboard the *Mayflower*. Their hope was to create a model society in the wilderness. This group founded the Plymouth colony in New England. They are the Pilgrims whose first Thanksgiving gave Americans that holiday. Over the following decades, thousands of pilgrims migrated to New England.[3]

Another Separatist group led by John Smyth (d. 1612) settled in Amsterdam. Smyth decided that he must break with the Anglican church entirely. He rejected infant baptism, baptized himself, and set up the first Baptist church in 1609. Smyth was aided in his task by Anabaptists from the Amsterdam area. He eventually left his Baptist congregation to become an Anabaptist. Others kept the congregation going, one of whom, Thomas Helwys (ca. 1550–ca. 1616), returned to England to establish Baptist churches. In 1612 he organized the first Baptist church outside London. His preaching was very successful.

Helwys' popular document, *A Short Declaration of the Mystery of Iniquity*, brought him to the attention of authorities who imprisoned and eventually executed him. In the *Mystery of Iniquity*, Helwys rejected infant baptism and accepted **general election** (Christ died for everyone, but some will not accept the salvation he offers). More important, he contended that all religious groups who have political power will abuse it. The king has power only over earthly matters. He has no rights in religious matters. His power must not be used to try to enforce religious orthodoxy. A person's beliefs are a matter of personal conscience. All religions must be tolerated. These doctrines of toleration and separation of church and state historically have been one of the distinguishing marks of the Baptist movement.

Because of the acceptance of general election the churches associated with Helwys came to be known as General (Arminian) Baptist churches. Another branch of the Baptist movement developed in the 1630s from the Calvinist Separatist congregations. One leader in this movement was Henry Jacob. These Baptists accepted the Calvinistic idea of the atoning death of Christ being for the elect alone. They came to be called *Particular Baptists*, and they eventually accepted baptism by immersion in water as the biblical method. Baptism by immersion would come to be the standard Baptist practice.

Roger Williams (ca. 1603–1684) established the first Baptist church in America after he broke with the Massachusetts Puritans to found Rhode Island. His *Bloody Tenent of Persecution*, which argues for separation of church and state and for universal toleration, is one of history's great documents.

Additional Conflict, Revolt, and Restoration. James I continued to have conflicts with Catholics, Puritans, Parliament, and others. The situation did not improve under his son, Charles I (1625–1649). Charles married a sister of King Louis XIII of France. In the process, he had to make concessions to English Catholics. These concessions enraged the Puritans who were already upset over the restrictive measures that had been taken against them. He also was in trouble with the Puritan-dominated Parliament. He dissolved Parliament and ruled eleven years without it.

Yet the English king had limited power to raise money through taxes without Parliament. That caused problems for Charles when the Scots revolted. The revolt occurred because the archbishop of Canterbury, William Laud (1573–1645), tried to impose the Anglican liturgy on the Presbyterian Scots. The Scots soon invaded England. Charles needed money to put down the rebellion, and he called together the Parliament. Thus began the Long Parliament, which met from 1640 to 1653. Parliament quickly assumed control of the government from Charles. When Charles sent troops to arrest the leaders of Parliament, an armed mob forced the king to flee from London.

Parliament moved toward abolishing Anglicanism and establishing a Presbyterian type of Puritanism. This was done partly to attract the Scottish rebels. Parliament was assisted in religious decisions by the Westminster Assembly, a remarkable group that produced the *Directory of Worship, Short Catechism,* and *Westminster Confession.* These documents are some of the best expressions of Calvinism. They formed the groundwork for later Presbyterianism. (Congregationalists, Baptists, and others also drew heavily on these documents in creating their theologies.)

Both the king and his enemies prepared for civil war. The king was supported by the nobles and bishops while Parliament received its support from the lower classes who had suffered under both James and Charles. Parliament found a military genius in Oliver Cromwell (1599–1658), a Puritan who felt called by God to his mission. Cromwell also extended acceptance of the **independents** (Anabaptist, separatist, and Puritans who rejected the national Church of England). His army included various types of dissidents such as Baptists and Quakers who had suffered at the hands of Anglicans and Puritans alike. Cromwell reorganized the army around a regiment of "godly men" who fought with the zeal of religious conviction. He also improved the rest of the troops. His efforts were rewarded when Charles was defeated and captured in 1646. Both Laud and Charles were imprisoned and executed by Cromwell.

Cromwell became the virtual dictator of England, although he refused the title of king. Instead, he chose the designation "Lord Protector." He successfully put down rebellions and defended the country against foreign enemies. Religious tolerance was extended to Presbyterians, Baptists, and others. The only ones excluded were strong advocates of the episcopacy and Catholics. The Puritans undertook social reform and produced legislation regulating the Sabbath and prohibiting various forms of "licentiousness," such as attending games, horse races, dancing, and heavy drinking. Christmas and other festivals were eliminated. Marriage was made a civil ceremony. Ornate church altars were desecrated. Opposition to the Protectorate grew.

When Cromwell died in 1658, his son was unable to hold England together. Parliament decided to restore the monarchy. It brought Charles II (1660–1685), the son of Charles I, back from exile in France, where he had acquired a taste for Catholicism and royal absolutism. Charles undid much of what the Puritans had accomplished. He restored the Anglican church and launched a severe attack on those not conforming to Anglican ways. He even entered a secret treaty with Louis XIV to restore England to Catholicism, a move Parliament prevented. Charles confessed Catholicism on his deathbed.

Charles' successor, James II (1685–1688), openly tried to bring Catholicism back to England. Parliament invited William of Orange and Mary, the daughter of James, to invade England. William and Mary were rulers in Holland. The Dutch army invaded and placed William and Mary on the throne. They issued the Act of Toleration in 1689, which extended toleration to all but Catholics and Unitarians. (**Unitarians** were a group who argued for the "oneness" of God and rejected the Trinity.) Puritanism was past its prime. The middle way of Anglicanism was firmly established.[4]

PROTESTANT ORTHODOXY AND PIETISM

New religions often develop from the intense personal experience of their founders. Yet a personal experience of God is very difficult to transmit to followers. It becomes especially hard to ensure that each successive generation has the same kind of experience that gave rise to the new faith. Oftentimes an emphasis is placed on right belief in determining who is among the "chosen" and who is not. Things that were mere speculations in the original teachings evolve into absolute truths that must be accepted by all true believers.

By the seventeenth century, this evolution was well under way in Lutheranism and Calvinism. Both Calvin and Luther had powerful conversion experiences that influenced their work. Although Calvin produced a great systematic theology, some argue that what drove his thought and action was the experience of justification by grace. Luther's thought was not as systematic. It came out of his personal encounter with the Gospel. Through a number of controversies, Calvinist and Lutheran theologians were defining the fine points of their theologies and writing "creeds" to be accepted by the faithful.

For instance, a distinguished Calvinist Dutch pastor and professor, Jacobus Arminius (1560–1609), came to doubt that God elected people for salvation or damnation "before the foundations of the earth were lain." In fact, God had decreed the salvation of all humanity through Christ. Some would choose to accept this salvation and others would not. Predestination was not a sovereign decree of God about the fate of individuals. It was God's foreknowledge of who

TULIP Theology

The Synod of Dort was called to deal with the challenges presented by Jacobus Arminius and his followers. The organizers hoped to secure the support not only of the Dutch Reformed church but also of Calvinists from all of Europe. As a result, delegates attended from Great Britain, Switzerland, and Germany. The synod met from November 1618 to May 1619. Arminius was condemned. The synod spelled out its theology in several canons that became the heart of Calvinistic orthodoxy. The essence of the synod's teachings is referred to as TULIP theology after the first letters in the key doctrines: Total depravity, Unconditional election, Limited atonement, Irresistible grace, and Perseverance of the saints. Total depravity means that because of Adam's fall humans are totally bound to sin. Even if some "light" exists in this world, humans are incapable of responding to it. Unconditional election means that being elected by God is predestined. It is not based on God's foreknowledge of who will respond to the call for salvation. Limited atonement teaches that Christ died only for the elect, not for all humankind. Irresistible grace goes back to the teachings of Augustine, as do many of the ideas surrounding predestination. It holds that predestination is so powerful it is impossible for people to resist the grace of God once it is given to them. Perseverance of the saints means that once a person is saved he or she cannot then be lost. It is impossible to fall from grace.

would choose to be saved and who would reject Christ. Arminius' teachings came to be called **Arminianism**.

These teachings produced a long-running conflict that continued after Arminius' death. Finally the Synod of Dort (1618–1619) defined five teachings that were the core of orthodox Calvinism. This came to be known as TULIP Calvinism after the first letters in the key words of the five doctrines. TULIP theology was supplemented by the more detailed Westminster Confession developed in England. The heart of Reformed orthodoxy was formed in the work of Dort and Westminster. Arminius' teachings had their greatest impact on the Methodists and certain Baptist groups who were noted for their efforts to convert the lost.

Lutheranism took a similar course. Through the seventeenth and most of the eighteenth centuries, Lutherans operated under what scholars call "Protestant

Scholasticism." Theologians fought Calvinists and Catholics, as well as one another, over who was most rigidly following the teachings of Luther. They refined their thinking by developing long, carefully reasoned systematic theologies. All of these efforts defined what Lutherans must believe.

Fox and the Quakers

The emphasis on orthodoxy, or correct belief, produced a religion that appealed to the intellect but that had little room for the feelings of the heart. Such a one-sided religion created reactions stressing the experiences of the Spirit. One of the earliest of these reactions is seen in the work of George Fox (1624–1691). Fox became disillusioned with the lack of spirituality and low morals he saw in the religion of his day. He felt called by the Lord to correct these shortcomings. He wandered about the English countryside searching for true spirituality and attending church services. When he found them lacking, he would stand and proclaim the truth he had received.

This public proclamation led Fox to be arrested and thrown into jail. On one occasion he and some of his followers were thrown into the lowest levels of the prison at Launceston. There they were forced to stand in the excrement of other prisoners. When they set straw on fire to help control the smell, the jailors dumped pots of excrement on them from above to extinguish the fire. Despite this persecution, Fox continued to preach in England, Ireland, the West Indies, North America, and Holland. Followers gathered around him. In 1668 he founded the Society of Friends, or Quakers as their enemies called them. The term *Quaker* was used because Fox's followers often appeared to quake when they were possessed by the Spirit.

The Quakers were pacifists who held for the equality and brotherhood of all. They believed that all revelation was produced by the Spirit. The Spirit gives inward revelations that are necessary for the forming of true religion. Revelations are superior to either Scripture or natural reason. The Spirit is available to everyone. If it is not resisted, it will produce true holiness. The Quakers rejected the outward sacraments and argued, for example, that true baptism was inward. They also rejected an organized ministry along with customs that catered to inequality, such as bowing to superiors.

The Pietists

Pietism, another movement that emphasized the importance of religious feelings, developed around the work of Philipp Jacob Spener (1635–1705). Spener was a Lutheran who became convinced that the ministry was lax and overly concerned with worldly status as well as dry orthodoxy. The established church

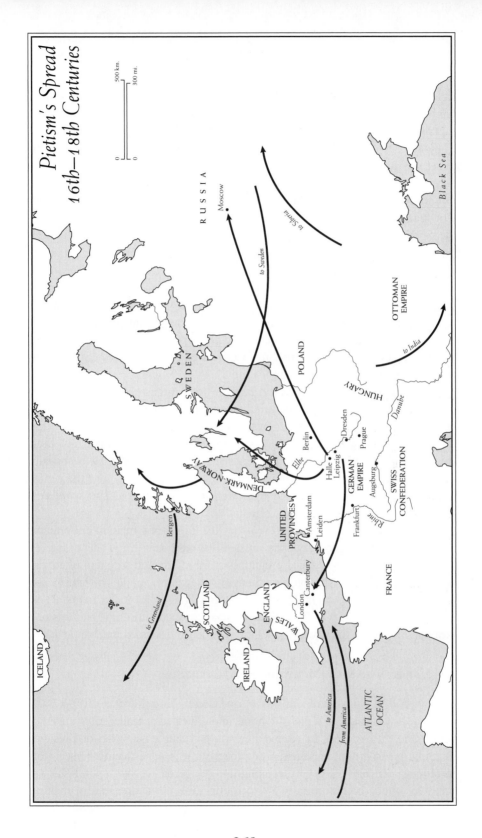

Pietism's Spread
16th–18th Centuries

500 km.
300 mi.

ICELAND

ATLANTIC
OCEAN

IRELAND

SCOTLAND

ENGLAND

WALES

London

Canterbury

FRANCE

UNITED
PROVINCES

Amsterdam

Leiden

Frankfurt

Rhine

SWISS
CONFEDERATION

Augsburg

GERMAN
EMPIRE

Halle

Leipzig

Dresden

Berlin

Elbe

Prague

Danube

HUNGARY

POLAND

DENMARK-NORWAY

Bergen

SWEDEN

RUSSIA

Moscow

OTTOMAN
EMPIRE

Black Sea

to Greenland

to America

from America

to Sweden

to Siberia

to India

called people to live a comfortable life in which people did little more than conform to the accepted morality of the day. Spener believed that Christian morality went far beyond simply doing what was good in the eyes of society. The old issue of Christ and culture plays an important role in Pietism. Right belief was useless unless it was accompanied by true **piety** (sincere devotion accompanied by acts of love). Spener did not disagree with Lutheran doctrine, but instead taught that right feeling was as important as right belief. The Christian faith must be a deep and persnal *living* faith.

Spener wrote the *Pia Desideria* ("*Devout Wishes*") as a guide to attaining piety. It advocated a number of practices to increase devotion, including active participation of laypeople in the priesthood of the believer by ministering to one another, intense study of the Bible, and a return to strong evangelical preaching. Increased piety in pastors as well as in professors and students at universities also was recommended. The movement spread partly because of small circles of believers who came together for prayer, Bible study, and increasing devotion. These gatherings were called *colleges* of piety. Spener saw these as the method for reviving the church.

An important figure in early Pietism was August Hermann Francke (1663–1727). Francke was from a well-to-do Lutheran family. He came to have teachings very similar to Spener but insisted to an even greater degree that the Christian life was a heartfelt, joyous experience. His ideas got him fired from teaching positions at the universities at Erfurt and Leipzig. He eventually secured a job at the new University of Halle, which he turned into the center for Pietism. Hundreds of young men were educated in pietistic ways and placed in pastorates throughout Germany.

Halle also became the source of the first Protestant mission movement. During the eighteenth century, sixty missionaries were sent from Halle to foreign lands. Francke developed social programs for the needy and a system of education for young children that brought them into the pietistic tradition. Pietism also deeply influenced German Lutheran and Reformed traditions. It had an impact on Roman Catholicism as well. It eventually spread throughout Europe and was one idea that influenced the Great Awakening in America discussed in Chapter 12.[5]

Moravians and Methodists

Pietism had a significant influence on Count Zinzendorf (1700–1760). Zinzendorf was raised in a pietistic home and educated at Halle. After traveling widely and studying law, he received an appointment at the court of Dresden. There he met a group of Bohemian Anabaptists who were fleeing persecution in Moravia. Zinzendorf gave these pilgrims refuge on his lands. In 1722 the brethren founded a community at Herrnhut. Zinzendorf dreamed of making

Herrnhut a college of piety to revitalize the Lutheran church. He left his job to join the community and soon became the head of Herrnhut.

Zinzendorf stressed a religion of the heart and ethics based on the Sermon on the Mount. The community soon became caught up in missionary zeal. Before long, the Moravians were sending missionaries to many places in the Old and New Worlds. Zinzendorf himself went to America where he founded Bethlehem, Pennsylvania, as a Moravian settlement. The Moravians were never a large group, but their missionary zeal helped inspire the great nineteenth-century mission efforts greatly influenced John Wesley and the Methodists.

John Wesley (1703–1791) had been raised in a devout home. He attended Oxford University where he distinguished himself as a scholar. He joined a religious club founded by his brother Charles. The group was ridiculed by non-members as the "holy club" or "methodists" because of the methodical way they organized their lives and devotion.

Wesley was ordained an Anglican priest. Early in his career he took a pastorate in Georgia in the New World where he hoped to convert the Indians. The pastorate was a disaster, but on the trip to Georgia he had several encounters with Moravians that changed the course of his life. A Moravian missionary challenged Wesley, "Do you know Christ [personally]?" This query caused Wesley to confront the state of his soul.

After returning to England, Wesley sought direction from other Moravians. Finally, on May 24, 1738, he had an experience at a prayer meeting at Aldersgate that changed his life. In this experience, he came to know beyond doubt that he was saved. Wesley eventually parted company with both the Moravians and the Calvinists. He did not believe in extreme predestination. He accepted the Arminian idea that Christ died for all, not just the elect. If that were not the case, then preaching was wasted. He desired to promote a vital practical religion that would generate Christians who would have the life of God increased in their souls.

Wesley soon found it difficult to find Anglican pulpits in which to preach. He was encouraged by an old friend from the Oxford holy club to adopt a different method. George Whitefield (1714–1770) was an Anglican priest who had an experience similar to Wesley's Aldersgate encounter. Whitefield pastored a church in Georgia but made frequent preaching trips back to England. In Georgia he had taken to preaching outside. He successfully adopted this method in England and came to be recognized as one of the great eighteenth-century preachers.

Wesley followed his friend's example. He began preaching in open fields and drew lots of people, many of whom experienced soul-wrenching conversions. His work was especially effective in the industrial city of Bristol where members of Methodist "societies" were organized by lay leaders to continue to develop their own inner spirituality. Because people did not have to be wealthy or educated to serve as leaders, new possibilities for lay participation opened up that had not existed for many in the Church of England.

Whitefield's and Wesley's efforts were particularly effective in reaching urban workers who had migrated to the cities from traditional farming communities. This migration had uprooted them from their traditional lifestyles and from the parish structure that was a big part of Anglicanism. Some scholars argue that the Methodist movement was one of the forces that prevented the type of political revolutions that would occur later in France, Russia, and elsewhere.

Whitefield and Wesley disagreed over Whitefield's strict Calvinism. The Methodist movement was left firmly in the hands of John Wesley and to a lesser degree his brother Charles. (Charles is best known for the many moving hymns he wrote.) John had no intention of breaking with the Anglican church. Throughout Wesley's life Methodism remained within the Anglican camp. As the movement grew, John rode thousands of miles each year on horseback, preaching and organizing his followers. The movement soon was organized into circuits under the direction of a superintendent.[6] Lay preachers, including women, provided leadership. Wesley's own example formed the basis for "circuit riders" who rode from place to place and preached to widely scattered congregations.

This approach proved particularly effective on the American frontier. John was especially concerned with the New World. In 1771 he sent a lay preacher, Francis Asbury (1745–1816), to preach in America. Asbury was a powerful force in spreading Methodism on the American frontier. In 1784 he ordained Thomas Coke (1747–1814) as the first superintendent in America. Asbury also was made a superintendent later. More superintendents were designated for other countries. Before long Asbury and Coke were calling themselves bishops; consequently, American Methodism has bishops and superintendents while in other places it only has superintendents. Wesley remained in the Anglican church all of his life and resisted efforts by other Methodists to withdraw from the Church of England. By the time of his death, however, Methodism was well on its way to becoming a separate denomination.[7]

THE SMILE OF REASON

Pietism, with its stress on feeling, was one of the trends that shaped the seventeenth and eighteenth centuries. Another influential movement was **rationalism**, the belief that reason alone can comprehend all truth and is sufficient to guide morals. The belief in reason had been growing for several centuries and reached its high point in the eighteenth and nineteenth centuries. Proving theological doctrines by reason alone was a major point in Scholasticism. The reintroduction of Aristotle, with his trust of information gathered by the senses, opened the door to study of the natural world. The process progressed through the Renaissance and the humanistic movement. While Protestantism did not abandon religion, many argue that evangelical thought tended to make religion more reasonable and understandable than it had been in the great mysteries of Catholicism. Gradually the universe came to be seen as a material realm governed by understandable natural laws, not by the mysterious will of God. Understanding these laws would allow people to control the world around them and to build a bright future. The rise of science was one area where confidence in reason would bear much fruit.

The Scientific Revolution

Nicolaus Copernicus (1473–1543) was the most important thinker who contributed to the rise of modern science. Copernicus used mathematical models to turn the universe upside down. Since the days of Aristotle, Western society had accepted the idea that the earth was the center of the universe. The stars, sun, and moon revolved around the earth, locked forever in a hierarchy of spheres. This idea had its impact on theology. The earth and humans were the center of God's concern. Copernicus argued that the sun was the center of the universe and the earth as well as other heavenly bodies revolved around it. He was afraid to publish his findings until the last year of his life. After his views were published, Protestant and Catholic authorities condemned them as incorrect and a threat to the Christian faith.

Another important step toward modern science was taken by Galileo Galilei (1564–1642). Galileo contributed to the science of experimental physics by calculating the speed of falling bodies. Galileo turned to astronomy using a telescope he built. He discovered the moons of Jupiter, sun spots, and imperfections on the moon. His observations supported Copernicus'. They also demonstrated that the universe was uniform and ordered. The earth was not special and different from other bodies in the solar system. Galileo was brought before the Inquisition for his views and forced to deny them.

The shift toward a new understanding of the universe was completed in the work of Sir Isaac Newton (1642–1727). Newton also used mathematics to study the fundamental structure of the universe. He is credited with showing that the material universe is held together by the attraction of gravity. He also set forth the four rules for reasoning, which became the foundation for all later scientific investigation. Newton's universe was an ordered one that operated according to measurable cause-and-effect laws. The universe was in essence a "machine" whose principles of operation could be understood by the human mind.

By the time of Newton, science was beginning to be widely accepted. Though Copernicus and Galileo had found themselves in trouble for their ideas,

Newton was knighted for his! Most European governments were racing to form national science academies. They were competing with one another for new scientific discoveries. Discoveries were made in mathematics, physics, chemistry, astronomy, anatomy, and a host of other disciplines. Catholic church officials generally reacted negatively to the new science but Protestants were more accepting.

By the end of the seventeenth century, the worldview that had formed the basis for society from the time of Aristotle had been replaced by the Copernican-Newtonian understanding of the universe. This understanding had wide-ranging implications for religion and philosophy and for politics and psychology. If the universe and its laws were understandable by reason, then there was no need for revelation or old authorities such as Scripture and church fathers who claimed special revelation. In fact, anyone claiming special revelation or miracles was just spreading superstition.

Theological doctrines were not worth fighting over. Many thought that reason alone could grasp the truth and would lead reasonable people to agreement and toleration, not conflict. Social ills and individual problems could be solved by the power of reason. If government was no longer ordained by God, then its basis must be a democratic contract between reasonable people designed to ensure individual rights. There was no need for God, the Bible, or revelation. The smile of reason spread over the eighteenth century. The eighteenth century is often referred to as the Enlightenment or the Age of Reason.

Rationalism in Philosophy and Religion

Rationalism also had a strong impact on religion and philosophy. René Descartes (1596–1650) was a great believer in the power of the mind. He felt there was nothing beyond human comprehension provided proper mental discipline was used. The correct method was to doubt everything until one reached the point that proof could be obtained with mathematical certainty. Searching for a firm foundation for his philosophy, Descartes doubted everything until he concluded that the only thing he could not doubt was the fact he was doubting. This realization gave him the starting point of his philosophy—"I think, therefore I am."

Descartes built his philosophical system from this unshakable base. God's existence was "proven" by the fact that the idea of God existed. For Descartes, the idea of a "more perfect being" could not have been produced by the mind itself. God must have put it there. Because God exists, the material world and the thinking mind must both have their origins in God. Human minds, like God's, can comprehend the laws that make the universe work. Nothing seemed beyond human grasp.

John Locke (1632–1704) was another figure who advanced the cause of rationalism. Locke wrote a number of important works, one of which was *An Essay Concerning Human Understanding*. Locke argued that at birth the human mind is a *tabula rasa* (blank page, white sheet of paper), which is then written upon by experience. People can know with certainty only three things: the existence of the self, the existence of things that are immediately before them, and God, upon whom the self depends and of whom people's ongoing experiences confirm.

For Locke, another great concept was probability. Probability allows us to function not on the basis of absolute certainty, but on judgments. For instance, individuals cannot prove with certainty that things not in our presence continue to exist. However, because they appear in the same place each time a person is there, individuals make the judgment that they continue to exist. This thinking has implications for faith. Faith is based on revelation, not reason. Revelation may be shown to be probably true but cannot be shown to be absolutely true. Many religious fanatics confuse faith with empirical reason. They wrongly think that revelation proves the tenets of faith with absolute certainty. Because this certainty is impossible, toleration must be extended to a wide variety of beliefs.

In the *Reasonableness of Christianity*, Locke held that there is nothing that is incredible or improbable in Christianity. Christianity is a simple, harmonious, and reasonable religion. Even miracles and revelation are not unreasonable. Yet Locke did not believe that Christianity added anything of importance that could not already be known by judgment and reason.

This type of thinking had been around for some time, but in its latest embodiment it eventually emerged in a religion called *Deism*. Lord Herbert of Cherbury (1583–1648) studied world religions and concluded that all religions contained five common ideas: (1) there is a God; (2) God should be worshiped; (3) virtue is the key part of this worship; (4) repenting for sin is a duty; and (5) there is an afterlife for reward and punishment. He found these five tenets to be the true essence of all religion.

The next important work in Deism's development came out in 1696 when John Toland (1670–1722) published *Christianity Not Mysterious*. Toland contended that there was nothing mysterious in Christianity. The idea that mystery is found in such doctrines as baptism and the Eucharist was promoted by church officials who had a self-interest in maintaining the air of mystery. Reason came before Christ and must be used to judge all doctrines. In 1730 Matthew Tindal (1657–1733) wrote *Christianity as Old as Creation*. In it he taught that all people need is the religion revealed in the natural order. God created an orderly universe. He gave humans reason to understand the laws by which the universe runs. Reason is all that is needed by humans for salvation and to guide their behavior.

Deists saw God as creating a perfect universe. He then withdrew from it. Because God had no further involvement with the material world, such things as miracles and incarnation were impossible. Humans had the capacity to comprehend the physical and moral laws on which the universe operates. Christ was to be respected only because he had lived according to these laws. Moral laws might include human rights or the law of sowing and reaping. Some held there was no judgment or hereafter. People could only reap what they had sown in this world. God may be understood as the Great Watchmaker who creates the perfect watch (the material world), winds it up, and lets it run on its own!

Deistic thought became widespread especially on the Continent. In France, it and other Enlightenment ideas were included in the thinking of Voltaire (1694–1778) and Jean-Jacques Rousseau (1712–1778), which gave rise to the French Revolution. In America, some of the founders of the Republic, including Thomas Jefferson and Thomas Paine, were Deists. It may surprise some to know that the Creator who endowed Americans with inalienable rights was the remote God of the Deists, not the compassionate God of Christ.[8]

Opponents of Rationalism

Rationalism was a major influence on Western thought in the seventeenth and eighteenth centuries, yet it was not without its critics. One important one, David Hume (1711–1776, was very pessimistic about reason's ability to grasp absolute truth. He thought that people learned through experience. Experience comes from observation, but observation does not give insight into the actual nature of things. Observations themselves are colored by the irrational mental customs. For example, people talk in terms of cause and effect, but no one can actually observe one thing causing another. Nor can a person actually observe the "substance" (essence) of a thing. All people have is a series of observations that are linked together in the mind.

These arguments undermined much of rationalistic thought, including the arguments used by the Deists. The Deists argued that the material world was a world of cause and effect. If the world existed, then it must have a cause. That cause was God. Hume showed that cause and effect had no basis in experience. Because "cause and effect" exist only as ideas in the mind, there is no necessary reason to assume a supernatural cause for the material world. Since that is the case, then one could not demonstrate the logical need for God. While the inability to demonstrate a logical need for God did not mean there is no God, it did show that the existence of God could not be proven. Neither doctrines, revelation, the superiority of the Bible, nor claims for church authority could be shown to be true without question. Hume's thought left people with little but skepticism (questioning) toward the natural world and their religion.

The deathblow to simple rationalism was dealt by Immanuel Kant (1724–1804). His *Critique of Pure Reason*, published in 1781, caused a tremendous stir in the intellectual world. He contended that people have no direct knowledge of things-in-themselves. They only "know" what they perceive through their five senses. The mind organizes input from the senses in terms of time and space in twelve categories such as causality, existence, and substance. Knowledge of nature is limited by these categories. We can only guess about religion as it is beyond the realm of pure reason (that is, time and space). That means that reason cannot actually know such things as the existence of God, the soul, or eternity.

Kant's other major works include *Critique of Practical Reason*, *Critique of Judgment*, and *Religion Within the Limits of Reason Alone*. In these works he deals with questions about morality and the existence of God and other issues. Just as people can have no real knowledge of nature, people cannot have an absolute knowledge of right and wrong. But if there is only limited knowledge of right and wrong, then even in trying to do right a person might actually do wrong. What standard should a person use to guide behavior? Kant answers this question with his **categorical imperative.** He says each person should act as if his or her behavior would become a universal rule. By this standard, such acts as murder, stealing, and lying would not be good as they would destroy society. On the other hand, such things as love, justice, and assisting the needy would be good.

While one cannot prove things beyond the realm of time and space, such things as the existence of God, freedom, the soul, and immortality are demanded by "practical reason"—it is such constructs that make life meaningful. If people are to be saved from meaninglessness, then virtue must be rewarded and evil punished. Yet in this world just the opposite often happens. A hereafter is thus demanded where evil *is* punished and good *is* rewarded. Moreover, there must be a judge to ensure this happens. Jesus was important to Kant because he was ruled by the categorical imperative. Kant reduced religion to the categorical imperative and to those concepts that could be derived from it. He believed that there might be more to religion, but reason could not understand more than the imperative.

THE ORTHODOX CHURCH OF THE SEVENTEENTH AND EIGHTEENTH CENTURY

Much of the Orthodox world defended itself against the Muslims and Western Catholicism during the seventeenth and eighteenth centuries. The rivalry between the Orthodox church and the Western church was particularly intense in Poland. Pamphlets and other religious literature were printed presenting

Greek positions. Orthodox schools that rivaled those of the Jesuits were established. Cyril Lucaris (1572–1638) carried on one interesting line of defense. As a young man, Cyril had been a representative at the Council of Brest that declared the Uniate union of Orthodoxy and Catholicism in Poland and the Ukraine. Later he became the patriarch of Constantinople. He then made it his lifelong mission to combat Roman influences in the Turkish Empire. He turned to the embassies from Protestant countries in Constantinople for aid. In the process, he fell under the influence of Calvinism. In 1629 he published his *Confession*, which was definitely Calvinistic in its teachings. Cyril's *Confession* was rejected in a series of Orthodox councils.

Church and State in Russia

The Russian church remained the most active part of Orthodoxy. As in the past, it played a significant role in affairs of state. In the late sixteenth and the early seventeenth centuries there was a period of turmoil in Russia known as "the time of trouble." The death of Ivan IV's childless son left the throne without a successor. A number of contenders presented themselves and civil war resulted. One contender received aid from the Poles and the Jesuits. The Jesuits saw an opportunity to bring the whole Russian church into submission to Rome. The Poles invaded, capturing Moscow.

During this time of trial, the Orthodox church served as a rallying point in resisting the foreigners and the attack by Rome. After the Poles were finally ejected, an assembly was called to restore order to the country. In 1613 the assembly elected the sixteen-year-old Michael Romanov as tsar. Romanov became the head of the dynasty that ruled Russia for the next 300 years. Michael's father, Philaret, was chosen patriarch of Moscow. For the next twenty-four years, state and church leaders worked cooperatively to assist the country in recovery and reform.

The situation changed at Michael's death. Alexis became tsar. One of the most capable men in Russian Orthodox history, Nikon (1605–1681), was eventually made patriarch of Moscow. Nikon undertook changes on many levels. For one thing, he was dissatisfied with the relationship between church and state. In theory, the Russian church operated under the same system of *symphonia* found in the old Byzantine Empire. In fact, however, the Russian church was dominated by the state, a condition Nikon found intolerable. He demanded absolute authority in religious matters and reserved the right to intervene in affairs of state. He even took the title "Great Lord," which previously had been applied only to the tsar.

At first Alexis submitted to Nikon's demands, but he soon came to resent the patriarch. Nikon's reforms in the liturgy were resisted by many religious people, as discussed below. Alexis asked for a council to deal with the patriarch. The council met in Moscow during 1666–1667 and deposed Nikon, but kept many of his religious reforms. It also affirmed the Greek system of *symphonia*; however, this balance of church and state did not last long.

When Peter the Great (1682–1725) became tsar, he was determined to break the power of the patriarch. Upon the death of the latest patriarch in 1700, Peter refused to appoint another. In 1721 he issued the *Spiritual Regulation*, which eliminated the patriarchate and placed the regulation of the church under the direction of a Holy Synod (also known as the Spiritual College). The twelve-member synod was composed of bishops, heads of monasteries, and married clergy. The tsar was seen as the "Supreme Judge of the Spiritual College." The *Spiritual Regulation* made the church a department of the state. The Russian church operated under this system until the Communist revolution in 1917.

The Old Believers Controversy

When Orthodoxy was accepted in Russia, the Greek liturgy was translated into Russian. In the process, a number of errors were made. As a result, Russian practices and rituals differed somewhat from those in Greece and other parts of the Orthodox world. For some time, attempts had been made to prepare new liturgy books that would be more in line with those in Greece. These attempts were resisted by many lower clergy and common people who saw them as a way of destroying their tradition. The reforms also were resisted by Josephites and other supporters of the Third Rome Theory who believed the Greek church was corrupt and the Russian church was the true bearer of Orthodox heritage.

Nikon was an admirer of the Greeks. As patriarch, he had sponsored new Greek translations of the liturgy. He then tried to impose them throughout the Russian church. The hierarchy generally supported the use of the new liturgy books and their revisions of Russian rituals, but many parish clergy, ordinary monks, and common people joined the Josephites in opposing them. The turmoil produced by Nikon's efforts to reform the liturgy helped lead to the council that resulted in his downfall.

Although the Moscow council deposed Nikon, it accepted his reforms in the liturgy. In turn, it tried to impose the new worship practices on the Russian church. Those who held to the old ways were ordered to submit or face excommunication and prison. This action inspired further resistance. These resisters came to be called the **Old Believers**, or **Raskolniks**. The Raskolniks were mainly drawn from the lower classes of society. The Old Believers controversy was, in part, a rebellion of the "have-nots" against the powerful.

The state vigorously persecuted the Old Believers. Thousands were hanged or burned at the stake. Many others chose to end their own lives instead of submitting to the new rituals. Despite extensive persecution and many deaths, the Old Believers persisted. They became fragmented into numerous groups with different beliefs and practices, but still remained a major division within Russian Orthodoxy (or perhaps alongside it). Their appeal to the dispossessed was one way the common people expressed their religious faith.

Even in the face of internal controversies and threats from Islam, Catholicism, and Protestantism, many Orthodox remained faithful to their beliefs. They continued to see themselves as the proper guardians of the true, ancient, apostolic Christian faith.[9]

THE CHURCH AT THE CLOSE
OF THE EIGHTEENTH CENTURY

At the end of the eighteenth century Europe was permanently divided into Protestant and Catholic sections. The religious wars that followed the Reformation failed to produce a clear victory for either side, and they left large sections of Europe devastated. Many became so disgusted with the fighting that they began to feel people might be better off without religion. Parts of Europe are less openly religious to this day than are other parts of the world, especially the United States. On the other hand, a "lasting peace" between Protestants and Catholics had been established. While Protestants and Catholics alike continue to experience discrimination and scattered violence, there has been no return of large-scale religious warfare between the groups. Instead the tendency has been toward increasing toleration and cooperation.

Despite reactions against it, Protestant Scholasticism remained strong. The Catholics engaged in their own forms of conservatism built around the reforms of the Council of Trent. Much of this conservatism centered around obedience to the pope and the rejection of Protestantism. Conservative Catholicism was supported by a powerful educational system that not only taught many students but also helped keep the faithful in the fold. Pietism and similar movements reacted against orthodoxy by insisting that right belief was not enough. Right feeling (deep devotion, the experience of Christ in the heart) which could be fostered by disciplined living, prayer, and Scripture reading, was needed also. These ideas influenced Catholics and most Protestant denominations. Pietism also became the forerunner of feeling-based movements such as romanticism.

Christianity followed the conquerors and colonists as empires spread. The Puritans tried to establish a godly society in North America. Protestant missions began as Moravians and Pietists took up the challenge of sharing the Gospel. Methodists soon attempted to win converts on the American frontier and in other distant lands. These efforts would reach their high point in the great Protestant mission movement of the nineteenth century.

At the same time, other changes were occurring that would remake the world. Industrialization and urbanization were under way and Britain was the first to experience these powerful social forces, which would have worldwide impact in the twentieth century. The urban industrial world was vastly different from the rural farming world in which Christianity had functioned for so long. Democracy was on its way to becoming a widely accepted political system. Equality, the right to vote, and human rights came to be expected and desired by many—a far cry from the hierarchical structure that dominated medieval society. Countries that are mainly Protestant have been more effective in adapting to democracy than have countries that are predominantly Catholic.

Rationalism also left a strong mark on religion and society. Many came to think of traditional doctrine as superstition. A religious person was often seen as narrow-minded. Solutions to human problems came through rational efforts, not divine intervention. The rise of modern science accompanied the emphasis on rationalism. New discoveries opened the universe to humans. There was little need for revelation. Moreover, some scientific discoveries seemed to conflict with religious teachings. For example, the discovery of geological strata (layers of dirt and sediment deposited age after age) demonstrated that the earth was millions of years old, not a few thousand years old as the church had traditionally taught. Fossils and dinosaur bones were discovered in early strata, which raised speculation about evolution as a means of producing life on earth.

Scientific discoveries resulted in issues that unbalanced the theological world. Copernican and Newtonian theories radically changed views on the material world and the place of humans in it. The universe was no longer limited and centered on earth where God could be passionately involved with human affairs. Instead it was limitless. The earth was not the center of the universe but simply one of many planets. Humans did not have the same importance they had in an earth-centered universe. Perhaps humans were just one of many intelligent species on a multitude of inhabited planets scattered in the vast expanse of space. If that were the case, how could Christians then claim that the death of Christ had implications for the salvation of all? As long as humans were the center of the universe, the death of Christ and human redemption seemed to have great importance. But what was the impact of the death of this would-be Jewish Messiah on a small planet of a small star in an infinite universe? As the scientific model of the universe unfolded, humans and the Christian Savior would seem less important in the scheme of things. The criteria for evaluating the correctness of things became more rational and scientific, not more religious.

Yet Kant had demonstrated that science and reason could no more discover absolute truth than could religion. Whether dealing with science, reason, religion, the future life, or morals, it was impossible to be totally objective. Kant opened the door to the subjectivism and relativism that characterize the twentieth century. **Subjectivism** suggests each person has her or his own definition of truth. **Relativism** suggests there are no truths that are correct in all times and situations. Instead, truth is always related to the time, place, or culture in which it is taught.

CONCLUSIONS

By the end of the eighteenth century, Christianity was experiencing two powerful trends that would continue to define it into the twentieth century. Its renewed vigor from such sources as Pietism resulted in deeper faith, revivalism, and mission efforts. This vigor helped Christianity to launch worldwide evangelistic campaigns and to confront social problems associated with urbanization.

At the other extreme, philosophical and scientific trends posed significant challenges to the faith. The skepticism of philosophy demanded new understandings of faith, reason, and historic doctrines, which would occupy the greatest of Christian minds. New scientific findings would continue to undermine traditional Christian teachings. More important, Christianity had to learn to operate within a worldview that was more and more dominated by the scientific perspective. Religion had to deal with both skepticism and science if it was to survive. These and other trends will be examined in Chapter 10.

Notes

1. For a good discussion of the Thirty Years' War, see Justo L. González, *The Story of Christianity*, vol. 2, *The Reformation to the Present Day*. San Francisco: Harper & Row, 1984, pp. 134–141.
2. Denominations have debated the New Testament pattern of church organization for centuries. In the New Testament, the Greek words for elders (*presbyters*) and overseers (*bishops*) seem to have much the same meaning. The development of the role of the bishop was discussed earlier in this text. The hierarchical episcopal structure emerged after the New Testament period. At the same time, the episcopal structure may have roots in the first century. For instance, Paul exercised "bishop-like" influence over the congregations he founded. Other congregations seem to have had a great deal of self-rule. Some had a presbytery structure. The bottom line is that the episcopal, presbytery, and congregational patterns may all have their forerunners in the fluid situation of the first century. In all likelihood, there was no single New Testament pattern, only New Testament patterns.
3. For a good discussion of the early Puritans in America, see Perry Miller, *Errand into the Wilderness*. Cambridge, MA: Harvard University Press, 1956.
4. For a good discussion of the Puritan revolt, see González, vol. 2, pp. 149–163.
5. For a good discussion of the emergence of Pietism in Germany, see Kurt Aland, *A History of Christianity*, vol. 2, *From the Reformation to the Present*, trans. by James L. Schaff. Philadelphia: Fortress, 1980, pp. 221–266.

6. Wesley knew that the Greek word for *superintendent* had the same meaning as the one for *bishop*. Yet he did not want to appear to be setting up a denomination separate from the Church of England by ordaining his own bishops.

7. Whitefield along with Wesley and the Methodists was a part of what would become a larger movement among Protestants known as *revivalism*. Revivalism began as a spontaneous renewal in the colonies during the early eighteenth century known as the Great Awakening. This movement was so successful at bringing new life to churches that it spread rapidly to England and the Continent.

8. For a good discussion of the political and social context of the Enlightenment, see Donald Kagan, Steven Ozment, and Frank M. Turner, *The Western Heritage*, 3d ed. New York: Macmillan, 1987, pp. 594–653.

9. For a good discussion of the Orthodox church during the sixteenth and seventeenth centuries, see Timothy Ware, *The Orthodox Church*. Baltimore: Pelican, 1973, pp. 119–128, and Kenneth Scott Latourette, *A History of Christianity*, vol. 2, *Reformation to the Present*, rev. ed. New York: Harper & Row, 1975, pp. 907–922.

Additional Readings

Aaron, Richard I. *John Locke*. 3d ed. Oxford: Oxford University Press, 1971.

Andrews, Wayne. *Voltaire*. Salem, OR: New Directions, 1981.

Bangs, Carl. *Arminius: A Study in the Dutch Reformation*. Nashville: Abingdon, 1971.

Bates, Arlo. *The Puritans*. Reprint. Ridgewood, NJ: Gregg Press, 1968.

Bostridge, Ian. *Witchcraft and Its Transformations, c.1650–c.1750*. New York: Oxford University Press, 1997.

Bradley, James E. *Religion, Revolution, and Radicalism: Nonconformity in Eighteenth-Century Politics and Society*. New York: Cambridge University Press, 1990.

Collinson, Patrick. *The Elizabethan Puritan Movement*. New York: Oxford University Press, 1990.

Cragg, Gerald R. *Reason and Authority in the Eighteenth Century*. Cambridge: Cambridge University Press, 1964.

Davies, Rupert E. *Methodism*. Baltimore: Penguin, 1963.

Descartes, René. *Discourse on Method and the Meditations*. Translated by John Veitch. Loma Linda, CA: Prometheus, 1989.

———. *Principles of Philosophy*. Translated by Valentine R. Miller and Reese P. Miller. Hingham, MA: Kluwer, 1984.

Eales, Jacqueline. *Puritans and Roundheads: The Harleys of Brampton Bryan and the Outbreak of the English Civil War*. New York: Cambridge University Press, 1990.

Fraser, Antonia. *Cromwell: The Lord Protector*. Reprint. New York: Donald I. Fine, Inc., 1986.

Gauchet, Marcel. *The Disenchantment of the World: A Political History of Religion*. Princeton, NJ: Princeton University Press, 1997.

Gay, Peter. *The Enlightenment*. New York: Random House, 1966.

Golden, Richard M., ed. *The Huguenot Connection: The Edict of Nantes*. Hingham, MA: Kluwer, 1988.

Hales, E. E. Y. *Revolution and Papacy, 1764–1864*. Garden City, NJ: Hanover, 1960.

Hall, David E., ed. *Puritans in the New World: A Critical Anthology*. Princeton, NJ: Princeton University Press, 2004.

Kant, Immanuel. *Critique of Pure Reason*. Translated by J. M. Meiklejohn. Loma Linda, CA: Prometheus, 1990.

King-Hele, D. G., and A. R. Hall, eds. *Newton's Principia and Its Legacy*. Vol. 42, No. 1. Port Washington, NY: Scholium, 1988.

Knecht, R. J. *Richelieu*. White Plains, NY: Longman, 1991.

LaPlante, Eve. *American Jezebel: The Uncommon Life of Anne Hutchinson, the Woman Who Defied the Puritans*. New York: HarperCollins, 2004.

Locke, John. *An Essay Concerning Human Understanding*. Translated by Peter H. Nidditch. Reprint. Oxford: Oxford University Press, 1979.

———. *The Reasonableness of Christianity*. Edited by George W. Ewing. Reprint. Washington, D.C.: Regnery, 1989.

McBeth, H. Leon. *The Baptist Heritage*. Nashville: Broadman, 1987.

Milton, John. *Paradise Lost*. Great Books of the Western World. Vol. 32. Chicago: Encyclopaedia Britannica, 1955.

Outler, A. C. *John Wesley*. New York: Oxford University Press, 1964.

Petersen, Rodney L. *Preaching the Last Days: The Theme of "Two Witnesses" in the 16th and 17th Centuries*. New York: Oxford University Press, 1993.

Pollock, John. *John Wesley*. Wheaton, IL: Scripture, 1989.

Rees, Helen G. *Guytons Galore: From French Huguenots to Oregon Pioneers*. Portland, OR: Binford and Mort, 1986.

Simpson, Alan. *Puritanism in Old New England*. Chicago: University of Chicago Press, 1955.

Stoeffler, F. Ernest. *German Pietism During the Eighteenth Century*. Leiden: Brill, 1973.

Torbet, R. G. *A History of the Baptists*. 3d ed. Valley Forge, PA: Judson, 1963.

Van Etten, Henry. *George Fox and the Quakers*. New York: Harper, 1959.

Websites

http://en.wikipedia.org/wiki/Puritan [Provides articles and links to a host of topics associated with the Puritans]

http://www.apuritansmind.com/ [Provides a gold mine of articles and links about a comprehensive range of subjects regarding Puritans and Calvinism as well]

http://www.fordham.edu/halsall/mod/modsbook10.html [Provides a very useful source of articles about the Enlightenment along with Enlightenment original documents]

http://www.lucidcafe.com/library/95sep/richelieu.html [Provides an article about Cardinal Richelieu and links to a variety of resources]

http://www.questia.com/library/religion/theology/theologians/john-wesley.jsp?CRID=john_wesley&OFFID=se1&KEY=john_wesley&LID=14578296 [Provides online library of articles and books about Wesley and Methodism]

IV

CHRISTIANITY IN THE MODERN AND GLOBAL ERAS

INTRODUCTION

Scholars debate when the modern era actually began. Some argue that it should be dated from the sixteenth-century Reformation. The Reformation established a clear break from the medieval understanding of church and society. The secular state started to come into its own as the source of authority in society. The importance of the church and of religion in people's lives began to decrease. Individualism, subjectivism, and secularization became more important after the Reformation.

Others argue that the modern era really began in the nineteenth century. It was then that many of the trends that started in the Middle Ages and the Reformation began to be felt. Moreover, many trends inspired by the Enlightenment bore fruit in the 1800s. At the same time, Kant's criticisms of reason and the negative aspects of the French Revolution had their strongest impact in the nineteenth century. In addition, capitalism, industrialization, urbanization, and the pressures from population growth, which are such a part of the modern scene, began to assert themselves in the nineteenth century.

Whenever the modern era actually started, it was obvious in the nineteenth century that a vastly different world was emerging. For at least the last 200 years the church has faced the challenge of dealing with this new world. Some parts of the church have tried to "make peace" with this new world by submitting to it and incorporating its concerns into Christian doctrine and practice. Others have rejected the modern world altogether, often demanding that modern Christians return to traditional ideas and practices that are considered vital to the faith.

By the early twentieth century, it was obvious that modernism was spreading beyond its traditional boundaries in the West to much of the rest of the world. In fact, most of the societies characterized as rural and traditional at the beginning of the twentieth century were transformed into urban, industrial, scientific ones by the end of the twentieth century. Almost all of those societies that had not changed completely were well on their way to becoming modern by 2001. As a result, many portions of the world were experiencing much the same turmoil produced by modernization as had accompanied the movement to modern societies we see in the West. The chaos produced by social change in these parts of the world has resulted in many of the same types of religious reactions that appeared in Western societies.

The early twentieth century also saw the recognition of yet another earth-shaking change. Intellectuals in a variety of disciplines began to talk about post-modernism. They believed that modernism had reached its limits and, perhaps, was causing more harm than good. While the emphasis of many of these persons was on the negative consequences, toward the end of the twentieth century, writers, commentators, business people, military persons, and politicians began to talk about post-industrial or advanced industrial societies. They also began to talk about an emerging global society. The process creating this new type of society is called globalization.

We discuss globalization and some of its implications in Chapters 11 and 12. At this point, we only wish to make one interesting observation. If we look at the bigger picture, we can say that major changes in Western European history have occurred about every 500 years:

1 C.E.	Birth of Jesus
500 C.E.	Collapse of Roman Empire/Early Middle Ages Begin
1000 C.E.	High Middle Ages Begin
1500 C.E.	Reformation Occurs/Start of Modern Period
2000 C.E.	Emerging Global Society

Each 500-year marker indicates a significant watershed in Western history as we have seen throughout this book. This pattern has implications for the current context for understanding Christianity because the period of colonialism that started with Christopher Columbus led to the eventual spreading of Western culture and the Christian faith around the world. To some degree, emerging global society is built on Western civilization and the modern period, but in other ways it represents a radical departure from them.

This part of the book departs somewhat from the form used in other sections. Given the importance of understanding the modern world and emerging global society, we dedicate most of Chapter 11 to discussing relevant elements of the modern period. We also address some of the more important reactions of Roman Catholicism to social, economic, and political changes associated the modernization and globalization. Chapter 12 deals mainly with various religious reactions to modernism and emerging global society. It then explores briefly the uncertain, but hopeful position in which Christianity finds itself as it enters the twenty-first century.

11

CHRISTIANITY FROM MODERN TO GLOBAL SOCIETY: MODERNIZATION, GLOBALIZATION, AND THE CATHOLIC REACTION

(1800–Present)

Charles Darwin

This chapter establishes the background of the modern period by examining important trends and events of the last two centuries. We then review some of the ways that the Catholic church has operated in this environment. In the next chapter, we concentrate on how Protestant churches have reacted to modern society over the last two centuries and assess the state of Christianity at the beginning of the third millennium since Jesus' birth.

THE WORLD IN THE NINETEENTH THROUGH THE TWENTY-FIRST CENTURY

The nineteenth and twentieth centuries were a period of great advance for Western culture. A new phase of empire building spread Western influence. Scientific discoveries continued to deepen the understanding of the universe. Technology was used to solve problems, from increasing agricultural output, to conquering illness, to improving production. All of these advances led to a tremendous period of optimism in the nineteenth century. It seemed as if humans were on the verge of conquering problems that had plagued them since the beginning of time. Human perfection seemed possible.

Forces were operating that would bring this optimism to an end, however. Philosophy was moving toward nihilism in Europe. **Nihilism** is the total rejection of the ability to understand any ultimate truth. It implied that there were no absolute morals or, at least, that humans could not discover them if they did exist. World War I was even more important to the destruction of nineteenth-century optimism. In World War I, the very science and technology that promised so much good created terrible tools for death, resulting in destruction and suffering never before known in human history. The years after World War I were characterized by worldwide economic and political chaos. In World War II the forces of death and destruction reached new heights. Since World War II, crises and new problems have caused many to despair of humanity's ability to deal rationally with a progressively hostile environment. Despite some rays of hope, humanity seems in danger of being overwhelmed as it moves into the twenty-first century.

Revolutions, New Powers, and the New Imperialism

The American and French revolutions of the late eighteenth century had a strong effect on the first half of the nineteenth century. On the European Continent, the French Revolution was much more important than the American revolt. The French Revolution began in 1789 and went through several phases over the next ten years. Many of the ideas underlying the revolution came from the Enlightenment. French citizens rallied around the cry "Liberty, Equality, and Fraternity" (brotherhood).

Despite such high ideals, the revolution drifted into rule by terror in which thousands of suspected "counterrevolutionaries" were put to death. The leaders of the revolution saw themselves as the commanders of a new order in which science and reason would overcome superstition and religion. As the revolution turned more radical, Christianity was seen as a threat. The leaders sought to replace it with natural religion. Traditional worship was discouraged. Priests and other Christians eventually were persecuted. The revolution created its own religion with elaborate rituals around the "cult of reason" and the "cult of the Supreme Being." A new non-Christian calendar was created. Liquor was poured out as offerings to statues of nature, which had been made a god. Political heroes were substituted for saints. Churches were made "temples of reason."

The French Revolution was founded on democratic ideals, which had become a part of Western culture. These ideals would continue to have great influence into the twentieth century. However, the excesses that resulted from the revolution caused many to fear uncontrolled rationalism. Many started appealing to the "purity" of feelings and longed for a simpler, more natural past. This sparked a movement among artists, writers, and poets called **romanticism.** The romantics emphasized feeling over thinking. They glorified nature and advocated abandoning civilization because it was an artificial creation of humans. The closer one could live to nature the better one was.

Despite such reactions, many ideas and goals of the French Revolution still had appeal. They influenced liberalism, which spread throughout nineteenth-century Europe. Liberals generally drew on the ideas of the Enlightenment and the French Revolution in advocating the extension of the vote to more people, free speech, and, later in the century, protection of the less fortunate. These ideas sparked significant reform and revolts in the mid-nineteenth century in a number of European countries.

Two new nation-states arose in the late 1800s. Italy was finally unified under the leadership of King Victor Emmanuel II in 1861. Strong currents of nationalism had pushed the nation toward unification throughout the nineteenth century. The move was opposed by the Austrians, who controlled many of the states that made up the new nation. It also was radically opposed by the pope, who feared a further decline of his power.

Germany achieved unification in 1871 under the direction of the Prussian ruler William I and his able chancellor, Otto Eduard Leopold von Bismarck. Bismarck took advantage of a wave of nationalism after defeating both the Austrians and French. Germany was then the most powerful nation on the Continent. It was a state dominated by military interests. Liberal opponents had been defeated by Bismarck. Germany set out to build empires.

By the late nineteenth century, most major world powers began a new phase of empire building. This time the expansion was into Africa, China, and the Middle East. Japan had been forced open by an American fleet in 1853.

Important Events of the Nineteenth through Early Twenty-First Centuries

DATES	EVENTS	SECULAR LEADER	CHURCH PERSON	WRITINGS
1734	Great Awakening begins in America	Edwards		
1789	French Revolution begins			
1792	Mission movement begins, Particular Baptist Society founded			
1793	Protestant mission in India	Carey		
1797	Second Awakening begins in America			
1799–1822	Liberal theology takes form		Schleiermacher	*Speeches on Religion, Christian Faith*
1830	Mormonism founded		Smith	*Book of Mormon*
1843	Existentialism begins		Kierkegaard	*Either/Or, Attack upon Christendom*
1848	Communism advocated	Marx		*Communist Manifesto*
1859	Evolutionary theory	Darwin		*Origin of Species*
1864	Many modern views condemned		Pius IX	*Syllabus of Errors*
1869–1870	Vatican I, dogma of papal infallibility		Pius IX	
1891	Problems of laborers addressed		Leo XIII	*Rerum novarum*
1895	Five fundamentals formed			
1896	Nihilism advanced	Nietzsche		*Thus Spake Zarathustra*
1907	American Social Gospel		Rauschenbusch	*Christianity and the Social Crisis*
1909	Dispensationalism advanced		Scofield	*Scofield Reference Bible*
1914–1918	World War I			

Important Events of the Nineteenth through Early Twenty-First Centuries

DATES	EVENTS	SECULAR LEADER	CHURCH PERSON	WRITINGS
1917	Communist Revolution in Russia	Lenin		
1919	Neo-orthodoxy begins		Barth	Commentary on Romans
1922	Fascism in Italy	Mussolini		
1925	Height of early Fundamentalist/Modernist controversy, Scopes "Monkey Trial"			
1932–1967	Neo-orthodoxy advanced		R. Niebuhr	Moral Man and Immoral Society
1932–1967	Neo-orthodoxy advanced		Barth	Church Dogmatics
1933	Fascism in Germany	Hitler		
1939–1945	World War II			
1945	Nuclear attack on Hiroshima, Bonhoeffer killed in German prison, Cold War begins		Bonhoeffer	Letters from Prison
1948	World Council of Churches founded			
1950	Assumption of Mary made dogma		Pius XII	
1961	Death of God theology emerges		Vahanian	The Death of God
1962–1965	Vatican II		John XXIII	
1965	Theology of hope appears		Moltmann	Theology of Hope
1970–1980	Fundamentalists and New Right become more active			
1972	Liberation theology advanced		Gutiérrez	A Theology of Liberation
1978–2005	Papacy of John Paul II		John Paul II	
1989	Berlin Wall torn down, new era between East and West begins			

By the end of the century Japan also was engaged in expanding its empire into China, Korea, and other Asian nations. In addition, the United States had gone through its own Civil War and was emerging as a major industrial, military, and colonial power.

While there certainly were pessimists, as discussed later in this chapter, nineteenth-century leaders were largely optimistic. Liberalism tended to be optimistic. It particularly believed in the ability to produce perfect people and perfect societies. Furthermore, almost everyone believed that Western civilization was humanity's highest achievement. The Western world felt a duty to share its enlightenment with the "backward" societies of the world. Much of the Western world felt the **white man's burden**, which was that people of European background had a special obligation (if not a calling from God) to share the benefits of their advanced civilization with their **brown brothers** (East Indians, Africans, Native Americans, and other dark-skinned peoples) around the world. The "brown brothers" were often seen as simple, uncivilized people who were incapable of ruling themselves effectively and who lived in societies characterized by superstition and immorality.

This attitude was (and probably still is) especially strong in the United States. From the time of the Pilgrims, some Americans felt that they had a special calling from God to be a light unto the world. This attitude had its origins in the idea that America was to be God's "righteous nation" where the example of a holy society would be created. Democracy and capitalism later would be added to the definition of the righteous nation. Thus, America has felt that its mission was to spread the good news of the "holy trinity"—Christianity, Democracy, and Capitalism—to a needy world! The white man's burden was used by Western societies throughout the period of new imperialism to justify the taking of native lands and the destruction of indigenous cultures.

These ideas fed into the increased missionary activities of the nineteenth and twentieth centuries. Many of the early modern missionaries seem to have understood Christianity as being much the same thing as Western society. As a result, as they spread Christianity, they sought to westernize native cultures as well. However, such attitudes lead to a rejection of westernized Christianity by many important native church leaders. These leaders created versions of the faith based on the ideas and practices of the indigenous cultures. We discuss these in greater detail in Chapter 12.

Industrialization, Urbanization, and Population Growth

Three significant changes created a tremendous, worldwide social revolution during the nineteenth and twentieth centuries: industrialization, urbanization, and population growth. While they held out great promise, they also subjected societies to terrible stresses. Like societies in general, Christianity has had to adjust to the consequences of these changes. The faith is operating in a much different world in the twentieth century than it was at the beginning of the nineteenth century.

The **industrial revolution** was a series of sweeping economic and social changes that began in England in the late eighteenth century. It eventually spread to the Continent, the United States, and much of the world. Industrial production moved to factories where larger groups of organized workers used machine power to increase output. An agricultural revolution had preceded the industrial revolution. Improved agricultural methods and scientific methods of food production allowed the production of more food by fewer people. The agricultural revolution permitted sufficient food to be grown for expanding urban populations and also freed large numbers of people from producing food to work in the new factories.

Industrial cities attracted people to work in the factories and mills. Many left the countryside hoping to find a better life. The population of the cities swelled. Great Britain became the first society to **urbanize** (more than one-half of its population lived in urban areas) in the nineteenth century. Other societies followed suit, but most industrialized nations did not urbanize until the twentieth century. Even the nonindustrial, or developing nations, are now urbanizing. Urbanization is a major problem in some developing nations because many of their cities have increasing populations but few industrial jobs to support the people. Nevertheless, by the year 2000 the vast majority of the earth's people lived in urban areas.

It is important to recognize the changes urbanization has brought. Throughout most of history, people have lived in rural tribal groups or small villages. People knew everyone they saw on a daily basis. On the one hand, they tended to help their neighbors in times of need. On the other hand, it was fairly easy to know other people's "business" and to control their behavior. Most people had the same or similar racial and ethnic backgrounds. They engaged in much the same activities and shared similar values. They had a sense of belonging to a common community. In the West the church was often the center of this community.

Many of these qualities changed with urbanization. Because vast numbers of people were living together, it was impossible to know everyone in the city personally. There was little sense of community. Methods of controlling people's behavior changed. Societies relied on law and formal agents like police to make sure people obeyed the law. People felt little responsibility for helping one another. To further complicate matters, the city brought together people from different backgrounds who often did not share common values or lifestyles. They were of different racial, ethnic, and religious groups.

When Will Christ Return?

The Second Coming of Christ has been expected since the early church. Much of the speculation about his return has centered around the millennium. The *millennium* is the thousand years of peace that the Revelation of John in the New Testament seems to indicate is associated with Christ's coming. Three different understandings of how Christ's return relates to the millennium can be found in church history.

The *postmillennial* (after the millennium) interpretation says life in this world will be getting better and better as the kingdom of God is progressively realized. Finally, things will be so good that 1000 years of peace and prosperity will result. After that, Christ will return and bring in the new heaven and new earth.

The *premillennialists* (before the millennium) believe conditions in the world will get worse and worse. Evil will become overwhelming. Christ will return, bind the devil, and establish the thousand years of peace. After the millennium, the devil will be loosened for a while to tempt all those who might still fall into his traps. He and his forces finally will be destroyed and thrown forever into torment. Then Christ will bring in the new heaven and new earth.

The *amillennialists* (no millennium) believe good and evil will continue to coexist until Christ's return. Life will get neither better nor worse. There will be no literal millennium. Because of that, Christ can return at any time to establish the new heaven and new earth.

Postmillennial ideas tended to dominate in the optimism of the nineteenth century. Premillennial teachings have been more obvious in the more pessimistic times of the twentieth century.

Especially in its early phases, industrial capitalism exaggerated the differences between those who were wealthy and in control and laborers who were poor and often exploited. Urban slums grew and were often filled with poverty, crime, prostitution, violence, child abuse, and alcoholism. Christianity had to try to cope with the urban situation. Traditional church structures like the parish did not work very well in an environment where people had little sense of community. Traditional methods of winning new converts were not very successful either. Problems seemed overwhelming. New methods of reaching the lost, dealing with social problems, and ministering to needs had to be developed. Some new methods were developed in the nineteenth century as the church started to adjust to the urban world; however, much still needs to be done. The church is still confronted with questions about how to extend the Gospel to the urban world.

Problems associated with industrialization and urbanization were enhanced by dramatic, worldwide population increases. Human population had increased very slowly ever since *Homo sapiens* (the scientific name for humans) first appeared on the scene about 50,000 years ago. Increased agricultural and industrial production and medical advances meant more and more people were surviving until their reproductive years. As a result, population started to skyrocket. It took until 1850 for the earth's population to reach 1 billion. Yet the second billion was added by the mid-1930s. The fourth billion was added by the mid-1960s. At present the earth's population is between 6 and 8 billion and is *doubling* every thirty to forty years. The population increase is most rapid in developing nations, where many people are crowding into already overpopulated, under-industrialized cities.

This rapid population increase has heightened existing concerns. Problems of poverty have been made even worse. Economic systems are struggling to meet the needs of ever-increasing numbers of people. Pollution from people and the industries needed to support them is threatening the existence of life on this planet. Wars and famines, as well as the push toward new worldwide political and economic systems, are fueled partly by population pressures. The church is forced to confront all these problems. It is also finding itself in a world that is more and more non-Western and non-Christian because much of the population increase is in areas where Christianity has played a limited role.

World Wars I and II

During the late nineteenth century and the early twentieth century tensions increased between the European powers. The European nations and Russia played dangerous games that brought them to the brink of war in Europe, Africa, and the Middle East. These were accompanied by a massive arms build-up.

World War I and Its Aftermath.   An incident in 1914 in the Balkans rapidly spread as the Central powers of Germany, Austria-Hungary, Turkey, and Bulgaria aligned themselves against the Allied powers of Great Britain, France, and Russia. World War I had begun. In time, Russia was forced to withdraw because of the 1917 communist revolution. However, more than thirty other countries eventually joined on the side of the Allies, including the United States.

During the four years of the war 65 million men were under arms. More than 9 million of these died and more than 21 million were wounded. Civilian casualties probably were at least as high. The technology and industrial production that had given the West such hope in the nineteenth century was turned to destruction. New inventions, such as chemical warfare, the submarine, the airplane, and the machine gun, made war even more horrendous. Pessimism and self-doubt began to settle on the Continent, although the United States escaped many of these reactions until after World War II.

The treaty ending World War I was seen as just, if not lenient, by the Allies. But the Germans felt it placed an unduly heavy burden on them. Many felt resentful and desired an opportunity for revenge. The German people felt deprived of their "natural" place of dominance in the community of nations. To make matters worse, economic, political, and social unrest were common in Germany, other parts of Europe, and North America. Economies fluctuated wildly and the world economic system was unstable. Unemployment and inflation were high. Labor unrest was widespread. When people feel threatened in such situations, the ground is fertile for the growth of political extremism.

The Rise of Fascism and World War II.   That is exactly what happened. Fascism came to the forefront under these unstable conditions. It developed first in Italy under Benito Mussolini. Fascist movements soon appeared in Spain, Greece, Japan, Poland, Austria, Hungary, Romania, and Bulgaria. Adolph Hitler's Nazi Germany rapidly became the dominant fascist power in Europe. The Fascists appealed to extreme nationalism and claimed that their nation had a special destiny to fulfill. They used racial, ethnic, and political minorities as scapegoats. This particular element was exploited most successfully in Nazi Germany where Hitler built upon the anti-Semitism that always had been part of the Christian West. Hitler offered a "final solution" to the existence of Jews and other "inferior" minorities in which he slaughtered several million innocent people. This shameful period, known as the **Holocaust,** is one of the saddest events in human history.

Fascists also glorified war and hated the weakness of those who desired peace. Strength, power, and dominance were to be pursued. Democracy and liberalism were enemies. Individualism, human rights, free speech, the free press, and the arts were attacked. Totalitarian governments that were ruled by one party and that persecuted all those who disagreed took control where Fascists came into power. They often were unethical in dealing with other governments. Agreements and treaties were made only to be violated when it suited the Fascists. They operated under the principle "might makes right." The Fascists came to power by promising security, law, and order in the instability of the 1920s and 1930s. Many people were willing to exchange their rights for the promise of a stable, orderly society.

The Germans, Italians, and Japanese formed the Axis alliance and began a series of military conquests that culminated in World War II. The war actually started in September 1939. In the long run, the combined power of the Allies (Great Britain, France, the Soviet Union, the United States, and those countries fighting with them) proved too much for the Axis. The Italians were defeated in 1943. The Germans surrendered in May 1945 and the Japanese in August 1945. The final victory over Japan was hastened by the dropping of atomic bombs on the cities of Hiroshima and Nagasaki by the United States. The terrible destruction wrought by these weapons ushered in a new and frightening age.

The Cold War. The victorious Allies were determined to prevent the economic and social instability that culminated in World War II from occurring again. The Soviet Union was given control of much of Eastern Europe. A liberal world economic order was created that stabilized currencies around the fixed price of gold and later around the value of the U.S. dollar. Trade regulations were created in a series of international conferences that tried to ensure free trade. Eventually most of the Western countries, developing nations, and Japan were integrated into this system. The communist countries formed their own trading block, which had only limited contact with the liberal economic order dominated by the industrialized nations.

The cooperation between the capitalistic democracies of the West and the communist dictatorship in the Soviet Union had been key to victory in World War II; however, this cooperation rapidly dissolved into hostility and mistrust. A peculiar mentality dominated thinking on both sides. Communist teachings advocated spreading the workers' revolution all over the world. Communist governments were installed in Eastern Europe. A revolution in China brought that country into the communist sphere. The West came to believe (often incorrectly) that every move the Soviets and their allies made was aimed at world domination. On the other hand, the Soviets inherited the Russian fear of the West and the Chinese continued their centuries-old suspicion of outsiders. They, too, were convinced that the capitalists were trying to destroy them.

This mistrust led to the so-called Cold War between capitalist and communist powers. The Cold War supported a loud war of words in which each side threatened the other. A massive arms race was undertaken out of fear, which became particularly menacing when the Soviets also developed nuclear weapons in the 1950s. Arms were stockpiled to the point that each side could destroy the earth several times over. Strangely world peace was ensured by a doctrine called MAD (Mutually Assured Destruction)! The Cold War dominated the world scene for almost forty years.

In the United States, fear of the "communist menace" was whipped into a frenzy during the early 1950s by Senator Joseph McCarthy of Wisconsin. McCarthy had a following of millions of Americans and was convinced that the American government, defense industries, educational system, artistic community, and military were filled with Communists and their sympathizers. Fear and suspicion overcame the country. To be a liberal meant that one was a Communist. Hundreds were hauled before investigating committees or were harassed by the Federal Bureau of Investigation (FBI). Thousands lost their jobs. McCarthyism demonstrated that even a "Christian nation" dedicated to liberty and justice for all could be caught in extremism.

Emerging Global Society

After World War II, most of the colonial powers freed their colonies or their colonies freed themselves through revolution; thus many new nations came into being. Most either were not yet industrialized or were in the process of industrializing. They were forced to compete in a world market dominated by the United States and other Western countries. That left many of them dependent on the very countries from whom they had so recently won freedom. As a rule, nations in the Northern Hemisphere were industrialized and prosperous. Nations in the Southern Hemisphere tended to be non-industrialized and poor.

For the most part this discrepancy in wealth has grown in the last forty years. Efforts to improve the standard of living in many non-industrialized, or "developing," nations have been overwhelmed by rapid population growth. At the same time, the world economy has become more and more integrated. In many ways, the industrialized nations are as much dependent on the developing nations as the developing nations are dependent on them. This trend toward interdependency has been fostered by political alliances and worldwide communications. Few societies are isolated. There is little doubt that one of the most important qualities of the twentieth century was the beginning of a truly global community. This process is referred to as globalization. **Globalization** is an ongoing process of social change that is radically remaking the way people interact, the social systems into which people are immersed, and the context in which they practice religion.

This process has advanced in recent years by the collapse of most parts of the communist world. In the late 1980s the communist system in the Soviet Union, Eastern Europe, and other places folded. Most of the socialist nations are attempting to convert to some form of capitalism and have taken steps toward democratic reform. Many are attempting to integrate into the liberal economic order of the West. They are seeking Western help and emphasizing cooperation with capitalistic societies. This left the United States as the sole surviving superpower and at the center of much of the world's economic, political, and cultural developments. While it is impossible to know just what it will look like, it appears that a new world order is emerging. We look at some of the perspectives of global society later in this chapter. For now, we review some of the challenges for Christianity posed by the modern period.

PERSPECTIVES OF THE MODERN ERA

Christianity had to deal with new intellectual trends in the nineteenth and twentieth centuries. Many of these trends originated in earlier periods and came into full force in the modern era. Christianity has had to adjust to these trends just as it has had to adjust to other cultural changes ever since its founding. Some Christian movements attempted to adjust by virtually surrendering to the changes. Others attempted to adopt new ideas while still maintaining the essentials of their faith. Still others rejected new concepts altogether.

Political Liberalism

Political liberalism was one such set of ideas that affected Christianity. Liberals advocated individual rights, free speech, and democracy. They were suspicious of the type of hierarchical authority upon which monarchies and many denominations had depended.[1] Eventually they would advocate the extension of the vote to all men and women. To some extent, liberals saw contemporary troubles such as poverty, divorce, crime, and alcoholism as societal problems rather than as individual failures. As a result, they advocated government protection of the poor as well as government involvement in creating new programs to deal with social problems created by industrial, capitalistic society. Protecting human rights became a major issue for many liberals.

Some saw these liberal concepts as a challenge to Christianity. If humans were evil, then they could not be trusted to make just decisions. Free speech could not be tolerated when new ideas opposed traditional Christian teachings. Democracy challenged the understanding that God spoke only to those in the hierarchy. It opened the possibility that there could be no absolute truth, but many different opinions. In addition, determining matters of faith and morals by popular vote undermined the control of popes, bishops, and ministers.

The idea that deviance could be rooted in societal problems seemed to deny individual responsibility for personal sins. It also placed the remedy for these problems in the realm of secular programs rather than to be achieved through personal spiritual redemption. The churches were challenged to regard sin as having corporate as well as personal dimensions, meaning that sin creates unholy societies as well as personal impurity. Finally, the church had to examine its relation to the rich and powerful. Traditionally, the church had sided with the powerful against the powerless, just as Luther had sided with the princes against the Peasants' Revolt in the sixteenth century. Some groups accepted the concepts of political liberalism while others rejected them.

The Pentecostals and Charismatics

Pentecostalism is a movement that gets its name from the New Testament outpouring of the Spirit at Pentecost (Acts 2:1–4). Pentecostals emphasize direct contact with the Spirit of God that results in receiving spiritual gifts. One of the most desired gifts is speaking in tongues, which is seen as a sure sign of the outpouring of the Spirit. Pentecostals also are characterized by a strict morality, an emphasis on missions and evangelism, and a belief in healing by faith alone.

Pentecostalism developed out of the nineteenth-century Holiness movement, which comprised Christians who believed in the possibility of complete sanctification or sinless living. Holiness tendencies were found in many denominations, but were especially strong in Methodism because of Wesley's emphasis on sanctification.

Direct outpourings of the Spirit were experienced within many nineteenth-century Holiness groups. In the early twentieth century, moderates within the movement moved away from the emotional, ecstatic experiences while retaining the Holiness emphasis. They formed into groups like the Church of the Nazarene. More radical believers continued to stress the direct experience of the Spirit and formed such Pentecostal groups as the Assemblies of God. The Holiness movement remained scattered in a number of relatively small denominations. However, the Pentecostals have been remarkably successful at rural and urban evangelism. Their missionaries have spread their version of the Gospel to other lands. They have been very successful in Latin and South America.

A different phase of Pentecostalism began in the 1960s with the emergence of the charismatic movement. Charismatics seek the Pentecostal outpouring of the Spirit. However, most charismatics stayed within their own denominations and tried to renew their denominations through their spirit-filled worship. At the same time, they often participated in ecumenical events with charismatics from other denominations. Almost all denominations, including Catholics, now have a charismatic element. Charismatic worship now is often accepted as simply an alternative form of worship in established denominations.

Scientific Advances

Advances in modern science were even more troubling to some Christians. In the late nineteenth and early twentieth centuries atomic theory came to the forefront of science: The universe is composed of tiny atoms, each like a tiny solar system, with negatively charged electrons that orbit around a nucleus. For some, atomic theory seemed to open the possibility that humans could unlock all the secrets of the universe. The work of Albert Einstein (1879–1955) proved even more challenging. Einstein provided the formula that opened the power of the atom and became the basis of the atomic bomb. He also developed his theory of relativity, which made time, space, and motion relative to one another and to the point of view of the observer. Thus, time and space were not absolutes as they had been thought to be. This theory of relativity contributed to the idea that morals and philosophical and theological concepts might be relative to the community that held them. Perhaps there were no absolutes in these areas, either.

Evolution presented an even greater threat to traditional Christian beliefs. Evolution simply means change. It indicates that all life goes through a gradual process of change. Evolutionary ideas had been around since the time of the ancient Greeks. However, the nineteenth-century rise of science caused a deepening desire to understand the origins of life based on empirical observation rather than religious myths. Recent geological discoveries had indicated that earth had existed for much longer than the 6000 years that the church had come to accept.[2] The discovery of dinosaur bones and other fossils buried in deep layers of ancient soil raised the possibility that life had changed gradually on the earth over long periods of time.

By the mid-nineteenth century, many educated people were open to the idea of evolution. In 1859 Charles Darwin published *On the Origin of Species,* in which he presented an evolutionary theory. According to Darwin the various species of plant and animal life evolved over eons. Life began with simple forms and became more and more complex and diversified over time. In part, this evolution was accomplished through natural selection, in which animals and plants that were most fit survived while those that were less well adapted to their environments did not continue. *On the Origin of Species* rapidly became one of the most important books in history. It was important not only because Darwin was the first to present evolutionary ideas but also because he had systematically gathered vast amounts of observational information to support his theory. In 1871 Darwin published *The Descent of Man* in which he showed that humans had evolved from earlier species like other forms of life.

While certain elements of Darwin's thought were immediately challenged (and continue to be challenged today) in the scientific community, his basic theory rapidly became the chief explanation of the origin of life. Few scientists today question whether evolution has occurred. Before long, evolutionary ideas were being applied to all sorts of phenomena. For instance, Herbert Spencer published his massive *System of Synthetic Philosophy* in which human social development was placed in an evolutionary framework. According to this framework, societies evolved from simple, primitive communities to complex, advanced societies. Moreover, within societies only the fittest survive. The fittest worked their way to the top while the less fit floundered at the bottom. This approach came to be known as "social Darwinism." In the late nineteenth and early twentieth centuries, it was used as a "natural" justification for "advanced" Western societies dominating "primitive" colonial cultures and for the continued exploitation of the poor by the wealthy. It also confirmed the belief that society was becoming progressively better—a belief that was widely accepted in the late 1800s.

Darwin refused to apply his ideas to religion; however, that was not the case with Thomas Huxley (1825–1895). Huxley was a distinguished British scientist who used evolutionary ideas to attack the claims of Christianity directly. His attacks were so devastating that he soon became known as "Darwin's bulldog." Although many scientific advances were challenging Christianity, evolution became the focus of the battle between science and religion. More than anything else it moved the fight from the world of intellectuals to the world of ordinary people. Although some scientific issues are almost too complex to understand, almost everyone could see the implications of evolution.

The theory of evolution directly challenges literal interpretations of the biblical account of creation. Creation did not occur in seven days, as Genesis says, but over eons. There is no need for a Creator who wills life into being. Evolution operates by chance according to the natural laws of selection and the survival of the fittest. Finally, humans are not the peak of creation only slightly "lower than angels," but rather just another random species that has survived for a brief time and that may be destined to disappear as so many species had before. Although many Christians tried to reshape their understanding of creation on the basis of the new ideas, others saw evolution as a direct threat to Christianity and rejected it. To them, the fight against evolution was nothing less than a battle for the Bible and their faith. This fight has continued into the twenty-first century.

The Social Sciences, History, and Philosophy

The rise of social sciences also presented a challenge to religion. Sociology and psychology tended to look for explanations of human behavior in natural phenomena, not in supernatural battles between good and evil. Some social scientists believed that religion was nothing but superstition that had to be eliminated if humans were to progress and deal with their problems. Other social scientists recognized some positive sociological or psychological functions for religion, but had no special place for Christianity. It was but one of many religions that operated by the same observable dynamics as other faiths. In the twentieth century, the social sciences became widely accepted as legitimate tools for understanding human behavior. Christianity had to confront their perspective.

The study of history made giant strides in the nineteenth century. Before then there had been some advances in critical history where efforts were made to separate fact from fiction. Much written history had been a mixture of truth and legend. That changed when German scholars began emphasizing writing objective history. Leopold von Ranke (1795–1886), one of the leaders of this movement, insisted on applying scholarly rigor to the study of history. He believed that the recording of history should be based on extensive study of documents and other source materials. Events should be assessed within the context of the time in which they occurred. They should not be understood from the point of view of later times. As much as possible, subjective interpretations of historical events should be eliminated so the events could be seen as they really were.

The methods of the German scholars were somewhat revolutionary. They quickly spread over the Continent and to the United States. Before long, they were applied to the Bible and Christian history. Objective study of source material quickly demonstrated that many cherished beliefs were based as much on legend and later interpretations as on what actually happened. For better or worse, modern people came to expect written history to be based on objective facts. History was expected to "tell it like it really was."[3]

Philosophy also was undergoing significant changes that would affect the modern mind. G. W. F. Hegel (1770–1831) disagreed with Kant (see Chapter 10) about the inability to know the reality behind observable phenomena. He felt that an absolute spirit, or reason, lies behind all occurrences. This spirit becomes known through a process of a thesis (a supposed truth) generating an antithesis (its opposite, which is also supposed to be true). The combination of thesis and antithesis formed a new synthesis that was a greater truth than either the original thesis or antithesis. This synthesis then became a thesis that in turn created another antithesis and so on. As the process continued, greater insight was reached into the underlying reason. Finally, all differences would be resolved and the absolute spirit would be apparent.[4]

Arthur Schopenhauer (1788–1860) was another student of Kant who reached quite different conclusions than Hegel. He held that behind this world there is a great irrational "will." The world people know is an illusion. Nothing as we know it actually exists. The best people can do is to end their struggle, cease to be, and be absorbed back into the great will. Friedrich Nietzsche (1844–1900) was a student of Schopenhauer who eventually rejected much of his teaching. He felt that the will to power dominated life. Ideas of good, beauty, humility, and love were rejected as illusory. Nietzsche considered them a part of the slave mentality that dominated the Jews. Through Jews these ideas had infected Christianity, and through Christianity, Western civilization. The sooner the West rid itself of these concepts, the better. His hero was the *Übermensch* (superman), who ruthlessly pursued power. Nietzsche's teachings contributed greatly to the German mindset that led to World Wars I and II. They also implied that life is meaningless. Only might makes right. This thinking added to the moral confusion of the twentieth century that persists today.

One other significant twentieth-century philosopher was Karl Marx (1818–1883), who wrote against the problems of early capitalism. In so doing, he developed a systematic understanding of history based on Hegel's ideas about the process by which truth is discovered. Marx saw history as a constant battle between the wealthy and those they exploited. The conflicts between industrialists and their workers were the latest and final phase of that battle. He felt history was moving toward a communistic state where the workers of the world would unite, overthrow the capitalists, and establish a classless society in which each person's needs would be met. There would be no private property in this paradise as well as no greed and no wants.

Marx saw religion as connected with the human alienation that resulted from the workers not having control of production. Religion was both a cry against this alienation and a factor that helped produce it. On the one hand, religion helped give people hope despite the terrible conditions in which most lived in capitalistic society. In this sense, it was the "opiate of the masses"—a narcotic that made the pain bearable.

On the other hand, religion contributed to alienation. God was nothing but a projection of human desires for good, equality, justice, and so on. Yet by projecting these desires into a supernatural realm, people were alienated from themselves and often prevented from taking steps to make their lives better. For example, they waited for God to meet their needs in the hereafter but did not rebel against those who were exploiting them in this world. Religion also was used by those in power to control the oppressed. It emphasized obedience to authority and acceptance of one's lot in life. For these reasons, Marx felt that the communistic paradise would have to be **atheistic** (denying the existence of God). Marx did not, however, advocate trying to destroy religion. Instead, he felt that in communistic society alienation would be conquered. Religion would disappear because it would no longer be needed.[5]

SHIFTING PERSPECTIVES AND STANDARDS OF GLOBAL SOCIETY

People and religions are still reeling today from changing standards and concepts of modernization. Now they must cope with a host of changes associated with globalization. There is a tendency for people to understand globalization merely as the growing interconnectedness of political or economic activity. Upon closer examination we see that globalization is more radically sweeping. In essence global society involves much different patterns of human interactions than we have experienced thus far. It involves the creation of a global culture that goes beyond the tribal or national cultures that have dominated human lifestyles to this point in history. This global culture seems to be centering around a number of key factors. One is the use of English as a near-universal language. Almost all international commerce, medicine, science, and government is carried out in English. Democracy and human rights are providing ideas that are driving the move toward global society. Human rights are an especially powerful tool that is remaking the way that people think about themselves, what they expect from their governments, and even how they understand their religions.

Human Rights, One Humanity, and Global Civil Society

The belief that all people have undeniable rights just because they are human is really quite new. It is a direct result of the Holocaust and World War II. Nazis on trial for their crimes against innocent persons argued in their defense that there was no internationally recognized standard that indicated how governments had to treat civilians. Because of this, the Nazis argued that they could not be punished for crimes against their civilian victims. Most of the Nazis were convicted for their crimes against humanity, but their defense pointed to a real global issue. To correct this, the newly formed United Nations passed the **Universal Declaration of Human Rights** in 1948. This Universal Declaration indicates that civil rights (freedom of speech and religion, right to vote, trial by jury, etc.) as well as economic and social rights (right to housing, food, jobs, education, health care, etc.) are necessary for humans to live dignified lives. Therefore, governments and agencies around the world have an obligation to protect these rights. The Universal Declaration became a major force for compelling societies to agree on standards of how people must be treated in their countries during the latter half of the twentieth century. It also popularized around the world the idea that there is a universal humanity that demands respect, but that transcends the limits of tribe, nation, or religion.

To some extent, the Universal Declaration is a fulfillment of humanistic ideas, but its widespread acceptance as a standard for judging the behaviors of individuals, governments, and religions is a step beyond the positions taken by most in the past. It probably is not far from correct to say: Today, people are starting to see themselves as part of one HUMANITY that has different expressions in tribes, nations, societies, religions, and the like. This replaces a "tribal" mentality that sees people first as members of tribes, nations, religions, and so on, and then as humans with whom they share common interests and goals. The Declaration also provides grounds for religions to cooperate with one another in facing humanity's problems. It does, however, undermine any particular society's or religion's ability to claim absolute truth for itself.

Other changes associated with globalization also are under way. One of the more important of these for religion in general and Christianity in particular has to do with the increasing importance of global civil society. Social thinkers have indicated there are three sectors upon which societies stand. The political sector has to do with government. The economic sector has to do with the way that society provides for people's livelihood. The **civil sector (or civil society)** has to do with the non-governmental and non-economic activities needed for a society to sustain itself. One part of the civil sector is families who not only contribute to economic activities, but also do any number of unpaid, but necessary activities that benefit society. For example, they may take care of elderly parents or help relatives who have lost their homes or jobs. Volunteer groups (Boy or Girl Scouts, the Parent Teachers Association [PTA], the Rotary Club, the local historical society, human or animal rights groups, religious organizations) are very important elements of the civil sector.

Obviously, globalization involves the growing interconnectedness of political and economic sectors along with the establishment of worldwide organizations to deal with political issues (i.e., the United Nations) and economic conditions (i.e., World Bank, International Monetary Fund, World Trade Organization). But the development of a powerful, independent global civil society (or sector) is one of the surprises of the globalization process. This **global civil society** is made up of international or global non-governmental organizations that attempt to influence different aspects of the world's political, economic, or environmental scenes. These might include organizations like Human Rights Watch, the Red Cross and Red Crescent (the Muslim counterpart of the Red Cross), Greenpeace, Physicians Without Borders, and numerous religious organizations. Some elements of this civil society, such as the Red Cross, were present on the world scene prior to the twentieth century, but the last hundred years saw the development of tens of thousands of organizations concerned with various aspects of the world's development. The majority of civil sector organizations have developed since World War II. Like other organizations in the civil sector, religion may impact global society in several ways, including the direct delivery of goods and services to those in need. For example, because of lack of funds or political conflicts governments often cannot or will not deliver food to starving people. Religious organizations may take food to those in need where secular agents cannot.

Global civil society impacts affairs through moral influence. Elements of the civil sector have little political organization or funds to change undesirable situations. But they can bring an undesirable situation before the "world court of public opinion," which often is enough to cause governments or businesses with power to make significant positive changes. Often, this influence relies on bringing the undesirable situation to the attention of the news media, who will bring it before the public. In this way religions also may use their moral authority to protect people's rights or the environment. That is, religions may draw upon their sacred ethical principles to impart a moral dimension to issues that others may see in strictly economic or political terms. For instance, capitalists may consider moving jobs to countries with a lower-paid workforce and fewer protections for workers as a simple way to increase profits; however, religions may call the power of moral condemnation on such profit seeking if it has potential detrimental impact on workers' lives. After all, are not people more important than profits? The sacred moral voice of religions may prove to be their most valuable contribution they bring to the emerging global society. Christian denominations as well as other religions have increasingly found themselves involved in these kinds of efforts.

Roles such as providing for the needy or bringing moral principles to bear are not new for religious groups. Yet, the immensity of the problems along with the necessity for a truly global reach to provide assistance presents new challenges. The problems themselves are global and have tremendous potential for global destruction. Environmental decay, weapons of mass destruction, and the possibility of a "doomsday" illness that spreads around the world all have the potential to destroy human life on the planet. It seems obvious that, when it comes to the survival of the human race, religions have to move beyond their differences to cooperate in trying to resolve pressing global issues. Christianity is building cooperation within Christian denominations as well as with other religions to try to address global problems.

Fluidity and Identity

Two other aspects of globalization must be mentioned. First, the global society seems to be based on fluidity. By **fluidity** we mean fewer rigid unchanging structures exist, but information lines and alliances between people, jobs, and the like shift readily. Institutions are attempting to adapt to this situation. For example, the U.S. military is evolving from an emphasis on heavily armed divisions intended to "slug it out" with Russian troops in a conventional land war to more smaller, light units that can be brought together in a proper mix to fit whatever configuration a particular situation demands. The temporary structure of these units will be dissolved and reconfigured differently when the situation changes. This fluidity is also apparent in Christianity. A good example is seen in temporary alliances of Christian groups as they come together to fight for or against certain issues, such as legalized abortion. These groups historically may have opposed one another violently, but they will cooperate on a particular issue. Their alliance dissolves if the issue is settled, or they may oppose one another on other issues, such as the death penalty. It very much feels like nothing is permanent in this globalizing world.

Fluidity is one of the factors that contribute to another problem that many encounter in global society—identity crisis. **Identity crisis** means that people have trouble maintaining a clear image of who they are and how they relate to others, whether they be neighbors or persons and groups on the other side of the earth. Baptists and Catholics are two Christian denominations that have significant animosity for each other. As long as there is significant tension between them, the groups have a reason to say clearly "I am Catholic" or "I am Baptist." People also identify themselves by who they are not. That is, "I am not a Baptist" or "I am not a Catholic." But what if changing theology means that Baptists and Catholics are encouraged to see one another as brothers and sisters in Christ. How do we now understand being Catholic or Baptist? Does this mean that we now have to accept one another's theologies or concepts of church structure (hierarchical or congregational), leadership patterns (priest or ministers), or sacraments (seven sacraments or two ordinances) as legitimate? What if we cooperate on some issues, but oppose one another on others? How now am I to understand myself as a Baptist or a Catholic Christian?

In addition, modern societies bring together persons of a variety of different national, ethnic, employment, educational, and religious backgrounds. Often these potential identities overlap in a perplexing fashion. For instance, your neighbor may be an American like yourself, but from a different ethnic heritage (European, African, or Asian), a different religion, and be educated at a school that is an archrival of your school. Which of these identities are you going to use to either identify with or separate yourself from your neighbor? Under what circumstances are you to identify with one or the other of your neighbor's characteristics and under what circumstances are you going to reject yet other of your neighbor's characteristics? Should you, for example, accept your neighbor at your common college alumni party, then reject him or her because of membership in a different religion? Such difficult questions are made even more confusing when they are applied to the global scene. Should we assist the Chinese government in treating an outbreak of disease because the Chinese are people like us? Or should we not assist them because they abuse human rights and persecute Christians? Which identity should dominate when considering assistance to the Chinese government—human, abuser of human rights, persecutors of Christians?

Some people, including Christians, embrace the stresses caused by the fluidity of globalization along with its "floating identities" as part of the necessary cost of living in a global society. They may even draw upon their religion to help them accept and deal with the pitfalls of global society. Still others have the opposite reaction. They root their identities ever more strongly in the supposed unchanging truths of their Christian (or Jewish, or Muslim, or Hindu) religion. For them, being their kind of Christian is the main identity that sets them apart from the secular world, other religions, and Christians of different denominations, values, or thoughts. Moreover, they may adopt a "siege mentality" that causes them to see the rigidity of their religious interpretation as a powerful wall to be defended from the hostile world around them.

These two reactions to globalization are common to the reactions of people to nearly all expressions of globalization. There are those who welcome globalization as a positive thing. To see globalization in a positive light they have to stress what is common among nations, people, and religions and, thus, they see globalization as a good thing because it is overcoming our tribalism. Those who find globalization threatening stressing their differences from those defined as not like themselves. They emphasize the superiority of what is particular to themselves and their country, their people, or their religion. We need to emphasize that these trends are not only found among Christians, but also among all religions. The stressing of the particular often leads to conflict. When the fervor of religion is added to this mix, passions can become inflamed and violence results. We see this occurring around the world as Christian particularists clash with those of other faiths. Muslims and others attack secularized Western ideas and systems. Hindu particularists persecute Muslims and Christians. And on and on such clashes go.

While there are hopeful trends, the twenty-first century also has begun with such overwhelming problems that many are fearful and uncertain. Poverty and starvation are widespread. Religiously motivated conflict is becoming more intense. This is especially true of conflict among fundamentalists of various kinds as well as fundamentalist attempts to defend against the encroachment of global society (see Chapter 12). Natural resources are being depleted. The quality of the environment is deteriorating. Many nations are seeing a decline in their quality of life. Doubt and anxiety seem to dominate the world scene.[6]

THE CATHOLIC REACTION TO THE MODERN WORLD

The political liberalism, scientific theories, and philosophical perspectives discussed above were all part of the modern mindset that was developing in the nineteenth century. Some Catholic theologians attempted to accommodate this new mindset by adopting methods and viewpoints present in the culture. They were called **Modernists**. Much of their work was eventually rejected and they were condemned by the papacy. Most of the confirmed Modernists left the Catholic church while others chose to ignore papal dictates.

Ultramontanism

Most nineteenth- and twentieth-century popes held to a philosophy called **ultramontanism,** which maintains that Rome alone has the right to determine matters of doctrine, morals, and culture. This attitude directly conflicted with trends that arose during the Reformation and that advocated a lessening of church authority. Ultramontanist ideas had existed since the twelfth century, but they reached their height in the late 1800s.

The nineteenth century involved a long series of battles between the papacy and the secular states. The papacy eventually lost all of its civil authority. The battles reached their climax during the reign of Pius IX (1846–1878). Pius fought both the efforts to unify Italy and the attacks of Bismarck on the rights of the church. In both cases he lost. His rule marked the end of the political power of the pope. In the long run, the pope was left to rule over only Vatican City, the small papal state within Rome.

As his political power declined, Pius seemed determined to assert his spiritual authority. In 1854, he proclaimed the dogma of the **Immaculate Conception of Mary.** According to this doctrine, Mary was protected from all sin, even original sin, because she was chosen to be the mother of Jesus. It was the first time in history that a pope had taken it upon himself to proclaim a doctrine without first consulting a council.

Another important step was taken in 1864 when Pius issued a *Syllabus of Errors* listing eighty propositions that Catholics must reject. These included modern tendencies such as rationalism, communism, liberalism, freedom of worship, freedom of speech, national churches without papal authority, the recognition of religions other than Catholicism, democracy, marriage as a civil institution, and secular schools provided by the state. The document rejected the idea that the papacy could be reconciled to progress, liberalism, and modern civilization.

Ultramontanism peaked at the First Vatican Council. This council was the first ecumenical council since Trent. It was convened by Pius in 1870 and he tightly controlled it. While many issues were discussed, the most important was the doctrine of papal infallibility. The council overwhelmingly approved a limited form of this doctrine. The pope is considered infallible only when speaking *ex cathedra,* which means the pope is infallible when he is speaking in his official capacity as the "pastor and teacher" of Christians in defining matters of faith and morals. In ordinary matters of faith, morals, or church administration, the pope is not considered infallible. The pope has spoken *ex cathedra* only once since Vatican I. In 1950, Pius XII proclaimed the dogma of the **Assumption of the Blessed Virgin Mary,** which holds that Mary was bodily taken to heaven at the end of her life.

The popes after Pius IX held ultramontanist views but were forced to make concessions to modern culture. One of the more positive of these was the bull *Rerum novarum* issued by Leo XIII (reigned 1878–1903). *Rerum novarum* dealt with problems resulting from the exploitation of laborers by capitalists. It recognized the injustice that allowed some to accumulate vast fortunes built upon the poverty of so many. It called for laws to protect workers and the formation of Catholic trade unions. On the other hand, Pius XI (1922–1939) and Pius XII (1939–1958) both sought to accommodate totalitarianism. Pius XI made treaties with Mussolini and Hitler only to be betrayed by both. Pius XII was condemned by many because he did not take a firm stand against the slaughter of millions of Jews and others during the Holocaust.

Second Vatican Council

A new phase in Catholicism's efforts to relate to the modern world began when Pope John XXIII (1958–1963) called the Second Vatican Council. Vatican II met from 1962 to 1965 and sought to build a bridge between the church and the modern world. The council issued decrees on a wide variety of administrative, moral, religious, and social issues. It dictated that the liturgy be said in the language of the people, or the vernacular, and not in Latin. It attempted to ensure greater participation of the laity in the life of the church. It supported freedom of conscience in religious matters. Protestants were recognized as fellow Christians, although they remained estranged from the church. It also generally supported a more positive attitude about the inherent dignity of people, which has resulted in active support for human rights. Efforts were made to address problems of the poor and powerless. However, the church did not change its basic doctrine or attempt to accommodate Protestant teachings. It left unchanged church teachings about a number of important issues that fly in the face of Catholics living in the contemporary world, including the ordination of women to the priesthood, allowing priests to marry, and the use of birth control even by married Catholic couples.

Since Vatican II, the Catholic Church has tended to remain conservative on theological issues but has been more liberal on social issues. Tensions between Protestants and Catholics have lessened in many parts of the world. Protestants and Catholics often have cooperated at least on local levels on different projects. Increasing dialogues with other Christian denominations have led to some degree of reconciliation with certain Protestant groups; fruitful talks with Orthodox Christianity have led to some positive steps. For instance, recently Catholic and Orthodox leaders took steps to heal the rif between the two major branches of Christianity that came to a head in the Middle Ages (see Chapter 7). Catholicism remains strong in Latin America although it is losing some of its influence in the area to rapidly growing evangelical Christianity. Both

Protestantism and Catholicism are growing rapidly in Africa; in fact, Africa represents the major success story for Christianity in the late twentieth century, as we will discuss in Chapter 12. The Catholic Church has shown itself to be very powerful in some of the former communist countries of Eastern Europe. It was one of the forces that helped overthrow communism in Eastern nations. The Catholic Church exerts considerable moral influence in several Eastern European countries where it has resisted abortion, gay marriage, and other "loosening" of moral standards. It has been particularly successful in Poland. The Church's efforts have helped heighten the split between conservative Eastern Europe and liberal Western Europe.

Nonetheless, many Catholics in the West do not feel that Vatican II went far enough. It failed to staunch the flow of people who were leaving the church in industrialized societies. In these societies, the Catholic church now faces many problems, including declining membership, few new people entering the priesthood and orders, and the feeling of many that the church hierarchy is not in touch with their needs. Negative feelings toward the hierarchy have been fanned in the first years of the twenty-first century by series of highly publicized sexual scandals involving the abuse of children by Catholic priests.[7]

Sexual abuse by priests and other church officials has a long history in the Catholic Church. In times past, because of the revered place of the priest and other officials, sexual abuse usually went unreported. But not reporting sexual abuse does not mean that it had no consequences. In fact recent revelations in relation to the sexual scandals indicate that victims often experience severe psychological damage as a result of the abuse.

Even when sexual abuse was reported to higher officials, the hierarchy often did little to address the situation. Bishops tended to move abusive priests around from parish to parish, often without reporting offenses to their new congregations. This was true even of priests who had a long history of reported sexual abuse. They also protected the priests against inquiries from within the church as well as inquiries from state authorities who were trying to investigate reports of cases that could result in criminal sexual abuse charges being filed against priests. We cannot go into detail about the cases and events that led to why this protective system began to unravel. We can only note that revelations associated with sexual abuse allocations have led to the criminal convictions of some priests. They also stirred many lay Catholics to demand that priests who abused along with the bishops who protected them be held accountable. This outrage along with the publicity generated by the protective system has forced some changes. The Catholic church is now more open in the handling of accused priests, priests are being removed from ministry in some cases when they are accused of abuse (pending the results of a thorough investigation of the charges), and church officials are now cooperating with law enforcement officials when they are investigating abuse charges. These changes may not be entirely successful in preventing or punishing future cases of sexual abuse, even if they are uniformly and diligently enforced. But, perhaps more than any other change since Vatican II, they indicate to the church hierarchy that it will be held accountable to the ordinary Catholics. This may well be one of the greatest accomplishments of Vatican II.

Pope John Paul II

No history of the last four decades is complete without a discussion of the papacy of John Paul II (1978–2005). Pope John Paul II was born in 1920 as Karol Jozef[11] Wojtyla. His early life was strongly influenced by the German occupation of Poland during World War II. His rise in the ranks of the church from priest to Cardinal was influenced by his own growing opposition to the communist government that dominated Poland during the Cold War. Any assessment of John Paul II's papacy has to include his mixed reaction to Vatican II. If some felt Vatican II did not go far enough, others felt that it went too far in seeking to modernize the Catholic Church.

There was strong conservative reaction to the changes advocated in Vatican II. Most of the opposition to Vatican II worked to limit the impact of the council's decisions, not to completely reverse them. For instance, Pope Paul VI (1963–1978), who presided over the council after the death of John XXIII, took a number of steps to affirm conservative principles against liberalizing affects of the council. The most important of these was issuing the encyclical *Humanae vitae* (*On Human Life*), a document that recognized that sex between couples served a number of important functions other than reproduction. It was part of the bonding that brought the couple together in love and was a natural and desirable expression of that love. It admitted that there might be legitimate reasons why couples might want to limit family size, but slammed the door to using contraceptive devices to prevent pregnancy. In taking this stance, Paul VI went against the advise of lay advisors as well as several well-known theologians.

John Paul II continued these generally conservative trends in issues of morals and theology. He condemned ideologies and movements he felt were leading to the decay of society, including communism, Marxism, feminism, imperialism, relativism, materialism, fascism, and consumerism. John Paul also took action to reign in liberal theologians. In one notable action, he worked with Cardinal Joseph Ratzinger, the head of the Congregation for the Doctrine of the Faith (the current name of the old Inquisition), to withdraw the license to teach of several widely acclaimed liberal Catholic theologians including Hans Küng[12], Edward Schillebeeckx, and Charles Curran. John Paul eventually condemned Liberation Theology from Latin America because of its close relation with Marxism (see Chapter 12).

To end our discussion of John Paul here would be a grave injustice to a man known as the People's Pope. John Paul had a powerful ability to excite and identify with ordinary people. He was by far the most-traveled pope in history. He took some 104 trips covering some 725,000 miles. Everywhere he went he drew large crowds. In one instance in Manila in 1995, he said mass to a crowd estimated at between 4 and 8 million. His messages opposed oppression and preached hope and encouragement. He was a particular favorite of young people who considered him a hero. His outreach to youth did much to renew their faith. He reached out to those of other faiths, including Buddhists, Orthodox Christians, Protestants, Jews, Coptic Christians, and Muslims. He also issued a long list of apologies to people wrongfully harmed by the Catholic Church, including Galileo Galilei, African slaves, women, victims of the Holocaust, Jan Hus, Orthodox Christians for the 1204 attack on Constantinople by crusaders, and the abuse of native peoples in various parts of the world at the hands of Catholic missionaries.

All-in-all, John Paul likely will go down in history as one of the most remarkable and beloved popes in history. Shortly after his death in 2005, his successor Cardinal Ratzinger (who became Pope Benedict XVI) put John Paul on the fast track to becoming a saint. The election of Cardinal Ratzinger as pope likely will ensure a continuation of John Paul's policies for the immediate future.

CONCLUSIONS

The last 200 years have created many new challenges for Christianity. The political liberalism, individualism, subjectivism, and new scientific discoveries undermined many traditional beliefs. Urbanization, industrialization, and nationalism created a world in which the Church was increasingly ill at ease. Modernism has evolved into a global society that raises new issues that Christianity must address. Two trends seem to reflect the dominant reactions of Christianity to global society. On the one hand, many Christians embrace globalization using their faith as a tool to expand links with persons of other faiths and cultures by finding things they have in common. On the other hand, many other Christians use their faith to stress what is peculiar to their religion, their denominations and their cultures.

During the nineteenth century, the Catholic Church became even stronger in its negative reaction to modernism. The church continued its ultramontanist pronouncements in the twentieth century but gradually made concessions to accommodate existing political and social conditions. The Second Vatican Council was convened to update the church. Significant changes were made, but many Catholics in industrial societies still feel the church has little understanding of their needs. Participation in the church has continued to decline in the West, but it is on the rebound in Eastern European countries as well as developing nations, especially Africa. Pope John Paul II was a key force in advancing Catholic renewal in the last quarter of the twentieth century. He also set the tone for Catholic theology and moral teachings into the twenty-first century.

The following chapter looks at major developments in Protestantism and the Orthodox churches as they try to navigate in the shifting environment of the contemporary world.

Notes

1. The term *denomination* means a branch of Christianity. To a large extent, the idea that Christianity can have "branches" reflects the peculiar nature of religion in the United States. The early Puritan colonies along with a few others had theocracies that established a certain group as the dominant church. Yet American religion soon evolved into a different model. Tolerance was extended to most church groups. No specific church was established. Participation in a given group was voluntary. It was a matter of choice. The Bill of Rights to the U.S. Constitution legalized this religious freedom.

This "volunteer church" is a peculiar American idea that has slowly gained wide acceptance. The term *denomination* assumes this approach. It implies that the real church is invisible. It is made up of all true believers. No denomination can claim to be the true church. They all are visible expressions of the invisible church that people voluntarily choose to join.

2. In the sixteenth century, Archbishop James Ussher (or Usher) traced the genealogies (the records of families and descendants) in the Bible. He concluded that creation took place in 4004 B.C.E

3. The idea that history is an accumulation of objective occurrences has become so much a part of modern thinking that this discussion may seem strange to readers. In fact, historians work with documents that reflect the subjective views of the writers. For instance, Luther and his work would be presented much differently from the viewpoint of the sixteenth-century papacy and Lutheran authors of that time. At the very least, historians have to sift through the subjective interpretations of the authors of documents to try to get at objective "facts." Because of the difficulties involved, many twentieth-century historians have come to believe it is impossible to write really objective histories.

4. Hegel has been discussed under philosophy because of the importance of his ideas about the process for discovering truth to later philosophers. He also is a Christian theologian of some importance. For a good discussion of Hegel, see James C. Livingston. *Modern Christian Thought: From the Enlightenment to Vatican II*. New York: Macmillan, 1971, pp. 143–157.

5. To some extent this explains the communist reaction to religion in the twentieth century. For instance, the constitution of the Soviet Union guaranteed religious freedom, but the controlling Communists often reacted negatively to religious participation. At times they have actively sought to destroy religion in the countries they dominate. In other communist countries, the church has been supported by state funds. For a good discussion of Marx on religion, see Livingston, *Modern Christian Thought*, pp. 188–194.

6. For a good discussion of the nineteenth and twentieth centuries, see John B. Harrison, Richard E. Sullivan, and Dennis Sherman. *A Short History of Western Civilization*, 6th ed.

New York: Knopf, 1985. pp. 507–768, and Donald Kagan, Steven Ozment, and Frank M. Turner. *The Western Heritage,* 3d ed. New York: Macmillan, 1987, pp. 625–1066.

7.   Sexual scandal and sexual abuse are not new to Christianity, nor are they limited to Catholic Christianity. Unfortunately, they are found in all branches of the Christian faith.

Additional Readings

Abbott, Walter M., ed. *The Documents of Vatican II.* Translated by Joseph Gallager. New York: Guild, 1966.

Beiser, Frederick. *Hegel.* New York: Taylor & Francis, 2005.

Bellitto, Christopher. *The General Councils: A History of the Twenty-One Councils from Nicaea to Vatican II.* Mahwah, NJ: Paulist, 2002.

Bonnot, Bernard F. *Pope John XXIII: An Astute, Pastoral Leader.* New York: Alba, 1980.

Bordin, Ruth. *Women and Temperance: The Quest for Power and Liberty, 1873–1990.* Philadelphia: Temple, 1981.

Carter, P. A. *The Spiritual Crisis of the Gilded Age.* De Kalb, IL: Northern Illinois University Press, 1972.

Cate, Curtis. *Friedrich Nietzsche.* New York: Overlook, 2004.

Cochrane, A. C. *The Church's Confession under Hitler.* Philadelphia: Westminster, 1962.

Easton, Stewart C. *The Rise and Fall of Western Colonialism.* New York: Praeger, 1964.

Ellis, J. T. *American Catholicism.* Chicago: University of Chicago Press, 1969.

Halloway, Mark. *Heavens on Earth: Utopian Communities in America, 1680–1880.* New York: Dover, 1966.

Hasler, August B. *How the Pope Became Infallible: Pius IX and the Politics of Persuasion.* New York: Doubleday, 1981.

Held, David and Anthony McGrew. *Globalization/Anti-Globalization.* Cambridge, England: Polity, 2002.

Huebsch, Bill. *Vatican II in Plain English: The Council.* Allen, TX: Thomas More, 1997.

Kaufmann, Walter. *Nietzsche: Philosopher, Psychologist, Antichrist.* New York: World, 1968.

Kellener, Ann and Laura Klein. *Global Perspective: A Handbook for Understanding Global Issues.* Upper Saddle River, NJ: Prentice Hall, 1999.

Kepel, Gilles. *Jihad: The Trial of Political Islam.* Trans. Anthony F. Roberts. Cambridge, MA: Belnap, 2002.

Kurtz, Lester. *Gods in the Global Village: The World's Religion in Sociological Perspective.* Thousand Oaks, CA: Pine Forge, 1995.

Latourette, Kenneth Scott. *Christianity in a Revolutionary Age.* Vols. 1–3. New York: Harper, 1954–1961.

Lewy, Guenther. *The Catholic Church and Nazi Germany.* New York: McGraw-Hill, 1964.

Pope John Paul II. *Crossing the Threshold of Hope.* Ed. Arnoldo Mondadori. New York: Knopf, 1994.

_____. *In My Own Words.* Ed. Anthony F. Chiffolo. New York: Gramercy, 2002.

_____. *Memory and Identity: Conversations at the Dawn of a Millennium.*New York: Rizzoli, 2005.

Ruprecht, Louis A., Jr. *Tragic Posture and Tragic Vision: Against the Modern Failure of Nerve.* New York: Continuum,1995.

Schlink, Edmund. *After the Council: The Meaning of Vatican II for Protestantism and the Ecumenical Dialogue.* Philadelphia: Fortress, 1968.

Sreinfels, Peters. *Adrift: The Crisis of the Roman Catholic Church in America.* New York: Simon & Schuster, 2004.

Tolley, Christopher. *Domestic Biography: The Legacy of Evangelicalism in Four Nineteenth-Century Families.* New York: Oxford, 1997.

Williams, George H. *The Mind of John Paul II: Origins of His Thought and Action.* New York: Seabury, 1981.

Young, Julian. *Schopenhauer.* New York: Taylor & Francis, 2005.

Websites

www.vatican.va/archieve-councils/il_vatican_council/ [Provides access to the important documents coming out of Vatican II]

www.vatican.va/holy-father/jphn-paul-ii/ [Official website of the Vatican. Provides access to biographical material in Pope John Paul II and access to archives of his writings]

www.vatican.va/phome_en.htm [Official home of the Vatican. Provides access to a trove of historical and contemporary materials on Catholicism]

www.vatican2voice.org/index.asp [Provides a brief history of Vatican II along with material to assist in understanding the context and implications of Vatican II]

12

CHRISTIANITY FROM MODERN TO GLOBAL SOCIETY

Optimism, Uncertainty, and Opportunity (1800–Present)

Christian Baptism in Africa

Science, secularism, democracy, urbanization, and industrialization have presented significant challenges to Christianity in the modern era. Globalization poses other problems and opportunities. The church has been caught in contradictory trends. On the one hand, it has witnessed tremendous vigor and expansion. On the other hand, it has moved into a situation where its interpretations of reality are severely questioned. Many in the industrialized world simply regard religion as irrelevant. Pessimism and uncertainty have dominated the last few decades of the twentieth century. The globalized world is changing the context for all human activities including religion. The issues of the twenty-first century will likely be as confounding as those of the twentieth century. All-in-all, optimism, uncertainty, and challenges abound as Christianity moves into the third millennium since Jesus' birth.

In this chapter, we look primarily at some of the ways Protestants have attempted to deal with this new social environment. We then examine some new trends in the faith that promise new life for Christianity: the ecumenical movement, emerging ideas from the dispossessed, and the explosive growth of the Christian faith in the developing world. We also discuss how the Orthodox Church has coped with the modern era. Finally, we assess the state of Christianity at the beginning of the twenty-first century.

THE PROTESTANT REACTION
TO THE MODERN WORLD

On the whole, the Protestant reaction to the world emerging in the nineteenth century was much more positive than the Catholic reaction. While the Catholic hierarchy engaged in fortress building—setting itself apart from the rest of the world—significant parts of the Protestant community engaged in bridge building—connecting itself to the world. Protestants either accepted the perspective of the secular culture and attempted to redefine church teachings or, at least, tried to answer questions raised by their culture.

Liberal Theology

Friedrich Schleiermacher (1768–1834) was one of the first Protestant theologians to attempt to address questions raised by Western culture after Kant. Schleiermacher was educated by the Moravians, whose piety and romanticism influenced his work. He became a hospital chaplain in Berlin and later a professor at the University of Berlin. There Schleiermacher found that educated people despised religion. They felt it had been thoroughly discredited by rationalism and was not worth serious intellectual consideration. He wrote *Speeches on Religion to the Cultured Among Its Despisers* to counter this thinking. Schleiermacher maintained that the essence of religion was neither knowledge as the rationalists and orthodox religion taught nor a moral system as had been implied by Kant; rather, the essence of religion was "feeling."

Schleiermacher defined this "feeling" in his great work, *The Christian Faith*. This essence is the sudden, profound awareness of dependency on something outside the self in which all life is grounded. This feeling is a sense of absolute dependence. It is expressed in action by religious ceremonies and in conviction by dogma. Each religious community tries in its own way to transmit this feeling to its members. Christianity is superior to other religions because its founder, Jesus Christ, experienced God-consciousness fully in himself. Jesus saved others by inspiring God-consciousness in them.

Schleiermacher developed an elaborate system based on the experience of dependence on God. His system investigates the implications of the felt relation to God for the self, for relations to others, and for the understanding of God himself. According to Schleiermacher, any Christian teaching that does not affirm this dependence may be harmful and should be avoided. For instance, Christianity may need to affirm the teaching about God's creation of life. However, the Genesis account of creation may not be historically accurate. This lack of accuracy should not concern the Christian as it has nothing to do with the feeling of dependence. The important concept is the affirmation that "In the beginning God created," not *how* or *when* this creation occurred!

Schleiermacher's system did not satisfy the rationalists because he kept too many traditional teachings; it did not satisfy the orthodox because he dispensed with too many traditional doctrines and modified others. Nevertheless, people found his system appealing in his day. In addition, he left a strong influence on theology. His search for Christian essentials guided many later thinkers who would struggle with the problem of what was vital and what was superficial to the faith. Almost all subsequent theologians have had to follow his example of dealing with the psychological element of faith. Schleiermacher's effort to accommodate Christianity to contemporary culture rightly earned him the title of the "father of liberalism." Albrecht Ritschl (1822–1889) and a host of others followed his lead.

Biblical Criticism and Historical Studies

Biblical criticism was another effort to accommodate religion to elements of nineteenth-century culture. New methods of historical research were soon focused on the Bible and theological studies. Ferdinand Baur (1792–1860) was the forerunner of this movement. Baur adopted Hegel's model for understanding the development of early Christianity. To him, Peter's Judaistic Christianity was the original thesis of the faith. Paul generated the antithesis when he made Christianity a universal religion. These contradictory trends were synthesized in the second-century Catholic church. Baur attempted to date the books of the New Testament and determine who wrote them by the way they expressed the struggle between Peter's and Paul's approaches to Christianity.

David F. Strauss (1808–1874) wrote an even more sensational work on the New Testament. Using Hegel's approach, Strauss came to believe that Jesus was a man on whom messianic expectations came to be focused. These expectations led to the creation of elaborate myths about him. Strauss questioned the historical accuracy of much of the New Testament. He questioned the virgin birth along with the accounts of the Crucifixion, Resurrection, and post-Resurrection appearances. Most of the sayings and deeds of Jesus were challenged also.

Ernest Renan's (1823–1892) *Life of Jesus* attracted wide attention throughout Europe. Renan, a French philosopher, dismissed all supernatural elements in the story of Jesus as unscientific and indefensible. To him, Jesus was a charming Galilean preacher who was a modern, enlightened man. He preached a message of love and died because of his high idealism. Julius Wellhausen (1844–1919) extended critical methods to the study of the Old Testament.

Biblical criticism brought the tools developed in historical research and literary analysis to the study of the Bible. Most of the early persons in the biblical criticism movement attempted to be objective—to tell it like it really was. Yet most were guilty of allowing their assumptions to influence their understandings of the past. As a result, they often developed confusing and contradictory images of biblical times. Later scholars have attempted to be more careful about allowing their biases to influence their work. Despite its early shortcomings, biblical criticism has dominated much of biblical studies since the nineteenth century. Even conservative students are careful to study biblical teachings in terms of their authors, the times of their writing, the social and political contexts in which they were written, the audiences for whom they were intended, the specific issues they were addressing, and so on. These considerations are the result of biblical criticism. Biblical criticism has contributed greatly to a better understanding of the Bible and its times.

Historical studies focused on the evolution of the church and its doctrines. The great church historians of the late nineteenth and early twentieth centuries included Ernst Troeltsch (1865–1923) and Adolf von Harnack (1851–1930). Some historians saw later developments in the church as evolving naturally from characteristics present in the New Testament period. Others saw later developments as departing from the original meaning of the faith. For instance, Harnack was convinced that the church had radically altered the simple teachings of Jesus. It had moved from the teachings of Jesus to teaching *about* Jesus. Even with such disputes, the nineteenth-century rise of historical studies significantly improved our grasp of the actual development of the church.[1]

The Mormons

The nineteenth century saw the rise of new religions related to the Christian faith. One of the most important of these was the Church of Jesus Christ of the Latter-day Saints or the Mormons as they are commonly known. Joseph Smith (1805–1844) was the founder of the Mormons. Smith claimed to find two golden tablets written in ancient hieroglyphs in Palmyra, New York. He translated these by the aid of two "seer's stones" and the angel Moroni. These translations resulted in the *Book of Mormon* (1830), which was supplemented by additional revelations to Smith and revelations to later leaders of the movement.

A number of followers soon gathered around Smith. They believed their religion fulfilled Christianity in the same way Christianity fulfilled Judaism. The Mormons believed Christ would return soon to establish his kingdom in the United States. They practiced communal living and questioned the jurisdiction of the United States over them. Conflict with the surrounding society led them to migrate west. Smith was killed by an unruly mob in 1844. Brigham Young (1801–1877) then assumed leadership of the main body of Latter-day Saints.

Young led them on a difficult trek to what is now Utah. In Utah they established an autonomous state that came under the jurisdiction of the United States in 1850 as that country expanded westward. In 1852, Young reported one of Smith's revelations that had been kept secret until then. This

REACTIONS AGAINST LIBERALISM

Liberalism was generally optimistic about the fate of humans and the future of society. It fit well with the attitudes of the second half of the nineteenth century and gained some degree of support on the Continent, especially among the better educated. In the United States, it appealed largely to the middle class and elite in New England. It had little effect on the less well-to-do in the Northeast and had almost no impact on the South and West. While liberalism enjoyed some success, it did not go unchallenged.

Strong opposition movements developed in both the Lutheran and Reformed churches. These conservatives felt that liberalism departed too far from traditional orthodoxy. They believed that it rewrote eighteen centuries of revelation reinstituted polygyny (the marriage of one man to several women). Polygyny and other Mormon teachings led to continuing conflict with the United States government and non-Mormon Americans who migrated to Utah. Utah eventually applied for statehood but was denied partly because the Mormons continued to practice polygyny. Finally, in 1890 the Mormons agreed to abandon polygyny, at least officially. (Some Mormons continue to practice polygyny in secret.) In 1896, Utah was admitted as a state.

Unlike many other Christians, Mormons do not believe revelation stopped with the Bible. Instead Christ continues to reveal himself through the channel of Mormon church leadership. Many Mormon doctrines are compatible with orthodox Christianity, but some Mormon beliefs are distinctive: Proxy baptism for the dead and marriage is for eternity when it is performed in a Latter-day Saints temple. They teach a form of **universalism** (everyone will be saved) but maintain there are degrees or levels of salvation. The Mormons contend their church structure is like that of the first-century church. As a result, they have church offices found in the New Testament such as apostles and prophets that are no longer part of most other Christian denominations.

Mormonism has grown steadily. Missionaries have spread the faith throughout the United States and the world. Today the Church of the Latter-day Saints is one of America's fastest-growing religions.

Christian doctrine, particularly in its interpretations of Jesus. These had little resemblance to the Savior and Redeemer that had been the focus of Christian faith. Conservatives staunchly defended orthodoxy. Liberal scholars often were dismissed from their positions because of their views. Other groups tried to mediate between the extreme liberals and conservatives.

Another movement was developing in the United States as a reaction against liberalism and biblical criticism. In the United States, liberal and conservative forces had been arguing for some time over a wide variety of issues. Presbyterian conservatives found an able advocate in Charles Hodge (1797–1878), a professor at the Princeton Theological Seminary. With the help of like-minded colleagues, he turned the school into a center of conservatism. He fought against any innovation in the Reformed tradition. His huge *Systematic*

Theology soon became a standard work that did much to advance the orthodox cause. Its influence spread beyond Presbyterianism to other denominations. The ideas from this seminary came to be known as Princeton theology.

Hodge felt that an infallible Bible was the cornerstone of the Christian faith and that it must be defended. Biblical criticism was especially troubling as it produced Scriptures in which there were contradictory trends and errors of fact. Hodge and other supporters of the Princeton theology believed that this criticism undermined the Christian faith's very foundations. To admit any error in the Bible meant that the faith was invalid. However, the evidence for contradictions in the Scriptures was so strong that the defenders of infallibility soon had to find new grounds.

They then proposed that the Scriptures may now contain errors but they did not in the original autographs. (**Autographs** are the original works from the hands of the original writers.) One could argue that this distinction made no difference because no one has these autographs. Yet the autograph argument served the needs of those who desired to hold to an infallible Bible. With time, supporters of this view developed the corresponding theory of verbal inspiration, which holds that God verbally told the original authors of the Bible exactly what to write. Verbal inspiration and biblical inerrancy (infallibility) became two of the main doctrines of fundamentalism as it emerged in the twentieth century.

REACTIONS AGAINST CHRISTIAN CULTURE

One of the most able thinkers in the history of the church in Denmark launched a violent attack on the prevailing nineteenth-century Christian culture. Søren Kierkegaard (1813–1855) was an unhappy, slightly disabled man who had been raised in a strict Lutheran home. His personal suffering led him to understand Christianity in a light much different from the view that prevailed then. The Christian culture he was born into tried to make Christianity easy for its many followers. That resulted in many "half-Christians" who had little understanding of, or commitment to, the New Testament faith. This easy Christianity was far removed from the radical call for commitment in the New Testament.

For Kierkegaard there was a tremendous contradiction between the goodness of God and the sinfulness of humans. Reason cannot close this gap. To erect systems, as did Hegel, that try to smooth the way to God is folly. The God of the Bible confronts humans and requires decision either for or against him. The true Gospel produces much suffering and struggle, not comfort, as humans stand naked before God. No system can prove God's existence or provide insight into ultimate reality. Insight is gained only when people go beyond reason through the leap of faith. Truth is subjective. Each person must make his or her own decision about what is correct. The big question is not what people believe, but how people live.

Because of the emphasis on living (existence) before God, Kierkegaard's system came to be called **existentialism.** Kierkegaard had little effect on the nineteenth century, partly because he wrote in Danish. Also his pessimistic ideas were not appealing in the nineteenth century. He has had wider influence on many twentieth-century theologies and philosophies.

REVIVALISM, MISSIONS, AND SUNDAY SCHOOL

Despite attacks on Christianity by "cultured despisers" and disputes among Christians themselves, the faith was remarkably vigorous during the nineteenth century. Three movements show this vigor especially well: revivalism, Protestant missions, and Sunday schools.

Revivalism

Revivalism and other forms of evangelism (efforts to reach the "unconverted" in the church and the lost outside the church) played key roles in the advance of aggressive Protestantism, particularly in the United States. Revivals involve a renewal of church life through the use of strong preaching. Stress is placed on the need to reject the devil and on the personal experience of the saving grace of God. Pietism, with its emphasis on close personal devotion, helped to generate revivals as did the need to adjust to sweeping social changes. Historians have yet to determine exactly why the revival movement began as it did.

The first large-scale series of revivals began in the British colonies in the early 1700s among Dutch Reformed churches. The movement spread to other denominations and became known as the "Great Awakening." Jonathan Edwards (1703–1758) was a great supporter of revivals among **Congregationalists** (the name the Puritan church took in America). The revivals were originally isolated and spontaneous as scattered pastors became convinced of the need for breathing new life into the church. The Awakening reached its height in the 1740s when George Whitefield undertook a mission of evangelistic preaching on the East Coast of the United States. By the late 1740s most revivals had ceased.

Whitefield, John Wesley, and others successfully used revivalistic methods in England in the second half of the eighteenth century. The movement was quite controversial and denominations split over whether or not the new methods were acceptable. Often the services were prolonged and involved emotional conversion experiences, even of people who already were deeply involved in church life. One issue that split denominations was whether emotional conversions were necessary for salvation. The movement also opened the way for Arminianism, which conflicted with the older, strict Calvinism. At any rate,

Jonathan Edwards

Jonathan Edwards senior was one of the most important people in American religious history. In fact, he was so important in the life of the colonies that some historians claim that understanding the man Edwards is a key to understanding the eighteenth-century New England mind. He was the son of a Reformed minister and the grandson of the preacher Solomon Stoddard. Edwards entered Yale when he was only twelve years old. There he developed a liking for science and perhaps Locke as well.

Edwards entered the ministry. His passionate preaching, concentrating on calls for a return to disciplined Christian living, helped spark the Great Awakening. When the revivals were attacked, Edwards staunchly defended them as the work of God, although he did believe that some of the emotional excesses accompanying the revivals were demonic.

Edwards also became a worthy defender of traditional Calvinism as it was presented in the Synod of Dort, the Westminster Assembly, and the early Puritans. Against such liberalizing trends as Enlightenment thought and Arminianism, he asserted a belief in original sin, irresistible grace, and the sovereignty of God. Yet these doctrines were modified somewhat by the "new thinking," especially Locke's ideas. He also opposed reducing the Christian faith to dry rationalism. He insisted that God be experienced in the "affections." For Edwards affections were those "parts" deep in the personality that move a person to possess or reject something. The greatest affection is love. Edwards shows a genuine mysticism in this insistence on the personal, deep experience of God.

new people were brought into the church and "old" churches received new vigor, leaving a deep impression on the Christian community.

The Awakening spread to all the American colonies. It fostered cooperation among colonies that previously seemed to have little in common. It helped give the colonies a common sense of identity, and in so doing, it indirectly helped produce the American Revolution. While almost all North American denominations participated in revivals, Baptist and Methodist churches were very good at using revivals on the frontier and in the South. Revivals contributed greatly to their membership growth in these regions. The memory of the Awakening deeply influenced the North American church. Certain parts of the American church eventually would make revivals a focus of their church life and their evangelistic efforts.[2]

A Second Great Awakening occurred in the early 1800s in the United States. Initially revivals were preached by local pastors. Some would preach in their own churches or they would exchange pulpits with nearby pastors. Sometimes the pastors would be of different denominations. Revivalism helped spark interdenominational cooperation.

By the nineteenth century, the character of revivals began to change. While the practice of using local pastors would continue, a new breed of professional evangelists began to emerge in the nineteenth century. Following the lead of Whitefield and Wesley, they would preach to large groups in prolonged meetings. At times they would rent large meeting halls to hold their "crusades," as the evangelist meetings came to be called. Specific techniques and formats were developed to stir up revivals. Meetings were emotionally charged and searing sermons called on people to reject the devil and accept Christ. Special music designed to increase the sense of drama was used. Praying aloud before the assembly for the conversion of "known" sinners was widely done. Sometimes these "sinners" were important members of churches and well-known community persons. The "anxious bench" also became a standard feature. It was a pew in front of the assembly where sinners wrestling with conversion would sit while the congregation prayed for their salvation. The atmosphere became so intense that some of those wrestling with their salvation would fall to the floor—rolling around, screeching, and moaning.

Later some of these evangelists started to transport large tents that they would erect on the edge of town to hold tent revivals. On the frontier, people were often very scattered and had limited access to churches. The revivals became an effective way of reaching them. A preacher would arrive in an area and proclaim a revival meeting to occur at a certain time and place. The places chosen were sometimes river crossings or the intersections of roads. A brush arbor (a "building" covered by tree branches) might be constructed. A "camp meeting" would then be held. People would come from miles around and camp for a week or so. The meeting would have long preaching and singing services interspersed with gathering times for eating and socializing. These camp meetings not only served as a way to evangelize but also provided an opportunity to gather for fun, which was often lacking on the rural frontier. Camp meetings and other forms of revivals served as standard forms of social life in many sections of the United States into the twentieth century.

Great American evangelists include Charles Finney (1792–1875), Dwight L. Moody (1837–1899), Billy Sunday (1862–1935), Aimee Semple McPherson (1890–1944), and Billy Graham (1918–). Protestants also responded to the needs of urban people by establishing several organizations that combined evangelism with work programs for the poor. Among these are the Salvation Army, founded by William Booth (1829–1912) and his wife Catherine Mumford (1829–1890), the Young Men's Christian Association (YMCA), and the Young

Women's Christian Association (YWCA). These associations were founded in England but soon spread worldwide.[3]

Revivalism and evangelists have remained controversial in the church. In part the difficulties are sparked by the relation of the evangelist to the local congregation. At times evangelists worked in close cooperation with local churches. For instance, denominations might come together to sponsor a citywide crusade by a noted evangelist. However, at other times the evangelists have competed with local churches. Some evangelists have developed such a following that they almost have their own "denomination."

This tendency increased in the twentieth century as evangelists started using radio and television to further their programs. This offered the convenience of having religious services in the home, but it also pulled members and funds away from local churches. By the latter part of the twentieth century, this trend had become so pronounced that scholars started talking about **"electronic churches,"** which are radio and television ministries with large followings that become substitutes for traditional congregations. Often these evangelists issue emotional appeals for funds and produce programs with all the hype of major network productions. In recent years, several American television evangelists have been convicted in court for misuse of church funds or publicly accused of sexual immorality. Even when there are no abuses by the evangelists, concerns are expressed about meeting the needs of people who have no contact with local churches. For example, where do members of electronic churches go for counseling, baptisms, weddings, or funerals? Where is the support for these people in times of crisis, which the local church family has traditionally provided? How are electronic church members encouraged to grow in the faith? How can they assure that the funds collected for evangelism or missions are actually spent on these types of projects?

Missions

Catholics had been involved in spreading the Gospel to foreign lands for centuries. Protestant involvement in missionary efforts had been limited. In the late eighteenth and early nineteenth centuries, Protestant denominations began to embrace a new missionary vision largely through the efforts of Pietists, Moravians, and Methodists. The new colonialism, along with ideas about spreading the many "superior" features of Western civilization, contributed to this vision. Revivalism, with its stress on converting the lost, also played a part.

The nineteenth-century mission effort was increased by the founding of mission societies in most European and North American countries. The purpose of these societies was to promote the Gospel among the heathen (nations not worshiping God). Many denominations also formed their own missionary

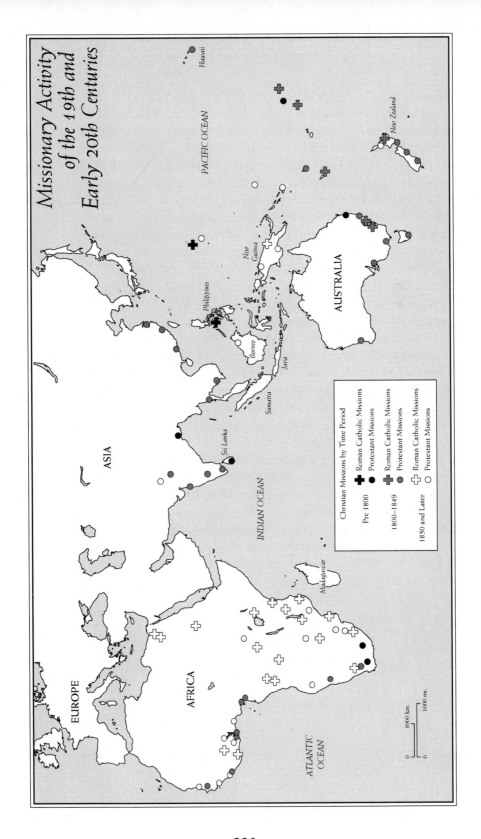

Missionary Activity
of the 19th and
Early 20th Centuries

EUROPE

ASIA

PACIFIC OCEAN

Hawaii

New Zealand

AUSTRALIA

New Guinea

Philippines

Borneo

Java

Sumatra

Sri Lanka

INDIAN OCEAN

Madagascar

AFRICA

ATLANTIC OCEAN

Christian Missions by Time Period

	Roman Catholic Missions	Protestant Missions
Pre 1800		
1800–1849		
1850 and Later		

1000 km.

1000 m.

boards to support evangelistic work in foreign lands. Much of the new emphasis on missions may be traced to the work of a truly remarkable man named William Carey (1761–1834). His influence was so great that he is called "the father of modern missions."

Carey was raised as an Anglican and was a shoemaker by trade. As an adult he had a conversion experience and eventually became a Baptist. He was convinced that his faith demanded preaching the Gospel in heathen lands. This conviction led him to form the Particular Baptist Society for Propagating the Gospel amongst the Heathen (later called the Baptist Missionary Society). The society raised funds and eventually sent Carey, his family, and a physician to India in 1793. The work was very difficult, yet that inspired Carey to work harder. One of his chief efforts was to make the Bible available to people in their native language. By the time of his death, he had translated the Bible or parts of it into twenty-five languages and dialects.

Written reports of Carey and his work inspired the founding of other mission societies and stimulated the creation of missionary boards in other denominations. Adoniram Judson (1788–1850) was one of the notable missionaries to follow in Carey's steps. Judson was sent to India by the Congregationalist's American Board of Commissioners for Foreign Missions. Upon arriving in India he converted to the Baptist faith. A mission society was organized among Baptists to support his work and it eventually became the American Baptist Convention. Because he was denied permission to minister in India, Judson migrated to Burma where he spent most of the rest of his life. Judson was supported in his efforts by his first wife Ann Hasseltine, who died in 1826, and his second wife, Sarah Boardman. Each of these women made remarkable contributions in her own right. Numerous other missionaries exhibited tremendous courage and dedication in their efforts in other lands.

Mission efforts continued throughout the twentieth century. At present, there are few, if any lands, that do not have some form of Christian witness in them. One of the characteristics of the twentieth-century church is that for the first time in history it is truly global. It is difficult to assess the general impact of the mission efforts. Missionaries have been accused of simply destroying indigenous cultures and extending the influence of colonial powers. Certainly this happened. On the other hand, at times missionaries were opposed by colonial governments because they spoke against injustice or would have forced the colonialists to treat Christian natives as equals.

Mission fields have been a source of change in the church. Women were very active in the mission societies, often taking the lead in efforts to support missionaries. More important, women played a key role on the mission fields themselves. On occasion women were sent as missionaries. More often, they accompanied their husbands. In foreign countries they not only supported the mission's work but also played a central role. They taught, preached, and otherwise ministered in ways that would have been denied them in their home countries. Mission work tended to increase the status of women in the church.

Missionaries of different denominations found it necessary to cooperate closely on the mission fields. This cooperation was partly for friendship. Missionaries of other denominations often were the only westerners available for companionship. The theological differences that seemed so important in the homelands were hindrances on the mission fields. Indigenous people could not understand how different groups could proclaim the same Christ and fight among themselves. Missionaries found it to their advantage to emphasize what they had in common and forget their differences. This was one of the sources of interdenominational cooperation that would become important in the twentieth century.

Sunday School

The Sunday school movement also took hold in the nineteenth century. Some organized efforts at religious instruction had been made in the past. However, the need for such teaching was increased by the industrial revolution. As large numbers moved to the cities, traditional ways of reaching many people broke down. Many came to feel that young people were not receiving instruction in the Bible and the Christian faith at home. In 1780, Robert Raikes (1735–1811) organized a Sunday school in his home parish of Gloucester, England, to teach poor children such elementary subjects as reading and writing as well as religion and the Bible. In the long run the Sunday school movement spread to become a standard feature of Protestant churches. It was also used extensively by missionaries. Many denominations chose to cooperate in the development of literature. Laypeople, especially women, played a key role in Sunday schools by serving as volunteer directors and teachers.

OTHER TWENTIETH-CENTURY MOVEMENTS

The nineteenth century had been an age of tremendous optimism. The industrial and agricultural revolutions held out the promise of freeing humans from needs. Modern medicine and science made advances in conquering disease. Evolutionary theory seemed to point to the possibility of ever-improving conditions in society. This optimism changed with the extensive bloodshed and destruction of World War I. A much more pessimistic mood started to characterize society, starting in Europe and spreading to the United States after World War II. In this section we look at some of the twentieth-century movements that either continued nineteenth-century trends or reacted against them.

Neo-Orthodoxy

Neo-orthodoxy was one reaction against liberalism. **Neo-orthodoxy** means "new orthodoxy." It is a rediscovery of many of the traditional themes of Calvinism and Lutheranism. While liberalism asserts faith in reason and human ability, neo-orthodoxy asserts the sinfulness of humans. Against liberalism's faith in progress, it asserts the necessity of God's saving intervention in history. Against liberalism's close identification of religion and culture, it asserts the God who stands outside and judges all human culture and human institutions. Against liberalism's belief in revelation that occurs in nature and human culture, it asserts a God who is so wholly other from human experience that he must reveal himself to people. Neo-orthodoxy did not reject the insights from historical studies and biblical criticism, but it did emphasize God's unique revelation in the Bible. The Bible confronts humanity with truth that cannot be found in the historical process alone. Neo-orthodoxy also is called "crisis theology" or "dialectical theology."[4]

Karl Barth (1886–1968), the father of neo-orthodoxy, is probably the greatest theologian of the twentieth century. Barth was the son of a Swiss Reformed pastor who also was a professor of theology. Early on, Barth was attracted to liberalism. While serving as a pastor in Switzerland during World War I, however, he became aware that liberalism could not explain the disaster that was taking place. Barth studied Paul's Epistle to the Romans in the New Testament, which would have a wide-ranging impact on him. In 1919 he published his well-regarded *Commentary on Romans*. The *Commentary* is a prophetic attack on prevailing culture and religion. The book caused a tremendous theological stir. Barth later presented his mature ideas in *Church Dogmatics,* a massive, thirteen-volume work written over four decades that was never completed.

For Barth, as for Calvin, God is totally other from human experience. A mighty gulf exists between God and his truth and the efforts of sinful humans. There is nothing humans can do to know God and there is nothing they can do to bring about the kingdom. They can only humbly accept the revelation of God, his salvation, and the coming of his kingdom. The truth about God is found in Jesus Christ, the cross, and the Resurrection. The Word of God is revealed in the Bible. All of this did not mean that humans should not strive to create a better society, but that they cannot identify those efforts at improvement with the workings of the kingdom of God.

Neo-orthodoxy initially came to America in the writings of two brothers—H. Richard Niebuhr (1894–1962) and Reinhold Niebuhr (1892–1971). H. Richard's works include *The Social Sources of Denominationalism* and *The Kingdom of God in America*. In these books he pointed to the impact of culture, social class, and nationalism on denominations, their theology, and their ethics. He warned about allowing Christianity and its ethics to become slaves to social forces.

While serving as a pastor in Detroit, Reinhold Niebuhr became convinced of the destructive powers in modern capitalism. This conviction led him to reject liberalism and to assert a powerful doctrine of original sin. Human societies are destructive and self-seeking. They are more evil than the sum of the total evil of their individual members. Salvation from sin and its social consequences can not come through human efforts. It depends radically on the unmerited grace of God.

Niebuhr's thinking does not mean that Christians have no responsibility for society. They are duty bound to work for justice in society although they realize that perfection in the temporal realm is impossible. Nevertheless, Christians are optimistic people. They have the hope of the coming of the kingdom of God. Niebuhr presented these ideas in books like *Moral Man and Immoral Society* and *The Nature and Destiny of Man*.

Paul Tillich (1886–1965) achieved something of a synthesis of liberal and neo-orthodox ideas. He was born in Germany and served as a chaplain to the German army in World War I. After the war he taught at several German universities. Life became increasingly difficult for Tillich when the Nazis came to power. In 1934 he was persuaded by Reinhold Niebuhr to join the faculty of Union Theological Seminary in New York City. He spent the rest of his life teaching at Union, then Harvard, and finally at the University of Chicago.

Tillich's thought is difficult to classify. He drew some ideas from existentialism and described himself as a theologian of culture. He tried to show how the Gospel responds to the most difficult questions raised by life in modern culture. For Tillich, God and the Christian faith address human anxiety about meaninglessness and death. God is the great "Ground of Being" in which all life is rooted. All religious practices, objects (including the Bible), and beliefs are symbols that point beyond themselves to that Ground. They can neither contain that Ground nor completely express it.

Tillich had a particularly strong doctrine of grace. The grace of God says to humans, "You are accepted unconditionally!" Faith is a matter of accepting the fact that you are accepted. The "religious experience" was the affirmation one felt when he or she experiences the unconditional acceptance from the Ground of Being. This acceptance may come through traditional religious channels, but it may also be found outside or even in spite of them. Wherever there is acceptance, there is God. Tillich's numerous works include *The Courage to Be*, *The Shaking of the Foundations*, *Love, Power, and Justice*, *The Eternal Now*, and his three-volume *Systematic Theology*. Tillich's thought has helped many find hope in the confusion and meaninglessness that marked the twentieth century. However, others believe that his "philosophical theology" departed too far from the core of Christian doctrine. His efforts to speak of God in a secular society contributed to the rise of death of God theology in the 1960s, which we will discuss shortly.

Martin Buber

Martin Buber (1878–1965) was a Jewish religious philosopher whose ideas have had a profound impact on social science, psychotherapy, and education as well as Christian theology. According to Buber, the essence of the human is found in the way the person relates to others and the world. People can either have I–It or I–Thou relations. In I–It relations, people or the material world are treated as objects to be studied or manipulated.

In I–Thou relations, there is a deep involvement with, commitment to, and identification with the other. The other person (or even the world) is not used or manipulated but is loved and appreciated. While I–It relations are necessary, it is in I–Thou relations where people become fully human. Martin pointed out the modern world unfortunately was more and more characterized by I–It relations.

Buber's ideas about relationships also influenced his understanding of God. He felt people too often try to treat God as an It. For example, people try to prove God's existence or manipulate God to get what they want by prayer or ritual. It is only when people treat God as a Thou by committing to him that God can be truly known. Interestingly, Buber taught that people do not have to encounter God in traditional religious activity. He is encountered in the everyday and ordinary. One of the most important places where God is encountered is in relationships between people. When one treats another as a Thou, the eternal Thou is experienced.

LIBERALISM AND FUNDAMENTALISM

Although liberalism has been continually attacked, it remained a powerful force in the twentieth-century church. Harry Emerson Fosdick (1878–1969) was a well-known advocate of liberalism. Fosdick, a Baptist, was one of the best-known preachers of his day. He spent most of his career as pastor of Riverside Church in New York City. Fosdick was committed to Christian evangelism but contended that Christians should also be committed to progressively eliminating ignorance, sin, and apathy. For him, contemporary needs were more important than ancient creeds. People should be committed to principles that promote free inquiry, personal development, and social progress.

The Social Gospel is an American movement that helped give liberal Protestantism a distinct form in the twentieth century. The **Social Gospel** involved the insistence that the Gospel must be expressed in social ethics. The movement had been developing for some time in American liberal Protestantism. Its roots are very complex and it includes the American tendency to think of itself as a righteous nation, the social action impulses in revivalism, the European Christian efforts to treat social ills, and the rise of secular social sciences. The Social Gospel was an effort to remedy the problems caused by urbanized, capitalistic, industrial society. Washington Gladden (1836–1918) often is considered the father of the movement. Yet in many ways the Social Gospel was but the end result of the recognition of the need for Christian social involvement that had been growing throughout the nineteenth century. Many of the major denominations had developed social action branches by the late 1800s.

In the early 1900s, a Baptist minister and theology professor named Walter Rauschenbusch (1861–1918) produced a theology that gave the best-known expression to the Social Gospel. Early in his career Rauschenbusch pastored a church in the Hell's Kitchen neighborhood of New York City, one of the poorest and most hopeless neighborhoods in the nation. Rauschenbusch became deeply involved in efforts to deal with the problems of the neighborhood and the city. His ideas evolved from this experience. Rauschenbusch's concepts are expressed in three major books: *Christianity and the Social Crisis*, *Christianizing the Social Order*, and *A Theology for the Social Gospel*. He attacked older approaches to Christianity for their lack of concern for the needy, presented a powerful doctrine of the "kingdom of evil," and pointed to the coming kingdom of God. According to Rauschenbusch, the long-awaited coming of the kingdom is truly Gospel as it will bring good tidings to all people. The coming kingdom rests upon the perfectibility of human beings. This perfectibility had been revealed in the quick evolution of the United States and the progress that had occurred since the Reformation. Christians must unite to bring the power of religion to break the kingdom of evil. The kingdom of God will come only when humans have taken control of social forces to direct them to the good.

The actual Social Gospel movement itself was small and was merely a subdivision of Protestant liberalism. All liberals did not support it. Yet it helped focus the attention of many Christians on social concerns, particularly the problems of industrialized urban society. Its concerns were expressed by the Federal Council of Churches of Christ in America, which was founded by thirty-three denominations in 1908. Many reforms advocated in the Social Gospel were enacted in the 1920s and 1930s. However, this success must be attributed more to the progressive ideas present in society at large than to any specific religious motive.[5]

Throughout the twentieth century, Protestant liberalism continued to build bridges to modern culture. It has adjusted the Christian faith to accept the viewpoints of historical studies, biblical criticism, and the social and natural sciences. It has emphasized social action. It has tended to subject traditional doctrine and church discipline to modern ideas of individual liberty and democracy. It has tried to adapt to a **pluralistic environment** (a situation in which there are many different people with many different faiths and ideas) by extending tolerance to almost all religions and philosophies. Some argue that in attempting to speak to modern culture liberal Protestantism has so diluted Christian teachings that it has lost the ability to say anything distinctive.

To another powerful twentieth-century movement these liberal trends are the tools of the devil designed to destroy Christianity and Christian society. **Fundamentalism** is an American movement that spread across denominational lines in the early twentieth century. It is largely a reaction against modern culture and various Christian attempts to adapt to that culture. Fundamentalists not only reject liberalism but also feel that neo-orthodoxy went too far in attempting to address the modern world. While fundamentalism developed in the United States, its concepts and attitudes are common to many Christians in various parts of the world. Most fundamentalists now prefer to call themselves *conservative* or *evangelical* Christians.

Fundamentalism developed gradually in the second half of the nineteenth century, starting with the Princeton theology of Charles Hodge. The movement received a further boost with the work of John Nelson Darby (1800–1882), who developed a theory of explaining developments in the Bible and Christian history in terms of seven dispensations. **Dispensations** were long periods of time in which God chose to relate to his people in a particular manner that was appropriate to the age. Christians were living in the sixth dispensation—the dispensation of grace. This age would end in judgment when God returned to establish his kingdom in the seventh and final period. The corrupt present civilization would be doomed. Only a small remnant of true believers would be saved. This viewpoint was furthered by the publication of the *Scofield Reference Bible* in 1909. This Bible soon became the standard tool for millions as they attempted to interpret the inerrant and unified Word of God. Premillennial dispensationalism would become one of the marks of the fundamentalists.

Through much of the second half of the nineteenth century, evangelical Christians labored to define the fundamentals of the faith that people were to affirm so they would not succumb to liberalism. There were five fundamentals:

1. The inerrancy of the Scriptures (often coupled with a theory of verbal inspiration).
2. The virgin birth of Christ.
3. The satisfaction theory of the Atonement (as the only one taught in the Bible).
4. The physical, bodily Resurrection of Christ.
5. The impending return of the Lord. (Others held his earthly miracles were essential.)

With slight variation, these doctrines are held by all Christian fundamentalists.[6] The movement was given further support when two wealthy laymen gave a large grant to write a series of pamphlets addressing present-day issues from a conservative perspective. The project drew together an international panel of noted conservative scholars, which began the publication of *The Fundamentals* in 1910. These pamphlets were distributed free of charge and resulted in converting many to the evangelical cause.

Battle lines soon were drawn between fundamentalists and Modernists (as liberals were sometimes called) in pulpits, seminaries, and colleges all across the country. In the early twentieth century, the Disciples of Christ and the northern branches of Baptists, Presbyterians, and Methodists were embroiled in the fundamentalist-Modernist controversy. Most of the southern branches of the major denominations were not touched by the early stages of the conflict. In the long run, most of these denominations implicitly or explicitly settled on a position that might be described as "broad churchmanship." **Broad churchmanship** is a "truce" in which liberals and conservatives agree to disagree on certain topics but to cooperate on such efforts as evangelism, missions, and other denominational programs. Some could not accept such an approach and broke with the major denominations. Many denominational seminaries and colleges began to adopt more liberal stances. Fundamentalists withdrew their support from these and formed their own seminaries and Bible colleges.

The fundamentalists believed that liberalism in all its forms had to be resisted. "Social Gospelers" especially drew their wrath. However, evolution was the one theory that average Christians saw as a threat to their faith. Evolution seemed to undermine the whole Christian revelation. Because of this, evolution became the focus of much of the fundamentalists' effort to resist modern culture. Fundamentalists tried with some success in southern states to pass laws forbidding the teaching of evolution in the classroom. They were successful in Tennessee. Both fundamentalists and Modernists were spoiling for a fight over evolution. The opportunity was provided in 1925 when a young high school teacher named John Scopes was charged with violating the evolution law.

The Scopes "Monkey Trial" was held in Dayton, Tennessee. Actually it was much more than the trial of a simple school teacher. The town fathers hoped to use it to put Dayton on the map. Fundamentalists hoped for a decisive defeat of modernism. Liberals hoped to show the ignorance, irrationality, and backwardness of the conservatives. Evangelicals and Modernists believed the case would end up in the United States Supreme Court where the issue would be settled once and for all. The trial attracted worldwide attention. Reporters and spectators poured into Dayton from all over. The trial came to resemble a circus more than a legal proceeding. Scopes was found guilty, but his conviction was overturned by a higher court on a technicality. The case never reached the United States Supreme Court.

Despite the conviction, liberals felt that the trial was a decisive defeat for fundamentalism. The foolishness of the fundamentalists had been shown to the world. It is true that the Scopes trial was one of the high-water marks of early, aggressive fundamentalism. There were few successful efforts to pass new laws. The ones that were enacted were not openly enforced. Conservatives seemed progressively reconciled to other elements of their denominations. Hard-core fundamentalists withdrew into their own associations and Bible schools. Yet this assessment is far from totally correct. Because of the controversy, publishers quietly withdrew sections on evolution from textbooks. The subject would not reappear until 1960. Moreover, many Christians in average churches remained very conservative, if not fundamentalist.

Fundamentalists have again become active on the national scene in the last three decades. They have taken over two major denominations (the Missouri Synod Lutherans and the Southern Baptist Convention) and deeply influenced others. They are asserting themselves on issues such as restoring prayer to schools, outlawing abortion, supporting "biblical" family values like male domination in the home, opposing gay marriages, and resisting secularism. Their conservative political agenda is expressed by the New Right. The New Right has been led by a number of individuals of whom television evangelist Pat Robertson and Baptist preacher and university president Jerry Falwell are two of the best known. By the 1970s, fundamentalists in the United States attacked the teaching of evolution with a new weapon called **creation science,** or **creationism.** Creationism claims that the gaps and inconsistencies in evolution make it a very poor theory for explaining the origin of life. They claimed that scientific evidence better supports the biblical account of creation than it does evolution. At the very least, they demanded that creation science be taught alongside evolution in public schools.

Creationism lost most of its influence in the 1990s after a series of court decisions held that creation science amounted to inserting religion into the high school classroom. This teaching of religion in the public school was seen by the courts as a violation of the First Amendment to the Constitution which guarantees separation of church and state. With the weakening of creation science, the "Darwin versus the Bible" struggle took another turn with intelligent design theory replacing creationism. **Intelligent design** believes that the universe is so complex, intricate, and closely integrated that an intelligent mind must have designed it. It could not have happened by blind change as evolution theory contends. This argument is not new. It is a modern variation of the teleological argument for the existence of God. The argument dates back to the ancient Greek philosophers. Christian writers have used it many times in the past.

The intelligent design advocates are careful to say that the "intelligent mind" that created the universe is not necessarily the Christian God. Their goals are much the same as those of the creationists—to get intelligent design taught along side of evolution as a scientific way of explaining the origins of the universe. Some state legislatures have passed laws requiring the teaching of intelligent design in biology classrooms as have a number of local school boards. Recently, court decisions have held that intelligent design, like creationism, is bringing religion into the classroom. It also is important to note that most scientists also believe creationism and intelligent design are not scientific at all; instead, they are attempts to teach religion disguised as science in public schools.[7]

Church Decline and Growth in the United States

It is worth mentioning that in the United States church participation was on the increase up to the 1950s. Since then almost all of the major denominations have experienced a decline in membership. This decline is particularly true of those denominations most influenced by liberalism, such as Presbyterians, American Baptists, Disciples of Christ, Episcopalians, and United Methodists. On the other hand, fundamentalists (or evangelicals) have increased their numbers. Two complementary trends seem to have contributed to the decline of mainline denominations.

The first of these is the rise of a vague spiritualism as a replacement for more traditional religious commitments. Many people have come to have negative images of denominations. They see denominational conflict, politics, and scandals as cheapening religion. There also is the idea that truth is relative so that no one denomination can claim to have all the truth. This may also contribute to the idea that one denomination is as good (or bad) as another. Thrown into this mixture is the growing idea that religion is an individual and private experience. Lost is the necessity of the church as supportive community where spiritual growth and discipline should occur. This trend is seen in people who make statements like, "I am spiritual, but not religious." Such people are unlikely to make a commitment to a denomination or to the Christian church in general.

The second related trend is the growth of nondenominational churches. Not only have new nondenominational churches appeared, but many churches with denominational ties have removed the denomination's name from their congregation. For example, many Baptist, Methodist, and Presbyterian churches and replaced it with a community church label (i.e., Bethel Baptist Church becomes Bethel Community Church). This is done to appeal to persons of other denominations or those repulsed by denomination labels, but it is another indication of the weakening of denominational ties.

This approach is fueled by the consumerism of modern times. We tend to see ourselves as needing goods and services which are tailored to our wants. When this carries over to religion, it takes the form of finding a church that "meets our needs," not one that holds a sound denominational theology. This does not mean that people who search for a church that "meets their needs" are looking for a church with a vague theology. In fact, as we saw above, those evangelical groups with the most rigid and the most clearly defined theologies have attracted the most members.

In some ways, the above trends come together in the rise of megachurches. **Megachurches** are those with an average weekly attendance of 2000 or more. There are about 800 Protestant megachurches in the United States and many others throughout the world. One Korean megachurch claims a weekly attendance of 250,000. In the United States, there are another 1700 or so Roman Catholic megachurches. Most of the research has been conducted on Protestant megachurches. Most Protestant megachurches have a very conservative theology and are presided over by a strong pastor. Some are denominational. Almost all of these are Southern Baptist or Assemblies of God. The rest are nondenominational. Some scholars believe the growth of megachurches is coming to an end, but others expect it to continue for some time.[8]

The Death of God and Process Theology

While fundamentalism is a rejection of contemporary culture, trends arose in the second half of the twentieth century that tried to redefine Christianity in terms of that culture. Much of the literature of the twentieth century had emphasized despair, relativity, and hopelessness. The world continued its march toward secularization. The scientific perspective dominated. Many Christians found themselves living in a situation in which the church-taught supernatural ideas, with their traditional categories of right and wrong, did not seem to square with the scientific, secular ideas of their daily world.

Liberalism lost much of its force after the first few decades of the century. Fundamentalism was also not a viable option for many who wanted to live consistently in the modern world. Neo-orthodoxy had provided an answer for many until the end of the 1950s. However, by the 1960s, many Christians felt that Christianity was providing few fitting answers to give their lives meaning. In the 1960s, a group of theologians attempted a radical break with the past by trying to express Christianity in secular terms. As a group, their ideas were known in the popular press as the "death of God theology" (although not all of them really proclaimed the "death of God").

The death of God theology said that Christianity must stop speaking of God in the supernatural terms inherited from the past. These older ideas did not fit in the modern world where the supernatural had little place and the idea of a transcendent God was dead. The proper way to understand God was in his actions. God acted in love and justice. Where these existed, God also existed. The church must stop talking of the transcendent God and start advocating social involvement. The daily concerns of people, not abstract ideas, were the legitimate focus of theology. When the church started addressing these concerns, it would be meaningful to moderns. Friedrich Gogarten, Gabriel Vahanian, J. A. T. Robinson, Thomas J. J. Altizer, William Hamilton, and Paul Van Buren are proponents of this theology.

The death of God theology drew upon the ideas of Nietzsche, who had proclaimed the death of God in the nineteenth century. It was also based on existentialism and the cultural theology of Tillich. However, its more immediate spiritual father was Dietrich Bonhoeffer (1906–1945). Bonhoeffer was a twentieth-century Christian martyr who was killed for his faith by the Nazis. While in prison awaiting death because of his involvement in a plot to assassinate Hitler, he wrote articles and letters that were later published in the 1950s as *Letters and Papers from Prison*. These letters presented a number of provocative, but undeveloped, ideas on "religionless" Christianity. Bonhoeffer viewed secular culture very positively. He believed God had raised humans to the point that they no longer needed him so he could establish a relation with humans based on love not dependency. People no longer needed God for explanations about the working of the universe because science provided tools for understanding it. Nor did people need God to solve their problems. They should take this responsibility on themselves. Because people no longer depended on God as they had done in the past, they could live in a responsible loving relation to God.

Process theology also had a positive attitude toward modern culture. For the most part, twentieth-century science regarded the natural world as continually involved in an evolutionary process. Tying into this idea, process theology sees the world, religion, and God in a constant process of development. To see God as the unchanging ruler of tradition is to introduce error into the faith. God and his world are forever evolving. In a sense, God is incomplete but is in the process of becoming more complete. Humans have a very special place in helping to complete God. God is not absolute, commanding the direction of the universe; rather, God depends on humans (and all other creatures and natural processes) to do his work. To be human demands that there be real freedom. To be free, people are left with the very real possibility that they will undermine the constructive work of God through destructive acts. In process thought, God is not necessarily in control. The universe may not move to the glorious fulfilling end that God appoints, but it may destroy itself. Process thought is built upon the work of philosophers Henri Bergson (1859–1941) and Alfred North Whitehead (1861–1947). Twentieth-century theologians who contributed to the development of process theology include Charles Hartshorne (1897–) and Teilhard de Chardin (1881–1955).

The Theology of Hope

The theology of hope is one of the more interesting theologies of the twentieth century. It grew out of the dialogue between Christians and Marxists. The Marxist philosopher Ernst Bloch came to believe early Christianity was a cry against oppression. Its most important feature was its "principle of hope." This hope was Christianity's greatest contribution to human history. It means people are not determined by the past but are open to the possibilities of their future.

These themes were developed into the theology of hope by several Christian writers. The leader of this group was Jurgen Moltmann. For Moltmann, hope is central to the Christian faith. In spite of all problems, God is still active in this world, drawing it to him. God meets us in the present but draws us toward him in the future. This hope of the "last things" of God is the beginning of Christian theology, not its ending chapter.

Christian hope is not individualistic but is the hope of a new order. Because God is active now and in the future, people can not just sit and wait on his final day. Instead, the faithful must be active in bringing about the peace and justice that characterize God's future. This emphasis on eschatology, hope, and involvement has been very important in twentieth-century theology.

THE ECUMENICAL MOVEMENT

The **ecumenical movement** was a major Protestant trend during the twentieth century. It refers to the efforts of various denominations to reunite or at least to engage in cooperative efforts. The ecumenical movement is the result of the interdenominational mission movement and worldwide councils that have occurred in the past two centuries.

The mission movement created interdenominational cooperation. Inspired by the work of William Carey, the London Mission Society was formed in 1795 by 200 ministers to further the mission enterprise. The London Mission Society was the most important of many interdenominational societies formed in numerous countries. The missionaries themselves recognized the need to cooperate on the mission fields. That led them to advocate large-scale interdenominational cooperation for evangelization.

This cooperation resulted in the calling of several world mission conferences in the nineteenth century. The World Mission Conference of 1910 met in Edinburgh, Scotland. That conference led to the founding of the International Mission Conference in 1927, which gave continuing direction to world mission efforts. The Edinburgh Conference produced additional conferences, which furthered interdenominational cooperation. One was the Universal Conference on Life and Work, which first met in Stockholm, Sweden, in 1925 under the leadership of the Lutheran archbishop of Uppsala, Nathan Söderblom. This conference tried to apply the Gospel to the social issues of the day. Subsequent conferences on life and work continued this concern.

In the World Mission Conference and the Life and Work Conferences, denominations set aside their differences on such issues as ordination, the sacraments, and church governance. At the same time, there was a growing recognition of the need to address differences between the denominations. That recognition led to the creation of the World Conference on Faith and Order in 1927. This and later conferences on faith and order studied the similarities in theology and church governance and established dialogues to resolve denominational differences in these areas. In 1948, the various conferences united to form the World Council of Churches (WCC). The International Mission Conference merged with the WCC in 1961.

The WCC contains over 300 different denominations. Many Protestant groups belong as does the Orthodox church. The Roman Catholic church has never formally joined the organization. A number of Protestant denominations also have refused to participate. Fundamentalists believe that the WCC stands for theological compromise and view it very negatively. Others are suspicious that a call for social involvement by the WCC is a masked form of communism. Since Vatican II, the Catholic church has engaged in dialogues with the Anglicans, Methodists, Disciples of Christ, and the Orthodox church. Although these dialogues have produced fruitful discussions as well as "substantial agreement" between the groups, no actual reunions have resulted.

The ecumenical movement has resulted in cooperation and reunions within national churches. The Federal Council of Churches of Christ in America was founded in 1908. This organization merged with several other interdenominational groups in 1950 to form the National Council of Churches in the United States. In the twentieth century similar national councils formed in France, Switzerland, Germany, New Zealand, Great Britain, Canada, and Australia. This ecumenical spirit also fostered the union of splinter groups within numerous denominations. Even when formal union has not occurred, the ecumenical spirit of the twentieth century encouraged dialogue and cooperation among Christians of different views and has led to increasing positive relations between Protestants and Catholics.

An extension of this process is seen in Christian groups with vastly different theologies putting aside differences to cooperate on items of mutual concern. For instance, Roman Catholics and Southern Baptists have united in public campaigns to oppose abortion. Still, each of these denominations has different theologies, theories of the church, and concepts of Christian morality. And they continue to oppose each other on other moral, religious, and political issues.

THE DISPOSSESSED AND THE PROSPECTS OF GLOBAL CHRISTIANITY

One of the most significant trends in the twentieth century was the rising importance of the "dispossessed." The **dispossessed** are those who have traditionally been excluded from positions of power and influence in society as well as the church. Western women increasingly made their presence felt in the twentieth century. For some time, they have been involved in mission efforts and Sunday schools and in such movements as the antislavery program and the Women's Christian Temperance Union. As their status in society improved, women demanded a greater role in the church. Some conducted campaigns to become ordained into the ministry. Few churches ordained women in the nineteenth century, and through the first half of the twentieth century, the church was still dominated by males. Since that time, a number of Protestant denominations have started ordaining women and a few have been made bishops.[9]

Women also have made contributions to theology and biblical studies. Some female theologians, including Letty M. Russell, Elizabeth Schüssler-Fiorenza, Rosemary R. Ruether, and Mary Daly, argue that theology traditionally has been written from a male perspective. They contend that a feminist theology has much to contribute. Some have argued that starting in the nineteenth century there has been a marked "feminization" of God. There has been a move away from the war-like, strong, judgmental, "male" view of God to a caring, compassionate, loving, "female" God. Undoubtedly, female scholars are adding deeper insight into the nature of God and the Christian faith.

The African-American church also asserted itself in the twentieth century. One area where the influence of the black church made itself felt is in the civil rights movement. The National Association for the Advancement of Colored People and the Southern Christian Leadership Conference were instrumental in dismantling segregation and securing civil rights for blacks. Both groups drew much of their leadership from the Christian church. Ministers like Martin Luther King, Jr. (1929–1968) and Adam Clayton Powell, Jr. (1908–1972) were strong leaders in the movement. One African-American Baptist minister, Jesse Jackson, was a serious presidential candidate in the 1980s. Church involvement

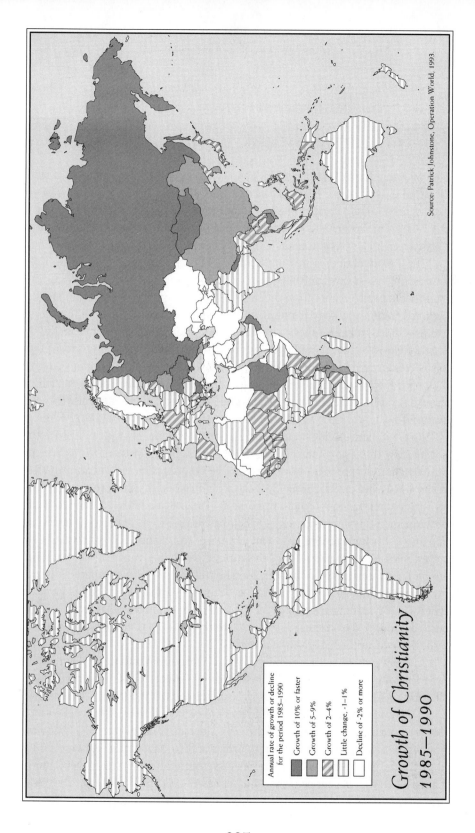

Annual rate of growth or decline
for the period 1985–1990

Growth of 10% or faster

Growth of 5–9%

Growth of 2–4%

Little change, -1–1%

Decline of -2% or more

*Growth of Christianity
1985–1990*

Source: Patrick Johnstone, Operation World, 1993.

in the movement also has started to generate a black theology that combines orthodoxy with themes from the black struggle.

Christianity in Latin America

The mission efforts of the nineteenth and twentieth centuries resulted in a truly universal church. As Christianity moved from Western society to non-Western nations, important contributions were made by those nations to the development of Christianity. Contributions from the "dispossessed" nations are altering how Christians conceive of the church as well as the way the church does theology.

The newer churches in non-Western societies have begun to make their presence felt. Not only do they participate in organizations like the WCC, but their theology also comes from different cultural, economic, and social perspectives. Liberation theology is one new theology that has had wide influence. It was developed in Latin America by a number of Catholic theologians, including Gustavo Gutiérrez and Juan Luis Segundo. The liberation theologians insist that it is necessary to do theology from "the bottom," that is, from the perspective of the poor. They claim that the Gospel demands liberation not only from sin but also from exploitative economic and social conditions. This emphasis has been mirrored by many Catholic bishops in Latin America such as Oscar Romero (1917–1980) and Helder Camara (1909–1999) who struggled against the exploitation that has characterized the region. Liberation theology led to the confrontation of repressive governments that controlled much of Latin America in the 1970s and 1980s. Some of those who opposed the powerful were killed for their efforts. Bishop Romero was among those whose faith led them to social activism and who were martyred for their beliefs. In recent years, the Vatican has taken steps to limit the involvement of priests and bishops in social struggles. Nevertheless, the social justice message of the Latin American church has affected Christianity worldwide. Liberation theology is particularly relevant because the influence of the church is declining in the North but is growing rapidly in developing nations of the "South." Liberation theology is a theology created among the disposed of the "South" that speaks to those without resources and influence around the globe.

In Chapter 9 we noted the movement of Catholicism into Central and South America with the arrival of the Spanish and Portuguese. In the long run, almost all parts of Central and South American became solidly Catholic. Central and South America are still largely Catholic. However, the twentieth century saw a steady increase in Protestantism in the area. The end of the twentieth century saw a very rapid increase in conversion to Protestantism. Mainline Protestant groups like Baptists, Methodists, and Lutherans have been joined by the newer denominations like the Mormons, Jehovah's Witnesses, and Seventh-Day Adventists.

Charismatic Christianity has had a particularly strong influence. This is apparent in the fact that the Assemblies of God is the largest Protestant denomination in the region. Charismatic styles of worship have also have carried over into Catholicism and branches of Protestantism not traditionally considered charismatic. Most branches of Christianity in Latin America are moving away from the Liberation theology style of confronting governments and demanding change to various smaller-scale projects designed to directly improve the life of the poor.[10] The Protestant groups are joined through conversion. Those who join claim a new purpose for their lives and have an identity in their faith that helps them navigate the uncertainty of rapid changes brought on by globalization.

Christianity in Africa

In Chapters 1 through 2 we saw that Christianity spread to North Africa early on. North African Christianity was closely associated with Rome and tended to join with Rome in opposition to Eastern (Greek) Christianity. By the eighth century, the region had been conquered by Muslim armies and was lost to Christianity. The Coptic Church is the only surviving remnant of Christianity in North Africa. The Coptic Church is the Egyptian church. It is named after the native language (Coptic) that was spoken in Egypt during the early centuries of Christianity. The Coptic Church tends toward monophysitism. In recent years, the Coptics have negotiated with both the Orthodox Church and the Roman Catholic Church over the divine and human natures of Jesus. These negotiations resulted in signing joint agreements on the natures of Jesus. The Coptic Church has been restored to fellowship with both Orthodox and Catholic Christians. The Coptic Church played a significant role in the conversion of Ethiopia to Christianity. Even today, the Ethiopian Church remains one of the oldest and most important Christian communities in Africa.

The story is different in Sub-Saharan Africa (that part of Africa south of the Sahara Desert). Christianity reached these regions rather late. The Portuguese made the first efforts to convert Sub-Saharan Africans as they worked their way down the coast of Western Africa seeking a sea route to India and China. Their greatest success was in the kingdom of the Kongo where a version of Catholic Christianity became firmly established. Other small missions were established in various coastal regions.

The biggest push toward converting Africa was begun in the nineteenth century as revivals in Protestantism produced missionary efforts and Catholics found renewed interest as well. On the whole, Africa was not colonized until the nineteenth and twentieth centuries. Missionaries flocked into the European colonies to spread the Gospel. Many missionaries felt it was their responsibility not only to convert the natives, but also to destroy their traditional cultures.

These native cultures were to be replaced by superior Western civilization. To their credit, missionaries did learn native languages, translated the Bible into the local language, established schools, and brought in modern medicine to assist the natives.

Although European and American missionaries were somewhat successful in introducing Christianity, the major success in evangelizing Africa has come at the hands of Africans themselves. Some of these became pastors or other officials in the colonial mission churches. However, many broke away from the Western churches to produce truly African varieties of Christianity. These came to be called **African Independent Churches (AIC).**[11] Some of these churches form into larger associations, but many stand alone, keeping their independence from other congregations and associations. There are two main categories of AICs: Ethiopian Independent Churches and Zionist Independent Churches.

The Ethiopian Independent Churches were not founded in Ethiopia or by Ethiopians. Instead, they get their name from their contention that the many times that Ethiopia is mentioned in the Bible are an indication that God has always been involved in Africa. These churches developed out of traditional mission churches and do not differ greatly in theology or worship patterns from them. They were founded by persons who felt racism in mission churches and were frustrated by the difficulty of native people to move into positions of leadership. Zionist Independent Churches are also called Spirit churches for their emphasis on the Holy Spirit, their charismatic style of worship, and their stress on direct physical and spiritual healing. These are distinctive characteristics of Pentecostal and charismatic Christianity. As in Latin America, charismatic Christianity is the dynamic force driving conversions. Some argue that Christianity has been so successful in southern Africa because the worldview in traditional Africa is closer to that of the Bible than that of modern societies. Certainly, the AICs do attempt to draw parallels between traditional culture and Christian teaching and/or redress African concepts into Christian terms.

In recent years, several African professional theologians have undertaken formulating theologies that seek to accommodate both African tradition and Christian theology. This effort to reconcile African traditions and religion with Christianity is known as **African theology.** For instance, these theologians argue that traditional African religions have a single supreme spirit that is all powerful. This is the equivalent of the Christian God. The multitudes of spirits in African tradition are similar to the angels and demons found in the Bible. Ancestor worship is much like veneration of saints and so on. African theology, on one level, is a logical extension of what we have seen throughout Christianity from the time of the New Testament and thinkers like Justin Martyr. They may be Christian writers trying to build a bridge between the faith and the surrounding culture. On the other hand, critics of African theology believe it has gone too far in making African religions kinds of "Old Testaments" leading to Christ. According to them, this dilutes and confuses the Christian message and undermines the uniqueness of God's revelation in Jesus Christ. Again, the old issue of Christ and culture asserts itself. We should also mention that part of the attraction of Christianity may come about because the worldview of the Bible is much closer to the worldview of traditional African religions than it is to the secular, scientific societies of the modern West.

Christianity is growing very quickly in Latin America as well as in Africa. In fact, because of population growth in these regions, Christianity is the fastest-growing religion in the world. With the decline of Christianity in secular Europe and the fact that Christianity is "holding its own" in North America, the future of Christianity is in the Southern Hemisphere countries. Some writers contend that Latin American and African churches may soon be undertaking missionary efforts to reconvert the North.

Christianity in Asia

Missionary efforts in Asia began with the Catholic missions to India, the Malay Peninsula, Japan, and China in the sixteenth century (see Chapter 9). Missionaries met with some initial success, but in the long run had much less success than they did in other sections of the world such as the Americas. Despite 400 hundred years of missions, Asia remains the least Christian area of the world. Prospects are not entirely bleak however. The *World Christian Encyclopedia* indicates that conversions are occurring at a rate of about 2.4 million per year in Asia. One country, the Philippines, was converted to Christianity while it was colony of Spain. Another country, Korea, is in line to become the second country in Asia with a Christian majority. Christian growth has come in part through missionary effort from the West, but like Africans, Korean Christians have been successful at converting their own countrymen. Prior to the communist take-over, there was considerable effort on the part of Westerners to evangelize China. The communist drove Christian missionaries out of China and suppressed those Christians who are not members of the officially recognized (and government controlled) Christian church. Because of the official control of religion and lack of access by outsiders, we do not have an accurate picture of the condition of Christianity in China. A form of Christianity has existed for a very long time in India. Because the legend of the origin of this type of Christianity holds that it was taken to India from Judea by the Apostle Thomas after Jesus' resurrection, its followers are known as Thomas Christians. Protestants and Catholics continue long-established missions and new outside groups continue to plant new missions. Still, only around 2% of Indians are Christians.

THE ORTHODOX CHURCH IN THE MODERN ERA

The collapse of the Ottoman Turkish Empire in the nineteenth century was accomplished largely as a result of the rising nationalism of the people of the Balkan Peninsula, although Russian intervention also contributed. The national churches of Balkan countries became focal points of the liberation movement. Under the Turks, the patriarch of Constantinople (the ecumenical patriarch) had been employed as a governmental official. He had appointed Greek bishops and priests to rule in religious and civil matters in many of the eastern European countries dominated by the Ottomans. These Greek clerics were viewed by many as foreign symbols of the hated Turks.

As a result, when nationalistic groups in the Balkans overthrew the Turks, they were unwilling to submit to rule by the ecumenical patriarch. They formed national churches headed by local people. This process continued in Bulgaria, Romania, Moldavia, Greece, and other regions. Ecclesiastical control was further limited by the fact that Catholics, Protestants, and other Christian groups also had followings in many of these countries. By 1914, the ecumenical patriarch found his effective control limited to those areas still controlled by the Turks—Constantinople and parts of Asia Minor.

The position of the Orthodox church in Russia was somewhat complicated in the nineteenth century. The church itself had been experiencing something of a revival. Yet Western influences, encouraged by Peter the Great, introduced new ideas into the country. The Jesuits had been allowed into Russia and were making inroads, which generated a reaction by some Orthodox Christians. The Jesuits were expelled from the country in 1819.

A group known as the **Slavophiles** also became active. They believed that the only true church was the Russian Orthodox church. Others had been corrupted by Rome or Protestantism. They advocated insulating the Orthodox church from outside influences. To make matters worse, the Holy Synod that ruled the church increasingly was controlled by the government and served as its instrument. Priests were even required to report to the police anything heard during confessions that might indicate disloyalty to the tsar. In spite of suspicion of the clergy, many of the Orthodox maintained a firm commitment to their faith and were sustained by the liturgy.

Although the church was corrupted by its connection to the state, a number of noted people did have a positive impact on spirituality. One was Pilaret Drozdov (1783–1867). Drozdov was the son of a priest and rose to be the metropolitan of Moscow. He was active in a movement to have the Bible translated into the everyday speech of the people, was a counselor to many in the state and church, and was instrumental in having the tsar free the peasants. A number of *startzi* also were active. **Startzi** were monks whose dedication to prayer and spiritual discipline commanded special respect. They served as "elders," whom many sought for counsel. Seraphim of Sarov (1759–1833) and Feofan of Vysha (1815–1894) were two of the best known of the *startzi*.

Vladimir S. Soloviev (1853–1900) was a mystic, philosopher, and theologian who dedicated his life to a search for Christian unity. Soloviev was schooled in the Western philosophies and he came to believe that philosophy was nothing and religious experience was everything. A whole host of Russian authors also influenced Russian spirituality. Drawing on their orthodoxy and their insight into the Russian soul, they vividly explored the depth of meaning and meaninglessness of the human experience. One of the greatest writers was Leo Tolstoy (1828–1910). In the middle of his life Tolstoy experienced a religious conversion that led him to a passionate commitment to his own brand of Christian anarchism. He rejected many of the dogmas of the church and advocated refraining from all forms of violence. Tolstoy had little following in his own country but was widely read outside Russia.

The church had been a dominate feature in the life of Russians for 1000 years. However, much of the official influence was lost in the twentieth century. The tsars had been losing control of the population throughout much of the second half of the nineteenth century. Russia's disastrous entry into World War I brought an end to tsarist rule. During most of World War I, the real power in the country was Grigory Rasputin, the "mad monk" (1872–1916). Rasputin's assassination in 1916 instigated a general revolt against the corrupt tsarist government.

Much of the turmoil surrounding the rebellion ended when the Bolshevik revolution of 1917 brought Nikolai Lenin (1870–1924) to power. The **Bolsheviks** were communists who interpreted Karl Marx's ideas through Lenin's eyes. Initially, it seemed as if the Orthodox church was going to fare better under the new government than it had under the tsars. The new Soviet constitution guaranteed freedom of religion. The Holy Synod dominated by the government was abolished. The patriarch of Moscow was restored as the head of the church.

The new optimism of the church was soon dimmed, however. It became obvious that the Bolsheviks were antireligious, and they systematically destroyed religion in the Soviet empire. Minority religious groups such as pagans, Baptists, and Muslims were persecuted. Church property was confiscated. Many Orthodox churches were closed or turned into museums of religion (many having an antireligious theme). Seminaries were closed. Religious instruction and efforts to win new converts were forbidden. Although it was not illegal to be a Christian, it was impossible to get a job if one was a practicing Christian. Initially, the Orthodox church tried to resist these efforts, but, eventually, the church decided to adapt to the new situation and work within the confines imposed upon it by the state.

Persecution was intense until World War II. During the war, the restrictions were relaxed partly because the church supported the government in the war. Since the war, the church continued to exist under severe restraints in the

Soviet Union. The church in Eastern European communist countries also experienced severe persecution. Christianity was not eliminated from communist countries, however. In fact, it remained very much alive. When priests and other leaders were absent, laypeople continued to pass on religious traditions to their children.

Since the collapse of communist domination, many former communist countries have seen a return of an active church life. In many republics of the former Soviet Union, a new openness has permitted churches to reopen and many to return to open worship. Nearly seventy years of atheistic communism failed to destroy the Orthodox church. At least 60 million still practice the Christian faith throughout many of the republics.[12]

CHRISTIANITY AT THE BEGINNING OF THE TWENTY-FIRST CENTURY

The church at the beginning of the twenty-first century finds itself in an uncertain position. In large measure this uncertainty reflects the state of society at large. Society has become progressively **materialistic** (judging the worth of things solely on their material value). The scientific approach continues to be a dominant philosophy. Much in science makes religion appear irrelevant, if not a throwback to earlier, more superstitious, times. Scientific breakthroughs continue to astound and hold great promise for solving human problems.

Yet science has proven as destructive as it is constructive. The same science that has cured so many traditional illnesses has also produced the atomic bomb, which can destroy all life on earth. Many scientific breakthroughs raise ethical questions about their use and even about whether science should be allowed to progress in certain directions. People seem to be more aware of the limits of the "god" of science. It is double-faced, both creator and destroyer. It cannot answer many of the questions it raises. These questions demand ethical and religious answers.

At the same time, the religious community is as infected with relativism and subjectivism as society. Despite the ecumenical movement, Christianity does not speak with one voice, but many voices. Few clear answers are provided. Some try to live with this situation by finding truths that work for them. Others react by staunchly defending the absolute "fundamentals" of the faith. This approach has proven attractive. Those denominations that claim to provide the simple answers to modern life have been growing. The more liberal, less authoritarian denominations have seen membership decline. Whether the absolute answers of the authoritarian denominations will dominate is still an open question.

The world is facing vast problems caused by industrialization and population growth. These are made more pressing by the destruction of the environment and the depletion of natural resources. Unfortunately, Christianity has contributed to this problem by emphasizing human mastery over the material world. This emphasis has led to an attitude in Western societies that the environment can be exploited regardless of the consequences. Western people have too often lived in conflict with the environment, not in harmony with it. The church is attempting to redefine its understanding of nature and the ethical human response to it, partly by joining a worldwide trend toward seeing the "spiritual" nature of the material world. Many denominations including evangelicals are reexamining their own traditions and are using such ideas as Christian **stewardship** (the believer's responsibility to care for what God has provided). This has spawned a new branch of theology called **Ecological Theology,** whereby Christians have responsibility not only for personal salvation and social issues, but also for acting ethically in relation to the natural environment itself.

The globalization process presents other challenges. As Western ideas, political systems, and ethical understandings associated with Modernism have come into contact with traditional pre-modern societies, forms of non-Christian fundamentalism have emerged. Jewish, Islamic, Hindu, or Buddhist fundamentalism differ in the specific theology they promote (Jewish, Hindu, Buddhist), but all have developed as reactions to modernism. They all teach a no-compromise doctrine and rigorous adherence to religious law. They see global society as a threat to their religion and to the "traditional" way their religion created. The image of warfare dominates their speech (Holy War, prayer warriors, etc.). They tend to see themselves as instruments for carrying out God's work even if this involves using violent measures against civilians. This provides an identity (I am a true Muslim or I am a true Christian.) as well as a purpose in life (to spread the true faith and oppose our religious enemies). Although many, if not most, fundamentalist reject violence, the spread of this approach to faith with no room for compromise and accommodation has led to increased violence and persecution among various religions worldwide.

Globalization poses a number of important questions: Can the power of the emerging economic and political world order be used for constructive purposes or will it further erode human freedom and dignity? Can the vast differences in wealth between industrialized and developing nations be directed toward a more just distribution or will the system lead to further exploitation? How can the former communist nations be integrated fairly into the new economic order? Can we develop means to use religions' moral authority as a way of dealing with the inequities of our planet? Can we lessen religious conflict and direct the power of religion to solve the world's social, cultural, religious, and ecological problems? The social awareness and concepts of social action developed over the last two centuries in Christianity may help bring hope to our planet. The fact that Christianity is universal and that Christians share many things in common in spite of the differences they hold may prove useful. The voices from the new churches in the developing nations may help bring different insight into the meaning of the Gospel in the global community.

CONCLUSIONS

The modern era has seen Western civilization move from an optimistic appraisal of the possibilities for perfecting humanity to a questioning and uncertain stance. In Western Europe, religion lost much of its power and drive in the twentieth century. Participation in many churches declined under the onslaught of secularization, materialism, and nihilism. In the United States, many mainline denominations have declined but charismatic and evangelical groups have helped offset these losses. The past several decades have witnessed the beginning of new religious searches for meaning, community, answers, and identity. These searches are not necessarily confining themselves to traditional Christian channels. Instead, new Christian movements are giving new vitality and diverse forms to the 2000-year-old faith. Christianity in Eastern Europe has remained viable even in the face of long decades of persecution at the hands of Soviet-style communist governments. Christianity is healthy in many developing nations. It is growing rapidly especially in Africa and Latin America. The growth in these areas help make Christianity the fastest-growing religion in the world. Christianity is the largest religion in the world with approximately 2 billion of the earth's 6 billion inhabitants belonging to some form of Christianity. Those churches that are developing most rapidly in the Northern and Southern hemispheres are those that stress direct access to God through the Holy Spirit, personal forgiveness and empowerment (the ability for a person to take control of his or her life), and personal morality that extends to strict family relations. In Africa and Latin America, the emphasis is not on stimulating governmental involvement to address social problems. Instead, it is on the churches' ability to change their societies through church-based programs and the formation of communities that meet social means. For instance, many Christian denominations run schools and health facilities that meet the needs of people where government cannot or will not take action.

In addition, there are many sections of the world in which Christians are in conflict with other religions or where they are being persecuted. Conflict with Muslims is particularly obvious at present. Such conflict likely will increase in the twenty-first century. Overall, the early twenty-first century sees Christianity in an uncertain period. Uncertainty is full of danger, but it is also full of creative possibility. Christianity has survived many crises in the last 2000 years. It has adapted to and changed many different cultures and social situations. Whether it has the inner strength to successfully meet the new challenges remains to be seen.

Notes

1. For a good discussion of nineteenth-century biblical and historical studies as well as reactions to them, see Kenneth Scott Latourette. *A History of Christianity*. vol. 2, *Reformation to the Present*. Rev. ed. New York: Harper & Row, 1975, pp. 1127–1134.

2. For a good discussion of the early history of revivalism, see Latourette, vol. 2, pp. 1018–1048.

3. In the nineteenth century, evangelism and social concerns were closely linked. People did not see a conflict between saving souls and helping with the material needs of people. Many important evangelists and conservative leaders were involved in meeting the needs of society's less fortunate through efforts such as the antislavery movement, help for "wayward women," programs to feed the poor and homeless, and the fight against alcohol abuse. It is largely in the twentieth century that a division has occurred between liberals concerned with social problems and conservatives concerned with saving souls.

4. Neo-orthodoxy is a very broad movement with contributions from a number of important theologians. They did not always agree with one another. One issue that caused much debate was the relation of faith to culture. Most agreed that Christian truth was unique and revealed finally by God. Yet many differed on the extent to which truth and valid religion could be found through human nature or culture. For instance, a great debate raged in the early twentieth century between Karl Barth and Emil Brunner over the question, "Is man by his very nature religious?" Brunner was willing to admit a natural tendency in humans toward being religious. This religious nature served as a "point of contact" for the work of grace. To this end, Barth wrote a short, defiant book entitled simply *Nein!* ("No!").

5. For a good discussion of the Social Gospel, see Sydney E. Ahlstrom. *A Religious History of the American People*. New Haven, CT: Yale University Press, 1973, pp. 785–804.

6. In the last decade or so, there has been a worldwide surge in what is described as "fundamentalism." Not only have Christian fundamentalists been more active, but Muslim and Buddhist fundamentalists have asserted themselves as well. For example, a fundamentalist regime gained control in Iran in the late 1970s and Muslim fundamentalism is now threatening moderate Arab governments across the Middle East. Certainly, these non-Christian movements do not hold the five fundamentals of Christianity. The question must then be raised, "Why are these non-Christian movements called fundamentalist?"

Sociologically, fundamentalism is a reaction cast in religious terms against the change, complexity, and uncertainty of the modern world. Perhaps it is best described as a mindset that rejects certain elements of modern culture. It seems to be an effort to escape the negative effects of contemporary life by returning to imagined "good old days" when "God was in his heaven and all was right with the world." This is often combined with a political agenda that attempts to establish a theocracy that governs society according to traditional "laws of God." While claiming to restore tradition, many fundamentalists ignore significant elements of their religious heritage.

7. For a good discussion of the Scopes trial and its impact, see Gary Wills. *Under God: Religion and American Politics*. New York: Simon and Schuster, 1990, pp. 98–120. For a good discussion of the Intelligent Design controversy see Niall Shanks. *God, the Devil, and Darwin: A Critique of Intelligent Design Theory*. New York: Oxford University Press, 2003 and William A. Dembski and Charles W. Colson. *The Design Revolution: Answering the Toughest Questions about Intelligent Design*. Westmont, IL: Intervarsity, 2004.

8. For a good discussion of megachurches see the Hartford Institute for Religion Research's project on megachurches (http://hirr.hartsem.edu./org/faith-megachurches.html)

9. The Catholic church still refuses to ordain women. However, it has taken some steps to ensure greater female participation in worship and other aspects of church life. Fundamentalists and certain other conservatives resist female pastors as unbiblical. Yet other generally conservative groups have women ministers. For example, women always have served as ministers in some Pentecostal groups.

10. For a particularly insightful book on the current role of globalizing Christianity in Latin America see: Anna L. Peterson, Manuel A. Vasquez, and Philip J. Williams, eds. *Christianity, Social Change, and Globalization in the Americas*. New Brunswick, NJ: Rutgers University Press, 2001.

11. AIC may also stand for African Initiated Churches and African Indigenous Churches. The terms are used by scholars to stand for those churches begun and maintained by Africans themselves.

12. For a good discussion of Orthodoxy in the nineteenth and twentieth centuries, see Latourette. vol. 2. pp. 1210–1225, 1396–1405.

Additional Readings

Barrett, David B. et al. eds. *World Christian Encyclopedia: A Comparative Survey of Churches and Religions in the Modern World*. 2 vols. New York: Oxford University Press, 2001.

Barth, Karl. *Dogmatics in Outline*. Translated by G. T. Thomson. New York: Harper & Row, 1959.

Bonhoeffer, Dietrich. *Letters and Papers from Prison*. Edited by Ebehard Bethge. Expanded ed. New York: Macmillan, 1971.

Brown, Robert McAfee. *The Ecumenical Revolution*. Garden City, NY: Doubleday, 1967.

Buber, Martin. *I and Thou*. Translated by Ronald G. Smith. 2d ed. New York: Scribner's, 1958.

Chidester, David. *Christianity: A Global History*. San Francisco: HarperSanFrancisco, 2000.

Costas, Orlando E. *The Church and Its Missions: A Shattering Critique from the Third World*. Wheaton, IL: Tyndale, 1974.

Gish, A. G. *The New Left and Christian Radicalism*. Grand Rapids, MI.: Eardmans, 1970.

Gutiérrez, Gustavo. *A Theology of Liberation*. Maryknoll, NY: Orbis, 1973.

Hambrick-Stowe, *Charles E. Charles G. Finney and the Spirit of American Evangelicalism*. Grand Rapids, MI: Eersmans, 1996.

Handy, Robert T. *A Christian America*. New York: Oxford University Press, 1971.

———. *The Social Gospel in America, 1870–1920*. New York: Oxford University Press, 1966.

Hogg, William Richey. *Ecumenical Foundations: A History of the International Missionary Council and Its Nineteenth-Century Background*. New York: Harper & Row, 1952.

Japinga, Lynn. *Feminism and Christianity: The Essential Guide*. Nashville, TN: Abingdon, 1999.

Jenkins, Philip. *The Next Christendom: The Coming of Global Christianity*. Oxford: Oxford University Press, 2002.

Kekes, John. *Against Liberalism*. Ithaca, NY: Cornell University Press, 1997.

Kierkegaard, Søren. *Attack upon "Christendom."* Translated by Walter Lowrie. Princeton, NJ: Princeton University Press, 1968.

Latourette, Kenneth Scott. *Christianity in a Revolutionary Age*. Vols. 4–5. New York: Harper & Row, 1961–1962.

———. *A History of the Expansion of Christianity*. Vols. 4–6. New York: Harper, 1941–1944.

Marsden, George. *Fundamentalism and American Culture: the Shaping of Twentieth-Century Evangelicalism, 1870–1925*. New York: Oxford University Press, 1980.

Marty, Martin E. *Righteous Empire: Protestant Experience in America*. New York: Dial, 1970.

Moltmann, Jurgen. *The Theology of Hope*. New York: Harper & Row, 1967.

Murphy, Nancey. *Beyond Liberalism and Fundamentalism: How Modern and Postmodern Philosophy Set the Theological Agenda*. Harrisburg, PA: Trinity, 1996.

Neill, Stephen. *Colonialism and Christian Missions*. London: Lutterworth, 1966.

Niebuhr, Reinhold. *Moral Man and Immoral Society*. New York: Scribner's, 1960.

———. *The Nature and Destiny of Man*. Vol. 1, *Human Nature*. New York: Scribner's, 1964.

———. *The Nature and Destiny of Man*. Vol. 2, *Human Destiny*. New York: Scribner's, 1964.

Peterson, Anna L., Manuel A. Vasquez, and Philip J. Williams, eds. *Christianity, Social Change, and Globalization in the Americas*. New Brunswick, NJ: Rutgers University Press, 2001.

Riggs, Marcia Y, ed. *Can I Get a Witness?: Prophetic Religious Voices of African American Women: An Anthology*. Maryknoll, NY: Orbis, 1997.

Sabev, Todor. *The Orthodox Churches in the World Council of Churches: Towards the Future*. Geneva, Switzerland: WCC Publications, 1996.

Sandeen, Ernest R. *The Roots of Fundamentalism: British and American Millenarianism, 1800–1930*. Chicago: University of Chicago Press, 1970.

Schliermacher, Fredrich. *On Religion: Speeches to Its Cultured Despisers*. Translated by Richard Crouter. New York: Cambridge University Press, 1996.

Schüssler-Fiorenza, Elizabeth. *In Memory of Her*. New York: Crossroads, 1983.

Segundo, Juan Luis. *The Liberation of Theology*. Translated by John Drury. Maryknoll, NY: Orbis, 1982.

Stavrianos, L. S. *Global Rift: The Third World Comes of Age*. New York: Morrow, 1981.

Tillich, Paul. *The Courage to Be*. New Haven, CT.: Yale University Press, 1952.

———. *The Eternal Now*. New York: Scribner's, 1963.

———. *The New Being*. New York: Scribner's, 1955.

———. *The Shaking of the Foundations*. New York: Scribner's, 1948.

———. *Systematic Theology*. 3 vols. in 1. Chicago: University of Chicago Press, 1971.

Websites

http://hirr.hartsem.edu.org/faith_megachurches_research.html [Provides access to an extensive survey of megachurches as well as links to other resources]

http://members.tripod.com/~Berchmans.chridx.hmtl [Provides access to a host of information about Christianity in India]

http://www.bethel.edu/~letine/AfricanChristianity/ [Provides a brief history of Christianity in various sections of Africa. Also has links to other web materials as well as a bibliography of printed materials] http://www.faithnet.org.uk/index.html [Provides access to reflection on a host of topics from the Ecumenical Movement to philosophy of religion, to theology. Spurs interest and critical thinking. Additional links and reading materials are included]

http://www.religion-online.org/ [Provides online books and articles on a wide range of topics relevant to the study of Christainty]

http://www.religion-online/showbook.asp?title=1553 [Provides a very interesting book on Christianity in various parts of the East in a short readable format]

Glossary

Abbot "father." The head or overseer of a monastery.

Absolution forgiveness for sins.

Adoptionism the teaching that Jesus was such a good man he was adopted by God to be his Son and carry God's message to the world.

African Independent Churches label used for a wide variety of Christian churches that broke away from European-based mission churches to form Christian churches based on African traditions.

African Theology a movement by professional African theologians that seeks to reconcile Christianity with traditional African theology.

Allah Arabic word for *God*.

Allegorical method interprets stories of the Bible as though they have hidden symbolic meanings.

Anabaptists "those who baptize again." This label was applied to diverse groups of sixteenth-century Reformers, most of whom wanted to return to the simple faith of the Bible. They rejected infant baptism, insisting on baptizing only believers who made a profession of faith. They also resisted the close cooperation between church and state that existed in most European countries.

Anchoress a devout woman living in seclusion and often attached to a parish church.

Anglican(ism) "English." The term is applied to the form that the Reformation took in England. There the Reformation eventually resulted in the Anglican Church or the Church of England.

Antichrist a representative of Satan who is Christ's great enemy on earth.

Antinomians Christians who believed they should not have to live by any set of rules or laws since they were saved by grace.

Anti-Semitism hatred of Jews.

Apocrypha "hidden" writings. Several books that were removed by Luther from the Old Testament when he formed the Protestant canon because they did not appear in the original Hebrew canon.

Apologists a group of early Christian theologians who defended Christianity against attacks by pagan writers.

Apostles people chosen by Jesus during his earthly ministry to be his closest followers and friends.

Apostolic Fathers a group of second-generation Christian leaders who were believed to have been taught by the twelve, inner core of disciples who were the closest friends of Jesus.

Apostolic poverty poverty like that experienced by the apostles.

Arminianism doctrines similar to those of Jacobus Arminius, who taught that Christ died for everyone, not just for the elect.

Asceticism severe discipline of the body for religious purposes.

Assumption of the Blessed Virgin Mary dogma that Mary, the mother of Jesus, was bodily taken to heaven at the end of her life.

Atheistic   denying the existence of God.

Autographs   the original works (Scriptures) from the hands of the original writers.

Baptize   to submerge in water as a sign sin has been washed away. John the Baptist required baptism of his followers. Christians later adopted baptism as a sign (or perhaps a means) of a person's forgiveness and as a way of admitting members to the church. Later Christians would baptize by sprinkling with water.

B.C.E.   before common era, or the time before the common era shared by Christians and Jews (that is, before Jesus' birth).

Benefice   see *fief.*

Black Death   bubonic plague.

Blaspheming   cursing God.

Bolsheviks   communists who interpreted Karl Marx's ideas through Nikolai Lenin's eyes and who came to power in Russia in 1917.

Broad churchmanship   approach to theological disputes in which liberals and conservatives agree to disagree on certain topics but cooperate on such efforts as evangelism, missions, and other denominational programs.

Brown brothers   term applied by many nineteenth-century light-skinned peoples of western European origins to East Indians, Native Americans, Africans, and other dark-skinned peoples around the world.

Bull (papal)   a serious written papal mandate.

Bureaucracy   a hierarchy of officials.

Canon   officially accepted list of Scriptures.

Cantons   Swiss states.

Capitalism   an economic system based partly on the idea that industry, agriculture, and trade should be operated to create a profit.

Cash crops   crops that are sold for money.

Categorical imperative   Immanuel Kant's teaching that morals were to be guided by each person acting as if his or her behavior would become a universal rule.

C.E.   common era, or the time after Jesus' birth that Jews and Christians share in common.

Celibacy   not having sexual relations.

Cells   simple rooms where monks or nuns live.

Christ   Greek term for Messiah.

Christendom   a Christian world.

Christology   the doctrine of Christ and his work.

Clerical vestments   special clothing worn by ministers during worship services.

Civil sector (civil society)   the nongovernmental and non-economic activities needed for a society to sustain itself.

Coequal   term to describe the relationship between the Father, Son, and Holy Spirit meaning the three are completely equal.

Coeternal   term to describe the relationship between the Father, Son, and Holy Spirit meaning the three have always existed.

Conciliarism   movement originating in the fifteenth century that called for a council to reform the church and stop papal abuses.

Congregationalists   the name the Puritan church took in America.

Consecrated   a ceremony to install one in a church office, for instance, making a person a bishop.

Consubstantiation   Luther's teaching that Christ is actually present in the Eucharist although the bread and wine do not become his body and blood.

Contemplative life   a life of prayer and devotion often followed by monks or nuns.

Covenant   the "contract" established between God and his people. It gave God's people privileges but also made demands upon them.

Creationism twentieth-century effort by fundamentalists to attack evolutionary theory. It teaches that evolution is an inadequate theory for explaining the origins of life and that scientific evidence supports the biblical account of creation.

Creation science see *creationism*.

Creed a statement of beliefs.

Crucifixion death by nailing to a wooden cross.

Crusades military ventures against the Muslims to free the Holy Land from Islamic domination.

Day of the Lord period at the end of time when God will judge people and nations.

Deductive reasoning reasoning that starts with a general principle and reasons down to specific applications.

Demiurge a flawed lesser god who created the material world in Gnostic thought.

Devotio moderna "modern devotion." A movement arising in the fourteenth century that focused on contemplating the life of Christ and imitating him.

Dioceses regions under the direction of bishops.

Dispensation an exception from church law granted by the pope.

Dispensations (in John Nelson Darby's thought) long periods of time in which God chose to relate to his people in a particular manner appropriate to that era.

Dispossessed those who have traditionally been excluded from positions of power and influence in society as well as the church.

Divine Office a series of prayers and readings to be said at appointed hours of the day and night.

Divine Word the eternal Logos.

Docetics a group of early Christians who believed Jesus was a spirit that only appeared to have a body.

Donatists fourth-century sect that believed the church is made up of pure saints; sacraments administered by impure bishops are ineffective.

Double predestination doctrine that God chose some for salvation and some for damnation before the universe was created.

Ebionites a sect of Christian Judaizers who instructed Christians to strictly follow Jewish law.

Ecological Theology new branch where Christians have responsibility not only for personal salvation and social issues, but also for acting ethically in relation to the natural environment itself.

Ecumenical council a meeting of church representatives from all parts of the Christian world called to decide important issues.

Ecumenical movement twentieth-century Protestant movement in which various denominations are reuniting or at least engaging in cooperative efforts.

Edict of Milan decree by Constantine and Licinius issued in 313 that extended tolerance to Christians and other groups.

Egalitarianism the teaching that all people are equal.

Elect (the) those chosen or predestined by God for salvation before the universe was created.

Electronic churches twentieth-century radio and television ministries with large followings that have become substitutes for traditional congregations.

Elizabethan Settlement the approach of Elizabeth I of England to settling the religious differences of the sixteenth century. The settlement established the Church of England as the "middle way" between Catholicism and extreme Protestantism. All religious views other than Catholicism and extreme Protestantism were tolerated.

Episcopal structure an organizational hierarchy in which bishops rule over the church.

Essenes   Jewish group at the time of Jesus who lived in desert communes and strictly observed the Law while waiting for the Messiah to come.

Establishment   making Christianity (or any other religion) the official religion of a country.

Evangelicals   term applied to Protestant Christians. In Europe, the term is used for any Christian in the reformed tradition. The term has been used in the twentieth century for conservative Christians who stress the need to convert nonbelievers.

Ex cathedra   the pope is infallible when he is speaking in his official capacity as the pastor and teacher of Christians in defining matters of faith and morals.

Existentialism   philosophy that emphasizes the responsibility of people to make their own decisions to create meaning in their lives. Truth and meaning do not exist independently of the decisions people make.

Exodus   the Hebrew departure from Egypt under the leadership of Moses and their wanderings in the wilderness. A central event in Jewish thought.

Faith   a response produced by the Holy Spirit in the believer in which the believer commits to God and becomes more like Christ.

Fasting   going without food.

Feudalism   a system of economic, social, and political organization centered in large self-sufficient manors.

Fief   estate granted by a lord to his vassal in return for the vassal's service.

Final judgment   God's judgment of people at the end of time in which some will be saved and others damned.

Flesh   humans' sinful nature in Paul's theology.

Fluidity   characteristic of global society where information lines, alliances between people, jobs, and the like shift readily. Few remain rigid and unchanging.

Friars   "brothers." Members of the new mendicant orders that arose in the twelfth century.

Fundamentalism   twentieth-century American religious movement that calls upon Christians to return to the fundamentals of the faith. It is largely a reaction against modern culture and Christian attempts to adjust to that culture.

General election   doctrine that teaches Christ died for everyone, but some will not accept the salvation he offers.

Gentiles   the nations or all non-Jews.

Global civil society   the international or global non-governmental organizations that attempt to influence different aspects of the world's political, economic, or environmental scenes.

Globalization   an ongoing process of social change that is radically remaking the way people interact, the social systems into which people are immersed, and the context in which they do religion.

Gnosticism (Gnostics)   early Christian philosophy that stressed believers acquiring *gnosis* of (secret) knowledge necessary for salvation. Gnostics emphasized the difference between the spirit (good) and matter (evil). Gnostic ideas were used by some Christians to understand Jesus and his mission.

Gospel   "good news." The early Christians referred to their message as the gospel (good news) about Jesus. A Gospel or the Gospels may also refer to a book that tells the story of the life of Jesus.

Grace   God's unearned and undeserved love toward humans.

Greco-Roman world   that part of the world controlled by Rome at the time of Christ.

Hebrews (Israelites, Jews) a term applied to God's chosen people in the Bible.

Hold all things in common refers to the practice of the early Christian church of believers giving their possessions to the Christian community.

Heresy a teaching that departs from accepted (orthodox) doctrine.

Heretic one who rejects the true (orthodox) faith.

Hermitage place where a hermit lives.

Heterodox unorthodox or those outside the orthodox faith.

Historical process the interactions of people, places, and events which cause the occurrences of history.

Holocaust term for the slaughter of millions of innocent Jews and other "inferior" persons by the Nazis during World War II.

Homoiousios "of a similar substance." A Greek word used to describe the essences of the Father and the Son by those who opposed the Nicene faith.

Homoousios "of the same substance." A Greek word used in the Creed of Nicaea to describe the essences of the Father and the Son.

Humanism movement originating during the Renaissance that held that study of the humanities could improve religion and society.

Icons drawings or paintings of Christ, the Virgin Mary, or saints.

Identity crisis the trouble people have maintaining a clear image of who they are and how they relate to others whether these are neighbors or persons and groups on the other side of the earth.

Immaculate Conception of Mary doctrine that Mary was protected from all sin because she was chosen to be the mother of Jesus.

Imputed justice Luther's idea that the justice of Christ is transferred to unjust sinners. Sinners are not made into sinless creatures when they become Christian. The righteousness of Christ merely "covers" their sinful unrighteousness.

Incarnate (incarnation) to be made flesh as when God or a god became human.

Incarnational theology theology that teaches Jesus was God made flesh.

Independents seventeenth-century anabaptist separatist Puritans who rejected the national Church of England.

Inductive reasoning reasoning that starts with specific instances observed in the material world and reasons up to general principles.

Indulgences waivers from temporal punishments for sin made possible through the church drawing upon its storehouse of merit.

Industrial revolution series of sweeping economic and social changes beginning in England during the late eighteenth century involving the replacement of hand labor with machines organized in factories.

Intercede to intervene or to plead with God for the sinner.

Islam "submission to God." Religion founded by Muhammad in the seventh century.

Israelites see *Hebrews*.

Jesuits the popular name for the Society of Jesus, a Catholic religious order founded by Ignatius Loyola in the sixteenth century.

Jews see *Hebrews*.

Justification how sinners "get right" with God.

Justinian Code set of laws developed by the Emperor Justinian in the sixth century. The code gave shape to Byzantine civilization.

Kerygma the proclamation or preaching of the early Christian church.

Kingdom of God age in which the rule of God appears on earth.

Koran the holy book of Islam.

Law the commandments of God to his people.

Lay investiture process by which an emperor or other political leader would install clergy in their offices and give them fiefs for their support. This allowed the political leaders to dominate the clergy.

Left wing of the Reformation see *Anabaptists*.

Linear view of history the idea that history has a definite beginning as well as a definite end.

Literalism an approach to understanding Scripture that insists that biblical passages must be taken as literally true. God speaks directly in the Scriptures. There is no need for interpretation.

Live according to the Spirit living according to the believer's relationship to God in Paul's theology.

Logos reason or "the Word." The Logos was the force through whom the world was created in several first-century philosophies. Christians eventually claimed Jesus was the Logos.

Love feast a meal held by early Christians along with the Eucharist.

Manicheism religion based on the teachings of Mani that developed in Persia during the third century of the common era. It taught a radical separation between the evil material world and the good world of the spirit.

Manor a large self-sufficient agricultural estate.

Mass the Roman Catholic worship service in which the Eucharist is celebrated.

Materialistic judging things solely according to their material worth without reference to spiritual values.

Melchiorites followers of Melchior Hoffman, a radical sixteenth-century Anabaptist who forecasted the rapid approach of the return of Christ.

Mendicant orders orders of friars who lived by begging.

Merit good or good works that may determine a person's rewards in eternity.

Messiah figure in the Hebrew Scriptures linked with the end of time. Christians believe Jesus was the Messiah.

Miracle an occurrence produced by divine activity in which the laws of nature are set aside.

Modernists Catholic theologians who attempted to accommodate the modern mindset of the nineteenth century.

Monarchians early Christians concerned with defending the unity (monarchy) of God.

Adoptionist or Dynamic Monarchians denied the divinity of Christ and held that he was the adopted Son of God.

Modalistic Monarchians taught that Father, Son, and Holy Spirit were convenient labels for the way God was known by people in history.

Monasteries places where monks live.

Monastics people who seek to live pure Christian lives by withdrawing from society; they usually live in communities where they dedicate themselves to disciplining the flesh and developing their spiritual nature.

Monk a male monastic.

Monophysites a sect that came into existence after the Council of Chalcedon. They taught that the incarnate Christ had only one divine nature, not human and divine natures.

Monophysitism a teaching that Jesus had a divine nature but no human nature.

Montanists a North African group that looked for Christ's immediate return and practiced asceticism.

Mortal sins serious sins that could result in the sinner being condemned to hell.

Mosque Muslim place of worship.

Muslims (Moslems) "submission to God." Followers of the Islamic religion.

Mystery religions group of religions arising in the eastern Roman empire that emphasized secret knowledge and initiation into religious mysteries.

Nationalism idea where people see themselves as loyal to a nation-state.

Neo-orthodoxy "the new orthodoxy." The term is applied to a twentieth-century theological movement that asserts a Bible-centered faith, human sinfulness, and the necessity of God's saving intervention in history.

Neoplatonism a philosophy popular in the Roman Empire that stressed a return to the One who is the source of all that exists.

Nihilism the total rejection of the ability to understand any ultimate truth.

Nun a female monastic.

Old Believers see *Raskolniks*.

Orders (holy or religious) monks, nuns, or friars who live in religious communities.

Pacifism refusing to take up arms or go to war.

Pagans worshipers of non-Christian gods.

Papal infallibility teaching that nothing the pope does is wrong. In the nineteenth-century the Roman Catholic church accepted the doctrine that the pope is infallible when acting in his official capacity as the church's teacher of faith and morals.

Papal primacy the concept that because the pope is the supreme leader of Christianity, all Christians should submit to his rule.

Patriarch (Christian) usually means one of the major leaders of the Eastern Orthodox church. The term may also refer to one of the early theologians of the church known as a group as the *church fathers*.

Patriarchs (Jewish) the founding fathers of the Jewish faith.

Patrimony of Saint Peter lands in Italy controlled by the pope that provided financial support for the papacy.

Patristic period from the Latin word for *father*, the time of the church fathers (100 C.E.– 500 C.E.) when most of the core ideas in Christian theology were formed.

Penance good works or penalties required by a priest or bishop as a condition for sinners receiving forgiveness for their sins.

Pharisees Jewish group at the time of Jesus that stressed strict obedience to the Law of God.

Philosophical schools lines of thought or approaches to philosophy. Often these are associated with a particular philosopher.

Piety sincere devotion accompanied by acts of love.

Pluralism one person might be pastor or bishop of several places at one time, leading to absenteeism.

Pluralistic environment situation in which there are many different people with many competing faiths and ideas.

Polygyny the marrige of one man to several women.

Pope "papa or father." In early Western Christianity, the term was applied to any bishop. Gregory VII had the use of the term restricted to the bishop of Rome in 1073. The Eastern Orthodox church still applies the term to all priests.

Predestination doctrine that God chose some people to be saved before the universe was created.

Primacy "supremacy." The term is often used in the church to refer to the teaching that the pope is superior to other bishops.

Prophet one of a group of men who claimed to speak for God. They recalled the Israelites and Jews to keeping the covenant of Moses and linked true religion with ethics.

Protestants originally Reformers who protested at the Diet of Speier in 1529 revoking privileges granted to them by Charles V. The term came to apply to all Christians whose denominations grew out of the sixteenth-century break with Roman Catholicism.

Purgatory   a place where the dead wait to be cleansed of their sins so they can enter heaven.

Puritans   group in sixteenth- and seventeenth-century England who felt the Anglican church needed to be purified of Catholic influences. They advocated making the church conform to Calvinistic doctrines and practices.

Radical Reformation   see *Anabaptists*.

Raskolniks (Old Believers)   Russian Orthodox Christians who resisted the reforms to the Russian liturgy instituted by Nikon in the seventeenth century.

Rationalism   the belief that reason alone can comprehend all truth and is sufficient to guide morals.

Reconciliation   coming together or bringing together two beings who were estranged.

Relativism   the teaching that truth is related to the time, place, and culture in which it is taught. There are no absolute truths.

Renaissance   "rebirth." The term may refer to any of several rebirths of culture and learning occurring at various times in western Europe. When used as "the Renaissance" it means the large-scale rebirth of interest in classical culture that reached its height in the fifteenth century.

Repentance   turning away from sin.

Resurrection   rising from the dead.

Revelation   self-disclosure, self-showing. God showing himself to people.

Rhetoric   public speaking.

Romanticism   nineteenth-century artistic movement that emphasized feeling over thinking and that glorified nature.

Royal absolutism   the monarch was placed on the throne by God with absolute power to rule.

Sacrament   a physical act that leads to participation in the divine. In Christian theology sacraments bring the grace of God to humans.

Sadducees   small but powerful Jewish party at the time of Jesus who rejected innovations in Jewish tradition and was closely associated with the Romans.

Saints   noteworthy Christians believed by Roman Catholic and Eastern Orthodox Christians to possess extraordinary powers. Protestants often claim that all saved Christians are saints of God.

Sanhedrin   Jewish ruling body at the time of Jesus.

Scholasticism   system of philosophical and theological thought originating in great cathedral schools and universities that dominated the twelfth and thirteenth centuries. Scholastics built elaborate thought systems based upon the conviction that reason could shed deeper light on the Bible and Christian doctrine.

Sect   a group that breaks away from an accepted religion.

Secular   nonreligious.

Secularization   the removal of human institutions from religious domination.

Serfs   people bound for life to their lord.

Sheol   the realm of the dead in Hebrew tradition.

Sign   an unusual occurrence that happens when the divine is present in the world.

Simony   purchasing of church offices.

Slavophiles   a group of nineteenth-century Russian Christians who believed the Russian Orthodox church was the only true church. They tried to insulate the Russian Orthodox church from Protestant and Roman Catholic influences.

Social Gospel   twentieth-century movement that insists the Gospel must be expressed in social ethics.

Startzi   Russian monks whose prayer and spiritual discipline commanded special respect; they were considered "elders" whom many sought for counsel.

Stewardship (Christian) the believer's responsibility to faithfully care for what God has provided.

Stigmata the wounds of Christ.

Stoicism (Stoics) first-century philosophy that emphasized the creation of the world by Divine Reason (the Logos) and humans' duty to live according to the natural law placed in the universe by Divine Reason.

Subjectivism the teaching that each person has his or her own definition of truth.

Symphonia "harmony." The idea for church–state relations in Eastern Christianity in which the church handles spiritual matters and the state handles temporal matters. The church and state are to support each other in their tasks.

Synod meeting.

Synoptic Gospels the New Testament books of Matthew, Mark, and Luke which tell the story of Jesus from a similar viewpoint.

Tenants people who work the land and pay rent to the landowner.

Testament see *Covenant*.

Third Rome Theory theory used by the Russians to claim Moscow was the capital of Orthodoxy. It held that Rome, the first seat of Christianity, fell to the barbarians and Constantinople, the second seat, became apostate. This left Moscow the capital.

Transubstantiation doctrine that the bread and wine become the body and blood of Christ in the Eucharist.

Trinity Father, Son, Holy Spirit.

Tsar the emperor of Russia.

Übermensch Friedrich Nietzsche's "superman" who ruthlessly pursues power.

Ultramontanism philosophy that Rome alone has the right to determine matters of doctrine, morals, and culture.

Unitarians a group who argued for the "oneness" of God and rejected the Trinity.

Universalism doctrine that everyone will be saved.

Urbanize process in which a society moves toward having more than one-half its population live in urban areas.

Usury the lending of money for interest.

Vassals lesser lords who had sworn allegiance to a greater lord.

Veneration worship.

Verbal inspiration theory that God verbally told the original writers of the Scriptures exactly what to write.

Vicar of Christ one who rules on earth as the representative of Christ. The title has been applied to the pope since the thirteenth century.

Visionaries people who felt they were called by God to accomplish a certain task.

Vulgate Latin version of the Bible used in the Roman Catholic Church.

Watershed a major turning point in history.

White man's burden concept shared by many nineteenth-century Westerners that light-skinned people of European origins had a special obligation to share the benefits of their advanced civilization with their primitive "brown brothers" around the world.

Words of consecration "this is my body . . . this is my blood." These words were spoken by Jesus at the Last Supper with his disciples shortly before he was crucified. When these words are spoken by a priest during the Eucharist, some Christians believe the bread and wine become the body and blood of Christ.

Yahweh an Old Testament name for God.

Zealots a Jewish group at the time of Jesus who believed the Messiah would be an earthly king and who was involved in plots against Roman rule.

Index

Credits

This page constitutes an extension of the copyright page. We have made every effort to trace the ownership of all copyrighted material and to secure permission from copyright holders. In the event of any question arising as to the use of any material, we will be pleased to make the necessary corrections in future printings. Thanks are due to the following authors, publishers, and agents for permission to use the material indicated.

Chapter 1. 1: © Culver Pictures

Chapter 2. 30: © Culver Pictures

Chapter 3. 54: Santa Maria Novella, Florence/Bridgeman Art Library

Chapter 4. 76: © Bettmann/CORBIS

Chapter 5. 111: © Culver Pictures

Chapter 6. 137: © Culver Pictures

Chapter 7. 166: El Paso Museum of Art, Gift of the Samuel H. Kress Foundation

Chapter 8. 196: © Culver Pictures

Chapter 9. 220: © Bettmann/CORBIS

Chapter 10. 247: © Bettmann/CORBIS

Chapter 11. 279: © UPI-Bettmann/CORBIS

Chapter 12. 310: © Ed Kashi/Corbis